William Watson
and the *Rob Roy*

ALSO BY WALTER E. WILSON
AND FROM MCFARLAND

The Bulloch Belles: Three First Ladies, a Spy, a President's Mother and Other Women of a 19th Century Georgia Family (2015)

James D. Bulloch: Secret Agent and Mastermind of the Confederate Navy (2012)

William Watson and the *Rob Roy*

The Adventures of a Civil War Blockade Runner

WALTER E. WILSON

McFarland & Company, Inc., Publishers
Jefferson, North Carolina

ISBN (print) 978-1-4766-9903-5
ISBN (ebook) 978-1-4766-5753-0

Library of Congress cataloging data are available

Library of Congress Control Number 2025048354

© 2026 Walter E. Wilson. All rights reserved

No part of this book may be reproduced or transmitted in any form or by any means, electronic or mechanical, including photocopying or recording, or by any information storage and retrieval system, without permission in writing from the publisher.

Front cover image: "Chase of a Blockade Runner" (*Harper's Weekly*, November 26, 1864, p. 760-761, Library of Congress Prints and Photographs Division, LC-USZ62-15554); *background* © Shutterstock.

Printed in the United States of America

McFarland & Company, Inc., Publishers
Box 611, Jefferson, North Carolina 28640
www.mcfarlandpub.com

Table of Contents

Preface   1

Introduction   5

1. The Adventure Begins   11
2. From Merchantman to Blockade Runner   22
3. De los Brazos de Dios a las Manos del Diablo   29
4. More Than a Sinking Feeling   39
5. Captain Dave's Exciting Sea Story   47
6. Ready, … Set, … Wait….   52
7. Secret Agents, Spies, and Betrayal   60
8. Men of Affairs: The Intelligentsia in Tampico and Havana   73
9. Back to Texas: "A Right Down Swindle"   85
10. Captain Dave's Exciting Sea Story: The Sequel   99
11. Preparing for Another Run Through the Blockade   108
12. From Galveston to Tampico and Havana   115
13. Phantom Voyages Part 1: From Havana to Texas   124
14. Phantom Voyages Part 2: Galveston to Vera Cruz and Havana   134
15. Phantom Voyages Part 3: Running the Gauntlet in Steamships   143
16. The Demise of *Rob Roy*, Blockade Running, and the Confederacy   153

Appendix 1. Rob Roy *and Henry Laverty, the Prequel*   159

Appendix 2. Blockade Running or Smuggling   161

Appendix 3. Blockade Runs of the SS Alice *(aka Matagorda)*   163

Appendix 4. Cast of Characters   165

Appendix 5. Naval Order of Battle	180
Appendix 6. The Civil War Voyages of Rob Roy	196
Appendix 7. Nautical Tonnage and Rob Roy *(Francis Marquez, Jr. and James Cartey)*	197
Chapter Notes	199
Bibliography	233
Index	239

Preface

My own true adventure with the blockade runners *Rob Roy* and William Watson began more than 10 years ago. Like many others, I was captivated by William Watson's entertaining memoir of his Civil War blockade-running exploits aboard the schooner *Rob Roy*. I purchased the Texas A&M University Press reprint of his book and then splurged on a copy of the 1892 first edition. Watson's invaluable eyewitness account of blockade running in the western Gulf of Mexico is as unique as it is intriguing. His narrative raises almost as many questions as it answers. I decided to write an article to share the insights I had gathered from my research about the man, his ship, and the events he described.

My efforts went in a new direction in the spring of 2019. I attended a Civil War conference at the University of Texas Rio Grande Valley in Edinburg, Texas. The subject was "War & Peace on the Rio Grande." The decision to make the trip to "The Valley" was an easy one for me. I have family living in South Texas, my father was born in Edinburg, and I had developed a close connection with Tom Fort of the Museum of South Texas History. The speaker of greatest interest to me was a postgraduate nautical archeology student named Samantha Bernard. She presented a paper on the schooner *Rob Roy* and her efforts to locate its wrecked remains on the coast of Florida. That paper eventually formed the basis of her East Carolina University thesis, "Searching for the Schooner *Rob Roy*: An Historical Archaeological Analysis of a Civil War Blockade Runner."

After her presentation, I asked if she had been able to unearth *Rob Roy*'s previous name or owner prior to May 1863 when William Watson purchased the schooner at New Orleans. She confessed that she had not uncovered *Rob Roy*'s antecedents. Her exasperated expression told me that she shared the same frustration at running into a historical dead end. Rather than being discouraged, I was more determined than ever to find the answer.

I followed the trail of Watson's vague hints using my database of ship locations, characteristics, cargos, personnel, activities, and movements. It is a compilation of contemporary reports and primary sources documenting Civil War maritime activity in the Western Gulf of Mexico. This simple spread sheet has more than 13,000 individual line entries and counting. As revealed in Chapter 1, these combined archival sources pointed me to the name of the schooner's first captain and *Rob Roy*'s previous incarnations. This discovery naturally led to more questions. There was a discrepancy between Watson's description of *Rob Roy*'s size and tonnage and the

Schooner *Rob Roy*. William Watson, *Adventures of a Blockade Runner; or, Trade in Time of War*. London: Fisher Unwin, 1892, p. 6 (author's collection).

official registration record. While these figures might be of great significance to a nautical archeologist searching for *Rob Roy*'s sunken remains, they are not particularly edifying for most historians.

My findings came too late to assist Ms. Bernard with her research, but they motivated me to continue digging into the particulars of Watson's story. If he could exaggerate or mis-remember basic information about the dimensions of his schooner, I wondered if other parts of his tale were imagined as well. They were. But to my relief, I found that Watson's story is mostly true.

Watson often interrupts the flow of his own story to share tales about other ships and captains. Each of these adventures helps illuminate the scope, danger, and excitement of the blockade-running business. I will follow the threads that verify or disprove his personal experiences and other assertions. My hope is that the reader will find the resulting narrative informative and engaging, with the added advantage of being historically accurate.

No work of this depth can be accomplished without the assistance of helpful family, friends and scholars. As suggested earlier, authors Karen Fort and Tom Fort (senior historian at the Museum of South Texas History in Edinburg, Texas) generously provided much-appreciated encouragement and advice. Author, editor, and historian Milo Kearney, Professor Emeritus, University of Texas Rio Grande Valley, encouraged me to contribute to his long-running series of studies in Lower Rio Grande Valley history. His university sponsors the Rio Grande Valley Civil War Trail project through its CHAPS (Community Historical Archaeology Project with

Schools) Program. Other helpful South Texas resources are the Texas Maritime Museum in Rockport, Texas, and the Brownsville Historical Association.

J. Barto Arnold, Director of Texas Operations, Institute of Nautical Archaeology, was generous with his time and research. It was his advice that first led me to explore the rich admiralty case files within the National Archives. He also provided valuable feedback on an early draft of this manuscript. Archivist Barbara Rust and her team at the National Archives and Records Administration, Southwest Region in Fort Worth, obligingly ferreted out their myriad records pertaining to *Rob Roy* and Civil War blockade running.

Andrew W. Hall, an accomplished maritime artist, archaeologist, fellow admiral in the Texas Navy, and author of books and blogs about Texas steamboats and blockade running, was generous with his time and knowledge. Andy provided detailed and insightful feedback on an early version of the text. He also provided the wonderful portrait of Ensign Paul Borner, a key figure in Watson's story. Casey Greene and Sean McConnell of Lauren Martino's Special Collections team at the Rosenberg Library in Galveston were especially helpful in sharing their documentary and photographic treasures.

Lisa Neely, author and archivist for the King Ranch Museum, guided me through their unique archives that provide insight into the Civil War activities of Richard King and Mifflin Kenedy. Lisa introduced me to Lori K. Atkins, the university archivist at the James C. Jernigan Library on the campus of Texas A&M University Kingsville. Lori welcomed me to another fine collection of M. Kenedy & Co. Civil War records.

The University of Texas at Austin's Dolph Briscoe Center for American History is a national treasure. Its collection of unique Civil War–era letters and documents proved to be indispensable in my research, particularly the relatively unknown papers of José San Román. Roland Stansbury and his team at the Young-Sanders Center in Franklin, Louisiana, curate a rich repository of Civil War history, and I am honored to claim them as friends. Their collection of Confederate Vessel Papers and digitized Louisiana Ship Registers are unsurpassed in their availability and helpfulness. Together with the San Román Papers, it was the Young-Sanders Center resources that allowed me to make the connection between the schooner *Rob Roy* and its earlier incarnation as the *Francis Marquez, Jr.* Thanks to the diligence of Dr. Germain J. Bienvenu, a manifest for the "*F Marquez*" within the Louisiana State University Libraries Special Collections provided meaningful insight on the schooner's activities before Watson's purchase.

Michael Bailey, curator of the Brazoria County Historical Museum, was generous with his time and introduced me to his valuable store of information, the photograph of Joseph Bates, and artifacts relevant to the Civil War in Brazoria County.

Acquiring relevant, high-quality contemporary images is always a challenge. With that in mind, I am particularly grateful to Sara Pezzoni, the photo collections coordinator for the University of Texas at Arlington Libraries, Special Collections. Elisa Welder McCune, the special collections and integrative projects librarian for Southern Methodist University, was equally professional and helpful. Finally, Edith Smith of East Bernard, Texas, graciously shared a photograph and the family history of Charles W. Austin from the collection of her late husband Vincent Eastman Smith, Jr.

Despite the best efforts of those mentioned above, there are, no doubt, imperfections within the following text. The responsibility for any errors or omissions lies solely with yours truly, the author.

Introduction

If there was a title of "Most Famous" blockade-running schooner of the Civil War, *Rob Roy* would be a top contender. The schooner's fame is not based upon its combat exploits or its association with famous people or memorable events. *Rob Roy*'s place in history is a result of a rollicking memoir that its owner and captain, William Watson, wrote about their adventures. This obscure but articulate Scotsman authored an insightful and richly detailed account of his experiences as a blockade runner, most of which were on board a small, two-masted schooner named *Rob Roy*. Since the publication of his *Adventures of a Blockade Runner* (cover title) in 1892, Watson's book has been a standard maritime reference for scholars and students of America's most tragic conflict.[1]

His exciting tale is one of the few that addresses blockade running. It is the only one that focuses on the activities of small sailing vessels in the Western Gulf of Mexico. It is more than just an informative reference, it is entertaining and amusing. As one especially knowledgeable observer noted, his story is "spellbinding." His descriptions of the events, people, places, and context of the times have been among the most cited of all contemporary resources about blockade running during the American Civil War.[2]

There are, however, three questions that a skeptical reader might ask upon picking up a first edition copy of Watson's 1892 book: (1) Was there really a blockade-running schooner named *Rob Roy*? (2) Was William Watson a real person? (3) Is the book a history or is it fiction? The answers to those questions are: (1) Yes. (2) Yes. (3) Yes.

At first glance, the book appears to be more fantasy than fact. Gold gilt lettering emblazons the book's red cover that features a medieval knight mounted on a rearing steed. The publisher further embossed the cover with banners and a sailing ship in the background. Watson's book was the London publisher's 13th installment of its "Adventure Series" of books. All the volumes in this late–19th-century series seem to be targeting adolescent British boys.[3]

A quick review of the preface and first chapter dispels the notion that Watson wrote about his adventures exclusively with youngsters in mind. Despite the book's appearances and Watson's occasional lapses, a check of the historical records leaves no doubt about the existence of the schooner *Rob Roy*, its captain William Watson, and many of their blockade-running adventures. Contemporary correspondence and newspaper accounts as well as official U.S. and British government records all

Front cover. William Watson, *Adventures of a Blockade Runner; or, Trade in Time of War*. London: Fisher Unwin, 1892 (author's collection).

mention Watson and *Rob Roy* by name. These records also verify many of Watson's assertions.

Rob Roy did, indeed, sail from the ports of New Orleans, Belize, Havana, Matamoros and Tampico in Mexico as well as Velasco and Galveston in Texas during the American Civil War. Watson ran the blockade five times with his schooner *Rob Roy*. He carried 146 bales of cotton out of the Brazos River in early 1864 and ran out of Galveston with 198 bales in September of 1864. Despite his protestations to the contrary, Watson was in command when he ran *Rob Roy* onto a West Florida beach and set the schooner afire in March of 1865. During its short but adventurous life as a blockade runner, *Rob Roy* was one of the many small schooners that helped sustain international trade in wartime Texas.

Watson stated that he sold *Rob Roy* at Havana after his final run out of Galveston. He claimed that when *Rob Roy* made its last run through the blockade in Florida, the Union Navy chased the schooner ashore. To prevent capture, the crew abandoned ship and burned the schooner to the water line. After bidding adieu to *Rob Roy*, Watson also said that he made two additional runs through the blockade at Galveston Bay onboard two different steamers. Despite reassuring validations of most of his blockade-running adventures with *Rob Roy*, the saga of his heroic exploits on steamers does not stand up to closer scrutiny.

The Gulf of Mexico and Western Caribbean (author's map).

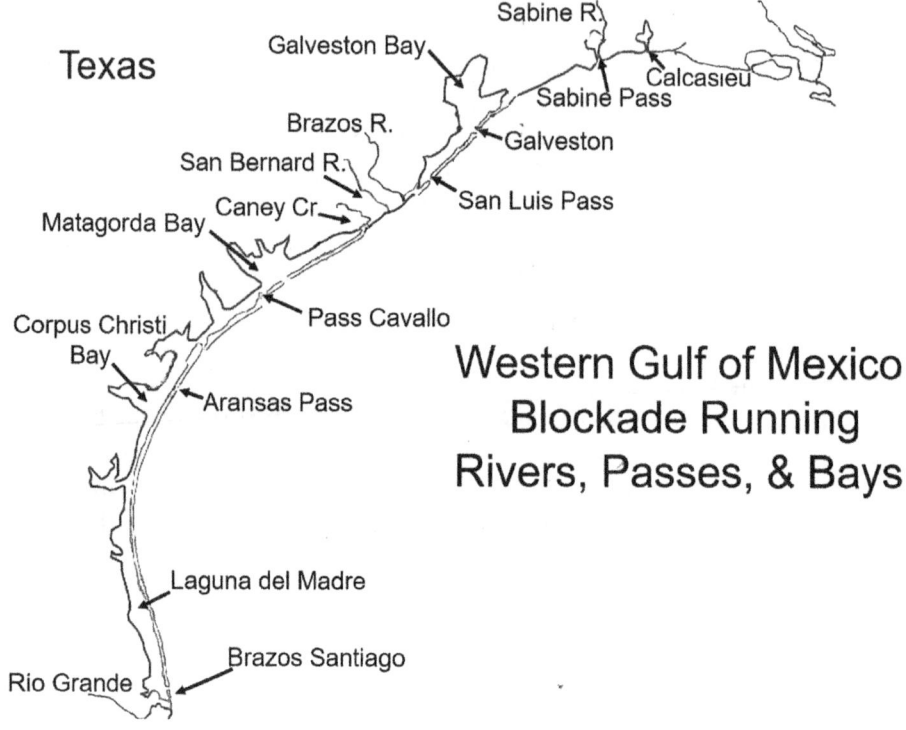

Western Gulf of Mexico blockade running rivers, passes, and bays (author's map).

To help jog his memory, Watson said that he retained many of his business and personal papers plus remnants of his logbooks. As was common during the Victorian era, Watson deliberately changed or abbreviated the names of some ships and individuals that he mentioned in his book. The intent was to avoid personal or professional embarrassment. There were, however, other more subtle errors, omissions, and exaggerations. One of the most obvious was Watson's description of the steam blockade runner *Phoenix*. There never was a blockade runner in the Western Gulf named *Phoenix* and there are no other blockade runners that match Watson's detailed description.

Although the inventory of steam blockade runners is well documented, historians have long vented their frustrations about the incomplete records of blockade-running operations. This deficiency is especially true in the Western Gulf of Mexico. There is no single compendium of blockade runner comings and goings in this distant theater of the American Civil War. Even the records of the National Archives and the U.S. Navy's 30-volume set of official records of the "War of the Rebellion" have significant omissions.

The relative paucity of reliable Civil War blockade-running information is one of the reasons why William Watson's book has been so important to historians. It is also one of the few first-hand accounts that provide unvarnished insights into the human dimensions of this secretive wartime business.

Watson's blockade-running sea story is exactly that: a sea story. It is part fact and part fiction, with liberal doses of exaggeration and omission. In fact, many of Watson's claims are verifiably true, but just as many are not. Some of his stories are essentially true, but he also interjected himself into others as a key participant when he was not even present. It was his story, after all, and he probably saw no harm in making himself the hero of his own story. Other events in Watson's memoir probably occurred pretty much as he claimed, even when he rearranged the times and places.

My purpose in authoring this book is less about setting the record straight and more about exposing the true history surrounding William Watson, his schooner *Rob Roy* and his blockade-running tales. By assembling widely dispersed contemporary accounts and official reports, and integrating them into the reliable portions of Watson's account, a reasonably clear picture emerges. The resulting blockade-running saga has the advantage of being a true adventure story. This narrative will also fill in the historical gaps that Watson left untold. The text and notes will identify Watson's exaggerations and misstatements as appropriate. It is the author's hope that the reader will find this Civil War blockade-running adventure story to be equally exciting, with the added advantage of being historically accurate.

1

The Adventure Begins

William Watson was born in 1826 about 25 miles west of Glasgow, Scotland, in the village of Skelmorlie in Ayrshire. His father, Henry, was a landscape gardener. The elder Watson had moved to Skelmorlie in 1820 to lay out the grounds of Ashcraig, the estate of a retired West Indies sugar planter. In that same year, Henry married Margaret Hamilton. They would have five children together. When William was only two, his mother died shortly after giving birth to her fifth child, Maria. His father remarried in April 1833, this time to a local girl named Robison Gilmour McLean. She not only took on the task of raising Henry's five children, but Robison also had four children of her own with Henry. The Watson family continued to live in the gardener's cottage until 1854, upon the passing of the estate owner Andrew Donaldson Campbell and his wife Janet Maria who died a few months later.[1]

After attending the local school at Skelmorlie, William trained as a shipbuilding engineer. Seeking more adventure, Watson abruptly emigrated to Bermuda around 1845, probably through the influence of Mr. Campbell. On the island, Watson worked as a civil engineer and an occasional ship's captain. About 1850, he moved to Louisiana. By 1859, he had formed a partnership with James W. Brown in a sawmill and a coal and steamboat business at Baton Rouge. As an expert mechanic and licensed third-class engineer, he often performed boiler repair and installation work at the sugar mills and refineries in the surrounding country. His clients included future Civil War generals P.G.T. Beauregard and Braxton Bragg, and the Louisiana governor Thomas O. Moore.[2]

Though a long-term resident of Louisiana, Watson was a proud Scotsman. His circle of friends in the Pelican State included many Scottish expatriates. He roomed at a boarding house owned by fellow Scotsman John McKenzie and his wife Isabella. He retained his British citizenship and could have been exempted from Confederate military service. He personally believed that slavery was an unhealthy institution for all concerned and he opposed secession. Like many men in the South who had similar misgivings, Watson still enlisted in the Confederate Army. His motivations were loyalty to his fellow working-class friends and his disdain for perceived Northern greed and arrogance. Perhaps more important was his thirst for adventure.[3]

While at Baton Rouge, Watson had joined a company of volunteers, "partly for pleasure and partly for policy." Shortly after the outbreak of fighting, Watson and his fellow militiamen enlisted in the Confederate Army. The unit joined as Company K, 3rd Louisiana Infantry, and included three officers, four sergeants, three corporals, and 66 privates. They were more familiarly known as the Pelican Rifles. Watson signed his enlistment papers on May 17, 1861, for a term of one year. At first, he filled the role of Third Sergeant. In anticipation of his prolonged absence from Baton Rouge, Watson gave another fellow Scotsman, John Hill his power of attorney to attend to the Bayou Sawmill's business affairs.[4]

His peers then elected him as the unit's orderly sergeant, a position equivalent to the executive officer of the company. He kept the company's roll-book, managed financial accounts, signed requisitions, managed discipline and morale, and was exempted from routine guard duty. As a foreigner, he was ineligible for an officer's commission. The prospect of a commission was tempting, but he was unwilling to forgo his allegiance to the British Crown and become an American citizen.[5]

After a brief period of training, his company fought at Oakhill, Missouri, a Confederate victory. During a bayonet charge, Watson suffered a minor saber wound to his wrist and narrowly avoided a fatal bullet wound during a subsequent assault. As he charged up a hill, a well-aimed minié ball struck the pit of his stomach and knocked him unconscious. Upon recovering his senses, he discovered a hole in his canteen and a severely dented brass belt buckle that had saved his life. Afterwards, he suffered a bout of fever that placed him on the sick list in October of 1861.[6]

His next taste of combat came at the disastrous Battle of Pea Ridge in northeast Arkansas. At least Watson emerged unscathed from that fight. His term of enlistment had come to an end, and since he was a British citizen, he was not compelled to extend his service for another two years like the rest of his company. He retained his paygrade as a First Sergeant until May 23, 1862, when he reverted to the rank of private. He finally received his discharge on July 16, 1862, at Tupelo, Mississippi. Four days later, he received back pay of $34.66, plus a $45.00 allowance for travel back to New Orleans. His pay receipt reflected a $3.25 deduction for shoes, yielding a net of $76.41 in Confederate dollars.[7]

Watson's discharge paper confirms his dates of service between May 17, 1861, and July 16, 1862. It describes him as being "aged thirty six years, five feet ten inches high, brown complexion, hazel eyes, and by profession an engineer." He was entitled to a discharge after his initial 12-month commitment and subsequent re-enlistment. Watson claimed that the reason for being excused from Army service was due to his British citizenship. While his eligibility for exemption as a foreigner was certainly true, the official reason for his discharge was something else entirely. Watson was allowed to leave the army because he was "over the age prescribed by the Conscript Act." A proud man, Watson apparently did not want to admit that the Confederacy considered him too old to be of further service.[8]

Upon his discharge, Watson left his unit at Tupelo, Mississippi, and headed back toward his former home in Baton Rouge. When he arrived at the outskirts of town, he found that it was occupied by Federal troops. He met up with his former partner and discovered that his sawmill was under Union control and out of business. As a discharged soldier and foreign national, Watson was under suspicion, but he was free to travel to New Orleans. There, he obtained a certificate of his citizenship from the British consul's office.[9]

Watson also managed to run afoul of Union authorities in New Orleans. The incident occurred shortly after General Robert E. Lee's Army of Northern Virginia inflicted a series of defeats upon General McLellan during the Seven Days Battles (Peninsula Campaign, June 26 to July 1, 1862). By mid–July, local New Orleans newspapers reprinted Northern reports of the McLellan's disorderly retreat as a "Change of Base." Watson was with friends who had gathered at a café where they observed a brief altercation between two dogs in the street. After the loser retreated from the fray with his tail between his legs, Watson joked that the hound was not running away, he was merely "making a change of base." This unguarded comment resulted in his arrest for, "Treasonable language."[10]

Watson's transgression earned him an audience with Major General Ben "Beast" Butler, who commanded the U.S. forces in New Orleans. A political general, Butler was a former Congressman and the future Governor of Massachusetts. He acquired his nickname in recognition of his corruption, petty looting, and beastly treatment of local citizens, particularly the women. While in New Orleans, Butler increased his personal worth over twenty-fold to over $3 million. Watson described his head as "large and flabby." He was the most "forbidding and ill-favoured personage" he had ever seen.[11]

To Watson's relief, Butler referred his case to a judge who he knew personally. He got off with an admonition to "abstain from making any remarks which would be irritating." When Watson received his wallet with only "half the money extracted," he hastily and gratefully departed New Orleans in August and returned to Baton Rouge. The ruined town was under nominal Confederate control, but there was no business being done and Watson had no prospects. Under these circumstances, he made the ironic conclusion that the "safest place to be was in the army."[12]

His old unit had scattered and many of his former officers and compatriots were dead or wounded. He joined a Confederate detachment in early October of 1862, as they were advancing to attack the enemy at the Battle of Corinth. Watson charged into the fray with his unit. Before he reached enemy lines, a Union minié ball struck him in the leg, and knocked him to the ground. The battle raged around him as he crawled into a recently dug fox hole. He bandaged his wound as best he could, and remained immobile. At nightfall, the battle subsided, and stretcher-bearers carted him to a field hospital where a doctor dressed his minor wound. His rescuers were all dressed in blue. The Union Army had won the day, and William Watson was a prisoner of war.[13]

Watson's wound soon healed, and he was placed on the parole list thanks to the intervention of a Scottish American major. He was released and allowed to return to Baton Rouge. As a wounded soldier on parole, he received deferential treatment from both sides of the conflict, including travel and accommodation at no charge. He made his way through the lines and back to Baton Rouge. He had a limp and no interest in rejoining the army. He found that business remained at a standstill, and it took several months for him to settle his commercial and personal interests. "It was now getting towards the summer of 1863," when Watson made his way back to New Orleans. He had decided to leave the country.[14]

Rather than purchasing passage back to Scotland, he invested in a schooner and naively decided to try his hand at blockade running. Thus began the second phase of his Civil War adventures, this time as a swashbuckling sailor. His plan was to sally forth from New Orleans in a small schooner bound for the closest British Colony at Belize, Honduras. He found a suitable vessel in New Orleans in June of 1863. He was no stranger to that city, having lived there before the war. After taking possession of the schooner, he chose the name *Rob Roy* in honor of the rebellious Scottish folk hero, Rob Roy MacGregor. He also obtained a temporary British registration for his newly acquired American schooner.[15]

When William Watson purchased *Rob Roy* at New Orleans in 1863, the schooner's name was *Francis Marquez, Jr.* (sometimes spelled *F. Marquez, Jr.* or *F. Marquis, Jr.*). New Orleans registry records show that its namesake owner constructed the schooner in 1855 at Madisonville, Louisiana. However, *Francis Marquez, Jr.* had begun its life six years earlier in Alabama. Mr. Marquez had only rebuilt the schooner in Louisiana. The ship's constructor used the keel and other materials from "an old schooner called the *James Cartey*" to create the new schooner. The hull of the original *James Cartey* began its life in 1849 at Bon Secours, Alabama, on a small lake connected to Mobile Bay.

The first owner was Mary B. Merrett of Bonfouca who registered her schooner at Mobile. The captain was her husband, C.H.B. Merrett. The Merrett's sold their schooner to Salvador J. Fronti (or Fonty) of New Orleans in March 1854. Fronti then sold it to Francis Marquez of Louisiana. The next year, the newly rebuilt *Francis Marquez, Jr.* set sail with the same physical measurements and tonnage as *James Cartey*. After initially trading between Mobile, New Orleans and Florida, the renamed schooner carried goods between Lake Ponchartrain and New Orleans under several different captains.[16]

After the Union capture of New Orleans, in April 1862, the schooner *F. Marquez, Jr.* became involved in an illicit scheme to move goods across enemy lines between New Orleans and Ponchatoula. Confederate military and customs officials on the northern side of Lake Ponchartrain seized the schooner for a short while. They released her after admonishing the schooner's captain to cease and desist trading with the enemy. With the lack of near-term trading prospects on the lake, the Marquez family decided to sell their schooner. The buyer was Antoine Laganne who registered *Francis Marquez, Jr.* in New Orleans on January 2, 1863, and listed himself as both the owner and master of the vessel.[17]

Mr. Laganne apparently did not go to sea in his new schooner, but hired the experienced sailing master, Henry Laverty, to take her to Matamoros. Laverty was a 45-year-old Irishman. Standing only 5 feet 5½ inches tall, Laverty had been dutifully practicing his maritime trade out of New Orleans since 1849. *Rob Roy* was the second schooner that he had commanded since the outbreak of the Civil War. The first was a 109-ton schooner, *C.P. Knapp*.[18]

Henry Laverty sailed the *C.P. Knapp* to the Rio Grande in January 1862 and loaded her with 150 bales of cotton bound for Havana. Over the next nine months, Laverty made several round trips between Havana and Matamoros as captain of the *C.P. Knapp*. By February of 1863, Laverty signed on as the captain of the schooner *Francis Marquez, Jr.* Captain Laverty sailed the smaller, 48-ton *Francis Marquez, Jr.* to the Rio Grande late that winter and returned to his home in New Orleans with 23 bales of cotton on April 4, 1863.[19]

It was at this point that the seafaring adventures of William Watson merged with those of the grizzled 14-year veteran of the sea, that he renamed *Rob Roy*. His schooner had a new name, but was still under the command of Henry Laverty. During his initial voyage from New Orleans to Belize, Watson's role in the adventure was that of owner and supercargo, or purser. It was his job to conduct the business aspects of the schooner's operations. Watson's primary purpose for sailing to Belize was to finalize *Rob Roy*'s permanent British registration papers. He then loaded a small amount of cargo and had Captain Laverty chart a course for the Rio Grande. He was optimistic that he could purchase a cargo of Texas cotton at the border town of Matamoros.[20]

The ploy of changing the registration of a vessel from the American flag to that of a neutral country was a widespread practice during the Civil War. It was a tactic that both sides of the conflict used to protect their investment. A vessel sailing under either a U.S. or Confederate flag would be susceptible to immediate capture or destruction whenever it encountered an enemy warship. To avoid the certain loss of the vessel and cargo, the "false flag" of a neutral country at least offered the owners a chance of release, escape, or government-to-government intervention.[21]

Watson naturally chose the British Red Ensign for his flag. As a British citizen, he did not have to employ the usual subterfuge of paying a foreign national to register the vessel on the American owner's behalf. To obtain a permanent registration, however, Watson had to sail his "whitewashed" schooner to a British port within the specified six-month period. This registration requirement helped explain why Watson's initial port of call was the British colonial port of Belize. The practice of changing flags and ship names complicates the investigation and analysis of Civil War blockade-running activities. This complexity is especially relevant for the hundreds of small sailing vessels that engaged in this inherently secretive business. Watson admitted to changing his schooner's name to "*Rob Roy*," but he never identified its previous owner or its former name.[22]

The Union blockade of Galveston had initially devastated the Texas economy. Galveston was the state's most important conduit for interstate and international trade, and its only deep-water port. There were five other Texas passes that accessed the state's large, but shallow, bays and lagoons (San Luis, Cavallo, Aransas, Corpus Christi, and Brazos Santiago). There were four other rivers (Sabine, Brazos, San Bernard, and Rio Grande) and a creek (Caney) that emptied directly into the Gulf of Mexico in the 1860s. The hydrography of the Texas coast had inherent advantages for small sailing vessels and light-draft steamers trying to avoid ocean-going U.S. Navy warships.[23]

No other Confederate state had a long, shallow coast and a border with a neutral country. The Texas coast offered unique blockade-running opportunities for shallow-draft sailing vessels and even small steamships that were not built for ocean travel. These vessels could hug the Texas and Mexican shoreline for safety and concealment. The geographic realities of the Texas coast meant that schooners remained a viable blockade-running option throughout the Civil War.[24]

The type of vessel favored by European traders attempting to run the Union blockade of the South by late 1862, was a fast side-paddle wheel steamer. In the open ocean, sailing ships bound for Nassau in the Bahamas and Bermuda were simply too slow and too dependent upon the winds. Distance alone made Galveston an unattractive blockade-running option. Texas ports were the most distant of all Confederate destinations from the primary international blockade-running havens, including Havana. Even Wilmington, North Carolina, the primary Confederate port on the east coast, was closer to Havana than was Galveston. Exacerbating the transportation challenge was the lack of a rail connection between Texas and any other state.[25]

The relative remoteness of Texas would remain a major disadvantage for the state until the Union began to occupy the other Confederate ports in the Gulf of Mexico and on the Atlantic coast. By January 1865, there were no other deep water Confederate ports available to larger blockade-running steamers. Beginning in the fall of 1864, and particularly during the last five months of the war, Galveston became the best and only port available to these sleek ocean-going blockade runners. During these last months of the Civil War, the notorious, but glamorous steamships competed with the workhorse schooners for cargos and space at the Galveston piers. One of those schooners was *Rob Roy*.[26]

William Watson's schooner made its first appearance in the public record under the name "*Rob Roy*" on May 8, 1863. Watson advertised his "Fast sailing schooner" in the New Orleans *Times-Picayune* newspaper. The ad ran for 12 days, and invited consignments of cargo bound for Belize. Watson's own account was not specific about his departure date or descriptions of his cargo. Fortunately, contemporary sources have filled in the gaps. *Rob Roy* cleared U.S. Customs at New Orleans on May

British merchant ship Red Ensign (ID 53420485 © Steve Allen, Dreamstime.com).

19, 1863. The schooner was loaded with barrels of molasses (57), pork (15), tar (37), and lime (5), plus 20 kegs of nails, 30,000 shingles, and seven packages of general merchandise.[27]

Watson said that just as they were leaving New Orleans, a harbor patrol vessel came alongside to inspect *Rob Roy*'s papers. Watson took care to note that the man in charge was an Irishman, "who seemed to possess more pride of his own importance than common intelligence or knowledge of his duty, trifling as that was." It was the official's duty to confirm that each vessel had the proper customs clearance that stated the name of the vessel and its port of origin (hailing port). Since *Rob Roy* had recently changed its registration from the United States to the United Kingdom, his Belize, British Honduras, registration was only provisional, which meant he did not yet have a hailing port.[28]

The obstinate official threatened to prevent Watson from leaving, but what he really wanted was a bribe. While Watson was a novice, his captain, Henry Laverty, was not. The petty tyranny of the government bureaucrat enraged *Rob Roy*'s captain, but not to the point of violence. As the harbor patrol official strutted around the deck, Laverty ordered their carpenter to take a paintbrush, and write "Of Belize Hon." on the stern. The crewman was no calligrapher, so the clumsy title looked more like "Balizehon." The official must have been incredibly ignorant since he misread the name as "Babylon." Laverty's quick thinking enervated the official who allowed them to proceed, as he entered "*Rob Roy*, of Babylon" in his ledger. Watson later learned that when a "more intelligent" customs official received this report, he suspected "that there must be come devilry under this, and at once telegraphed the forts [Fort Jackson on the West Bank and Fort St. Philip on the East Bank of the Mississippi] to stop the vessel until further inquiry." Watson claimed to have evaded this extra delay by "slipping away from under the forts during the night."[29]

Rob Roy soon exited the river and entered the open waters of the Gulf of Mexico, about 60 miles south of New Orleans. The sailing distance from the mouth of the Mississippi River to the colonial port of Belize in British Honduras was about 1,090 miles. With a fair wind, the voyage could take between five and seven days. Winds and currents, however, were rarely fair or consistent. *Rob Roy* often slowed to a crawl and was sometimes completely becalmed, with nary a puff of wind. At the other extreme, frequent storms might rage for days and blow the schooner off course, creating added delays.

Rob Roy was nine days into its voyage to Belize when Watson and his crew spotted a warship on the horizon. At first, he thought that the steamer might be the HBMS (Her Britannic Majesty's Ship) *Rinaldo*. This Royal Navy frigate had called at New Orleans and lingered near Galveston earlier in the year 1863. As the unidentified warship drew near and came alongside *Rob Roy*, the crew saw that the steamship was flying a Confederate flag. The vessel's boarding officer took a brief look at Watson's papers. He saw that registration papers verified that *Rob Roy* had a provisional register as a British vessel, a manifest that listed its cargo, and a U.S. Customs clearance for Belize.[30]

After sharing his recent New Orleans newspapers with the frigate's boarding officer, Watson and his crew watched as the warship steamed over the horizon. The captain and crew of *Rob Roy* surmised that the unidentified steamer was the famous Confederate cruiser CSS *Alabama*. This commerce raider, under Captain Raphael Semmes, had blasted the Union warship *Hatteras* to the bottom of the Gulf off Galveston Island the previous January. Although Watson's description of this encounter clearly echoed his own beliefs, he was careful to cite the speculation of his crew and not his own opinion that the mystery gunboat was the *Alabama*.[31]

Unfortunately for Watson's credibility, not only was HBMS *Rinaldo* not in the Gulf of Mexico at the time, neither was *Alabama*. In fact, there were no Confederate commerce raiders or privateers within hundreds of miles of his location. From mid–May through June of 1863, the CSS (Confederate States Ship) *Alabama* and all other Confederate raiders were in the South Atlantic Ocean. Joining *Alabama* in these southern waters were the CSS *Florida* and the steel-hulled CSS *Georgia*. In short, there were no candidates to substantiate Watson's claim about being stopped by a Confederate cruiser. The episode was either a complete fabrication or the misidentification of a Union warship disguised as a Confederate commerce raider.[32]

Despite this apparently bogus brush with the famous Confederate warship, British port authorities do confirm that *Rob Roy* arrived at Belize in 1863. These records show that William Watson obtained a permanent British registration for his schooner on Saturday June 13, 1863. Its official ship register number was "46416" and the schooner measured 37.92 tons. The tonnage figure used the British Moorsom system to determine the internal volume of the vessel and then subtracting the spaces used for fuel, the crew, and other non-revenue producing areas.[33]

Following normal registration procedures, the British surveyor at Belize marked those identifying numbers on *Rob Roy*'s main beam. While seemingly straightforward, this official tonnage registration for *Rob Roy* was considerably different than the tonnage listed in, or derived from, Watson's information and other contemporary sources. In his first chapter, he described *Rob Roy* in detail. She was a schooner with a retractable centerboard, ideal for navigating the shallow inlets, bays, and rivers of the Gulf Coast. He said that she measured 78 feet in length, 22 feet 6 inches abeam, with a loaded draft of 4 feet 9 inches and a hold that was 6 feet deep. He did not provide the vessel's tonnage, but those dimensions yielded a standard British gross tonnage figure of 92 60/94 tons. The tonnage figures for *Rob Roy* found in numerous other references range from 30 to 92 tons.[34]

The vagaries of various mid–19th-century systems for calculating vessel tonnage created confusion about tonnage a vessel's size and carrying capacity. Official reports also inconsistently applied existing tonnage measurement criteria. However, dozens of Belize-registered schooners with smaller dimensions than *Rob Roy* (as described by Watson) had greater tonnage figures. A sailing vessel with *Rob Roy*'s stated dimensions should have at a Moorsom value of about 55 and not 37.92 tons. Something is clearly amiss with Watson's description of *Rob Roy*'s dimensions, particularly its length. The reason for the inconsistency is simple. Watson's numbers were in error, at least for the dimensions that surveyors used to determine tonnage. (See Appendix 7.)[35]

This seemingly esoteric discrepancy about *Rob Roy*'s dimensions set a tenacious researcher and former U.S. Navy intelligence analyst on a quest to solve the mystery

1. The Adventure Begins

of *Rob Roy*'s antecedents. It was a question that had baffled researchers for over 100 years. The result of that search was the positive identification of *Rob Roy*'s original name, its true dimensions, and its adventurous life prior to Watson's purchase. Although Watson never mentioned the schooner's former name or owner, he did drop several clues. This meager trail of evidence began in New Orleans and then ran to Belize and Matamoros, Mexico.

At Belize, the government registrar recorded William Watson as the owner of *Rob Roy*, but that official did not name its captain. The clue to the captain's identity came from Watson when he reported that his next port of call after Belize was Matamoros. As his schooner made its approach to this Mexican port on the Rio Grande, Watson made an offhand remark that provided an important hint about *Rob Roy*'s history. He said that his captain and most of his crew had been aboard the schooner when it last called at the Rio Grande in the winter of 1862–1863. Although Watson provided no additional information, contemporary newspapers had identified *Rob Roy*'s master when it cleared from New Orleans in May 1863. The papers named him as "Capt. Leverty" and according to Watson, he retained this man as captain when he headed for Matamoros.[36]

Mid–19th-century newspapers were notoriously inconsistent with their spelling of names, so it was not surprising that the name "Leverty" did not appear in other editions of the New Orleans papers. The captain's name was Henry Laverty. A letter written to a Matamoros merchant after *Rob Roy* had reached the Rio Grande in July 1863, revealed the captain's true identity. Shortly after his six-day voyage from Belize, Captain Laverty signed this brief letter on behalf of William Watson while they waited at the mouth of the Rio Grande for a cargo.

"Boca Del Rio July 13th, 1863
Messrs. San Román & Co.,
Matamoras [sic]

Gentlemen,

My owner has agreed to take the cotton to Havannah [sic] at 2 ½¢ per ft. for eighty bales provided the cotton is here within eight days. The vessel is now ready to receive it. Please to send an answer by return of stage.

Yours resply,

Henry Laverty
Capt. Schooner *Rob Roy*
For William Watson"[37]

The letter to José San Román confirms that the captain of William Watson's schooner *Rob Roy* was Henry Laverty and not "Capt. Leverty" or "Lafferty" as the New Orleans newspapers sometimes spelled his name. It also was not "Enrique Laverty" as Spanish language documents would translate his name. Following this important clue, a check of the 69 schooners known to have called at the Rio Grande during the previous winter, revealed that only one had a captain with a name that was phonetically similar to Laverty. It was *Francis Marquez, Jr*. This 48-ton schooner was home ported in New Orleans, and like its captain, its name was often misidentified. Spelling variations included *F. Marquez, Jr.*, *F. Marquez, Jr.*, or *P. Marquez, Jr.* The schooner *Francis Marquez, Jr.* under the command of Captain Laverty had delivered a small load of Texas cotton from Matamoros to New Orleans in early April 1863. This was a legal way to bypass U.S. Customs laws and get Texas cotton into U.S. cotton mills.[38]

The schooner *Francis Marquez, Jr.* was the namesake of its former owner and captain who had registered the vessel at New Orleans in June 1855. The New Orleans registration stated that *Francis Marquez, Jr.* had a flush deck, two masts, a square stern, and a plain hold. An additional, important biographic detail was that Mr. Marquez had constructed his schooner at the Lake Pontchartrain port city of Madisonville, Louisiana, in 1855. It measured 58 feet in length, was 22 feet 4 inches abeam, had a depth of hold of 6 feet, and a draft of 4 feet 7 inches.[39]

The dimensions that William Watson gave for *Rob Roy* were approximately the same as those of *Francis Marquez, Jr.* except for the length. The New Orleans surveyor registered *Francis Marquez, Jr.* at 48 4/95 Gross Registered Tons (GRT). This figure matches the GRT calculation that can be derived using the measured length of 58 feet. It also more closely matches the dimensions of similar Belize-registered schooners that had Moorsom tonnage totals similar to *Rob Roy*'s. (See Appendix 7.)

The association of Captain Henry Laverty with both *Rob Roy* and *Francis Marquez, Jr.* and the more accurate dimensions and tonnage figures would convince most analysts that the two vessels were, in fact, the same schooner. However, there is one more piece of evidence that definitively confirms that Watson's *Rob Roy* had been named *Francis Marquez, Jr.* when he bought the schooner. This information is in an obscure series of volumes that lists small British-flagged merchant vessels that were registered between 1849 and 1977. Titled the *Mercantile Navy List*, this annual publication recorded all British-registered vessels measuring one quarter of a ton and over. These vessels included those registered in colonial ports such as Belize during the American Civil War.

Rob Roy made its first appearance in the *Mercantile Navy List* in 1872, over seven years after it last sailed the seas. The publication confirms that *Rob Roy*'s owner was William Watson of "Largs, Ayshire" (Ayrshire, Scotland) who registered his 38-ton schooner at Belize in 1863 as vessel number 46416. The entry shows that the schooner had been built in the United States at Madisonville (Louisiana) in 1855. An additional annotation at the bottom of the page is tagged to *Rob Roy*. It simply says, "Foreign name: *F. Marquez, Jr.*" The "Foreign name" designation on British ship registration documents represented the vessel's previous name, if any, prior to its current British registration.[40]

These official British records match the other primary sources that link *Rob Roy* to *Francis Marquez, Jr.* The owner had only rebuilt the schooner in 1855 at Madisonville, Louisiana. It was first christened in Alabama six years earlier as *James Cartey*. After initially trading between Mobile, New Orleans and Florida, the original owners sold their interest in their vessel in 1854. The next year, the newly rebuilt schooner set sail under the name, *Francis Marquez, Jr.*, but it retained the same physical measurements and tonnage as *James Cartey* (Appendix 7, Table 1). After reconstruction, it routinely shuttled between Lake Ponchartrain and New Orleans under several different captains until the Civil War intervened.[41]

1. The Adventure Begins

After the Union capture of New Orleans, in April 1862, *F. Marquez, Jr.* ran afoul of Confederate officials for trading with the enemy. The Army detained the schooner and admonished its captain for his illicit activity. Foiled in this profitable enterprise, the Louisiana owners sold the schooner to another Southerner who hired Henry Laverty as Captain. Trade with Matamoros and other neutral ports under the Stars and Stripes was the only viable alternative. Captain Laverty navigated the 48-ton, U.S.-registered, *Francis Marquez, Jr.* into the Rio Grande late in the winter months of 1862–1863. He returned to New Orleans with a small load of cotton in early April 1863. (The backstory of Captain Laverty and the earlier incarnations of *Rob Roy* can be found in Appendix 1.)[42]

Watson's account of his maritime adventures began at New Orleans the following month. At first, he was just an ordinary commercial shipper, but the tantalizing lure of quick profits soon enticed him to risk running the blockade.

2

From Merchantman to Blockade Runner

Watson's often quoted descriptions of Bagdad, Matamoros, and the anchorage off the mouth of the Rio Grande captures the chaotic energy of the time and place. He was, however, "very far from being favorably impressed with the place." In part, because Matamoros was continuously "enveloped in a cloud of dust." Men looked like "millers, with clothes, hair, and beard saturated" with grayish-white dust, making it hard to recognize one from the other. He observed that "there must certainly be some strong inducement for people to live in such a place."[1]

He also noticed that the flat-roofed one and two-story buildings in the town were ominously and "thickly pitted with bullet-marks," most of them recent. He learned that there had been an attack on the city as part of the on-going Mexican Civil War. The town's defenders prevailed, and as a tribute, Mexican officials reinforced the city's pride by recognizing its official name of "Heroic Matamoras" [sic] (that it had earned over a decade earlier). When Watson asked a long-time resident about how many people were killed in the recent battle, the man said, "Oh, no! They are great people here for shooting the houses; they don't shoot the people so much."[2]

With the obvious signs of violence that was typical of a frontier border town, Watson expected an equally haphazard level of law and order. To his surprise, he observed just the opposite.

> I cannot say, however, that lawlessness, riot, or violence to person existed to any extent. The Mexican authorities maintained peace and good order in that respect, and let the trade go on. They took care to exact their moiety in duties and charges, and a rich harvest they made.[3]

The same could not be said for the Texas side of the border. It did not appear that Watson's curiosity was sufficiently piqued to venture across the Rio Grande to investigate. Even Confederate officers confessed "that Brownsville was about the rowdiest town of Texas, which was the most lawless state in the Confederacy. But they declared they had never seen an inoffensive man subjected to insult or annoyance." Lieutenant Colonel Sir Arthur James Lyon Fremantle, an observer from the United Kingdom's Coldstream Guard, reported that the Texans had a practical attitude toward prompt justice. They reasoned that the shooting down and stringing-up of desperadoes was a necessity in such a thinly populated state. It was also helpful to understand local customs to avoid any action that might be reckoned as giving offense when none was intended.[4]

2. From Merchantman to Blockade Runner 23

Watson's colorful observations seem authentic and add zest to the often-impersonal historical accounts of the Rio Grande frontier. As usual, Watson was imprecise about the timing and duration of his stay at the border. Fortunately, the previously quoted letter from *Rob Roy*'s captain, Henry Laverty that he wrote to José San Román, verifies Watson's presence at the Texas-Mexico border in mid–July 1863. Within his narrative there are several other events that help identify the general timeframe. He voiced his displeasure at the lack of British resolve following the Union capture of the British steamer *Sir William Peel*. That incident took place within or near the neutral waters off the Rio Grande on September 11, 1863. *Rob Roy* went to sea shortly after that event, which places Watson at the Rio Grande for about two months.[5]

Watson had accurately surmised that there were strong inducements that brought people to the Rio Grande. Amid this bustling frontier boom town, there were hundreds of opportunists out to make a quick dollar, some by hard work and others through moral or fiscal corruption. For the naive and inexperienced, "prospects of an advantageous trade in that direction were entirely visionary." As the novice blockade runner William Watson observed, everyone was trying to "grab what they could, and many schemes there were to make money out of the crisis." As he would learn, the summer of 1863 at its best offered only financial ruin, with death running a close second.[6]

Between July and September, the flow of cotton to the border was at a standstill. Disruptions to cotton supply chains due to political and military disputes were common, but this time it was a result of a South Texas drought. Mule and oxen trains could not survive the trek across the Wild Horse Desert to reach the Rio Grande. As a result, there was a surplus of imported goods at the border, but no cotton to pay for them.[7]

Dozens of larger vessels had to anchor offshore, impatiently waiting for their agents to send them a load of cotton. Very shallow draft vessels like *Rob Roy* were fortunate to cross the Rio Grande bar and reach the meager port facilities at Bagdad. The crossing was hazardous, and the lucky ones were able to reach safety, but there was no cotton to be had.

The Mexican City of Bagdad had sprouted up almost overnight to accommodate the cotton trade at the mouth of the river. The former fishing village had grown to a population of almost 20,000 who lived in rough wooden shanties that passed for hotels, boarding houses, and billiard-saloons or "rum mills." These hastily constructed buildings were no more than sheds. They were in danger of collapse whenever the sudden, gale-force winds of a Texas norther rolled into town. Most of Bagdad's crude restaurants were open to the elements. Their only protection from the sun, wind, and sand, was courtesy of tarpaulins, loosely spread over poles to form a roof that was constantly flapping in the wind.[8]

Watson made note of the numerous unemployed lighters that were lying about. These small craft were dedicated to transferring cargo to and from the deep draft vessels anchored offshore. They would then carry their freight over the sand bar protecting the entrance to the Rio Grande. All were under the protection of the Mexican flag on these neutral waters, but several were Confederate owned. A few of the lighters were steam powered, most only had sails, but they all had shallow drafts. Lighters usually offloaded their inbound cargos at Bagdad, Mexico on the banks of the Rio Grande.[9]

Most inbound and outbound cargos traveled to and from Bagdad by ox and mule carts. There were also several smaller river steamers that were able to navigate the notoriously crooked Rio Grande between Matamoros and Bagdad. Those river steamers included at least two of Richard King and Mifflin Kenedy's Mexican-flagged steamers that could cross the bar and steam all the way to Matamoros.[10]

The stack of imported goods and lack of cotton at the border did not bode well for Watson's prospects, particularly as his supply of cash began to dwindle. Laverty's letter to José San Román confirmed that blockade running was not his first choice. He truly had intended to load cotton at Matamoros and clear for Havana. It was only after *Rob Roy* had languished at the Rio Grande for six weeks without obtaining a load of cotton that Watson decided to consider other, more dangerous, options.[11]

Watson's inspiration for overcoming this dilemma by running *Rob Roy* into Texas came from another blockade runner. This confident captain had just arrived from the port of Velasco on the Brazos River in a small schooner with a nice load of cotton. Watson misidentified the man as "Captain Shaeffer." He was Captain Henricus "Henry" Ervin Scherffius, a 27-year-old Texan of German ancestry who was the older brother of a fellow blockade runner. He was one of the most successful of the blockade runners in the Western Gulf of Mexico and later achieved prominence as the mayor of Houston.[12]

Watson never mentioned the names of the two blockade-running schooners that Scherffius sailed into and out of the Rio Grande, but the first was *Cora*. She sailed from the Brazos and arrived at Bagdad just after *Rob Roy*. Henry Scherffius had purchased *Cora* earlier in the year from a swindling group of partners who were attempting to run Texas cotton into New York.[13]

Captain Scherffius was so enthusiastic about his prospects for success that he sold his schooner to Captain John E. Hulburt. He then purchased a second one at Matamoros on behalf of Thomas W. House. His new schooner was a "beautiful, swift-looking vessel" appropriately named *Deer*. Scherffius would command *Deer* as he set off for a return trip to the Brazos in company with *Cora*.[14]

Captain Laverty was not as excited about the idea of running *Rob Roy* through the blockade into Texas. His unhappy experience with Yankee warships and prize courts while captain of *C.P. Knapp* had dampened his enthusiasm for blockade running. Watson was disappointed, but empathetic when Laverty and most of his crew refused to stay with *Rob Roy*. The need for a new crew only added to Watson's problems. To pay off the crew and cover his mounting expenses, Watson had to take on an unidentified partner who had contacts in Galveston. His meager financial circumstances forced him to sell half the cargo and a half interest in *Rob Roy* to an unnamed merchant in Brownsville.[15]

Watson also had to recruit a new captain in Matamoros. At the Rio Grande, the demand was high for qualified sailing captains who were willing to run the blockade. When Captain Scherffius hired John E. Hulburt to temporarily take over command of his schooner *Cora*, the supply of available captains was reduced even further. Watson eventually found a suitable candidate in another Irishman, a powerfully built man who had served as first mate on a British-flagged bark. Watson identified him as an Irishman named "Captain J." He was most likely from the larger British sailing bark (barque) named *Laura Edwards* that had arrived at the Rio Grande from New Orleans in early August. Watson knew little about the man other than he was qualified as a ship's master, able to recruit a crew, and willing to run the blockade. It was only after he had signed the shipping papers, that Watson received a warning that his new captain was a man of poor character. By then, it was too late to make a change. There were no other available options.[16]

Rob Roy departed the Rio Grande a few days after the capture of *Sir William Peel* on September 11. Ideally, the voyage to the Brazos River would have taken only two to three days, but *Rob Roy* suffered weather delays. Another problem surfaced a few days after getting underway. The new captain became seriously ill with yellow fever. The captain's pugnacious first mate, and former shipmate of the captain when they both served aboard the British bark, took command of *Rob Roy*. William Watson, who knew how to use a sextant and chronometer, took over the navigation duties.[17]

Watson said *Rob Roy* had been at sea for five days when they sighted a three-masted U.S. Navy schooner that he identified as "Kittitinie." Although she was also a sailing schooner, the USS *Kittatinny* carried six guns and at 461 tons, was considerably larger than *Rob Roy*. The 39-year-old Isaac D. Seyburn was *Kittatinny*'s captain. He was a Welsh-born master mariner with years of civilian experience at sea. The wizened captain sent a boarding party over to check Watson's papers. The Union sailors quickly retreated in their boat when they discovered that the captain had contracted the dreaded and deadly yellow fever. They gladly sent *Rob Roy* on its way unmolested.[18]

After weathering a gale for three days and convincing the Navy of his innocent intentions, the wind literally went out of Watson's sails. *Rob Roy* was becalmed for two days as was the nearby *Kittatinny*, which like *Rob Roy*, had to rely on the wind for propulsion. They slowly drifted apart as the sun set and the next morning *Kittatinny* was nowhere in sight.[19]

When the breeze finally picked up, Watson made a dash for the Brazos just as another gunboat came into view. Unfortunately, this one was a steamer. *Rob Roy* raced away from the Union warship as it bombarded him with rifled cannon balls fired at maximum range. The low trajectory of the shots caused them to ricochet across the Gulf waters. Watson avoided them all, except the last one. It skipped across the water and struck *Rob Roy*'s hull near the stern at the waterline. The damage did not appear to be serious, as the schooner finally sailed across the bar guarding the river, and beyond range of the gunboat. The Spanish had named the river *Los Brazos de Dios*, "The Arms of God," as a thanksgiving for their deliverance from the elements. The river's name was shortened, but not Anglicized like many of the Texas rivers. Appropriately, Watson and his crew experienced a similar feeling as the early Spanish when they experienced their first embrace of the Brazos' saving waters.[20]

The official records confirm that *Rob Roy* reached the Brazos River by September

"Very Nearly Captured in a Calm." William Watson, *Adventures of a Blockade Runner; or, Trade in Time of War*. London: Fisher Unwin, 1892, p. 118 (author's collection).

24, 1863. They also confirm the identity of the pilot who guided Watson across the shallow bar at the mouth of the river. He called himself the British Lion. He was a predictably colorful character named Samuel C. Lyon. The 52-year-old sailor was originally from Liverpool, but had come to Texas while it was still an independent nation. A long-time resident of Brazoria County, Lyon had been the sailing master for the Rio Grande portion of the ill-fated Mier Expedition in the winter of 1842. Mexican soldiers captured him and his fellow Texians, but Lyon escaped execution by not drawing one of the 17 black beans. The Mexicans finally released him in 1844. By 1861, Lyon was serving on the staff of the local Confederate Army commander in his familiar role as a Brazos River pilot.[21]

The equally confident character who had been Watson's inspiration for venturing into the blockade-running business was not as fortunate on his voyage from the Rio Grande. While at Matamoros, Watson had befriended Henry Scherffius, the owner of the schooner *Cora*. Scherffius had opted to take command of his newly purchased schooner *Deer*. He sent *Cora* back to the Brazos River under a different captain, and loaded *Deer* for a similar voyage. He and Watson both set out for the Brazos at about the same time. Like much of Watson's account, his telling of this episode was essentially correct, but he placed the incident slightly out of sequence and inaccurately remembered some of the specifics.[22]

Like Watson, Captain Scherffius and *Deer* were hounded by the three-masted schooner USS *Kittatinny* as they approached the Brazos River. Unlike *Rob Roy*, *Deer* was too far away from the mouth of the river and its protecting forts on either side

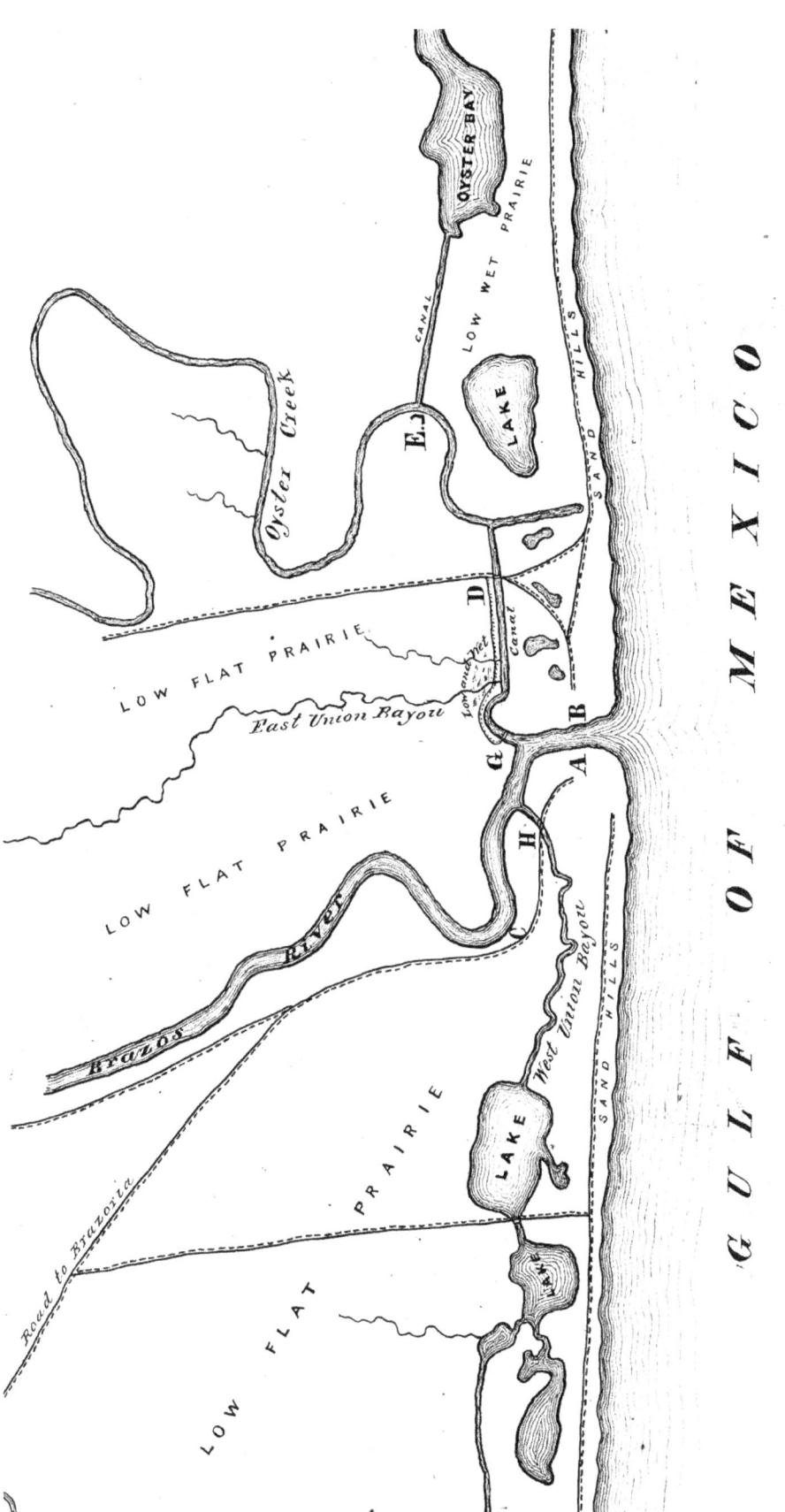

Locations of works at the mouth of the Brazos River (courtesy Jeremy Francis Gilmer Papers #276, Southern Historical Collection, Wilson Library, University of North Carolina at Chapel Hill).

to make its escape (see illustration on page 27 points labeled "A" and "B"). Instead, Scherffius pointed the bow of *Deer* toward the shore and set his schooner on fire even before he reached the sandy Texas beach. The captain thought it better to destroy everything than to risk allowing the Yankees to capture *Deer*, its cargo, and most importantly, himself and his shipmates. *Kittatinny* fired several broadsides that overshot their mark and hit the beach. *Deer*'s crew narrowly escaped the flames and cannon fire as they scrambled over the dunes near the mouth of Caney Creek located about 15 miles southwest of the Brazos.[23]

To salvage the schooner and its cargo, Captain Seyburn of the *Kittatinny* sent a boat ashore. As the sailors neared the flaming wreck, six Confederate soldiers on picket duty greeted them with a volley of musket fire. One bullet hit a sailor in his back and exited his chest without striking any vital organs. The schooner *Deer* belonged to the prominent merchant Thomas W. House of Houston. The schooner and its cargo were a total loss. The date was September 22, 1863, which was within a day of *Rob Roy*'s arrival from the Rio Grande.[24]

After celebrating his exhilarating dash through the blockade and into the Brazos River, William Watson took time to assess the damage. He discovered that *Rob Roy* was taking on water. Without prompt action, it would sink in the middle of the river. He deliberately ran the schooner aground on the riverbank, but at least he was mostly above water. His crew made temporary repairs to the damage inflicted by the Union cannonball and then continued 30 miles upriver to the railhead city of Columbia (now a community within the City of West Columbia). From there, Watson had to make several trips to Houston and Galveston to meet with Confederate customs officials and the agent who was managing the sale of *Rob Roy*'s consignment of cargo. (See Appendix 2 for an explanation of the differences between blockade running and smuggling, and the consequences of "violating" the blockade.)[25]

According to Confederate officials, *Rob Roy*'s cargo consisted of 36 barrels of molasses, 12 barrels of pork, 19 barrels of roofing tar, 20 kegs of nails, 4 boxes of matches and $1,400 in specie (hard currency). This tally was similar to the cargo he brought out of New Orleans and indicated that he had sold the shingles and a portion of the molasses, pork, and roofing tar. He still had all the kegs of nails. Watson's accounting of his cargo was less specific. According to his description of the items that did not sustain severe damage, there were, "…barrels of salt port, crates of earthenware, nails, and ironmongery." He bemoaned the loss of the cases of matches, chests of tea, and sacks of coffee that were destroyed by salt water that filled *Rob Roy*'s hull.[26]

After *Rob Roy* made its exciting escape into Texas, Watson's problems were just beginning. Confederate Army officers were initially suspicious about *Rob Roy* due to the minimal cargo that the schooner brought into port. Ship captains rarely risked running the blockade with so little cargo to sell and convert into cotton, unless they were up to no good. The soldiers also learned that the schooner had been built in Louisiana and was now owned by its supercargo, William Watson of New Orleans.[27]

Watson and *Rob Roy* would spend the better part of four tediously trying months attempting to depart the Brazos River. Watson would have to contend with Confederate officials, a damaged schooner, and an aggressively dishonest captain.

3

De los Brazos de Dios a las Manos del Diablo

Watson traveled by train from Columbia on the Brazos River to Galveston where he submitted his crew list and vessel registration with the British consul there. When he returned on September 30, the Scotsman discovered his first major setback. He had escaped the clutches of the U.S. Navy only to be driven into the hands of the Confederate Army. Army engineers had seized *Rob Roy* and its crew for government service. While he was away, Confederate engineers had cut away a portion of *Rob Roy*'s port and starboard rails. When Watson arrived, the soldiers were preparing to install a pile driver on deck. The army needed the schooner as a platform for placing obstructions at the mouth of the river. Their objective was to prevent Union vessels from running past the two forts that protected the entrance.[1]

The gentlemanly colonel in command at the forts said that the army's seizure of *Rob Roy* was nothing personal, and not because he suspected Watson of any illicit activities. The colonel assured Watson that the army would pay for the use of his schooner, albeit in devalued Confederate dollars. Watson identified this officer as Colonel Evans.[2]

The gentleman commanding Fort Sulakowski at Velasco on the north side and Fort Bates at Quintana on the south side of the Brazos was not Colonel Evans. The commander of the forts and all the troops in the area was Colonel Joseph Bates. Standing six feet two inches tall and weighing well over 200 pounds, Bates had a commanding physical appearance and excellent public speaking skills. These attributes complemented the courteous demeanor that Watson had observed in the colonel. He had been in Texas since 1845 after serving four terms in the Alabama legislature. Three years later, he served a single term as Mayor of Galveston and then received a presidential appointment as the U.S. Marshal for Eastern Texas. In 1854, he moved to a large plantation on the west side of the San Bernard River, where he became a farmer and rancher before he joined the Confederate Army.[3]

A year prior to his meeting with William Watson, Bates had endured a petty, but testy confrontation with Colonel Xavier B. Debray, his immediate commander at the time. Debray objected to Bates' use of the title "Colonel" when he was only entitled to the rank of Lieutenant Colonel. Colonel Debray was a naturalized Frenchman with military training and connections to Texas Governor Edward Clark. Debray had quickly risen from the rank of Captain to Colonel within a year. Bates, on the other hand, had been a Major General in the Alabama militia prior to the war. His wartime appointment at the rank of Lt. Colonel was only temporary until Richmond approved his permanent promotion. That approval finally came in March 1863. Major General John Bankhead Magruder who commanded Confederate military forces in Texas at the time, backdated his promotion to September 1861, which gave Colonel Bates seniority over the spiteful Debray. Magruder's support reinforced the portly colonel's loyalty and eagerness to promptly carry out the general's instructions.[4]

When Watson arrived in Texas, Major General Magruder was concerned that after the failed Union naval attack at the Sabine earlier that month, the Brazos might be next. Colonel Bates was under added pressure to mount a successful defense to match Captain Dick Dowling's brilliant victory at Sabine Pass on September 8, 1863. Dowling's small artillery company had defeated a Union invasion fleet and captured the gunboats USS *Clifton* and USS *Sachem* during the assault.[5]

Colonel Joseph Bates (Brazoria County Historical Museum Collection, Angleton, TX).

Lieutenant Abraham Cross was the Confederate engineer in charge of constructing defenses at the Brazos. He was the individual who set the chain of events in motion that led to the seizure of *Rob Roy*. In mid–September, the lieutenant wrote to Colonel Bates asking him for a schooner suitable for driving piles at the mouth of the Brazos River. He was acting on instructions from Colonel Valery Sulakowski, Magruder's Polish American chief engineer who had designed the battle-tested defenses at Sabine Pass.[6]

Lieutenant Cross needed a vessel that was sturdy enough to mount a steam pile driver and small enough to operate at depths of only four feet. Since there were no suitable vessels at hand that were already in government service, Cross wanted the colonel to impress one for Army use. The schooner would strategically place wooden piles that would partially obstruct access and prevent unimpeded travel on the river.

The obstructions would at least cause steamers to carefully navigate around them. The wooden piles would enable the gunners at the forts to take deadly aim at the slower moving targets.[7]

After Lt. Cross made his request, General Magruder issued a special order on September 23 directing Colonel Bates to impress a "small schooner" for the purpose. He was to choose one belonging to a Texas citizen "in preference to a foreign vessel if such can be done at once." The general's order to obtain a suitable schooner went out just before *Rob Roy* arrived on the scene.[8]

Watson was naturally upset by the loss of his schooner. He had hoped to run out of Texas with a load of cotton as soon as possible. Delays would cost him money and lost opportunities. He made his way straight back to the British consul to protest the seizure. Other than the personal annoyance, Watson's grievance was that he was a British citizen and the owner of a British-flagged vessel. Consequently, his schooner should not have been subject to forced impressment by a foreign government. The consul agreed and said he would "reason the matter" with General Magruder.[9]

Although Watson never mentioned the consul's name, Her Britannic Majesty's Consul in Galveston was Arthur T. Lynn. He was the only British consul in Texas and had served in the same position since 1846. Lynn was well established in the community having married a local girl in 1853. Not only was he a Freemason, but he also held the position of grand prelate of the Galveston Knights Templar. He would continue as the British consul for Galveston until 1882 and lived out the remainder of his years there. General Magruder was not fond of diplomatic matters in general or Consul Lynn in particular. But as the representative of the world's greatest economic and naval power, the British consul could not be ignored.[10]

As Lynn had suggested, Watson returned to Galveston one week later to check on the status of *Rob Roy*. The consul said that he had seen the general and lodged a protest, but had not heard back. Watson reported that the consul handed him a letter and recommended that he try handing it directly to General Magruder in the event that his earlier letter had been mis-routed. However, just because Watson had a letter from the British consul and a burning desire to see General Magruder did not mean that he would gain an audience with the commanding general.[11]

His attempt to call on the general at his headquarters in Houston got off to a bad start. Magruder's staff officers and the quartermaster were annoyed at his presence. They were obviously prepared to brush him off. Watson then had a chance encounter with a familiar Confederate officer who was visiting the general's headquarters to say goodbye to a friend. That friend happened to be the very man Watson wanted to see: the quartermaster for the District of Texas. Watson recognized this visiting officer as a Captain who had been with the 2nd Texas Regiment. Like Watson, the man had suffered a minor leg wound and was left behind on the battlefield at Corinth and taken prisoner in October 1862.[12]

Watson said that both he and the captain had been released from a "Yankee hospital." Since that time, his friend had been promoted to Major and was now back in Texas on furlough. This chance meeting occurred as the major was about to return to his newly formed unit. As Magruder's staff officers looked on, the two former prisoners from the battlefield at Corinth, Mississippi, caught up with their adventures since their last, forced meeting. The major then asked the quartermaster and all the other officers present to show Watson "all the kindness they could and charge it to his account."[13]

As usual, Watson did not name the major whose timely appearance helped advance his case. A review of all possible candidates reveals that the officer's name was George Washington Lafayette Fly. Major Fly had been a captain with the 2nd Texas Infantry Regiment when he was wounded and captured at the Battle of Corinth. As Watson claimed, official records confirm that both men had been sent to a Union Army hospital with leg wounds. Reported as killed in action, Fly's family mourned their favorite son's death for at least three weeks. They were relieved to learn that he had only been wounded and captured. Fly was duly exchanged, and returned to his command.[14]

Fly was promoted to major in January 1863 before the siege of Vicksburg, where his regiment was serving. He was again captured upon the surrender of Vicksburg on July 4, 1863. Exchanged a second time, he was briefly ordered to Alabama and Mississippi. He returned to Texas in November to help reorganize the regiment. With the forces he raised, Fly joined the expeditionary forces in south Texas under Col. John S. "Rip" Ford.[15]

According to Watson, his friendly exchange with Major Fly transformed the atmosphere in the room. The district quartermaster took an immediate interest in his case and introduced him to a general officer who Watson believed to be the quartermaster general for Texas. Watson may have met with a general officer, but he was not the quartermaster general. The senior quartermaster for the District of Texas was an Army major.[16]

Major Benjamin Seton Bloomfield was originally a bookseller from New Orleans. Although he was opposed to secession, he accepted a commission as a quartermaster with the 2nd Louisiana Infantry. He soon joined General Magruder's staff in Virginia before being transferred with the general to Texas in 1862. It

Major George Washington Lafayette Fly, 2nd Texas Infantry (courtesy Lawrence T. Jones III Texas Photographs Collection, DeGolyer Library, Southern Methodist University).

appears that it was Major Bloomfield who introduced Watson to the brigadier general who was part of Major General John Bankhead Magruder's staff. The general that Watson met was probably William Scurry, who had just been relieved as the commander of the Eastern Sub District of Texas. The general quickly ushered Watson into the office of the district commander.[17]

Watson had little to say about this meeting with General Magruder, but he did mention handing the commanding general the letter from Consul Lynn. After reading the letter and hearing Watson's story, the general dictated an order to Colonel Bates and allowed Watson to hand deliver the order. According to Watson, the order directed Colonel Bates (whom he again misidentified as "Colonel Evans") to return the schooner to its owner, "if the same could be done without material detriment to the public service." In addition to mixing up the colonel's name, Watson's telling of the story does not exactly match the facts.[18]

The official records have the actual letter that Magruder (via his aide) wrote to Colonel Bates. He dictated it on October 8, 1863, and it read as follows:

> The Major Genl. comdg. directs me to inquire why a British vessel [*Rob Roy*], in preference to a vessel belonging to a citizen of Texas was impressed by you for the purpose of driving piles, under Special Order No. 258, paragraph 13 authorizing an impressment to which order your attention is invited. A prompt reply requested.[19]

Colonel Bates responded to the commanding general three days later. He reported that all the vessels entering the Brazos were discharging their cargo 30 miles upriver at Columbia. Accordingly, he had dispatched a capable quartermaster corps sergeant there to procure a proper vessel. The sergeant was guided by an order that General Scurry had issued while he was still the Eastern Sub-District commander. Scurry's order was dated September 20, which was three days before General Magruder's Special Order No. 258. Scurry's earlier order directed Colonel Bates to hire a schooner if possible. Otherwise, he was to impress one; but the initial order said nothing about avoiding foreign-flagged vessels.[20]

Colonel Bates' quartermaster sergeant "selected the *Rob Roy* as the most suitable vessel," even though "the captain and supercargo [William Watson] were both absent at the time." Bates then explained why he did not promptly release *Rob Roy* after receiving General Magruder's order. He essentially had no other good choices. "All vessels coming into this port are under foreign flags…. Very few of them belong to our own citizens, or at least they will not acknowledge ownership in the Confederacy." Bates reasoned that since *Rob Roy*, "having at the time no cargo on board and being well adapted to the purpose" and was needed, "as I supposed, but for a short time," he placed her into pile-driving service.[21]

Only after receiving this report from Colonel Bates, did the Confederate Army agree to return *Rob Roy* to Watson's custody. The recently appointed commander of the Eastern Sub-District, acting Brigadier General Philip N. Luckett, initiated the order. Major General Magruder did not issue the order to release *Rob Roy* as Watson had claimed. The effect was the same, however. Colonel Bates had already caught the gist of Magruder's intent when Watson delivered the commanding general's inquiry. Bates went ahead and released *Rob Roy* prior to receiving any official order.[22]

When Colonel Bates ordered a Confederate steamer to tow the schooner back upriver to Columbia, *Rob Roy* was at the mouth of the Brazos River. It had been driving piles under the supervision Lieutenant Cross since late September. His schooner was waiting at Columbia when William Watson arrived there on October 12. He was pleased to have his schooner and crew back, but he was not happy with *Rob Roy*'s condition. Part of its running rigging and stores were missing, the starboard rail was cut down, and its port bulwarks were damaged (the extension of the schooner's sides above deck-level). In short, *Rob Roy* was "totally unfit to receive cargo until repaired." To top it all off, his small yawl boat was also missing.[23]

Watson said that he easily located the same carpenter who had repaired the damage to *Rob Roy*'s hull that a Yankee cannon ball had inflicted, but his problem was lumber. There was plenty of fine seasoned oak available. Unfortunately, all of it belonged to the government. Only an order from the brigadier general commanding the sub-district in Houston could authorize the release of the necessary wood for civilian use. Watson identified the acting brigadier as "Colonel L." who had been civilian prior to the war.[24]

The man who had relieved Brigadier General Scurry as commander of the Eastern Sub-District of Texas and issued the order to restore *Rob Roy*, was acting Brigadier General Philip N. Luckett. As Watson had reported, Luckett, like most Confederate officers, had been a civilian before the war, but he did have military experience, albeit as a doctor. During the Mexican War, Luckett had served in Rip Ford's Texas Ranger Company as a surgeon. Just prior to the outbreak of the Civil War, Doctor Luckett was one of three commissioners who successfully negotiated the surrender of U.S. Army equipment and facilities in Texas. The State of Texas then appointed Luckett as a colonel in the army and assigned him to serve under Colonel Ford once again at the Rio Grande. Luckett had replaced Ford as the commander at the border prior to his selection as an acting general and his posting to Houston.[25]

To obtain the needed lumber, Watson set off once again to Houston to joust with the Confederate military bureaucracy. This time he would have to deal with General Luckett and his staff. Feeling a sense of urgency, he traveled on horseback since the last train of the day had already left Columbia. In Houston, he met up with his Brownsville partner's representative that he only identified as "Mr. P." The man was well known in Texas, and Watson hoped he might help offset the suspicious regard that many Texans held for foreigners like himself. "Mr. P." was most likely Ernest Parizot, a partner in the firm of Wegmann & Parizot & Co. Parizot was also in partnership with Bernard (Barney) Tiernan of Tiernan and Parizot & Co. Both partnerships operated out of Galveston and together they had interests in several blockade runners. Of the two, Tiernan appears to be the most likely person who had invested in *Rob Roy*. Tiernan was the Galveston agent for G. Pauvert & Son, cotton and wool merchants in Matamoros and Brownsville.[26]

When Watson and Parizot arrived at the headquarters of acting Brigadier General Luckett, there was a "commotion arising out of some drunken spree." Sensing that it was a bad time to present the irritated commander with another problem to solve, Watson and Parizot attempted to leave. But they had been spotted; and the general called them back into his office to state their case. Watson reluctantly complied, trying to make himself heard above the unruly ruckus coming from the inebriated officers. Luckett said he could not grant any request for wood from a perfect stranger without some kind of recommendation.[27]

The drunken officers chimed in as well, accusing Watson and Mr. P. of being spies who were selling their cotton to the Yankees. This accusation caused Parizot to angrily respond that his accusers were liars. An instant later, he had to dodge a poorly aimed dagger that was offered in rebuttal. Luckett intervened before there was any bloodshed, but emotions were running high. Luckett's half-drunk quartermaster repeated some of the same insults, calling the two men speculators who had done nothing for the Confederacy. Watson heatedly said that he had battle wounds to document his own service, and that General Magruder could attest to the truth of his claim. This statement quieted the room a bit and introduced an element of doubt about the righteousness of their assumptions. Most of the officers remained unconvinced. More importantly, Watson was no closer to obtaining the lumber he needed.[28]

Luck was with Watson again when he ran into another comrade who had served with him in Louisiana and Arkansas. Watson described him as "Lt. Tom M." with the 3rd Louisiana Infantry. The lieutenant had been captured at the Battle of Pea Ridge, Arkansas, but had joined a Texas unit after he had been exchanged. Official regimental records reveal that the lieutenant was Thomas E. Mason, a 27-year-old from Alabama, who stood almost six feet tall. He had been promoted to captain and happened to be in Houston to attend a ball that had been held the previous evening. Since Mason was also a unit quartermaster, it was no surprise that he had dropped in to visit his counterparts.[29]

According to Watson, Captain Mason's testimonial as to Watson's bravery and service to the Confederacy had almost the same effect as Major George Fly's endorsement a few days earlier at General Magruder's headquarters. The rowdy rebel officers now wanted to toast Watson's service and urged him to have a drink with them. General Luckett also treated him with a level of respect due to a fellow soldier who had sacrificed his blood in combat. The commander was willing to listen attentively to Watson's request this time around. But to the business at hand: Luckett was embarrassed by the behavior of his officers. He quickly wrote out an order to the manager of the sawmill to provide Watson with the wood he needed for repairs. At least that was the story that Watson related in his book. The actual events were a bit less clear, and were certainly more formal.[30]

While his meeting with "Colonel L." and "Lt. Tom M." may have taken place just as he described, Watson failed to mention another letter that he had sent to General Luckett. He addressed it to the general's adjutant, Captain Robert S. Reid, on October 13, 1863. Watson wrote the letter in Houston and laid out the damage the Confederates had inflicted upon *Rob Roy* while it had been in government service. In the letter, he also reminded "Genl. Luckett" that it was his order that released the schooner back into Watson's custody.[31]

Watson's written request did not, however, make any mention of his need for wood. He only asked for a carpenter, since it was "impossible to find a carpenter out of government employ either to ascertain the extent of damage done or do the necessary repairs." He therefore requested, "the assistance of a carpenter to ascertain the extent of damage done and do the necessary repairs." Watson offered up his crew to help and promised to detain the carpenter for as short a period as possible.[32]

The endorsements on the letter show that Luckett sent it to Colonel Bates for comment on October 17. Three days later, the colonel received another letter from Magruder on the same subject. The general told Bates to investigate the case. If Watson's complaints were valid, he was to make the necessary repairs and reimburse any expenses. Bates was "expected to give your personal attention to this matter." He was advised to acknowledge receipt at once and report when the job was completed. The commanding general also admonished Colonel Bates that "in future you will not impress any foreign vessel for any purpose unless it be impossible to procure a vessel belonging to some of our citizens."[33]

On the same day that he received Magruder's latest directive, Bates sent General Luckett's order to Lieutenant Cross for comment. The next day, the engineers at Velasco responded to Watson's letter and acknowledged that they had cut "away a portion of her starboard bulwarks which was absolutely necessary in order to admit the piling machine in a position to work properly." They claimed innocence regarding any other injuries to the schooner and said that they must have been sustained after they had returned *Rob Roy* to her captain.[34]

Obviously irritated by this latest complaint, the engineers pointed out that Watson pronounced himself, "pleased to see everything had been so well taken care of" at the time of delivery. They also promised to return the yawl boat in good condition and would send it upriver to Columbia by the next trip of the steamboat. The next day, Colonel Bates added a note that he had detailed a carpenter to Columbia with instructions to repair any damages that may have been done to the Schooner *Rob Roy* while it was in the service of Lt. Cross.[35]

By comparing Watson's story with contemporary sources that describe the same events, it is apparent that Watson generally painted a much more collegial picture of his relationships with the senior Confederate officers than was the actual case. After dealing with the unruly officers at General Luckett's headquarters, Watson said that he was reluctant to make a second call on General Magruder. An examination of Magruder's delayed response to Consul Arthur Lynn's protest letter concerning William Watson and *Rob Roy* helps to explain why.

While Watson did not mention the specific contents, Arthur Lynn's complete letter can be found in the National Archives and the Official Records of the Navy. The British consul's protest to General Magruder of October 3 was far less cordial than Watson suggested. Lynn was upset with both the seizure of *Rob Roy* and the enlistment of British citizens into the Confederate Army. Enclosed within the letter was a copy of the order that Colonel Bates had given to William Watson. That order documented the appropriation of his schooner for government service at Velasco. The general did not take Consul Lynn's rebuke well.[36]

In the letter, Lynn reminded the general of his January proclamation that the ports of Lavaca (now Port Lavaca) in Matagorda Bay and Velasco at the Brazos River were no longer blockaded. Magruder had invited "friendly neutral nations to resume commercial intercourse with those ports." The frustrated British consul thought that it "would be an act of deep deception should they be induced to enter these ports, to be thereafter forcibly detained for the purpose of aiding your military defenses."[37]

Major General Magruder wisely delayed his response to the British consul until October 20, after he had fully understood and resolved the problem. By waiting, he was able to assume the legal and moral high ground. Through his adjutant, the now equally indignant general told Lynn that he found the tone and language of his letter "highly objectionable." He said that the schooner *Rob Roy* had been seized as a military necessity, but had been released "as soon as she was ascertained to be a British vessel."[38]

As for the damages to *Rob Roy*, Magruder said that Colonel Bates would pay for "such repairs as may be necessary to place her in precisely the same condition as she was in before the seizure and which may be presented by the captain." In a final flourish, General Magruder assured the British consul that "he has ever been as careful to respect the rights of neutrals as he is resolved to defend his own and those of the country [that] he has the honor to serve."[39]

That seemed to settle the matter, but Major General Magruder went one step further. He wrote a personal letter of complaint to James Mason, the Confederate Commissioner to England, and William Henry Gregory, a pro–Confederate member of the British Parliament. Gregory had formed his sympathy for the South during a visit to the United States in the autumn and early winter of 1859. He traveled extensively, initially to Niagara Falls via Canada, and then to Chicago and St. Louis, "just on the outposts of savagedom."[40]

After visiting Louisville and Cincinnati, the MP headed back east to Virginia. Just days prior to his arrival in the state, John Brown's band of radical abolitionists briefly occupied Harper's Ferry. Continuing to Washington, D.C., Gregory had office calls with President James Buchanan and Vice President John Breckenridge. He concluded the northern portion of his tour via Baltimore, back to New York, Toronto, and Illinois, before heading south. Along the way, he met important southerners including Virginia Senator, and future Confederate Commissioner to the United Kingdom, James Mason.

From Richmond, Gregory traveled through Montgomery, Alabama, before ending his stateside tour in Louisiana. He described New Orleans as a "murderous, blood-stained city." In the previous four months, eight men had met violent deaths at his otherwise fine hotel. Despite it all, Gregory admitted, "I like New Orleans and the people." His view of the northern states and their citizens was not as generous. He was disgusted by the region's "mob tyranny," rowdyism, and the rampant corruption of their elected officials.[41]

Upon his return to the United Kingdom, these sentiments carried over into Parliament, where Gregory introduced legislation to challenge the legality of the Union blockade in 1862. If successful, the act could have set in motion a chain of events that might have led to British recognition of the independence of the Confederate States. The British, however, had no intention of contesting the U.S. blockade, even when it was clearly illegal. That practical position was firm, unless or until it became clear that the Confederacy would prevail on the battlefield.[42]

It is possible that at some point during his extensive travels in the United States,

Gregory met up with Magruder. The only hint of a personal relationship, however, is in the letter's salutation. The general used the familiar "My dear Gregory," to address the MP, but did not reference any earlier meetings. Magruder thanked Gregory for his support for the Confederacy and enclosed copies of the letters that he had exchanged with Consul Lynn. He expressed his belief that the British consul was, "trying out of small things, to create mischief."[43]

Knowing that Gregory represented County Galway, Ireland, Magruder's letter to the MP carefully pointed out the success of Captain Dick Dowling at the Battle of Sabine Pass. Dowling just happened to have been born in County Galway and all his men were of Irish descent.[44]

> With (41) forty-one men (Irish Texas) we repulsed at Sabine Pass, the other day, 15,000 of the enemy on board the transports and four War Steamers which attacked us, captured two (now in our possession), crippled one and drove off the fourth, besides taking nearly 400 prisoners. Incredible but true![45]

On the same day that he wrote to Gregory, Magruder registered the same complaint in a separate letter to the Confederate Commissioner in London, James Mason. He invited both men to "make such use of my letter as may seem best." Nothing would come of the general's appeal. By the time Magruder's words reached London, Gregory was no longer taking the lead in Parliamentary initiatives to promote pro-Confederate motions and the Confederate Government had withdrawn Commissioner James Mason from London. The only support Magruder received in London was a sympathetic ear. Arthur Thomas Lynn, on the other hand, would continue to serve as Her Britannic Majesty's consul in Galveston until 1882 when he stepped aside after 32 years of service. His remains are buried in Galveston's Trinity Episcopal Cemetery.[46]

As exemplified by glossing over the annoyance he engendered within Confederate Army leadership circles, Watson usually told the truth, but not the whole truth. Events rarely unfolded as quickly or as precisely as he claimed, but the essence of his ordeal concerning *Rob Roy*'s impressment, damage, and release in Texas were correct. By October 22, 1863, all seemed to be going well when Colonel Bates detailed a carpenter to make the necessary repairs to Watson's schooner. Unfortunately for Watson, his troubles in Texas had just begun.[47]

4

More Than a Sinking Feeling

After the repairs to *Rob Roy* were completed, Watson's first mate supervised the loading of cotton into its hold. The mate used screw jacks to squeeze as much of the already compressed bales into the hold as he could. After calculating the total number of bales that could be stowed below and above decks, Watson prepared to set off for Houston and Galveston. Before he could depart Texas, he needed to obtain official military and customs clearances. He did not say when this all happened, but the official records fill in that gap and more. On Saturday, November 14, 1863, Watson paid Galveston customs duties of $89.93 for 150 bales of cotton weighing 67,145 pounds (about 448 pounds per bale) loaded on board *Rob Roy*.[1]

With his clearance in hand, Watson hurried back to Columbia, fully expecting to finally sail away from Texas on the first dark night. At the Columbia train station, however, he learned that his schooner had suffered another catastrophe. It had sunk at the pier. It seems that his first mate was inexperienced in the stevedore trade and had overloaded the hold. Though "reckless overpressure of the screw jacks" the mate had created a separation in the upper portion of the casing that housed the schooner's retractable centerboard. When the crew loaded cotton on the deck, *Rob Roy* settled low enough for water to pour into the hold and caused it to sink to the bottom of the Brazos River.[2]

Watson was at a loss about what to do. All his possessions were either invested in or literally on board a schooner which now was only visible above the tops of its deck rails. The rest was underwater. Like buzzards circling a wounded animal, opportunists were quick to offer Watson their self-serving advice. Foremost among them were a small group of individuals who were associated with a schooner that Watson identified as *Catherine*. He named Mr. L. and Captain B. as the men who conspired with Watson's Captain J. to steal away *Rob Roy* for their own gain.[3]

Uncovering the full names of these men that Watson only identified by a single letter is complicated by the fact that there was no schooner named *Catherine* or *Catharine* in Texas at the time. There was, however, one named *Eliza Catharine* that seems to match the events that Watson imperfectly described.[4]

Eliza Catharine had experienced troubles comparable to *Rob Roy*'s. It had cleared from the Brazos in August 1863, but did not depart until late January 1864. Watson said that "Mr. L." had recently purchased *Catherine* from "Captain B." after it had sunk in the river about the time Watson first arrived at the Brazos. The official records do not confirm whether the schooner had sunk as Watson claimed, but the calamity of a sinking would explain the delay in its departure. *Eliza Catharine* had arrived from Havana under the ownership of August Turbert, a French citizen with Alex McBurney as her captain. It is likely that he was Watson's "Captain B."[5]

Mr. L. teamed up with Captain McBurney to encourage Watson's Captain J. to help them purchase the distressed *Rob Roy* in the same manner as *Eliza Catharine*. The identity of "Mr. L." is probably "E. De Launey" who was also the consignee of *Eliza Catharine*. At first, Mr. De Launey tried to convince Watson that his schooner was poorly constructed. Watson knew that allegation was false, but the supposed owner of the *Catherine* said that the authorities were likely to declare it a wreck and charge him to have it removed. Mr. De Launey said it would be an exceedingly difficult and expensive proposition to raise *Rob Roy*. He advised Watson to sell it immediately to salvage whatever he could for it.[6]

Watson got much better advice and encouragement from a blockade runner captain that he identified as an old salt named Captain Downs. The helpful captain said that Watson could spend the night with him onboard his small schooner that was preparing to run out of the Brazos with a load of cotton the next day. Downs also said that *Rob Roy* could be raised easily enough, but that he should do it soon, in part to keep it out of the hands of the men who were trying to swindle him.[7]

Unlike the mis-identified *Catherine* and its vaguely identified usurper and captain, contemporary records readily confirmed the activities of Captain Downs and his small schooner. At the time of Watson's story, Francis Downs was the captain of a schooner named *Eureka* that was located on the Brazos River. Downs had gotten a provisional British registry from Consul Arthur T. Lynn in Galveston for the schooner, formerly known as the U.S.-flagged *Enriquita*. Like Watson when he first sailed *Rob Roy* out of New Orleans, Downs had to proceed to a British port by May 7, 1864. Only in a British port could he get *Eureka*'s permanent registration as a British-flagged vessel.[8]

Consul Lynn and the Galveston Customs House cleared *Eureka* for Havana on November 11, 1863, which was three days before *Rob Roy*'s clearance. Downs and his crew of three had a load of 76 bales of cotton, which was about half the capacity of *Rob Roy*. *Eureka* was consigned to John Mills, a Yale-educated nephew and junior partner of Robert & David G. Mills. The Mills Brothers were wealthy merchants who also owned cotton and rice plantations situated near Columbia and the Brazos River. As a complementary adjunct to their business enterprises, they were heavily invested in small blockade runners like *Eureka*.[9]

Watson bid Captain Downs and *Eureka* adieu as they made their way down to the mouth of the Brazos in preparation to run the blockade. After he returned to his sunken schooner, Watson encountered his "Captain J." from County Cork in Ireland. The captain had fully recovered from his bout with yellow fever and had been spending a good deal of time with Captain McBurney and Mr. De Launey. They persisted in the hope that they could manipulate Captain J. into helping them pull off the same fraud with *Rob Roy* as they were trying to do with *Eliza Catharine*.[10]

Legally, Captain McBurney had no authority to sell *Eliza Catharine*, just as "Captain J." lacked the authority to sell *Rob Roy*. After Mr. De Launey and Captain McBurney were discredited, Watson said that Mr. De Launey was unable to take possession of *Eliza Catharine* and that Captain McBurney was relieved of command by the true owner and had to find other employment. The schooner's owner, August Turbert, personally assumed command of his schooner *Eliza Catharine*. Alex McBurney would later achieve additional notoriety as first mate of a leaky U.S. steamer named *Ike Davis* that a small band of Confederates captured coming out of the Rio Grande. He was among the crew members rescued from the steamer after it sank in a storm shortly running the blockade out of Matagorda Bay in December of 1864.[11]

At the time, however, the outcome of this attempt to wrest away control of the two schooners from their rightful owners was less certain. Watson went to Houston to seek the assistance of the merchant responsible for *Rob Roy*'s cargo. Watson identified a Galveston storeowner named "Mr. C." as his consigning agent. He was a "plain quiet honest man, but not a very extensive merchant with little to do with blockade running and no great influence with the officials." Watson was referring to Matthias Dayton Conklin, the principal owner of M.D. Conklin & Co. and the consignee of *Rob Roy*'s cargo. Conklin was inexperienced in shipping matters and was unwilling to risk any more capital. Watson lacked the necessary funds to restore *Rob Roy* to operational status and continue to pay his crew.[12]

Conklin was only willing to provide some block and tackle equipment that Watson would need if he hoped to raise his schooner from the depths. When he returned to Columbia with the gear, he "found her as he had left her." But he also confronted another artificially manufactured problem. His captain had conspired with Mr. De Launey and Captain McBurney and gotten *Rob Roy* declared as "abandoned." *Rob Roy* was now facing condemnation and sale at a public auction.[13]

"Captain J." said that "Mr. L." was willing to buy the schooner from Watson at a fraction of its value. He said that he and the rest of the crew had abandoned the vessel and that it would be difficult and expensive to raise it. Captain Downs had forewarned Watson of their likely attempt to steal the schooner away from him. He was fully aware that *Rob Roy* could be raised with relative ease and minimal cost. Watson categorically rejected the scamsters' offer and turned the tables on them. He told the captain and his first mate that since they had abandoned the vessel, they could have nothing more to do with it. He would visit the British consul in Galveston and make arrangements to discharge them all and pay them off. Watson's confidence was commendable, but it was partially a bluff. He had no money.[14]

With the help of Mr. Parizot, his Brownsville partner's representative (G. Pauvert & Son), and supercargo, Watson went to work to solve his financial shortfall. He agreed to terms with "R. & D.G. M. and Co." in Houston. This, of course, was the firm owned by the Mills Brothers. Robert and David Graham Mills were also the true owners of Captain Downs' *Eureka*. The brothers agreed to advance Watson enough money to cover his expenses in exchange for a part-ownership interest in *Rob Roy*. Watson had already sold half of his investment in the schooner at the Rio Grande. His arrangement with the Mills Brothers, left him with only a one-eighth interest.[15]

With this infusion of cash, Watson was able to hire "Captain S., of Galveston" to help him raise *Rob Roy*. He described him as "a stalwart man both in body and resources, a thorough Southern steamboat man." There were several candidates who may have been the resourceful and immensely helpful "Captain S." One possibility was Watson's friend from his recent visit to the Rio Grande, Captain Henry Scherffius. Scherffius was in the area during this timeframe, but Watson had previously identified him as Captain "Shaeffer." Since Watson was meeting "Captain S." for the first time when he arrived at Columbia with his men and equipment, Scherffius was not the helpful steamboat captain.[16]

There were other candidates for this mysterious benefactor, but there is one southern steamboat man from Galveston who stands out as the most likely. He was William C. Scrimgeour, who had come to Galveston from New York in 1857. Captain Scrimgeour was a highly respected career sailor, steamboat man, and harbor master who lived in Galveston during and after the war. Perhaps the most important attribute as far as William Watson was concerned, Scrimgeour was the son of a Scottish immigrant.

William Scrimgeour had been the first mate on the Confederate steam gunboat *General Rusk* under Leon Smith in March 1861. He was aboard the steamer when it sailed to the Rio Grande as part of an expedition to seize military supplies from the U.S. Army. With the help of Scrimgeour and *General Rusk*, soldiers under Colonel John S. "Rip" Ford successfully occupied the Federal arsenal at Brownsville. It was the first military action of the Civil War in the state of Texas. In appreciation, the soldiers of the Rio Grande Regiment presented Scrimgeour with an engraved silver-plated pitcher that he proudly displayed the rest of his life.[17]

Captain Scrimgeour remained with *General Rusk* as first mate when the steamer was renamed and converted into the British-flagged blockade runner, *Blanche*. On its return trip to Havana after having made one successful roundtrip out of Texas, the *Blanche* ran aground to avoid capture by the USS *Montgomery*. The U.S. Navy boarding crew illicitly burned *Blanche* in Cuban waters along with part of its load of cotton. This afront to Spanish sovereignty created an international incident and resulted in the court martial and sacking of the *Montgomery*'s captain.[18]

Scrimgeour ("Captain S.") made his way back to Galveston in the fall of 1862, but would not return to government service for another two years. He finally

Captain William C. Scrimgeour (courtesy Rosenberg Library, Galveston, Texas).

assumed command of another government-owned blockade-running steamer named *Alice* (formerly *Matagorda*) in August of 1864. In the meantime, Scrimgeour was one of the few experienced "Southern steamboat" men with a last name beginning with the letter "S" who was available to assist William Watson and *Rob Roy*. "Captain S." immediately went to work on the slow process of raising *Rob Roy*. He had access to large pumps, blocks and tackle "made fast to trees high up the bank," teams of oxen, and several slaves from a nearby Mills Brothers plantation. While men, beast, and equipment went about their work, Captain J. was perched nearby in constant company with his fellow vultures, De Launey and Captain McBurney.[19]

On the day *Rob Roy* finally floated to the surface, Watson crossed over to the populated side of the river where there was a blacksmith's shop in the city of Columbia. Captain J. swooped in and intercepted Watson in an isolated spot that was out of view from the streets of the city. According to Watson, Captain J. angrily confronted him, demanding money. When Watson refused, the burly man attacked him with a knife.[20]

Just as Watson was about to subdue the inebriated sailor, one of the captain's local friends intervened. As a Scotsman, Watson went out of his way to mention that both Captain J. and his henchman were Irish. Looking up, Watson saw a cocked pistol pointed at his head, from a distance of about two feet. The interloper ordered Watson to let the captain go or else he would "blow your brains out." Watson refused, but before the man could act, Captain Scrimgeour suddenly appeared. He and Parizot had seen the ruckus from across the river and hurried over to help. Calling the man, a "cowardly dog," Scrimgeour took the gun from the townsman, and placed him in a chokehold until the Irishman almost passed out. Scrimgeour then threw the man into the mud of the riverbank "like a piece of offensive carrion."[21]

Watson and Captain Scrimgeour made their way to the local provost marshal's office and laid the matter before him. Rather than have Captain J. arrested, Watson was satisfied with the public disgrace that he had heaped upon himself and his friends. Watson was satisfied that there would be no more problems emanating from his former captain. His assessment of the unruly sailor proved to be correct, but Watson's difficulties were far from over.[22]

Watson and *Rob Roy* had been at the Brazos River since late September of 1863. By November, he had experienced the tribulations of having his schooner sunk twice, seized and damaged by the Confederate Army, and condemned by greedy conspirators. With help, he also narrowly thwarted a vicious attempt on his life. While Watson was confronting these personal difficulties, the Texas Confederates were having problems of their own.

In November, Union Naval and Army forces had invaded and occupied the Texas coast from the Rio Grande to Matagorda Bay. It appeared as if the Yankees were preparing to occupy the entire coast including the blockade-running outlets at Caney Creek, the San Bernard River, and most importantly, the Brazos River. The U.S. Navy also had been testing the defenses at the Brazos. Warships periodically lobbed a few shells in the direction of the two forts guarding the mouth of the river at Quintana (Labeled "A" on illustration on page 27) and Velasco (Labeled "B" on illustration on page 27). The soldiers called them Forts Bates and Sulakowski respectively. They were named after the Polish-born Confederate engineer and designer of the forts, Col. Valery Sulakowski, and the local commander Col. Joseph Bates.[23]

In the meantime, military authorities had not issued any permits for vessels to pass through the blockade since November 17. Their intent was to prevent Texas cotton from falling into the hands of invading troops or swarming warships. It would be almost a month before the threat had lessened enough that government officials were willing to issue permits to blockade runners allowing them to pass the forts and exit the Sabine and Brazos Rivers, or Galveston Bay. The permits to proceed to sea were conditional upon proving that all custom duties had been paid and verifying that none of their crewmembers were liable for military service.[24]

The numbers and vigilance of the Union fleet had also increased, leading to the capture of several blockade runners that had departed Texas in mid–November. Watson had heard that even Captain Downs had been captured. He was correct, but Watson's new friend was not easily deterred. Captain Downs would make his way back to the Brazos two months later, and continue his blockade-running business. When he arrived, Downs would regale Watson with a retrospectively amusing tale of his dealings with the Union fleet.[25]

Until then, the Confederates scrambled to remove all but essential fighting forces from the immediate area of the coast. In response to the threat of invasion, those troops had to be kept properly supplied and equipped. As supplies went downriver, the most important commercial commodity, cotton, was removed from coastal areas. This additional logistic demand was taxing the limits of the two government steamers on the Brazos, *Mary Hill* and *Era No. 3*. The Confederate government had leased *Era No. 3* from the Mills Brothers to use as a military transport. They eventually purchased *Mary Hill* and were using it as both a gunboat and for logistic support.[26]

Both steamers were in a poor state of repair, as stated by Watson and confirmed by official reports. Their limited availability increased the government's need for additional river transportation. Together, these factors made it unlikely that Watson would soon receive another clearance to go to sea. When the Mills Brothers told him that it would be several weeks before they could acquire some more cotton to load *Rob Roy*, Watson agreed to hire out his schooner. He would retain command, but work under the direction of the Army quartermaster. The mission was to haul timber and supplies down river to the forts. On the return trip, he would remove sugar and cotton to Columbia to keep those commodities away from potential Yankee invaders. With luck, he thought his service to the government might place him in good standing when the opportunity to obtain a pass resurfaced.[27]

Watson had experience as a ship commander prior to the war, as well as his recent stint in his own schooner as navigator. Recalling the problems with his former captain and mate, he took command of *Rob Roy* himself. He kept two of his former crew members, Frederick Jansen, the cook, and George Thomson, who acted as his first mate. Watson needed additional hands to help with the loading and unloading of cargo. In Civil War Texas, manual labor most often came in the form of slaves, and deckhands were no exception.[28]

His new partners, Robert and David Mills of R. & D.G. Mills & Co. happened to own about 800 slaves who worked on the Mills Brothers' sugar and cotton plantations in the vicinity. Robert managed the cotton brokerage end of the business while David took care of the plantations and the people living there. Watson readily obtained the manpower he needed and set about his work, while staying out of range of the U.S. Navy's long-range cannons.[29]

Not all slaves serving on board vessels in the Texas Marine Department were laborers. For example, of the 14 crewmen on board *Era No. 3*, seven of them were slaves. Their occupations were steward, mess boy, cook, watchman, two foremen, and a "3d Engineer." Their pay ranged from $40 to $50 per month, which matched the rate of pay for non-slaves performing the same tasks. The difference, of course, was that the slave owners were the recipient of the salaries, and not the individuals. On board *Era No. 3*, the seven slaves belonged to four different owners. Two of the men belonged to R. & D.G. Mills, the cook and one of the foremen.[30]

As for William Watson, he thought that slavery was detrimental to everyone involved, the individual slave, the slave owners, and the Southern economy. But he did not revile those owners who treated their slaves well. Despite this somewhat enlightened outlook among his peers, he was a bit surprised and pleased by the work ethic and reliability of the eight men under his charge. The men even said they liked working on a schooner, which was a break from the routine at the plantation.[31]

On Christmas Eve, the last day of their employment. Watson was "astonished" at the energy and enthusiasm of the "negroes" as they went about their work. They were anxious to get back to the plantation to for a ball and the entire Christmas week holiday celebration. They had invited George, the first mate, to accompany them. To their surprise, Watson gave each of the men a small gratuity. The men said that they would be envied back at the plantation for having worked on a blockade runner.[32]

As the men went away singing, Watson thought, "This war may bring you freedom, but I question much if it can bring you more happiness." Watson noted that the sentiments of the slaves in Texas about the war seemed to be aligned with those of the White population. He saw them celebrate Confederate victories and heard them express their confidence in defeating the Yankees. He opined that perhaps this sense of loyalty was prevalent before President Lincoln shifted the narrative about the purpose of the war. At first, Lincoln said that his primary goal was to save the Union. In a letter to Horace Greeley, the newspaper editor, dated August 22, 1862, the president said, "If I could save the Union without freeing any slave I would do it…." It was not until his Emancipation Proclamation of January 1, 1863, that the stated purpose of the war shifted from saving the Union to abolition of slavery within the Confederate States.[33]

For Watson, his immediate objective remained unchanged: to run *Rob Roy* out of Texas with a full load of cotton. Contemporary records offer little to confirm Watson's story about his difficulties in achieving that end. There was no direct evidence about *Rob Roy*'s sinking, his confrontation with his Captain J., or his service as a logistics vessel for the Confederate Army. However, the Galveston customs record does show that on January 2, 1864, the owner of *Rob Roy* paid duties for 72 bales of cotton plus another 74 that had been re-landed. The process of offloading and onloading cotton, brought the total cargo to 146 bales that were consigned to R. & D.G. Mills & Co.[34]

Despite the lack of specifics, the timing and content of the Galveston customs records are consistent with Watson's claims. The re-landed bales of cotton represent those that he had to exchange for the ones that had been underwater within the hold of *Rob Roy*. The records verify Watson's new partnership with the Mills Brothers, who had replaced M.D. Conklin. They also confirm that Watson received a customs clearance to Belize, but he did not yet have a military permit to pass the forts.[35]

The customs records offer reassuring information, but not all of Watson's observations and assumptions were accurate. For example, he said that Galveston was "so closely blockaded ... that entrance or egress were deemed impossible, and that no vessel had yet attempted it." It is true that very few vessels tried to run out of Galveston Bay for several weeks after the Union invasion of the Texas coast, but blockade running had been a regular activity out of Galveston before and after the tightening of the Union blockade. The only exception was during the U.S. Navy occupation of Galveston Bay between October and December of 1862.[36]

It is often difficult to determine with precision the exact date that a blockade runner ran through the cordon of blockading warships. As seen with *Rob Roy*, a customs clearance did not necessarily mean that the vessel departed on that date or that it ever left the port at all. All clearances to depart the Brazos River were issued out of Galveston, which often makes it difficult to determine a vessel's exact port of departure. Military-issued permits to pass the forts were usually more reliable in reflecting the actual departure location and date. Even then, the captain may have delayed departure for a variety of reasons. Tides, weather, visibility, equipment issues, or the presence of blockading warships frequently postponed departures.

Even considering these uncertainties in the historical record, at least 30 vessels had attempted to run the blockade at Galveston Bay in 1863. Twenty-four of these were successful outbound runs (one steamer, 21 schooners, and 2 sloops). The schooner *Nina* made the last confirmed outbound run from Galveston Bay in 1863. Just prior to Christmas, *Nina* received a permit to pass the forts with 32 bales of cotton that were bound for Tampico via Matamoros.[37]

Blockade runner arrival dates are even more difficult to figure out. There are fewer official and unofficial records regarding arrivals. When a vessel experienced some type of difficulty, such as being captured or running aground, there was usually some mention of the event in the official reports and contemporary newspaper accounts. Otherwise, the arrival dates must be derived from invoices, or comments made in other contemporary letters, special orders, and reports.

Even considering the difficulty in specifying precise dates of arrival and departure, Watson's assumption that the blockade of Galveston made it impossible for "entrance or egress" was clearly incorrect. However, the Union's occupation of Brownsville and its threatening advances up the Rio Grande temporarily interrupted cotton shipments to Matamoros. General Magruder's Special Order Number 308, paragraph 13, of November 12, 1863, stated, "Hereafter no cotton will be allowed to be passed to Mexico at any point lower down the Rio Grande than Eagle Pass." The general's concern about Yankee efforts to capture cotton also gave impetus to increased blockade-running attempts at the Brazos.[38]

5

Captain Dave's Exciting Sea Story

While Watson was having *Rob Roy* loaded with cotton, he met a fellow blockade runner and Scotsman he identified as Captain Dave McLusky [sic]. The 34-year-old David McClusky was a kindred spirit who had just sailed into the Brazos River, having narrowly escaped the clutches of the blockading fleet. He was a man who had those "peculiar traits of character which made and retained warm friends."[1]

Captain Dave, as he was known to his friends, had been a mariner from his earliest childhood and a resident of Galveston since 1842. At the outset of the Civil War, he served as the pilot on the steamboat *Josiah H. Bell*. *J.H. Bell* had been a coastal steamer that made regular passenger and cargo runs between Texas and New Orleans. Like most of these small steamers, it was taken into the Texas Marine Department. When the blockade disrupted normal commercial operations, McClusky did not follow his steamer into government service. He turned his attention to blockade running.[2]

In addition to being a capable seaman, Captain Dave was a first-class raconteur. He always had an exciting story to tell for anyone who would listen. He told Watson that he sailed his schooner from a port in Mexico in December of 1863, but as he approached the Brazos, a Union warship had overhauled and captured him. According to Watson's version of his story, the seizure took place on Christmas Day. The unnamed Union gunboat had secured McClusky's unnamed schooner with a tow line and placed two sailors armed with cutlases on board. Their assignment was to take charge of their prize and oversee the captain and his small crew. The two Navy crewmen were highly displeased at not being properly relieved of their detached duty. The sounds of a holiday "jollification" being celebrated on board the warship only increased their irritation.[3]

Apparently sympathizing with the sailors' plight and acknowledging that all his cargo would be lost anyway, Captain Dave offered the two Yankee crewmen access to his stash of high-quality brandy. The sailors happily obliged. The two men became knee-crawling drunk before passing out below deck. Up on deck, McClusky's first mate continued to call out "all's well" at the proper intervals to the satisfaction of the sailors on the larger gunboat; thus, assuring the deck watch that nothing was amiss onboard the schooner. Seizing his opportunity for escape while obscured from view during a passing rain squall, McClusky ordered his men to cut the tow line. He quickly set sail and made a dash for the mouth of the Brazos.[4]

Captain Dave said they made it safely across the bar without incident. When the two groggy sailors awoke from their stupor the next morning, they were hungover, disoriented, and confused. After another bracing shot of brandy, they staggered topside. Upon reaching the main deck, they saw land all around them, where before there had been mostly water. Bewildered, they exclaimed, "We have got into h-ll or some other port." Their situation only came into focus when Confederate soldiers came on board and took the sailors into custody as prisoners of war.[5]

This colorful story that the equally colorful Captain Dave McClusky told William Watson was an exemplary "sea story" in the finest tradition of nautical yarns. It had at least two parts of fable for every part of truth. Captain Dave McClusky's capture and escape, as retold and embellished by Watson William, appear to be a collation of two separate events. The first occurred in December 1863 on the schooner *Sarah* and the second in May 1864 on a different schooner. The separate adventure will be covered in a subsequent chapter.[6]

There were disconnects in Watson's timeline, exaggerations, and the inclusion of elements from his subsequent capture and escape. His tale about the schooner *Sarah* inaccurately described how the crew overpowered and imprisoned a drunken prize crew before escaping and sailing into the Brazos. Watson must have felt that McClusky's tale could be improved with a few added scenes of drama and comedy. Such a story, naturally, needed a grand finale that concluded in complete triumph. Despite these imperfections, his Christmas sea story about Dave McClusky and *Sarah* was partially true.

Captain McClusky's exploits of late December 1863 would not appear in the U.S. Army's or Navy's multi-volume, official records of the "War of the Rebellion." Perhaps Union officials were embarrassed by the incident, or did not think the escape was worthy of even a brief mention. Without the benefit of other archival records, this omission would normally indicate that Watson's yuletide story was a complete fabrication. However, Confederate Army field reports, consular dispatches, and first-hand newspaper accounts that were printed during and after the war tell a similar story. McClusky's Christmas fairytale had elements of truth.

The reality of McClusky's escape was equally dramatic and much more life-threatening than Watson's fictionalized version. What follows is the true story of Captain Dave McClusky and his escape from the Union blockading fleet off the Brazos in the schooner *Sarah*.

David McClusky was indeed the captain of a small blockade runner that had run the blockade from Texas to Tampico, Mexico in late October 1863. Contemporary records also confirmed that McClusky was in command of a schooner named *Sarah* that escaped from a U.S. man-of-war off the coast of Texas. Just as Watson had claimed, the encounter took place near the Brazos on *Sarah*'s return trip from Tampico during the Christmas holiday period of 1863.[7]

The adventure that began with *Sarah*'s run into Tampico was documented in the correspondence of U.S. Consul Franklin Chase. He reported *Sarah*'s arrival from Galveston on the 5th of September 1863. One of her passengers said that they had departed from Galveston along with three other vessels on August 3. This report confirmed a Confederate special order dated September 27, that read,

The Schooner *Sarah*, McClusky Master is hereby permitted to proceed to sea with about one hundred and forty-one bales cotton from the mouth of the Brazos River or San Louis [sic] Pass.[8]

In addition to naming Dave McClusky as captain, the special order showed that *Sarah*'s draft was sufficiently light for it to pass through the shallow canal that connected West Galveston Bay with the Brazos River (see illustration on page 27). It also helps highlight the difficulty in determining whether a schooner ran the blockade out of Galveston Bay or the Brazos River. All clearances for both Galveston Bay and the Brazos were issued out of Galveston. A customs clearance from Galveston did not necessarily mean that the vessel actually departed from Galveston Bay. It may have slipped through the canal and departed via the Brazos River.

Consul Chase confirmed that the schooner was laden with 141 bales of cotton when it arrived at Tampico from Galveston. It was "owned by the Swiss Consul at that port, Mr. J.C. Kuhn." Like most of the consular representatives of the era, Jacob Conrad Kuhn had other business interests. In this case, he was a cotton trader and merchant. Originally from St. Gall, Switzerland, he opened his store in Galveston while Texas was still a Republic. The land-locked Swiss Confederation (the official name for the nation of Switzerland) appointed him as their consul to the State of Texas in 1846.[9]

By 1861, Jacob Kuhn owned a large 3-story brick store on the Strand and was the principal owner of Kuhn's Wharf complex in Galveston Harbor. With the outbreak of the Civil War, he invested in numerous small blockade-running schooners that included *James Williams*, *Reserve*, *Mack Canfield*, and *Wave*, in addition to *Sarah*. Despite some unfounded reports that he had left Texas in 1861, Kuhn would remain in Galveston until May 1864 when General James E. Slaughter gave him permission to leave the Confederacy via Mexico.[10]

When J.C. Kuhn's *Sarah* arrived at Tampico, captain McClusky forwarded his load of cotton to a ship headed for Liverpool. He also switched the schooner's registry to the British Red Ensign. The nominal British owner of *Sarah* was David Jolly who approached U.S. Consul Chase for a clearance from Tampico to New Orleans. Chase refused the request, reasoning that Captain McClusky and other blockade runners intended to use this clearance as a safety valve in case they encountered the blockading fleet. Chase said that the blockade runners would "touch off the port of Matamoros for information as to the movements of our vessels of war." If the situation warranted, they would then run into a Texas port to load more cotton. If not, they could continue to New Orleans and try again without fear of being seized.[11]

When *Sarah* departed Tampico on November 16, 1863, Consul Chase surmised that she was headed for Galveston to pick up another load of cotton. In late December 1863, Confederate sources confirmed Chase's suspicions about *Sarah*'s destination. Despite its absence from the U.S. Navy's official records, other reporting of this incident is remarkably complete. A Union gunboat, not identified in the Confederate reports, did indeed capture *Sarah*. The schooner was under the command of Captain Dave McClusky, and it subsequently escaped the grasp of the U.S. Navy. However, contrary to Watson's claims, the schooner did not survive the encounter. Additionally, Captain McClusky did not aid in the capture or arrest of any Yankee sailors.[12]

Sarah's arrival off the coast of Texas in late December 1863 coincided with a volatile and worrisome period of the Civil War for that region. Union forces had established several beachheads along its southern coast and were expanding their foothold from the Rio Grande up to Matagorda Bay. In response to the Union invasion, Major General Magruder had moved his headquarters out of Houston and into the field. He feared that an attack on the Brazos was imminent. To get a tactical update, the general sent Captain Edmund P. Turner from his personal staff to conduct a reconnaissance of the coast southwest of Galveston Bay. Turner happened to be in the area between the San Bernard and Brazos rivers when *Sarah* ran ashore on December 29.

In the early morning hours of December 30, the Confederate signal officer at the mouth of Caney Creek reported that the enemy had landed a force nearby. As Confederate troops and cavalry rushed along the beach to repulse the attack, they found the report to be incorrect, "having arisen from the beaching of a Confederate States vessel consigned to Messrs. Ball, Hutchins & Co." Captain Turner was one of the first officers on the scene. According to Turner, *Sarah* was from Tampico and "laden with Mexican blankets, salt, and sundries." He also said that the schooner carried "no arms or ammunition."[13]

McClusky told the Confederate officers on the beach that after he was captured, the Union warship's boarding officer removed the passengers and took the ship's papers to the gunboat's captain for examination. With the departure of the Union boarding officer, Captain McClusky "took advantage of the occasion under the cover of the darkness and put directly to shore, beaching her about 5 miles from the mouth of the Bernard [sic]." Long after the war, a former Union sailor named George L. Smith named his gunboat, the USS *Virginia,* as the victim of McClusky's escape. None of these reports, however, mentioned the fate of any Union sailors who may have been on board as part of the prize crew when *Sarah* slipped away.[14]

Shortly after his arrival at the wreckage on the beach, Captain Turner assisted the local commander, Colonel August Buchel. The colonel was a grizzled veteran of the German and Turkish armies, the French Foreign Legion, and the Mexican War. Buchel confirmed that *Sarah* was a total loss, "being now covered with sand." Captain Turner supervised the salvage of the cargo and was able to save most of it. He also got to work dismantling *Sarah*'s valuable sails, spars, and rigging, and recovered its small "yawl boat." On New Year's Day, Colonel Buchel reported that he had sent the rescued merchandise to the Army quartermaster at Columbia where the captain and crew had also gone for shelter.[15]

A correspondent for a Houston newspaper later caught up with Captain McClusky and his crew. He was happy to elaborate on Colonel Buchel's terse official reports of the incident. The reporter repeated the essential facts, but was careful not to reveal the names of the schooner, its owners, or crewmembers. These omissions were probably for security reasons and to protect the crew in case they were captured in the future.[16]

The newspaper version provided an accurate summary of *Sarah*'s escape.

> The Yankees, feeling so jubilant over the day's exploits, forgot to put a sufficient guard on their prize. The captain of the schooner took advantage of the darkness, and beached his

vessel near the mouth of the San Bernard, her entire cargo will be saved, and was removed to a safe place.

The writer also commended the gallant actions of the Virginia-born Capt. Edmund Turner and Lt. Col. Francis R. Lubbock (the former Governor of Texas) in pushing forward to the scene of action.[17]

A few days later, Colonel Buchel and Captain Turner submitted "a list of articles constituting the cargo of the Schooner *Sarah*" that he sent to Columbia. His inventory included: "50 sacks salt, 2 bales blankets, 1 bbl. flour, 4 bales merchandise, 31 boxes raisins, 5 boxes segars, 2 boxes merchandise." The cargo had been consigned to Messrs. Ball, Hutchins, & Co. Colonel Buchel kept the Mexican blankets and salt for the use of his troops, no doubt to the consternation of the Galveston merchants.[18]

All Confederate sources confirm that *Sarah* was a complete loss and never sailed again into the Brazos or anywhere else. None of the reports mention drunken sailors or any Yankee casualties. Similarly, there were no naval prisoner lists that correlate with this location or the Christmas-New Year holidays of 1863–1864. The newspaper correspondent was the only source that mentioned the failure of the Yankees to place a "sufficient guard" on *Sarah*. In light of subsequent events, the lack of adequate precautions on the part of the Navy seemed obvious. It was unlikely that the prize schooner was left unguarded. Captain McClusky and his crew probably overpowered their captors. They may have simply tossed them overboard before heading for shore.[19]

After the loss of *Sarah*, McClusky soon gained command of another small vessel and quickly made his way back to Tampico in an unnamed sloop or schooner. Of the three known small blockade runners that arrived at Tampico from Texas in mid–February 1864, only one had an unidentified captain. It was a sloop that belonged to Thomas House named *Mary Louise*. It had departed from Galveston Bay via San Luis Pass on February 8 with 60 bales of cotton. According to Watson, Captain McClusky sold his small sloop in Tampico, and booked passage to Havana in search of a larger vessel. *Mary Louise* disappeared from contemporary records at this point and may have been kept for use at that port or renamed.[20]

6

Ready, ... Set, ... Wait....

After sharing Captain Dave's sea story about *Sarah*, Watson pointed out one administrative change that was a direct result of McClusky's actions. Blockade runners who attacked their captors were at risk of being branded as mutineers or pirates. To remedy this situation, Watson said that General Magruder issued an order to appoint blockade runner captains as acting Masters in the Confederate naval service. There was no practical consequence of this subterfuge and there is no evidence that any such order was acted upon or officially issued.[1]

On Christmas Eve of 1863, fully five days before McClusky's escape, the General did issue a similar order to Captain James R. Marmion who commanded Marine Department forces at Matagorda Bay. The order did not appear to address the blockade runner problem. Instead, it allowed conscription-eligible men who were performing important roles as merchant mariners to continue in that role without fear of being drafted into the infantry. The order stated that Marmion was to enroll and swear in all men in the merchant marine service who are liable to conscription. They were "not be removed from their places of occupation or interfered with in any manner."[2]

With his bogus commission in hand (either real or imagined), Watson turned his narrative to his own situation, which finally began to look promising. The new year brought new hope as the likelihood of an expanded Union invasion began to wane. With the reduced threat came increased pressure to regenerate the blockade-running business at Galveston Bay and the Brazos River. The persistent presence of the Federal troops at the Rio Grande and their marauding cavalry raids in South Texas only added to the demand for maritime commerce from the still-viable ports.

As he was awaiting his permit, Watson opined that schooners like *Rob Roy* were the best option for running the blockade in Texas. He made this off-hand comment to support his belief that "up to this time there had been no attempts made by steamers to run into the Texas ports. There was no place except Galveston where they could enter, and that place was supposed to be hermetically sealed." He was mistaken. Through December 31, 1863, a total of 16 different steamers had made a total of 35 runs into or out of Texas ports since the initial Federal implementation of the blockade on July 2, 1861.[3]

If Watson had qualified his statement to indicate that no steamer had attempted to enter a Texas port since April of 1863, he would have been correct, and his point would have been no less valid. However, there had been numerous other Texas blockade runs prior to that time, and most were successful. There were 16 runs into Texas, and all were successful. Of the 19 outbound runs, The U.S. Navy only seized one, and four others were wrecked. For those that wrecked or burned, at least a part of the cargo was saved in every case. Many of these runs were made early in the war when the blockade was not fully implemented along the Texas coast. Most of these vessels were small river or coastal steamers. However, seven of the 16 different blockade runners were designed for open ocean commerce. These larger steamships included the *Austin, Arizona, Union, Black Joker* (*C. Vanderbilt*), *Blanche* (*General Rusk*), *Victoria*, and *California*. The smaller, coastal steamers that ran the blockade were *Texas Ranger, Grampus No. 2, Josiah H. Bell, Belle Sulphur, Southern Flora, Sabine, Indian No. 2*, and *Cora*.

Watson's assumption that Galveston was the only viable port for these ocean-going steamers was also in error. Through 1863, Galveston had the fewest number of attempted blockade runs by deep-water steamships. Sabine Pass recorded the highest number of successful runs for these seven vessels with six runs (*Black Joker, Matagorda, Victoria*). There were four runs each at Matagorda Bay (*Blanche* and *California*) and Brazos Santiago (*Austin* and *Arizona*), and three at Galveston Bay (*Union* and *Blanche*). (See Table 1 "Steamship Runs for Texas Ports July 2, 1861–December 31, 1863" for details and citations.)

Table 1. Steamship Blockade Runs at Texas Ports: July 2, 1861–December 31, 1863

Steamer Name	Texas Port	Arrived	Departed	Comments
Texas Ranger	Galveston Bay	7/3/61†	7/19/62	From Berwick Bay; out: 449 b/c; wrecked, Mexico, 50 b/c saved[4]
Josiah H. Bell	Sabine Pass	7/7/61†	n/a	Fm Berwick Bay; carrying mail; taken into Texas Marine Dept.[5]
Grampus No. 2	Brazos Santiago	7/15/61*†	7/15/61*†	From Rio Grande; loading brig *Rosa*[6]
Austin	Brazos Santiago	9/1/61†	9/7/61†	General cargo from/to New Orleans[7]
Arizona	Brazos Santiago	10/3/61†	10/18/61†	Passengers & mail from/to New Orleans[8]
Union	Galveston Bay	10/3/61	8/18/62	From Havana, USS *James S. Chambers* Captured on 8/25/61; 350 b/c[9]
Grampus No. 2	Brazos Santiago	10/4/61†	10/8/61†	From the Rio Grande; lightering for brig *William R. Kibby*[10]
Black Joker (*C. Vanderbilt*)	Sabine Pass	12/29/61	2/15/62	From/to Havana with powder, caps; 406 b/c out[11]
Belle Sulphur	Sabine Pass	Prior to blockade	2/12/62†	Sugar to Berwick Bay; wrecked on return 5/8/62[12]
Southern Flora	Galveston Bay	Prior to blockade	2/12/62†	From Galveston Bay to Brazos[13]
Southern Flora	Brazos	2/12/62†	2/23/62†	At Brazos for salt[14]
Southern Flora	Galveston Bay	2/23/62†	6/1/62*†	River steamer to Galveston Bay[15]
Matagorda	Sabine Pass	3/15/62*†	4/15/62*	From N.O.; to Havana, 995 b/c[16]
Sabine	Sabine Pass	10/21/61†	3/20/62†	Ran ashore off Calcasieu & burned[17]
Blanche (*General Rusk*)	Galveston Bay	Prior to blockade	5/26/62	550 b/c to Havana[18]

Steamer Name	Texas Port	Arrived	Departed	Comments
Indian No. 2	Sabine Pass	5/30/62*†	7/17/62†	From Vermilion Bay, captured on return, but released[19]
Victoria	Sabine Pass	6/26/62	9/17/62*	From/to Havana with Guns & powder; 700 b/c out[20]
Blanche (General Rusk)	Matagorda Bay	8/24/62	9/29/62*	From Havana with arms/ammo; 583 b/c out: partially burned in Cuba[21]
California	Matagorda Bay	8/31/62*†	10/2/62†	From Havana with hospital stores, arms & ammo; outbound wrecked at Sisal 10/15/62; 137b/c saved[22]
Cora	Brazos	Prior to blockade	4/24/63†	100 b/c to Corpus Christi Bay via Matagorda[23]
Cora	Matagorda Bay	4/25/63*†	3/24/65†	USS *Quaker City* captured 3/24/65 off Rio Grande[24]

* Estimated date.
† Blockade runs omitted in the primary reference on Civil War steam blockade runners.[25]

Although he was unaware or misinformed about the recent history of blockade running in Texas, Watson was optimistic. He worked *Rob Roy* down the Brazos River from Columbia in anticipation of making a dash into the Gulf. To carry out his objective, he had to satisfy three critical physical needs. First, *Rob Roy* had to be structurally sound, and fitted out for an open-ocean voyage. Watson had made considerable progress in restoring *Rob Roy*'s structural integrity. In addition to those efforts, sails, rigging, anchors, food, water, and sufficient spares had to be acquired, checked, and double-checked, prior to getting underway.[26]

The second requirement was a skilled and dependable crew. Most sailors of the era only signed shipping articles for a single voyage. They were paid for the time spent onboard, which usually began a few days before sailing and continued for a brief time afterwards to account for loading and unloading cargo. When their obligation was complete, the sailors often did not wait around for the same vessel to complete the cycle of selling and buying cargos and gaining departure clearance. If another captain was prepared to sail and needed a crew, they would set off again on a different vessel. National or ethical affinities played little role in a seaman's employment decisions. As a result of *Rob Roy*'s prolonged delay at the Brazos, and Watson's conflicts with his captain and first mate, there was considerable turnover in his crew.

Watson was sufficiently skilled as a navigator and seaman that he had no problem getting the Mills Brothers to approve his appointment as captain. When he set sail from Columbia toward the mouth of the Brazos, he was anxious to get to sea. But he still lacked some necessary paperwork. He made fast to the riverbank about halfway to Velasco and awaited the long-delayed, but necessary permit. He named the remaining five members of his crew as able-bodied seamen George Thomson and James Hagen, ordinary seaman Appolonaria Barrios, cook Frederick Jansen, and A. Brotherton. Also aboard were two supercargoes that he only identified as "Mr. P." and "Mr. F."[27]

The first of Watson's two supercargoes was probably Ernest Parizot. He had joined *Rob Roy* at the Rio Grande. Parizo had been previously captured and released off Brazos Santiago while running the blockade in a small sloop named *Blazer*. He represented Watson's partner (G. Pauvert & Co.) who initially purchased a one-half ownership. With Watson's new arrangement with Robert and David G. Mills & Co., Parizot's partners only owned a one-quarter share in *Rob Roy*. William Watson's personal share was reduced to one-eighth. The Mills Brothers decided to place Mr. A.F. French (Alonzo Frank French) aboard as a second supercargo to look after their three-quarter interest. A.F. French had been the purser on the steamer *Era No. 3* that the Mills Brothers had chartered to the Marine Department on the Brazos. As the partner with the majority ownership of *Rob Roy*, placing their employee Mr. French onboard was a logical step.[28]

Both seaman George Thomson, a middle-aged Scotsman, and Frederick Jansen, the Swedish-born cook, had been with Watson prior to his arrival at the Brazos. Watson said that the other three crewmen were new. Watson named James Hagan as a seaman who had sailed into Texas on a blockade runner, but hurt his leg and had been left behind when it departed. The man's actual name was James O'Hagan, a 44-year-old Irishman who would later serve as the cook for another blockade runner. The most junior crewman was Appolonaria Barrios, a young man from Chile, that Watson nicknamed Polly.[29]

It turned out that the fifth member of his crew, the first mate who called himself A. Brotherton, was using an alias. According to Watson, the man's real name was George Taylor. He had known the man as Taylor, but Watson noticed that his mate had signed the shipping articles as "A. Brotherton." This subterfuge became a problem when Confederate soldiers boarded *Rob Roy* on the banks of the Brazos. They had an order from Commodore Leon Smith directing them to arrest Taylor as "a dangerous and suspicious character."[30]

Taylor had allegedly come into Texas on a blockade runner, but then joined the Confederate Naval Service (i.e., the Texas Marine Department). Taylor later had a falling out with Commodore Smith. Watson said he advised the man to turn himself in. His best course would be to show deference to Commodore Smith and throw himself on the mercy of a court martial, where he would likely receive a fair hearing.[31]

Watson's unstated motivation for giving this advice was to avoid his own arrest and detention. Before leaving port, every ship captain had to swear that he was not harboring a deserter or anyone else who was subject to conscription. The penalties for violating General Order No. 74 were severe and Watson had enough problems of his own without adding another that he could easily avoid.[32]

A more specific identification of George Taylor from the fragmentary and incomplete records of the Marine Department is problematic. To fill out the ranks of Commodore Smith's department, the commanding general often approved the temporary assignment of soldiers from various army units. At times, an entire company would be detailed to a Marine Department vessel. Other orders were more specific, detailing individuals for naval service based on their specialized skillsets and the needs of the service. These assignments were not always well documented and were often short-term. Among the men known to have served in the Texas military forces or Marine Department, there were no good candidates that fit the circumstances of *Rob Roy*'s George Taylor.

There was, however, a man named F.K.A. Taylor (aka Fred Taylor) of the Marine Department who may have been the sailor in Watson's story. General Magruder levied charges and specifications against this man and filed them with the Confederate Judge Advocate on March 3, 1864. This date was a few weeks after "George Taylor" was removed from *Rob Roy*. Two weeks later, the sailor named Fred Taylor attempted to depart the Brazos as captain of Thomas House's schooner *John*. Fred Taylor was a likely candidate for Watson's imperfectly remembered first mate since a sailor who was qualified as a first mate often served as a ship captain. Major General Magruder prevented Taylor's departure by pointing out that he was "taken from the military service by writ of Habeas Corpus." He also asserted that Taylor was liable for military duty, just like Watson's George Taylor. The schooner *John* would soon find its way into another one of William Watson's sea stories, but Taylor would not.[33]

With the removal of his first mate Taylor, Watson was even more short-handed than before. He was left with just four crew members, however, all were eager to leave Texas, as were the two supercargoes. Each man was equally willing to pitch in as best he could. The one thing Watson still lacked was permission to go to sea. He needed two departure clearances. The first he had just recently obtained was from the Customs House in Galveston. The customs agents documented his cargo, 146 bales of cotton. Other customs information included the date (Jan 2, 1864), the declared destination (Belize), the Consignees (R. & D.G. Mills), total weight of cotton (about 67,145 lbs.), and the custom duties paid ($83.93).[34]

With a customs clearance in hand, Watson still needed a military permit to pass the forts. He called this permit a "passport." The purpose of the military permit was to notify the forts that a vessel was fully approved to depart port. This added step was necessary to avoid friendly fire, ensure that no unauthorized personnel were attempting to leave the country, and (sometimes) arrange signals for nighttime identification. While a valuable cargo was not essential for getting underway, *Rob Roy*'s 146 bales of cotton provided ample motivation to do just that.[35]

Hopeful that he would soon receive his permit, Watson positioned his schooner farther down river, near Velasco at the mouth of the Brazos. Two other schooners accompanied *Rob Roy* with the same aspiration. Watson and his fellow ship captains had been observing the activities of the Union blockaders and planning their escapes. Early one morning as he was watching and waiting for an opportunity to make a run through the blockade, Watson said he saw a large schooner aground within two hundred yards of the forts. The harbor pilot, Sam Lyon, was on his way to render assistance. The stranded schooner was in grave danger of destruction from Union cannon-fire or the wind and waves. In either case, the wreck of a large schooner in the narrow channel would be an obstruction that might prevent or delay *Rob Roy*'s departure.[36]

Watson said that he and his three crewmen impulsively jumped into the pilot's boat with as much cordage (line or rope) as they could find. They hoped to pull the schooner off the bar. When they reached the stranded vessel, Watson was surprised to see his "old" friend Francis Downs that he had met on the Brazos the previous November. While *Rob Roy* was resting at the bottom of the river, Downs had graciously played host to William Watson who spent the night onboard *Eureka*. The next day, November 19, 1863, Downs had sailed his schooner down the Brazos and out to sea. The blockading fleet had discovered and captured *Eureka* shortly after its departure from the Brazos. The Navy prize crew took the schooner to New Orleans to stand trial at the admiralty court with Downs onboard as a witness.[37]

Over the roar of the roiling surf, Capt. Downs shouted for Watson to secure the line to one of the piles that *Rob Roy* had driven into the riverbed. Collectively, they hoped to be able to heave his schooner over the bar and into the river. Meanwhile, the Union gunboats had taken note of the vulnerable schooner, were closing the distance, and preparing to open fire. Fortunately, the tide began to shift. The pilot Sam Lyon urged the crew to "Heave away heartily, and the British lion will soon take you over" and he did. All sail was set, and the large schooner finally began to move. As she slipped off the bar and into the Brazos, her crew raised a loud cheer of relief to celebrate their survival.[38]

After his narrow escape, Captain Downs took time to catch his breath. Like most sailors, he regained his energy by spinning yarns about his adventures. Watson eagerly accepted his friend's offer to bring him up to date since the two men had parted ways in November. Downs said that he was captured soon after sailing from the Brazos, but had come within a hair's breadth of bluffing his way to freedom. When boarded, he was able to convince the Union gunboat captain that he was already a prize to the "*Ponobscot*" (USS *Penobscot*). There was no prize crew onboard the schooner because the "*Ponobscot*" had hurried off in pursuit of two larger, and even more lucrative schooners. The enticement of capturing another cotton-laden blockade runner temporarily clouded the Union captain's judgement. The warship sailed off to the west like an easily duped cartoon predator in pursuit of his prey. Upon reflection, the captain realized that the wily Captain Downs had fooled him. The gunboat quickly reversed course and took Downs and his schooner into custody.[39]

When he initially greeted the Navy's boarding party, Downs said the name of his schooner's was *Iniquity*. It was the ever-mischievous captain's way of referring to *Eureka* which had also been known as *Enriqueta*, *Enriquita,* and *Enrequita*. Downs did not identify his captor. However, official records confirm that the Navy warship the USS *Aroostook* captured *Eureka* and Captain Downs on November 19, 1863. *Aroostook* was one of the 90-day, *Unadill*a-class steamers. This time, it was Downs who was called into account for his iniquities. The New Orleans admiralty court condemned *Eureka* and its 73 bales of cotton for a total of $27,273.88.[40]

The truth of this part of Watson's story unfortunately means that Captain Francis Downs could not have been onboard a schooner trying to enter the Brazos in early 1864. Downs gave his testimony to the New Orleans admiralty court on December 15, 1863. It would have taken several days before Union officials would have released their witness. Downs then would have had to make his way to Havana or another Mexican port. He was back on the Brazos River prior to September 1864. Unfortunately, the historical record does not record when or how he got there. It is, however, highly unlikely that he was able to cross enemy lines. It simply was not possible for him to take command of another schooner in a neutral port and run the blockade into back into Texas by January 1864.[41]

Other than the identification of the schooner's captain (Francis Downs), the location of the grounding (Brazos River), and the approximate time of the event (early January 1864), Watson provided very few clues about the identity of Captain Downs' large new schooner. Once again, the official Civil War naval references are equally silent about the schooner's identity.

Francis Downs did command a large schooner that was briefly stuck at the mouth of the Brazos, but the time and circumstances do not match Watson's tale. Downs did not command the 102-ton schooner until late summer of 1864. He was captain when *John* grounded heading out of the Brazos on September 11, 1864, nine months after Watson and his crew had assisted what had to have been a different schooner or a different captain.

The schooner *John* had arrived at the Brazos in September 1863. The schooner departed the Brazos bound for Belize via Tampico with a load of cotton on October 16, 1863, under Captain Andrew Jackson (Jack) Moore. He then sailed to Havana and back to the Brazos River. Captain Jack Moore was in command both times that *John* arrived at the Brazos. If Watson's story about helping rescue a stranded schooner as it entered the Brazos was true, he and his crew aided Captain Moore and not Captain Downs in September or October of 1863.

Although Confederate authorities refused to let Fred Taylor take command of *John* in March, Jack Moore was able to turn *John* over to William Rogers Tucker on July 1, 1864. Captain Moore left for Havana via another vessel. Tucker was equally unsuccessful in getting *John* to sea and gave up command to Francis Downs two months later. Downs would have better luck getting the schooner across the bar, but little else.[42]

John had been bottled up on the Brazos for a full year due to its relatively deep draft. Two different captains (Moore and Tucker) had tried and failed to get *John* out of the Brazos, but it was not for lack of effort. It was extraordinarily difficult to find the proper combination of conditions to sail the large schooner over the shallow bar guarding the Brazos. Captain Downs would eventually make the attempt with a light load of only 81 bales of cotton on September 10, 1864.

Predictably, even with a minimal cargo, *John* grounded at the bar. The schooner remained stuck for over 12 hours, but eventually worked its way off. Captain Downs then wrote a brief a note to Thomas W. House asking him to pay the three men who helped him clear the bar. He had to hurry, "for the jack [jackstay] is raising and pitching like a bone tied to a gate post." He hoped to write again when he reached Vera Cruz. Captain Downs and his schooner would not be that fortunate. They were captured the next day when the winds died down. Captain Francis Downs would once again be hauled before the New Orleans admiralty court, and have his vessel and cargo condemned.[43]

There were other vessels that had difficulty getting into the Brazos, during the period of Watson's story. These incidents may have inspired Watson's tale about rescuing Francis Downs and his schooner. Some of the vessels were captured, and there were two schooners that succeeded in getting across the bar, after first running aground.

Blockade runners that received aid from Confederate shore parties or steamboats usually found mention in official reports and newspaper articles. Four different schooners ran into the Brazos and San Luis pass between December 1863 and January 1864. Three of them experienced the kind of trouble that Captain Downs reportedly experienced.

The schooners *Agnes* and *Charles Russell* both arrived at the Brazos River on December 20, 1863 (see Table 2). *Agnes* had sailed from Belize under Captain George N. Hubbard, and *Charles Russell* cleared from Vera Cruz under Captain Joseph Davidson. They both ran onto the beach about six miles below the river to avoid capture. The shallow-draft Confederate steamboat *Mary Hill* came to their rescue. This four-year-old, side-paddlewheel steamer promptly raced out of the Brazos and by hugging the coast, safely towed *Charles Russell* into the river. The steamer soon returned and repeated the process with *Agnes*. Another Confederate river steamer, *Lone Star*, then towed both schooners upriver to Columbia. There was no mention of either vessel getting stuck at the bar.[44]

The schooners *W.D.S. Hyer* and *Ann Giberson* also arrived at the Texas coast from Havana on December 23, 1863. *W.D.S. Hyer* briefly ran aground and received assistance from forces out of the Brazos. However, the schooner grounded again at the San Luis Pass into Galveston Bay. When it got under way, *W.D.S. Hyer* then passed over the bar at the mouth of the Brazos River. The other schooner, *Ann Giberson*, also entered the Brazos, but did not have any issues at the bar. Given the available facts, it appears that Watson's tale about helping rescue Captain Downs at the mouth of the Brazos, was more fiction than fact. The grounding occurred long after Watson and *Rob Roy* had left the Brazos. *John*'s heroic entry into the river may have been true, but Watson either confused the names and dates, or simply interjected himself into the story after the fact.[45]

With the stories of daring escapes and rescues fresh on his creative mind, William Watson returned to his own situation. He prepared to test his own skills at outwitting the blockading fleet. He understood that no amount of skill could guarantee success, but he was confident in his ship, crew, and most of all, himself.

7

Secret Agents, Spies, and Betrayal

Although his crew was now short-handed, Watson impatiently awaited his permit to go to sea from the military authorities. Fortune finally smiled upon him in the form of a Confederate officer who galloped up to the Velasco wharf where *Rob Roy* was docked. The man carried a surprising message from Major General Magruder. The general had a special task for him. The uncertain situation at the border resulting from the Union Army's occupation of the lower Rio Grande, created an opportunity for Watson and *Rob Roy*.[1]

As Watson related the story, the General, "having confidence in my integrity, had decided to entrust to my care some despatches [sic] of great importance. They were intended for the Confederate States Consul in Havana." Carrying the official letters would be no great burden, as long as they were not in his possession if he was captured. More importantly, this duty promised some beneficial perks, i.e., an expedited clearance for sea. What Watson did not know was that this simple request would immerse him in the sinister domain of secret agents and spies.[2]

Watson confessed to the courier that wind conditions would make it difficult for him to take the dispatches directly to Havana. He planned to first sail for Tampico or Vera Cruz and then to Belize before striking out for Havana. That detour was not a problem for General Magruder or his staff. These ports were on the regular Royal Mail steamer circuit that made routine deliveries to Havana. This circuitous, but safer route also meant that *Rob Roy* and General Magruder's correspondence were less likely to be captured.[3]

Watson felt honored by the trust placed in him. He carefully preserved the letter from Major General Magruder for almost 30 years and proudly quoted it in his book. Except for minor spelling and punctuation variances, Watson's transcription closely matches the letter recorded in the National Archive's Confederate files for the District of Texas. The only discrepancy was the cited date. Watson recorded Magruder's letter as written on January 13, 1864, instead of the actual date of "January 3rd, 1864."[4]

The instructions to Watson stipulated that he was to ensure the delivery of a package of letters to Major Charles J. Helm, the Confederate procurement agent in Havana. Since Spain had not recognized the Confederacy as a nation, Major Helm was technically not a consul, even though he functioned as one. His responsibilities included obtaining credit, removing trade barriers, making purchases, and influencing public opinion on behalf of the Confederacy. The major was also adept at obtaining and passing along vital intelligence, much valued by blockade runners and the Confederate government.[5]

Helm was well qualified for his job. He had fought in the Mexican War and served one term in the Kentucky legislature. Immediately prior to the Civil War, he had been the U.S. Consul accredited to both the Danish Virgin Islands, and to Havana, Cuba. Now that he was working for the other side, Union military officers, politicians, and newspapermen, complained that Helm had converted his office and home into a "regular resort for all rebels."[6]

Along with Magruder's personal letter to Watson, the Confederate courier handed him a large, sealed packet. Unknown to Watson, there were three letters inside the bundle. Watson was clearly flattered by Magruder's confidence in his "… good judgement, zeal, and patriotism" in the important mission entrusted to his care. However, Magruder's testimonial that Watson was "selected as the most suitable person to whom these papers can be entrusted" needs a bit of clarification.[7]

Watson's selection was based only in part on his fidelity. The timing of *Rob Roy*'s departure was perhaps the most important factor. A day before contacting Watson, General Magruder had asked the commander at Velasco, Colonel Philip N. Luckett, to find a schooner that was ready to sail from the Brazos River to Havana. He wanted Luckett's recommendation for "the first good vessel whose captain is a safe, reliable man." That vessel happened to be Watson's *Rob Roy*.[8]

When it became clear that *Rob Roy*'s first port of call would not be Havana and that his sailing was delayed into February, Magruder found another "most suitable person" to entrust copies of the same letters. That person was Emile Alvin Huke, the supercargo of the schooner *Ann Giberson*. His schooner was also headed to Havana, but like Watson, the sailing conditions would probably force him to make an intermediate stop. Huke was in good standing with Confederate officials for having fulfilled a contract to import arms and ammunition from Havana. These arms had arrived at the Brazos a few weeks earlier in the previously mentioned schooners *W.D.S. Hyer* and *Ann Giberson*.[9]

Huke had been a sergeant with Company "C" in Woods' Regiment of Texas Cavalry Volunteers at San Antonio. In June 1863, he requested a demotion to the rank of private. The reason for this unusual petition became clear when the Army furloughed him to run the blockade. He would be the supercargo on a schooner named *Sarah Jordan*. At just over 40 tons burden, it was slightly smaller than *Rob Roy*. As with Watson's schooner, R. & D.G. Mills were the primary owners of *Sarah Jordan*, and it was on the Sabine River in June 1863, preparing for a voyage to Havana. Given the ensuing activities of *Sarah Jordan* and its association with E.A. Huke, it is important to know the schooner's history as a blockade runner.[10]

Levi Jordan had built the schooner before the war and named it after his wife, Sarah (Stone) Jordan. Levi and Sarah owned a plantation near Columbia, Texas, situated between the San Bernard River and Caney Creek. Jordan and his partner Captain Caleb Letts had used the schooner to transport sugar and cotton down those waterways to market.[11]

When the Union Navy initiated the blockade of Texas in July 1861, *Sarah Jordan* was seemingly bottled up in Galveston Bay. At this early stage of the war, however, the Union fleet could only cover the main channel at the eastern end of Galveston Island. This coverage limitation left the other passes and rivers of Texas open for shallow-draft vessels. This included San Luis Pass at the far southwestern end of Galveston Island. From there, *Sarah Jordan* was able to make an undetected voyage into the San Bernard River where it continued to provide transportation for Levi's products.[12]

Robert and David G. Mills approached Levi about buying his schooner for use as a blockade runner in March of 1862. He was reluctant to sell, but was open to other options. As he explained to the Mills Brothers, "I do not wish to sell Her [sic] as she is all my dependence in getting my produce to market, when the blockade is removed. But if you wish to run Her [sic] and risk the blockading fleet, you can do so." It appears that rather than sell his schooner, Levi was willing to lease her. There were two conditions. The brothers had to carry cotton from his plantation and cover the schooner's value in case it was lost while running the blockade. But first, Levi needed to consult with his partner Caleb Letts.[13]

Captain Letts had become an unreliable and quarrelsome partner. Earlier, he had ignored Levi's request to move his sugar from Caney Creek to Matagorda Bay. Letts was also upset with Levi's lease arrangement with the Mills Brothers. He thought it was costing too much to outfit *Sarah Jordan* for a cruise. In short, he wanted Levi to buy out his share for $2,000. Levi asked the Mills Brothers what they were willing to pay for his partner's interest in the schooner. He explained that Capt. Letts "still owes me about $1,200 & since Capt. Letts appears to be dissatisfied, I would give a little more than the Schooner was actually worth to be rid of him."[14]

Levi Jordan and the Mills Brothers were able to complete their deal in July 1862, and successfully ran *Sarah Jordan* to Belize with 140 bales of cotton. Like much of the cotton shipped out of Texas, those bales eventually ended up in New York. With the proceeds of the cotton, *Sarah Jordan*'s supercargo bought "dry goods, boots, shoes, powder, ball and shot." *Sarah Jordan* then ran those goods into Sabine Pass, Texas, on September 18, 1862.[15]

Since that time, the Union Navy had increased its presence off the Sabine, and effectively stymied blockade runners trying to enter or exit the Sabine. However, by June 1863 *Sarah Jordan* was preparing to return to sea under the command of a 24-year-old German-American Captain named August A. Johnson with a crew of four. It is at this point that the 26-year-old Polish-American E. Alvin Huke also joined the crew as the new supercargo.[16]

Huke's schooner had received its initial clearance out of Sabine Pass in mid-July, but was delayed until early October 1863. While he was waiting for an opportunity to run the blockade, Huke decided to become an agent for the Confederate Government. General Magruder agreed, and gave him authority to make contracts on behalf of the Confederate Army when he reached Havana. Huke's authority included the unnecessary option of purchasing a light draft steamer that could carry any arms and ammunition he might be able to acquire in Cuba.[17]

Although the specific movements of *Sarah Jordan* after its clearance from

7. Secret Agents, Spies, and Betrayal

Sabine Pass are unrecorded, it did make a successful voyage to Havana in the fall of 1863. After his arrival, Huke was busy executing contracts for munitions of war and engaged at least two additional schooners to carry them. *W.D.S. Hyer* and *Ann Giberson* had recently arrived from Matamoros and were available and willing to run the blockade. In late December 1863, these two schooners returned to Texas. They ran into Galveston Bay and the Brazos River respectively and were consigned to Thomas W. House. E.A. Huke also reappeared in Galveston at about the same time, suggesting that he had been onboard one of those two vessels, or perhaps *Sarah Jordan*.[18]

Huke's return to Texas from Havana was just before General Magruder penned his letters for Watson to carry. A month later, the general sent Huke duplicate copies of those same letters for him to deliver on the schooner *Ann Giberson*. He had one other letter from Magruder dated February 6, 1864. This letter was addressed directly to Huke and emphasized that the package contained "papers of extreme importance." The general wanted to ensure that Huke was prepared to add heavy weights and jettison the package into the sea in the event he encountered an enemy vessel. Supercargo Huke would leave in the schooner *Ann Giberson* for Havana about two weeks behind *Rob Roy*.[19]

There is no record of exactly when *Rob Roy* finally went to sea. The Customs Office in Galveston had granted its clearance on January 2, 1864, for his cargo of 146 bales of cotton destined for Belize. It would be at least a month before *Rob Roy* actually sailed. Watson stated that he finally departed the Brazos River on a dark, stormy night near the "new," or dark phase, of the moon, which was February 7. That night, two other schooners followed him into the Gulf. A simultaneous departure increased the collective odds for the three schooners to evade the blockading fleet if they all scattered in different directions. The first schooner behind *Rob Roy* was the smaller *Mary Elizabeth* which was carrying 75 bales of cotton. The second was a larger schooner, that Watson believed was named *Hind*.[20]

Mary Elizabeth is a well-documented, 23-ton schooner owned by T.W. House who named it after his wife. The captain was Henry Scherffius's younger brother George (Georgius Scherffius). Unfortunately, there are no schooners with a name similar to "*Hind*" that cleared from Texas during this timeframe. Among the schooners that did sail from Texas at about the same time as Watson, only two were slightly larger than the 48-ton *Rob Roy*. They were *Eliza Catharine* and *Agnes*.[21]

Eliza Catharine received her permit on January 28, and ran the blockade out of the Brazos with over 201 bales. Watson remarked that he believed that the blockading fleet captured *Hind* before she was able to reach port. If his recollection that the third schooner was slightly larger than *Rob Roy* and was captured after it left the Brazos was correct, the schooner was probably *Agnes* (see Table 2 and Chapter 6). She was another blockade runner in the fleet of R. & D.G. Mills and carried 233 bales of cotton. At 53 registered tons, *Agnes* was about five tons more than *Rob Roy*. *Agnes* did not receive a permit for sea until February 21 which suggests that either *Rob Roy* did not sail until after the new moon, or that Watson's third sailing companion was not *Agnes*. The U.S. Navy captured *Agnes* as she departed the Brazos three months later. *Eliza Catharine* avoided capture, but after making several additional runs, she tragically ran aground in April 1865. Five members of the schooner's eight-man crew

"A Blockade Running Schooner Loaded with Cotton." William Watson, *Adventures of a Blockade Runner; or, Trade in Time of War*. London: Fisher Unwin, 1892, frontispiece (author's collection).

perished while attempting to run out of the Brazos.[22]

Upon the departure of the schooners *Rob Roy* and *Ann Giberson* for Havana, Magruder must have felt confident that his letters would find their way to Major Charles Helm in Havana. The seemingly reliable supercargo E.A. Huke was a backup for Watson and *Rob Roy*. At least one of the general's packages of sealed dispatches would surely reach its destination. Watson never revealed the contents of the letters that he carried, apart from the one expressly addressed to himself. He may not have even known what information they held that made them so important.[23]

The official Confederate letter files, however, reveal the contents of Magruder's secret correspondence in its entirety. The first letter was a direct appeal to Major Helm. The general wanted the major to use his influence to support an audacious plan for a Confederate naval offensive against the U.S. Navy's fleet on the Texas coast. The general was itching to go on the offensive. He proposed launching a series of attacks in the Western Gulf of Mexico. The Confederate ocean-going cruisers CSS *Alabama* and CSS *Florida* would spearhead the proposed offensive. The general offered up his small fleet of coastal gunboats under Commodore Leon Smith to coordinate simultaneous attacks from the shore for maximum effectiveness. Magruder hoped these combined operations against Union warships and transports would disrupt the blockade, open trade, and isolate the enemy troops encamped along the Texas coast between Matagorda Bay and the Rio Grande.[24]

The other two letters in the packet were virtually identical. The general asked Major Helm to forward them to the commanders of the two best known and most successful Confederate commerce raiders operating on the high seas, Captain Raphael Semmes of the CSS *Alabama* and Commander John Newland Maffitt of the CSS *Florida*. The general spiced up those two letters with the prospect of prize money. He minimized the dangers and pointed out the availability of the ports of Texas for sending in prizes to admiralty courts convened at "Sabine, Galveston, Velasco," and other ports. These courts would order the sale of all captured vessels at "very high rates." In addition to inflicting "serious injury upon the enemy" Semmes and Maffitt would garner considerable profit "in the way of prize money."[25]

CSS *Alabama* had executed a similar, but isolated, attack on the Federal Fleet as it was bombarding Galveston in early January 1863. Semmes had intended to attack Union troop transport ships, but when he realized that Confederate forces had recaptured the city, he changed his plans. Semmes mimicked the actions of a frightened blockade runner and successfully lured USS *Hatteras* away from the rest of the blockading fleet. After slowing *Alabama* enough for *Hatteras* to catch up with him, he patiently waited until the gunboat lowered its boarding party into a small boat. At that point, Semmes suddenly revealed his identity as a Confederate warship and opened fire. The wary Union warship returned fire, but after a violent exchange of broadside volleys, only the masts of the *Hatteras* were visible above the waves. All surviving Union sailors became prisoners, except for the bewildered *Hatteras* boarding party that Captain Semmes left adrift. The CSS *Alabama* went merrily on its destructive way, but never returned to the waters of the Western Gulf of Mexico.[26]

None of the vessels that Semmes, Maffitt, or the other Confederate commerce cruiser captains captured ever resulted in any prize money. The Confederate captains either had to set their prizes free on bond (only collectible if the Confederacy won the war) or sink them. Thus, the sinking of the *Hatteras* resulted in no profit for the Confederate States or the *Alabama*'s crew other than bragging rights and the reduction of one warship from the enemy's blockading fleet. Magruder was offering an opportunity to change all that, albeit one that had little chance of success.

Not knowing of the letters' contents or the futility of Magruder's request, Watson pressed ahead with his promise to deliver the package into reliable hands for Major Helm. That opportunity occurred shortly after Watson arrived in Tampico where he met a previous acquaintance from Matamoros that he knew to be a dependable Confederate agent. The man was probably John O'Sullivan, the brother-in-law of the British merchant John Maloney of Matamoros. O'Sullivan was an agent for Confederate General Hamilton P. Bee who was on his way to Havana. O'Sullivan's mission was to recover Confederate arms and ammunition that the French had taken from Mexico to Cuba.

The French had blockaded Bagdad/Matamoros on behalf of Emperor Maximilian to prevent the importation of arms for Benito Juárez. They had seized 24,000 Confederate Enfield rifles from the schooner *Love Bird* and brig *Caroline Goodyear*. The Confederates were only able to take possession of 4,000 of the rifles before a French warship intervened, thinking that the weapons were intended for the Juárista loyalists. After seizing the guns and munitions at the Rio Grande, the French gunboat escorted them to Vera Cruz before French authorities sent them to Havana. For his own safety, O'Sullivan was traveling in one of the British mail steamers.[27]

Before Watson handed off the package, he described an encounter with a man who was working on behalf of U.S. interests. Watson used several pages to detail the man's approach and motives. Watson was intrigued, and a bit disgusted, by this brush with the shadowy world of espionage, greed, and betrayal. The Union spy was a stranger who had just arrived in Tampico from Texas. The man was friendly, but was obviously trying to work his way into Watson's confidence. He did not know the contents of Watson's letters, but he was fully aware that a package from Major General Magruder was onboard *Rob Roy* and that it was intended for Major Helm in Havana. The confidence man finally got around to offering Watson a bribe to turn over the confidential dispatches. It was an offer Watson felt obliged to refuse.[28]

Watson offered very few clues about the secret agent's identity, but the man was clearly not the original source of the leak within Confederate channels. It had to be somebody within Magruder's inner circle or one of the men with direct knowledge of the packages that were intended for the Confederate agent in Havana, Major Charles Helm. A possible source of the leak was the former Confederate Army sergeant and blockade runner supercargo, E. Alvin Huke. Huke might not have shared the same scruples as Watson.

The circumstantial case against Huke is strong, but the only evidence of his possible betrayal (or loyalty, depending upon perspective), was a letter from the U.S. Consulate in Havana. In late July 1865, Vice-Consul Thomas Savage penned a letter to Secretary of State William H. Seward about a report from his mysterious "Secret Agent H." This secret agent had alerted the consul's attention to the plantation owners, blockade runners, and arms dealers, R. & D.G. Mills and Company of Texas. The agent focused on Robert Mills, the nemesis of William Watson. Robert, the older brother of David Graham Mills, was based in Havana, but fled to Europe at the end of the war. Victorious Union officials were eager for retribution against disloyal Confederates, especially against those who were overseas and had assets of value, making Robert Mills an obvious target.

Secret Agent H reported that Robert Mills had "done more than any one in Texas to assist the rebellion." Consul Savage touted his agent's first-hand knowledge of the gun running activities of the Mills family, saying "H" had personally carried a cargo in the schooner *Sarah* [and] the blockading fleet chased ashore near the San Bernard River. After the Union gunboat departed the area, "H" managed to save the whole cargo, except five Enfield rifles. "Half of the cargo he sent to Columbia per Stmr *Mary Hill* and the other half he took in carts or wagons to Mills' plantation (the Low Wood) 15 miles from the Mouth of the Brazos River...."[29]

Either Secret Agent H was spinning a tale of half-truths or Consul Savage got his facts slightly confused in his report. He correctly described the brothers Robert and David, and their nephew John Mills, as well as their travels and roles in supporting the Confederacy in Texas. Savage's letter also revealed the name of Huke's schooner. He said it was "*Sarah*," a shortening of its full name, *Sarah Jordan*. Although Emile Alvin Huke appears to fit the profile of "Secret Agent H," he may have had an accomplice. In September 1864, Huke died in Galveston, a victim of the dreaded yellow fever. Huke may have been involved or perhaps accidentally exposed the contents of Magruder's letters, he could not have been Consul Savage's secret agent in 1865. In a letter written much later, Savage identified his secret agent as Samuel Barker Haynes, who was using his middle name as an alias.

7. Secret Agents, Spies, and Betrayal

The Mills Brothers were particularly active as arms importers. They dispatched several schooners from Havana between late December 1863, and January 1864. During this period, there were numerous attempts to run the blockade into San Luis Pass, the San Bernard River, Caney Creek, and the Brazos River. Most were successful, but several captains had to run their vessels onto the beach in the process. Table 2 lists the 10 blockade-running schooners that were in this area of Texas during this period. There was ample documentation of all these voyages in the *War of the Rebellion* official records except for *Sarah Jordan*.

Table 2. Galveston & Brazos River Blockade Runners, Dec 20, 1863–Jan 4, 1864

Schooner Name	Date	From	To	Captain	Cargo
Charles Russell*	12/20/63	Vera Cruz	Brazos	Jas. Davidson	Gunny cloth, cotton cards, nails[30]
Agnes*	12/20/63	Belize	Brazos	G.N. Hubbard	Arms, ammunition[31]
W.D.S. Hyer†	12/23/63	Havana	Galveston	C.P. Marsden	Rifles, powder, rope[32]
Ann Giberson	12/23/63§	Havana	Brazos	Unknown	Rifles, powder[33]
Exchange	12/24/63	Vera Cruz	Captured	J.H. Ashby	10 mi. west of Brazos[34]
Sarah	12/29/63	Tampico	Wrecked‡	D. McClusky	blankets, salt, & sundries[35]
Stingray	01/03/64§	Kingston	Brazos	G.W. Little	Unknown[36]
Cora	01/03/64§	Belize	Brazos	J.E. Hulburt	Axes, spades, shovels, nails[37]
John Douglas	01/03/64§	Belize	Brazos	J.A. Kenney	Powder, shot, hardware[38]
Sarah Jordan	01/04/64§	Havana	Wrecked‡	A.A. Johnson	Rifles & bayonets[39]

* Chased, beached, towed in by SS *Mary Hill*
† Beached near San Luis Pass, cargo & vessel saved.
§ Estimated arrival date.
‡ Beached 7 mi. southwest of Caney Creek; cargo saved.

As detailed in Table 2 and in previous chapters, William Watson and other contemporary sources confirm that Union fleet did, indeed, chase the schooner *Sarah* onto the beach near the San Bernard River. In response, Confederate soldiers raced to the scene and saved the cargo. The contemporary reporting of this incident is remarkably complete. Just as all these schooners were arriving in Texas, Major General Magruder had moved his headquarters out of Houston and into the field. He was responding to the Union invasion of the southern coast of Texas, and feared an attack on the Brazos. Captain Edmund P. Turner from the general's staff was conducting a personal reconnaissance of the area between the San Bernard and Brazos when *Sarah* ran ashore on December 29.

Captain Turner was one of the first officers on the scene where *Sarah* had run onto the beach. The schooner was from Tampico and had escaped from a U.S. Navy prize crew in the night. According to Turner, it was "laden with Mexican blankets, salt, and sundries." He also said that the schooner carried "no arms or ammunition, nothing but the above-mentioned articles. Every article of value was being removed when I left."[40]

As General Magruder's adjutant, Turner had no reason to withhold any of the cargo for local troops and needed to give his boss an accurate report. Colonel Buchel, the local commander, was a small, quiet man with unassuming, courteous, and gentlemanly manners. He retained the salt and blankets from *Sarah* for his own troops, and had the rest of the cargo sent up the Brazos to Columbia.[41]

Sarah did not originate out of Havana. Instead, it sailed out of Tampico under the Swiss flag, with a cargo consigned to Ball, Hutchins & Co. These factors made it unlikely for it to have been one of R. & D.G. Mills & Company's vessels. Additionally, there were no known arms available for export out of Tampico at the time. These armaments had been transferred to Havana where John O'Sullivan, Robert Mills, E.A. Huke, and Confederate agents and merchants were working to acquire them. Neither Huke nor the Mills Brothers had any known affiliation with *Sarah*, or its consigning agents, Ball, Hutchins, & Co.[42]

In Havana, E.A. Huke had contracted for arms and ammunition that travelled on at least two schooners. Therefore, Huke's arms shipments would have originated from Havana. The first to arrive was *W.D.S. Hyer*, whose captain ran it ashore about one mile from San Luis pass. Thanks to the aid of soldiers and sailors from Velasco, both the cargo and vessel made it safely into the Brazos River. The schooner was carrying "8,000 pounds of powder & three hundred & fifty Spanish Rifles." The second was *Ann Giberson* (also *Anna Gibberson*), that made a less dramatic voyage to Texas when it entered the Brazos River at about the same time.[43]

As described in the previous chapter, the steam gunboat and transport *Mary Hill* was an important Confederate asset at the Brazos. A few days before the arrival of *Ann Giberson*, the steamboat had raced across the Brazos River's bar and along the beach to rescue the schooners *Charles Russell* and *Agnes*. Union warships had chased both schooners onto the beach. The boarding parties were on the verge of capturing the schooner when *Mary Hill* pulled them off the sand. The steamer then towed the schooners to safety under the guns of the Confederate forts that protected the entrance to the river. Confederate authorities were eager to rescue both vessels because they believed they were carrying valuable armament cargos from Havana. However, they had originated from Vera Cruz and Belize, respectively. The arms were on board *W.D.S. Hyer*, *Ann Giberson*, and (probably) *Sarah Jordan*.[44]

Mary Hill was active in moving military supplies up and down the river. These trips often included down-river loads of government owned cotton. Upriver cargos of government-contracted arms, ammunition, and supplies offloaded from blockade runners were also common. It is likely that Confederate authorities at the Brazos River would have loaded any armament imports onto *Mary Hill*. The steamer would deliver them to the railhead at Columbia for forwarding to the Ordnance Department.

Sarah is not the vessel that Consul Savage mentioned in his story about Secret Agent H's beached schooner. *Sarah Jordan* is the better candidate. Levi Jordan's schooner had a cargo consigned to R. & D.G. Mills and appears to have made an undocumented return trip to familiar territory on the San Bernard River in early January 1864. Consul Savage probably shortened the schooner *Sarah Jordan*'s name to *Sarah* in his letter to Secretary Seward. Colonel Joseph Bates did the same thing that spring when he reported the status of 195 Enfield rifles and 188 bayonets from "*Sarah*" that he had shipped to Houston from Columbia. These weapons must have come from *Sarah Jordan* instead. Captain Turner had definitively stated that *Sarah* did not have any ordnance onboard, but *Sarah Jordan* may have.[45]

Ralph J. Smith corroborated the arrival of an unrecorded schooner in his little-known Civil War reminiscences. The grounding occurred near the San Bernard in early January 1864 and was most likely *Sarah Jordan*. At the time, Smith was a private assigned to Fort Cedar Bayou, which was located about halfway between the mouths of Caney Creek and the San Bernard River. Shortly after he arrived there, a federal gunboat ran a Spanish schooner onto the beach near the fort. The crew, "all Cubans, being much frightened, abandoned her and took to the woods. Our officers took possession of the boat and cargo, consisting of coffee, Irish potatoes, salt fish, calico, washbowls and pitchers, bar iron and some few barrels besides numbers of cases of various tonics, which we called soothing syrup consigned to R. & D.G. Mills of Galveston." The soldiers salvaged the cargo, confiscated the "soothing syrup" and became roaring drunk.[46]

Smith did not report seeing any rifles, but this oversight was probably due to the soldiers' interest in securing the intoxicating liquors above all else. They buried the remaining barrels that they were unable to consume that day. Unfortunately for the thirsty soldiers, they were so drunk while digging in the sand, none of them could remember where they had hidden their treasure the next morning.[47]

If Private Smith got his dates, locations, and names correct, there were no good candidates for this vessel mentioned within in the official records. *Sarah* was consigned to Ball, Hutchins & Co. and ran aground on December 29, seven miles south of the Caney and far beyond visual range of Smith's Fort at Cedar Bayou. The two other schooners associated with E.A. Huke and known to have originated from Havana, *Ann Giberson*, *W.D.S. Hyer*, did not run aground near the San Bernard.

Sarah Jordan had been consigned to the Mills Brothers and would have originated from Havana in the Spanish colony of Cuba. Since the soldiers from Private Smith's regiment were able to siphon off part of the cargo, it is also possible that some of the cargo was diverted to the Mills' plantation on the Brazos before it reached the army warehouse at Columbia.

If E.A. Huke was indeed a secret agent working on behalf of the Union, it is likely that the contents of Magruder's confidential war plans that he had given to Huke and Watson became known to U.S. Consul Savage and the rest of the Federal leadership soon after Huke's arrival in Havana. Given William Watson's later dealings with the unscrupulous, or perhaps parsimonious, Robert Mills, it may be that Huke became disgruntled enough to become an informant for the U.S. government. However, even if Huke did turn General Magruder's letters over to the U.S. consul in Havana, the damage to the Confederate cause would have been minimal.

Despite Magruder's high hopes, nothing ever came of his grandiose naval plans. Confederate commerce raiders were not designed or intended to conduct attacks against well-armed enemy warships. In fact, their captains deliberately avoided such engagements unless cornered or there were other compelling factors that weighed heavily in their favor. Commerce raiders were not intended to slug it out against an enemy warship; there were far too few of them. Unlike the Union Navy, the Confederate ports were blockaded and unavailable for needed repairs, and equipment or personnel replacement. The Secretary of the Confederate Navy, Stephen Mallory would never have approved such a scheme, and neither Semmes nor Maffitt would have been foolish enough to try it.

Time and distance alone made Magruder's request for a naval campaign impossible. There were no Confederate warships in the Caribbean in early 1864 when Magruder placed his letters to Major Helm in William Watson's care. Raphael Semmes and the CSS *Alabama* were in the Indian Ocean. The war-weary Captain and his warship had seen two long years of continuous action and tension on the high seas. They were returning from an epic cruise through the South Atlantic, Indian, and South Pacific Oceans. The *Alabama* was headed for a much-needed refit at a dockyard in Cherbourg, France.[48]

By the time the letter for John Newland Maffitt reached William Watson, the CSS *Florida* was at Brest, France where it had been undergoing repair and refit since August 1863. Captain Maffitt had been relieved due to ill health. *Florida* and her new Captain would not venture into the open seas again until February 1864. After leaving France, the Confederate commerce raider would come no closer to Texas than Martinique in the Windward Island chain. It is one of the eastern-most Caribbean islands, and is over 2,300 miles from Galveston.[49]

Captain Maffitt would recover from his illness, but his cruiser would not survive the war. The U.S. Navy illegally captured the CSS *Florida*, while it was making a port call in Brazilian waters under a different commander. The United States then "accidentally" scuttled and sank the notorious commerce cruiser to avoid having to return it to the Confederacy. Maffitt's final command at sea was the blockade runner *Owl*. After finding North Carolina's Fort Fisher in the hands of Federal troops, he

"Scenes on Board the *Alabama*, Raphael Semmes." *Illustrated London News*, October 10, 1863, p 361 (author's collection).

diverted to Havana. From there, he left for Galveston in April of 1865. Arriving off the Texas port, Maffitt found 16 Federal blockaders guarding Galveston Bay. After braving a barrage of shot and shell, he was on the cusp of making his escape, when *Owl* ran aground at the northernmost entrance to the bay. *Owl* finally slid off the sandbar and steamed safely into the bay, with the help of a towline from one of the Marine Department's vigilant gunboats.[50]

This exciting version of *Owl*'s entrance into Galveston Bay first appeared in a 1901 newspaper article. Emma Maffitt repeated this story in her 1906 book about her husband. Other firsthand and contemporary reports suggest that *Owl* ran aground during a gale and remained there for almost three days during bad weather and poor visibility. Although *Owl* was within range of the fleet's guns, the seas were too rough for accurate firing. *Owl* may have been undetected until the weather improved enough for her to slide off the shell bank. Like William Watson, story tellers who are personally invested in an event or simply want to add excitement to their tale, tend to exaggerate the facts for dramatic effect. As the newspaper reporter said in John Ford's film, *The Man Who Shot Liberty Valance*, said, "This is the West, sir. When the legend becomes fact, print the legend."[51]

Commander John Newland Maffitt, CSN (Library of Congress, Prints and Photographs Division, LC-DIG-ppmsca-72018).

After the steamer's narrow escape and having been aground for three days, *Owl* needed repairs. During this time, Capt. Maffitt stayed with his younger sister, Henrietta Lamar. Henrietta was the second wife of former Texas President Mirabeau B. Lamar. She ran a popular boarding house in Galveston. She had moved to Galveston with her now-deceased mother Ann and her twin sister Caroline Matilda.[52]

As a renown naval commander and blockade runner, all of Galveston warmly welcomed "the celebrated J.N. Maffitt." He stood with Magruder when the general ordered a grand military review to boost the morale of his troops. History does not record whether Magruder mentioned his scheme to combine their forces in a grand naval offensive. Maffitt and *Owl* finally left Galveston for Havana on May 5, 1865, with 956 bales of cotton. Despite the fanciful notions of newspaper editors, and perhaps, Confederate generals, *Owl* was more prey than predator. Its visit to Galveston was just days before the final collapse of the Confederacy.[53]

But in the early days of 1864, Watson was glad to be rid of his secret packages and back in the business of trying to make a living in maritime commerce. He tended to the normal chores of preparing his schooner for sea, signing on a crew, and making arrangements for his cargo. The disposition of his load of cotton and the likelihood of acquiring goods suitable for Texas would be the primary factors in determining his next destination.

8

Men of Affairs

The Intelligentsia in Tampico and Havana

Rob Roy arrived off Tampico, Mexico, in early February of 1864, after several days at sea. The mouth of the river leading to Tampico had no distinguishing landmarks. It was the masts of the larger vessels lying at anchor offshore that told approaching vessels that they had reached their destination. Like Matamoros, this anchorage was vulnerable to the elements. The city was about six miles upriver, and, like the Brazos and Rio Grande, a shallow sandbar protected its entrance. The French had occupied the city, but there was no apparent impact on maritime commerce, particularly for a blockade runner loaded with cotton. After one night at the anchorage, a Mexican river pilot safely guided *Rob Roy* across the bar and into Tampico. It was a quiet end to a tumultuous sojourn at, on, and in the Brazos River.[1]

On the way to Tampico, Watson said that he had been discovered and pursued by a U.S. Navy sailing bark named *John Anderson*. Although there was no such vessel in the Navy's fleet, there was a sailing bark that was part of the blockading fleet off the Texas coast. The warship's name was USS *William G. Anderson*. Watson's description of this close encounter, and the general perils of life at sea onboard a small schooner were superb. He captured the hopes, fears, and superstitions of his sailors as well as the tactics of a small 19th-century schooner that was trying to evade enemy warships.

His narrative helps explain why it would sometimes take weeks to sail to a port and at other times it would only take a few days. Every voyage was an adventure, fraught with danger, and subject to the vagaries of the wind and waves. Even the routine maritime bills of lading had standard cautionary language about transporting cargos. The captained guaranteed the delivery his cargo, subject to "the dangers and accidents of the Seas and Navigation, of whatsoever nature or kind, excepted." All major seaport newspapers had a regular column for "Marine Disasters." A sea voyage in a sailing vessel was a hazardous endeavor at any time, but during the Civil War, the risk was compounded by the prospect of being captured or killed by shot and shell hurled from a U.S. Navy warship.[2]

In addition to *William G. Anderson*, Watson had another encounter on his way to Tampico. He said that it was with the schooner *Sylvia*. According to Watson, the schooner had originated from St. John, New Brunswick with a cargo of lumber and

View of Tampico. *Le Monde Illustre*, January 11, 1862, p. 24 (author's collection).

arrived at the Tampico anchorage shortly after *Rob Roy*. Watson normally tried to avoid all contact with other vessels while he was at sea for fear that each one might be a Union warship. In this case, however, Watson was able to aid *Sylvia*'s captain with his navigational calculations. In payment for Watson's help, *Rob Roy*'s crew got a nice supply of potatoes and codfish in return. There is no independent verification that a schooner named *Sylvia* arrived in Tampico during this period. There was a British-flagged schooner from Nova Scotia named *Sylvia* under a Captain Comstock operating in the Gulf by the spring of 1864. However, the movements of this *Sylvia* never overlapped with the locations and dates of Watson's tale.[3]

After he discharged *Rob Roy*'s cargo, Watson paid off his crew. Each man received a bonus for performing extra duty on board the short-handed *Rob Roy*. Watson did not plan to tarry in Tampico and wanted to quickly re-ship his current crew. Frederick Jansen, the Swedish cook, joined at once. James O'Hagan and Polly (Appolonaria Barrios) rejoined shortly thereafter. However, the first mate, George Thomson, went on a drunken bender. He was flush with cash and eager to spend it. Playing the role of the proverbial drunken sailor, Thomson was last seen in a café enjoying the company of some occupying French soldiers and shouting "Viva Napoleon!"[4]

It was about this time that Watson said he met the Union spy who offered him a bribe for the package that General Magruder had entrusted to his care. He also met a fellow blockade runner named "Captain Currie." Watson had heard of the "old gentleman" (he was only 51 years old) and knew him to be trustworthy. Captain Curry was not acquainted with the furtive man who turned out to be a Union spy. To Captain Curry, the man seemed to be one of those shady characters, "whose sympathies are always very strong with the South when they meet up with blockade runners."[5]

Watson reported that Curry was part owner of a schooner that had made three runs through the blockade. As a result, he had made a bit of money and decided to retire from the business and remain in Tampico at least until the war was over. Curry recommended two of his former crewmen, a mate and an able-bodied seaman. Watson readily agreed to take them onboard. The helpful captain's name was John M. Curry (sometimes identified as John Currie or James M. Curry). Curry had settled in Tampico with his wife and sisters, but like Watson, had retained his British citizenship. Even so, the career sailor did not lead a settled life.[6]

J.M. Curry had registered a schooner named *Alma* at Belize in 1861, but it was uncertain whether he ever ran the blockade in this schooner. The blockade historian Marcus Price has no record of *Alma* ever making a successful blockade run. A contemporary Louisiana paper did credit a schooner named *Alma* with a successful run into Mobile from Havana in late March 1863. However, her captain's name was Mitchell and not Currie or Curry. Additionally, the blockading fleet captured a schooner named *Alma* in mid–April 1864 trying to run into Galveston Bay. This *Alma* had sailed to Matamoros from New Orleans in February flying the Mexican flag. It had departed the Rio Grande just prior to being captured. This *Alma* also had a Mexican citizen named Francis Celda as the nominal captain. The schooner's true captain was a devious American named William Lee who signed the shipping articles as pilot and navigator. Although sparse, these records confirm that *Alma* was not the schooner that Curry was referring to when he claimed to have run a schooner into the Rio Grande once and Tampico twice.[7]

John Curry was also the captain of the schooner *Sylphide* (sometimes spelled *Sylfide*, *Selphide*, or *Sylphyde*). Curry sailed *Sylphide* from New Orleans to Matamoros in February 1863. By August, Curry had run the schooner into the Brazos River. There, Confederate authorities issued a permit for *Sylphide* "to clear the Mouth of the Brazos Coast of Texas ladened with cotton, [with] John Curry Master." By February of 1864, *Sylphide* was in Tampico under a new captain and owner. The schooner had already left port by the time Watson arrived. These records confirm that *Sylphide* made at least two of the runs that Captain Curry mentioned to William Watson. There were numerous schooners that ran the blockade into Tampico that the U.S. Consul Franklin Chase did not name, making Curry's story entirely plausible. On the other hand, the old captain's dream about retiring from the blockade-running business and living in Tampico did not quite play out that way.[8]

Captain Curry's motivation for returning to the sea is unknown. It may have been for money or perhaps he missed the thrill of the chase. In any event, he was back in the blockade-running business by October 1864. He signed on as master of the recently reflagged and renamed schooner *Lone* (formerly the Mexican-flagged *Cuca*). He successfully sailed to the Rio Grande later that month, but the blockading fleet captured him in early November when he tried to run into the Brazos.[9]

Even after the New Orleans admiralty court condemned his schooner and cargo, Captain John Curry was still not ready to quit. He was back in command of another schooner by February of 1865. This time, he was part owner and captain of the schooner *Richard H. Vermilyea* (usually identified as *R.H. Vermilyea*) that sailed from Tampico to Havana. As with the schooner *Lone*, Curry's luck ran out when he tried to run into Texas. The blockading fleet captured him on the Ides of March and sent *Lone* to New Orleans where the schooner and cargo were condemned for a net total of $6,220.89. This was Captain Curry's last attempt at blockade running, most likely due to the end of the war rather than any real desire to retire from the exhilarating business.[10]

As for William Watson, he finally had a full and trustworthy crew and was pondering his next move. Tampico was not an ideal commercial port. Its primary attribute was proximity to the Texas blockade-running ports, but it had little in the way of goods that were suited to the Texas market. Besides, the winds were poor for a return voyage to the Brazos. Tampico was equally unsuited to overhaul or refit vessels like *Rob Roy*. Those limitations left Havana as the best choice for his next port of call. The Spanish colonial port city had shipyards, a variety of exportable merchandise, and helpful Confederate agents. Robert Mills, a principal partner in the firm of R. & D.G. Mills & Co., and the majority stakeholder in *Rob Roy* was there as well.[11]

Prior to sailing for Havana, Watson said that he reshipped and stowed 21 bales of cotton below deck to serve as ballast. The extra weight would help *Rob Roy* sit lower in the water to avoid being tossed around the Gulf like a cork. He also took onboard three unidentified passengers who were southern men on their way to Havana. When he got underway, Watson set *Rob Roy*'s course to follow the coast down to the eastern tip of the Yucatan Peninsula. From there he would make the short jaunt across the strait to Cuba. He wanted to lessen his chances of being seized and detained by the Yankee admiralty courts in New Orleans or Key West.[12]

At this point, Watson's narrative about *Rob Roy*'s voyages matches the historical record. He said that he left Tampico "about the beginning of March" and arrived in Havana "about the middle of March." In between, he had some heavy weather, but much to his relief, no encounters with the U.S. Navy. It took about 15 days for a schooner to reach the tip of the Yucatan Peninsula. He would have crossed the 135-mile-wide Yucatan Channel and covered the remaining 185 miles to Havana in two or three days. A Havana newspaper confirmed *Rob Roy*'s arrival at Havana from Tampico on March 21, 1864, after a passage of 15 days. Captain William Watson had a load of 21 cotton bales and three passengers. The steamer *Denbigh* arrived the same day with 424 bales of cotton and two passengers after a three-day run from Mobile.[13]

Watson's description of *Sylvia*'s movements was less certain. The previously mentioned schooner *Sylvia* and Captain Comstock were in Havana in early April of 1864. But this *Sylvia* arrived in New Orleans from Nassau on the same day in early May that Watson sailed *Rob Roy* out of Havana. Watson had his facts confused when it came to the schooner he identified as *Sylvia*. Perhaps he deliberately misidentified the schooner's name, or he was simply embellishing his story. John Curry's former schooner, *Sylphide* sailed from Tampico about the time that *Rob Roy* left. However, *Sylphide* did not go to Havana, and she had not sailed from Canada. Thus, the historical record offers no good candidates that fully match Watson's description of *Sylvia*.[14]

Watson, like most people who sailed into Havana, made note of that harbor's formidable Castle Morro (*Castillo de los Tres Reyes Magos del Morro* or Castle of the Three Magi Kings of the Moor). Initially constructed in 1589, Castle Morro protected the entrance to the harbor. It was a monstrous bastion with tall towers, a lighthouse, and "teeth of guns." Inside the harbor, *Rob Roy* had to wind its way through a forest of masts that formed a nautical belt along the edge of the city. Rather than take up more space by lying alongside the piers, ships that were able find a berth at the piers had their bows pointed toward the street.[15]

Watson's literary forte was not lyrical prose that could frame the sights and smells of Havana. He was most inclined to describe the character of the people he met, particularly the opportunists that he called land sharks. It was an apt description. When a blockade runner entered port, it created a minor spectacle, the business equivalent of blood in the water. Agents, merchants, and chandlers (dealers in nautical supplies and equipment) all circled the vessel, vying for the captain's attention and favor.[16]

Rather than giving into these speculators who were "mostly of the Anglo-Saxon race," Watson trusted his cargo to a "respectable old-standing Spanish house." He later named his Havana consignment agents as "A. & Co." which was shorthand for the Avendaño Brothers (Hermanos). The firm had a long-time presence in New Orleans, but also had offices in Havana. During the war, Francisco (more commonly known as Peregrino) managed the office in New Orleans with his brothers Miguel and Teodomiro. José Maria Avendaño (aka Luis Maria Avendaño) ran the business in Havana. Despite their long-term residence in New Orleans, the brothers remained citizens of Spain.[17]

After consigning his cargo, Watson checked in with Confederate Major Charles Helm to confirm that he had received the sealed dispatches from General Magruder. With assurances that the Confederate agent (probably John O'Sullivan) had kept his promise to deliver the secret letters, the two men dined at a restaurant that was popular with Confederate officers and blockade runners. Watson then concentrated on settling his accounts with his partners and getting *Rob Roy* to the shipyard. It needed to be "thoroughly examined, caulked, and otherwise be put in the best sailing trim preparative for another voyage."[18]

Despite the exorbitant expenses and the "sharp" dealings of Robert Mills, the senior partner of R. & D.G. Mills & Co., Watson was able to buy back his three quarters interest in *Rob Roy*. He also got back the power of attorney that the supercargo A.F. French had held on behalf of the Mills Brothers. He was once again the majority owner of *Rob Roy*.[19]

Now that he was back in control of his schooner, he had to decide what to do with it. *Rob Roy* certainly needed refit, but acquisition of a cargo and the choice of a destination was more difficult. March had turned to April with the attendant longer days, shorter nights, and fickle winds. These conditions translated into a higher risk of being captured. On the other hand, to sit and wait for the steady winds of September would be ruinous both financially and materially. In tropical climates, sea-worms would soon eat away at the hull of a wooden vessel. Watson decided that he had rather risk facing the guns of a Union warship than to have *Rob Roy* "wheedled away" from him by the literal and figurative parasites of Havana.[20]

With his inevitable decision to run the blockade, and *Rob Roy* safely in the shipyard's slip-dock undergoing repair, Watson set about acquiring a cargo. He would need to find goods that met Confederate requirements for a "full and valuable cargo." The Confederate Congress had enacted a regulation on March 5, 1864, that, among other stipulations, required blockade runners to allocate half their inbound and outbound cargo space to government supplies. This type of government-imposed allocation was not new for Texas. In late January, General Magruder ordered Lt. Col. William J. Hutchins, Chief of the Cotton Office, to require all vessels taking out cotton to agree to return with "anthracite coal, bar iron, axes, spades, & percussion caps," as part of her cargo. The highest priority was "small arms, cannon powder, & cartridge flannel."[21]

These new regulations meant that blockade runners had to accept greater risk by investing in expensive inbound cargos with the prospect of lower profits from the sale of military supplies. As a result, shippers were more reluctant to ship cargos on consignment, preferring to sell them outright to the owners of the blockade runners. With the expenses Watson had incurred buying back his shares from the Mills Brothers and repairing *Rob Roy*, he did not have enough cash to buy the needed cargo. He had to find a merchant who was willing to consign a cargo on board *Rob Roy* for delivery to Texas. Given the hazards of a sea voyage and the likelihood of capture, it was a risk not many merchants were willing to take. Instead, he met a number of speculators who "sympathized excessively" with the Confederacy in general, but none were interested in taking a risk to alleviate his personal plight.[22]

Watson cited one individual as an example of these "pretended friends." The unnamed merchant invited Watson to his Havana office that served as a gathering place for Confederate exiles. Watson responded at once. He was hopeful that this ostensibly supportive agent would help him strike a favorable deal. The man specialized in outfitting and owning smaller schooners of the Gulf. He had a lengthy list of his small vessels that had run the blockade into Texas. The man was known for offering helpful advice about navigating bureaucratic procedures for running the blockade. He was also well versed in the types of cargos that would sell well in the Confederate States. Naturally, this "ardent patriot" just happened to have those same supplies available for sale. His touted motivation was a heartfelt desire to aid the Confederate cause. Any pecuniary advantage that he derived from his patriotic zeal was mere coincidence.[23]

Watson saw through this feckless scoundrel, but he did not share his name. Watson's self-righteous war profiteer was almost certainly George Panton Bell. Without Watson's colorful descriptions, Bell would have been a wooden historical figure, lacking personality, or any other human quality other than presumed greed. George P. Bell was a British citizen who was a ship owner and merchant who operated out of Havana before, during, and after the Civil War.[24]

Bell had ownership interests in other vessels, but his Civil War specialty was schooners, just as Watson said. Bell usually took a controlling interest in these vessels, but he was also willing to serve as the nominal owner. He willingly signed registration papers as a British citizen to give the vessel the protection of a neutral flag. These schooners travelled throughout the Gulf, including Matamoros, but the greatest potential profit was in blockade running. At least eight of his schooners tried to run the blockade into Texas. All but one of them succeeded at least once. His schooners made 16 successful runs inbound and 12 outbound runs in Texas waters. Three of the eight schooners survived the war without being captured. (See Table 3.)

Table 3. Texas Blockade-Running Schooners Owned by George Panton Bell[25]

Name(s)	Tons	Blockade Runs		Captured
		In	Out	
Ann Giberson*	99	3	2	n/a
William D.S. Hyer*	100	1	1	n/a
Belle (Gipsey and Zouave)	45	1	0	Dec 27, 1864
Indian	41	0	0	Apr 30, 1864
Agnes (John Arthur)	53	2	1	May 2, 1864
Richard H. Vermilyea (R.H. Vermilyea)	101	1	1	Mar 12, 1865
Mary Elizabeth (Mary Eliza)	33	5	5	n/a
Chaos (Vigilant, Fairy, Velocity, Nellie Blair)†	92	3	2	Apr 21, 1865

* A. Isaac, Levy & Co. were part-owners, Dec 1863.
† George P. Bell was probably the nominal owner on behalf of Thomas W. House.

One day after his encounter with George Bell, Watson checked on the progress of *Rob Roy*. While at the shipyard, he ran into his former partner, "Mr. R. M-----" (Robert Mills). Mills made him an offer to provide a suitable cargo of arms and army supplies, plus highly desirable commodities such as coffee, tea, cheese, sewing necessities, and medicinal brandy. The value of the invoiced goods would be equal to the value of the of *Rob Roy*. In return, Mills would become an equal partner. Watson accepted his proposal, but knew that his schooner's hold would accommodate even more cargo. Lacking funds to buy more on his own, Watson approached Major Charles Helm. He offered the Confederate agent the use of the remaining space at no charge. Helm readily agreed and placed 400 guns on board along with some dispatches for Major General Magruder.[26]

On another day at the shipyard, Watson met his old friend Captain Dave McClusky who had recently arrived in Havana. As described in an earlier chapter, Captain Dave had run the sloop *Mary Louisa* (*Mary Louise*) from Galveston to Tampico. He then hitched a ride to Havana to buy a larger schooner. Coincidentally, *Rob Roy* was laid up adjacent McClusky's latest blockade runner. Although Watson never identified Captain Dave's vessel by name, it was the schooner *Stingaree* (sometimes identified as *Sting Ray* or *Stingray*). Contemporary sources were silent about *Stingaree*'s dimensions and its arrival in Havana, but McClusky evidently acquired his new blockade runner at a bargain price.[27]

Watson delighted in playfully mocking McClusky's make-shift schooner. He derisively nicknamed it "*Scow*." McClusky unapologetically said that he had known about the vessel during his days on Galveston Bay where *Stingaree* had served as an inland waterway barge. It delivered cordwood from the Trinity River to Galveston. The vessel had somehow made its way to Havana despite its flat bottom and boxy, rectangular shape. *Stingaree* had been fitted up as a make-shift schooner with two masts, a long pole that served as a bowsprit, and a retractable centerboard keel.[28]

Even though *Stingaree*'s open-ocean sea-keeping capabilities were suspect, Captain Dave was confident that it could run the blockade into Texas. He reasoned that since the schooner had safely made its way from Galveston to Havana via Tampico, it could make the return trip with him in command. Besides, its price ($500) was about 1/10th the cost of a comparable blockade runner. McClusky concluded that if he bought a more expensive, but safer vessel, he would suffer a much larger financial loss if he was captured. Trusting in his skills as a sailor, it was a risk he was willing to take.[29]

That evening, Captain Dave invited Watson to join him for dinner at a large, "higher class" cafe named "The Louvre." The Louvre Café was indeed, the most fashionable restaurant in Havana. It rivaled the best in Paris or Naples in size and elegance. It was spacious, with a lofty ceiling, wide doors, and an attached bathhouse. It had just opened in 1863 and was one of the most popular gathering places in Havana. Its sophisticated clientele gathered there for dinner, cigars, and conversation while sipping their cooling drinks, amidst "wafting circles of sweet-scented smoke."[30]

The Louvre Café was a place for "men of affairs and the intelligentsia" to gather. Its literate clientele included "…writers, poets, artists, and journalists." According to Watson, the uninterrupted stream of visitors included "partisans of both sides" of the American Civil War. Rather than the heated contretemps that might be expected among ideological factions in more modern times, the Louvre Café was a neutral setting where civil discourse rather than uncivil warfare was expected. Watson described it as a dignified oasis where active participants "in the American Civil War often met, exchanged courtesies, and often entered into conversation." Sharing in this feeling of conviviality, Watson and his blockade-running companions invited three Union naval officers to join them for a drink.[31]

Watson remarked that U.S. Navy officers of the blockading fleet were generally, "very good fellows." The primary purpose of his dinner meeting, however, was not to enjoy a pleasant evening of good-natured banter with the enemy. Dave McClusky and Watson had come to Café Louvre to dine with Captain "M." The captain had intimate knowledge of the U.S. Navy blockade tactics and the hydrography at the main entrance to Galveston Bay. Watson had recently met the blockade-running steamboat captain at a dinner party with Major Helm. Captain M. was tall, well-built and possibly from Baltimore. He was anticipating taking command of a steamer that he would run into Galveston. One candidate that partially fit Watson's vague description of the mysterious Captain "M" was Captain James Britton McConnell.[32]

McConnell was an experienced steamship captain and blockade runner from New Orleans. He and his steamer *Susannah* (sometimes spelled "*Susanna*" and later renamed *Mail*) had arrived at Havana from West Florida in late April 1864. *Susannah* did not sail for Galveston until April 30, giving McConnell six days of overlap in Havana with McClusky and Watson. As would become clear at Galveston a few weeks later, Watson and McConnell may have later become trusted shipmates.[33]

However, there were several factors that suggest the Irish-born, 51-year-old McConnell was not Watson and McClusky's dining companion in Havana. At the time, he was not awaiting an assignment to another steamer since McConnell kept command of the *Susannah* during his entire stay in Havana. He was a long-time resident of New Orleans and not Baltimore as Watson remembered. Although he may have been familiar with the approaches to Galveston Bay, his knowledge was not intimate. Finally, he only stood 5 feet, 8 inches tall. Since Watson measured was two inches taller, it was unlikely that he would have described the shorter McConnell as "tall."[34]

Another possibility for Watson's "Captain M." was Appleton Oaksmith. He was the prospective captain of the *Carolina* and called himself John McDonald. Oaksmith needed the alias to avoid unwanted scrutiny. In 1856, he helped overthrow the Government of Nicaragua on behalf of the short-lived government of the American filibusterer "General" William Walker. As a reward for his fundraising services, "President" Walker appointed him as his de facto Ambassador to the United States. Oaksmith managed to resign prior to Walker's execution by firing squad in 1860. In 1862, Oaksmith had been arrested and convicted in Boston for outfitting a ship intended as a slave runner. Due in part to the personal intervention of Secretary of State William H. Seward, the court incarcerated Oaksmith at Fort Lafayette in New York harbor and briefly at Fort Warren in Boston Harbor.[35]

After eight long months, Oaksmith escaped from Boston's civilian-run Charles Street Jail. He quickly made his way to Havana in late 1863, with the intention of becoming a blockade runner. Sometime in April or May 1864, he took command of the steamer *Carolina* at Havana. *Carolina* (sometimes identified as *Caroline*) had been captured twice before under different names, first as *Union* and then as *Rosita*. The most recent capture occurred near Key West on January 28, 1864, as *Rosita* tried to run into Mobile from Havana. The admiralty court ordered the auction sale of *Rosita* that occurred on April 21, 1864, at Key West, Florida.[36]

Oaksmith adopted the alias John McDonald and took command of the steamer in Havana. He sailed the *Carolina* for Galveston on June 1, 1864, where he successfully arrived a few days later. Despite the coincidence of his alias last name, the timing of his presence in Havana, and his pending appointment as captain of a steam blockade runner enroute to Texas, Oaksmith was not Watson's Captain "M." He had never been to Texas and lacked familiarity with its coast. A *carte de visite* (CDV) of Oaksmith showed him to be of average height, and his biographer confirms that he stood five feet eight inches. Most importantly, Oaksmith was originally from Maine and had been living in New York and Boston prisons since the beginning of the war and he was pretending to be an Englishman. It was unlikely that Watson would mis-remember Oaksmith as a southerner.[37]

The person who most closely matches Captain M.'s profile was Andrew Jackson "Jack" Moore. The most important clue that points to this conclusion appeared in Watson's meeting with Union Navy officers at the Louvre Café in Havana. Captain M. made an obscure reference to a friend of his, "Captain C. of the L. who had been captured." The only viable candidate for "Captain C. of the L." was a Texan named William S. Cooper of the schooner *Lilly*. Cooper had been in command of the 44-ton *Lilly* since April 1863. He had successfully run out of the Brazos in July and again in November, but ran afoul of the blockading fleet on his return trip from Belize. Cooper was obviously a person who was well known to Captain M.[38]

The USS *Penobscot* captured *Lilly* and Captain Cooper on February 28, 1864, on their return trip from Belize to the Brazos. Cooper would later be freed and captured a second time with the schooner *Mary Ella* (*Mary Ellen*). But at the time of Watson's story, he was still held captive in New Orleans. Watson failed to mention that Captain Cooper and his schooner *Lilly* had been at the Brazos on September 24, 1863. Not coincidentally, Watson and Captain Jack Moore were there at the same time onboard their schooners *Rob Roy* and *John*. All three blockade runners would overlap at the Brazos River for almost two months. William Cooper and *Lilly* were the first to leave when they successfully ran for Belize in late November. *Rob Roy* remained stranded in Texas as a result of its various mishaps. *John*'s deep draft prevented the schooner from crossing the shallow bar at the mouth of the river. Frustrated by the inactivity, Captain Moore turned *John* over to William Rogers Tucker and left Texas for Havana. As discussed in a previous chapter, the schooner *John* would remain at the Brazos until September 1863, when Francis Downs unsuccessfully tried to run past the blockading fleet.[39]

Captain Moore arrived in Havana sometime prior to his meeting with Watson and McClusky in April/May 1864. As Watson had suggested, Jack Moore was awaiting command of a steamer that he would run into Galveston. A Galveston merchant and former Mayor of Houston named Cornelius Ennis engaged him to buy and command *Josie*, an iron-hulled steamer that was in New York. *Josie* had been captured and condemned for trying to run the blockade using the name *Eagle*. Ennis bought the steamer for $40,000 with the intent of returning it to the blockade-running business. To avoid suspicion, Capt. Jack Moore was not in command when *Josie* left New York in early September 1864. Instead, he took charge in Havana where he renamed and registered the steamer in honor of Ennis' wife Jeannette (the former Jeannette Ingals Kimball). Moore loaded *Jeannette* with 1200 Enfield rifles, gunpowder, and percussion caps, shoes, blankets, and other army supplies that he delivered to Galveston in October 1864.[40]

Watson's left a final clue concerning Captain M.'s identity that appeared to have been inadvertent. Watson explicitly mentioned "Captain M." on eight different pages (151, 152, 154, 157, and 186) of his book. On only one occasion did he slip up in trying to conceal the man's identity. On page 179, he quoted his slippery friend, Captain Dave McClusky who related the saga of his second capture and escape from the blockading fleet. During the melee onboard his schooner, Captain Dave said that he lost all his personal possessions. Among them were his collection of photographs (CDVs) of blockade-running captains. When Watson and McClusky met again in Galveston, Captain Dave admitted that he had "lost the one you gave me, as well as that of Captain Moore."[41]

Captain Jack Moore was originally from North Carolina rather than Baltimore. But he had been a pilot and ship captain at Galveston Bay since the early days of Texas statehood. He had been the captain of at least two U.S. lighthouse tenders that served on the Louisiana and Texas coasts and may have performed coast survey duties as well. Prior to the Civil War, the U.S. Light House Establishment operated under the control of U.S. Customs under the Treasury Department. Those seafaring experiences gave him intimate knowledge of Galveston Bay and its approaches. His first U.S. lighthouse tender command was a small schooner named *Essayons*, but his first run through the blockade was on *William R. King*.[42]

The Confederates had seized *W.R. King* from U.S. Customs authorities in Louisiana. Those same officials assumed identical roles within the Confederate government and retained Jack Moore as commander of the schooner. After conducting a special reconnaissance mission in the Gulf, Captain Moore left the Confederate Lighthouse service to command R. & D.G. Mills' blockade runner *Mary Ella* (*Mary Ellen*). He made a successful run to Kingston, Jamaica, where he delivered over 300 bales of cotton and renamed his schooner *Orion*. On the return trip in late July 1862, the U.S. Navy captured him onboard *Orion* just north of the Yucatan Peninsula. The admiralty court at Key West condemned his schooner three months later and Moore was set free to resume his blockade-running career. From Key West, he made his way to Kingston, Jamaica where he signed on as Captain of the Schooner *John* on January 3, 1863.[43]

Moore's biographic sources do not confirm Watson's observation that he was tall and handsome. They do, however, affirm that he "followed the sea all his life" and was "a plain, blunt-spoken man, loving all and fearing none." Notwithstanding his physical attributes, McClusky and Watson were most interested in Captain Moore's intimate knowledge about the optimum route to enter Galveston Bay.[44]

Captain Moore recommended approaching from the east, along Bolivar Peninsula, which was the windward side. There were three prominent sand dunes about 30 miles from the entrance to the bay. Not only were the hillocks good navigational references, the location was a safe, isolated area to anchor or beach the schooner and wait for nightfall before making a run through the blockading fleet. Captain Dave planned to take his schooner *Stingaree* in farther south, at "St. Louis Pass" [San Luis Pass]. He knew this entrance to the Bay had about four feet depth at bar and he believed that Yankee warships would not bother with trying to blockade it.[45]

With *Rob Roy* in good repair and his destination set, Watson needed a reliable crew for the voyage. He specifically named Fred the Swede (Frederick Jansen, the Swedish Cook), Hagan the mate (James O'Hagan), another Irishman named Jim Hyland, one man from Tampico, plus one other. Another able-bodied seaman was a 35-year-old named George (whose surname was Thompson or Thomson) whom Captain John Curry had recommended at Tampico. Watson made no mention of Polly (Appolonaria Barrios) who had also joined the crew at Tampico. With his crew complete, Watson's final task before sailing was to complete loading out his schooner.[46]

His partnership with Robert Mills gained him a partial cargo of arms and army supplies and consumer goods that included coffee, tea, cheese, sewing necessities, and "medicinal" brandy. Even after Major Charles Helm consigned 400 guns, Watson still had some available space. To fill it, he got some pickled mackerel, potatoes, raisins, a case of gin, and a dozen bottles of port wine. Finally, he carried a small package of official dispatches from Major Helm and civilian mail for Texas citizens eager to hear from their loved ones who lived beyond the Confederate States.[47]

After loading the cargos obtained from Robert Mills, Major Helm, and on his own initiative, Watson and *Rob Roy* were ready to sail and run the blockade into Texas. Just prior to departure, he mentioned witnessing the arrival of *Harriet Lane/Lavinia* and *Matagorda/Alice*. Watson's information about these steamers was essentially correct, but his story had some important omissions and inaccuracies.[48]

Watson said that the steamers *Harriet Lane* and *Matagorda* arrived at Havana from Galveston on the same day. He noted that their appearance was the source of considerable excitement in the city. This observation was especially true for *Harriet Lane*. The Confederates had rammed and captured this famous Navy warship during the Battle of Galveston in the early morning hours of New Year's Day, 1863. *Matagorda* had been part of Charles Morgan's Southern Steamship Company's merchant fleet. Prior to the war, it had operated in the Western Gulf of Mexico.[49]

When Watson saw the arrival of the two steamers, neither of them were actually named *Harriet Lane* or *Matagorda*. In February 1864, the Confederated government sold *Harriet Lane* to private owners at Galveston. They renamed the steamer *Lavinia*, removed all armament, and converted her into a blockade runner. Similarly, Confederate officials had seized the merchant transport *Matagorda* in 1861. They renamed the steamer *Alice* between July and August of 1862. But Watson was confused about more than just name changes. *Alice* (*Matagorda*) did not arrive at Havana on the same day as *Harriet Lane* (*Lavinia*). *Lavinia* and *Alice* had both departed Galveston on the evening of April 30, 1864, in company with a third steamer. The added blockade runner was *Isabel*. It was the steamer *Isabel* that arrived at Havana with *Lavinia* (*Harriet Lane*) on Thursday, May 5, 1864. *Alice* (*Matagorda*) arrived at Havana two days later, on Saturday, May 7.[50]

Watson also commented about the future activities of *Harriet Lane* (*Lavinia*) and *Matagorda* (*Alice*). He said that *Harriet Lane* would remain in Havana and forgo any other attempts at blockade running. Her deep draft made this steamer less suited for the shallow Gulf ports than *Matagorda*. Watson recalled that *Matagorda* would make one or two more attempts, but would eventually be captured.[51]

Lavinia (*Harriet Lane*) would indeed languish in Havana throughout the rest of the war. She and her cargo would be sold to finance the purchase of the blockade runner *Pelican* in England. *Alice* would make its eighth successful inbound blockade run when it arrived at Galveston from Havana on July 5, 1864. The U.S. Navy then captured the steamer on September 10 during its eighth and final outbound run. (See Appendix 3. Blockade Runs of the SS *Alice Matagorda*.)[52]

Isabel suffered a similar but more catastrophic fate. She left from Havana later in May but fell prey to the USS *Admiral* off San Luis Pass after braving multiple salvoes. The cannonade punctured *Isabel*'s iron hull at least twice. One of its officers lost his left arm and three fingers of his right hand during the attack. After finally surrendering to a prize crew, *Isabel* sank to the bottom of the Mississippi River a few days later, a residual effect of the pummeling she had received. As Watson prepared to leave Havana, he could only hope that the same fate would not await him or *Rob Roy*.[53]

9

Back to Texas

"A Right Down Swindle"

Watson did not say when he left Havana. He did say that Captain Dave McClusky and his make-shift schooner *Stingaree* left port at about the same time. Watson also noted that the mysterious *Sylvia* and another schooner came out on the same evening as *Rob Roy*. Although the flow of Watson's narrative is a bit out of sequence, his departure from Havana, Cuba and arrival at Galveston, Texas, can be accurately determined when combined with other contemporary and eyewitness reports. *Harriet Lane/Lavinia* (May 5, 1864) and *Matagorda/Alice* (May 7, 1864) had arrived just prior to Watsons departure. A Galveston newspaper report documented the appearance of McClusky's schooner *Stingaree* on May 23. The article said that Capt. McClusky had sailed from Havana 15 days earlier. The Havana newspaper *Diario de la Marina*, reported that *Rob Roy* cleared customs bound for Belize on May 7. The fusion of these sources would suggest that both *Rob Roy* and *Stingaree* departed Havana on May 8. However, that was not the case. The Havana newspaper *Diario de la Marina* verified the sailing of both *Rob Roy* and *Stingaree* as May 11, 1864. Four days elapsed between *Rob Roy*'s clearance on May 7 and the schooner's actual departure from Havana. (See Appendix 6 for a summary of *Rob Roy*'s voyages.)[1]

Proud of his clever ability to avoid detection, Watson described his voyage from Havana to Galveston in considerable detail. Believing himself to be a master tactician, Watson took his sails down at sunrise and always kept a sharp lookout posted at the masthead. To minimize his visibility to enemy ships, he only unfurled his sails when the horizon was clear of contacts and at night. His progress was slow, but he believed his caution was worth the delay. *Rob Roy* made it to within 150 miles of Galveston before the crew sighted another vessel. When about 120 miles from shore, they spied an enemy steam warship. The gunboat's lookouts did not spot them even though they approached within five miles. Watson's men jumped into their small boat and used the sweeps (oars) to keep the *Rob Roy*'s bow, and two masts aligned with the warship. This bow-on aspect angle made it difficult to distinguish a low-profile schooner, particularly when haze or rain further reduced visibility. There were several other similar near-encounters, but *Rob Roy* remained unseen.[2]

He was particularly concerned about the dubiously identified *Sylvia*. This was the schooner he allegedly had first encountered off Tampico and that had departed

Havana at the same time as *Rob Roy*. When Watson spotted *Sylvia*, he said that it was on a course that would take it to New Orleans. The schooner then shifted its heading to intercept *Rob Roy*. Just in case *Sylvia*'s navigationally challenged captain was merely lost again, Watson took one of his large hatch covers and wrote their latitude and longitude in chalk. Through his spy glass, it appeared to Watson that the few sailors visible on deck had the look of prize crewmen from a U.S. Navy man-of-war.[3]

Watson believed that he could out-sail *Sylvia*, but he was taking no chances. In the event there was no wind, a greedy Yankee prize crew might try to board and overpower *Rob Roy*'s crew. To prevent any such attempt, his men agreed to break out the Enfield rifles they were carrying in the hold. They made a show of fixing bayonets and preparing to repel boarders. The display had the desired effect when *Sylvia* reversed course to the east ... or so his sea story went.[4]

The truth of the situation may never be known, but there was no vessel named *Sylvia* in the Western Gulf of Mexico during this timeframe. The previously described schooner named *Sylvia* under Captain Comstock was at New Orleans from May 9 to 21, 1864, and there were no other schooners with a similar name in the vicinity during this period. There was, however, another possibility.[5]

A Mexican schooner named *Amanda* of about 59–60 tons had sailed from Havana on May 6, 1864. Its declared destination was Matamoros. The USS *Kanawha* then captured *Amanda* on May 14, about five or six miles off the Texas coast near Espiritu Santo Pass (probably referring to the very shallow pass below Pass Cavallo, Texas, that separates San Jose and Matagorda Islands). Two of *Amanda*'s captured mariners testified that the captain was a poor navigator and had strayed 100 miles west of his intended course.[6]

Captain José Rodriguez had dropped anchor and landed a shore party to determine his latitude. This was a risky maneuver that made him subject to capture by both Confederate and Union forces. At this time, the Union Army was still in possession of the desolate and featureless barrier islands of the South Texas shore. A U.S. cavalry unit on Matagorda Island under Major A.C. Matthews spotted *Amanda*. He assumed it was a blockade runner, as did their Navy counterparts on the USS *Kanawha*.[7]

For the previous two years, Captain Rodriguez had been captain of *Amanda*. He had a three-quarter ownership interest as well. He had been hauling goods consigned to the Avendaño Brothers of Havana and José San Román of Matamoros. On this most recent trip, Rodriguez had arrived in Havana from Matamoros on March 19, 1864, and loaded a cargo on Apr 28th. He left on May 6 with a crew of four, plus two passengers who were bound for Matamoros. The captain's intent was to use *Amanda* as a lighter upon his return to the mouth of the Rio Grande, just as he had done the previous April.[8]

In his testimony, *Amanda*'s prize master William A. Purdie made no mention of any near encounter with *Rob Roy*. This omission is not surprising. It would not have been in his interest to admit being so easily deterred from capturing a blockade runner. On the other hand, another Navy warship, the USS *Bermuda* intercepted Acting Ensign Purdie and his prize crew aboard *Amanda* as they were sailing toward New Orleans. *Bermuda*'s location at that time was about 150 miles west of Galveston. The boarding occurred at 8 p.m. on May 20 which was the evening after *Amanda* may have crossed *Rob Roy*'s path.[9]

Acting Ensign Purdie arrived at New Orleans in early June and turned *Amanda* over to the U.S. prize commissioner, Thomas B. Thorpe, who was a close associate of General Ben "Beast" Butler. Four weeks later, the New Orleans admiralty court released both *Amanda* and its cargo. Unfortunately for Captain Rodriguez, he did not receive any compensation for damages or expenses related to the seizure. The judge ruled that the captain of *Kanawha* had reasonable cause for the capture due to *Amanda*'s proximity to enemy territory.[10]

Amanda was the only inbound schooner that the U.S. Navy captured in the Gulf during the time of Watson's story. Additionally, no other schooner with a name similar to *Sylvia* called at Matamoros, a Texas port, or New Orleans in May or June of 1864. The lone exception was Captain Comstock's *Sylvia* that was at New Orleans, May 9–21, 1864. Watson's version of his encounter with a schooner while on his journey to Galveston may have been true, but his conclusions about the identity of the schooner as *Sylvia* were in error. If this story is true, the captured blockade runner could only have been the Mexican-flagged *Amanda*.[11]

After watching *Amanda* sail over the horizon toward New Orleans, Watson continued on his course to the west. The next morning, he reported arriving at a point near the shore and about 30–40 miles south-southeast of Galveston. Although far from his planned landfall, northeast of Galveston Bay, he was well south of the normal track of U.S. Navy gunboats between New Orleans and Galveston. He stayed in this relatively safe spot throughout the day to refine his exact position and get a good measure of the current, wind, and waves. That evening, he planned to arrive off Bolivar Peninsula about 30 miles east of Galveston. This was the spot that Captain M. (Jack Moore) had recommended during their meeting in Havana. Watson was positioning *Rob Roy* for a run along the coast and into one of the shallow channels leading into Galveston Bay.[12]

Watson got *Rob Roy* underway about sunset. He needed fortune to smile on him and his crew for he was sailing under a full moon. At sunrise, he was relieved to discover that their movements were partially concealed by a low-hanging haze. As the horizon cleared, his lookout gave the welcome cry of "Land ahead!" Watson said *Rob Roy* was about three miles from shore when he sighted three mounds "about thirty miles to the east of Galveston," just as Captain Moore had foretold. Jack Moore had described the mounds as "lumps or hillocks near each other."[13]

Historical and topographical resources do not readily verify or identify the three mounds of Watson's story. Other than unremarkable sand dunes, the Texas coast between Galveston and Sabine Pass had very few significant elevations of any kind. There are, however, plausible candidates for the natural landmark that Watson depended upon for navigation. On Bolivar Peninsula about 25 miles north northeast of Galveston is Caplen Mound. It was an ancient burial ground of the Atakapa tribe of Native Americans. It is and was a small natural hill made larger by shell refuse. It rose only five to six feet above sea level and was about 45 feet across.[14]

A better candidate was a tall salt dome at High Island, about 35 miles north northeast of Galveston. It was 38 feet above sea level making it the highest point on the Gulf of Mexico between Mobile, Alabama, and the Yucatán Peninsula. The mound was also over a mile in diameter where its elevation was at least 10 feet. Today, the salt dome is a single geographic feature, but it is possible that in 1864, when seen from the Watson's perspective, it could have appeared as if there were three lumps rather than one mound.[15]

After establishing their position, Watson sailed to within one mile from shore and anchored in 3 fathoms of water. Watson thought that this position still left them vulnerable to detection and capture. He carefully moved even closer to the shore by taking down sails, using oars and grapnels, and paying out more chain and line. *Rob Roy* finally came to anchor about a half mile from the beach in nine feet of water. His tactics of using the backdrop of the shore for concealment, keeping a bow-on aspect angle, and anchoring in water that was too shallow for enemy warships to approach proved successful. That morning, a passing Union cruiser came to within seven miles of *Rob Roy*, but gave no sign that it had sighted the nearly invisible blockade runner.[16]

The Confederate cavalry that patrolled the area had no problem detecting the schooner, but they also had no way of reaching her. Their presence, however, was a deterrent for any Union warship that might have contemplated sending in a boat to attempt a seizure. Watson decided to go ashore and consult with the troops. He surmised that they were part of Colonel Debray's Regiment who had previously patrolled this section of Bolivar Peninsula between Sabine Pass and Galveston Bay. By the time of Watson's arrival, the Regiment was in Louisiana shadowing the retreat of Major General Nathaniel P. Banks after the Union general's disastrous Red River campaign.[17]

Watson said that he went in by boat to deliver letters and dispatches to the mounted troops. Major General Magruder was keen to receive all possible intelligence from blockade runners. Even Union newspapers were highly prized. On May 25, Magruder had composed a letter to Colonel Joseph Bates at the Brazos emphasizing the "great importance of information concerning the movements of the enemy." He directed Bates to "always forward without delay" to his headquarters "all newspapers published within the enemy's lines that may fall into your hands." Confederate records do not confirm that Watson's correspondence reached Galveston, but the dutiful soldiers would have delivered the letters promptly. In return for his thoughtfulness, the soldiers offered Watson some relevant intelligence. There were 13 blockaders guarding the entrance to Galveston Bay.[18]

Undaunted by this news, Watson started out in the early evening, and by midnight had gone about 20 miles. He was moving slowly and carefully, with *Rob Roy* running under low canvas to avoid detection. He was hoping to work his way past the Union gunboats between 3:00 and 4:00 a.m. This late hour was the end of the midnight watch (mid-watch, 2400 to 0400) when lookouts were most likely to be tired, with heavy eyes. Tensions were high, but *Rob Roy* safely passed through the blockading fleet unnoticed. Just as the schooner reached the main channel into Galveston Bay and the crew began to relax, a bright light flashed on their port bow. A loud voice cried out from that direction, "Schooner ahoy! Heave to quick or we will sink you."[19]

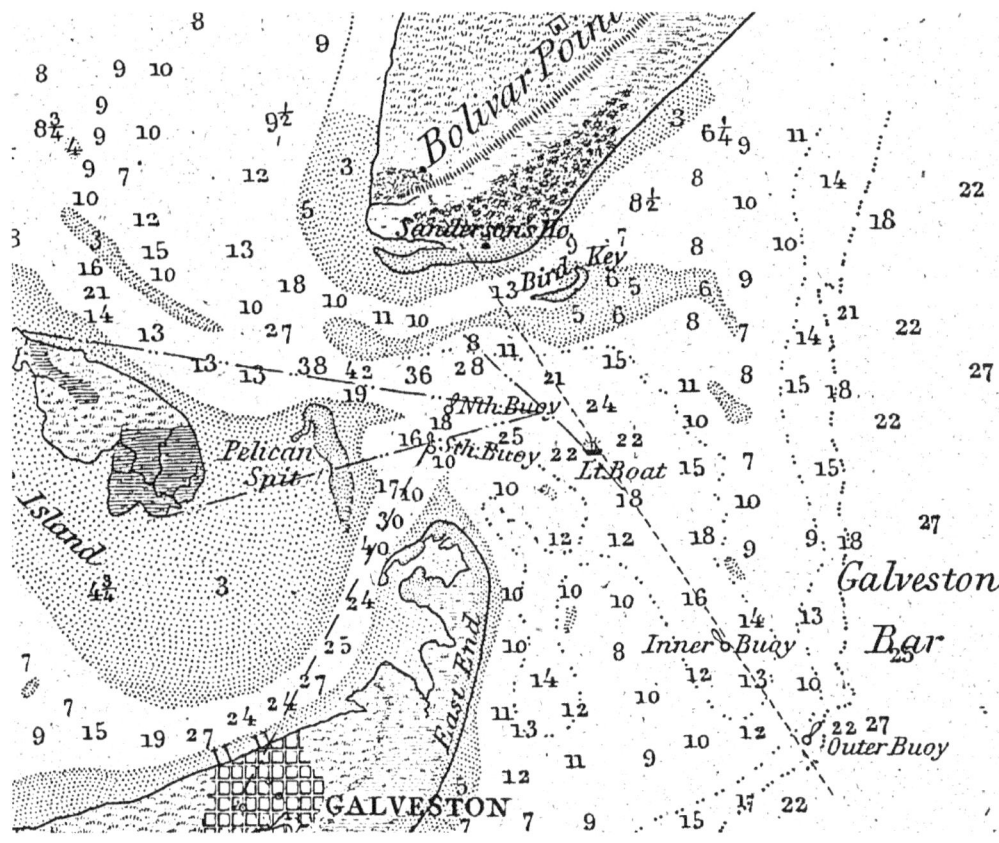

Preliminary sketch of Galveston Bay, Texas. U.S. Coast Survey, 1852 (author's collection).

At first, the crew feared they had stumbled upon an armed boat from one of the Union cruisers, but a sailor correctly asserted that no enemy boat would have come in that far. It turned out to be a Texas inland steamer that the Marine Department had fitted out as a guard boat. The Confederate ship threatened to sink *Rob Roy* only because they were about to sail right into the wreck of the former USS *Westfield*. The guard boat's crew needed to get the schooner's attention quickly and force the approaching schooner to heave to. The *Westfield* wreck was a deadly hazard that would have surely sunk *Rob Roy*, if they had not stopped immediately.[20]

Prior to settling into its final resting place, the USS *Westfield* had been the flagship for a U.S. Navy fleet of warships under Commodore William Renshaw. Along with an Army company of soldiers, the U.S. Navy had occupied Galveston Bay from November 1862 until January 1, 1863. However, in the early morning hours of New Year's Day, Texas, forces led by Major General John Bankhead (Prince John) Magruder, recaptured Galveston. The most important Confederate force in the attack was an improvised flotilla of "cotton-clad" river steamers under Commodore Leon Smith. Two of the steamers had their decks piled high with bales of cotton for protection. They proceeded to ram and capture the USS *Harriet Lane*. The loss of this famous warship caused panic among the Union fleet. In the confusion, Commander Renshaw ran the *Westfield* aground off Pelican Spit as it got underway in a futile attempt to intercept the Confederate cotton-clads. Seeing that he was hopelessly stuck, Renshaw ordered the destruction of *Westfield* to prevent it from falling into the hands of the Confederate forces. When the fuse did not detonate his flagship, Renshaw angrily returned to *Westfield* to set things right. He and several other sailors lost their lives when the delayed explosion obliterated the warship and everyone on it. The wrecked remains of *Westfield* remained a fixture in Galveston Bay for several months. Rather than clearing the debris, the Confederates spent months salvaging its guns, driveshaft, and coal bunkers.[21]

Other than rescuing wayward blockade runners, the Confederate ship standing guard near the wreck of *Westfield* had several other responsibilities. It was charged with discouraging enemy small boat incursions, enforcing customs and health regulations, and policing the waters of Galveston Bay. Watson did not identify the guard boat that saved him from disaster, but there were two candidates. One was the wooden side-wheel river steamer *Bayou City*. It was the primary cotton-clad steamer that rammed and captured *Harriet Lane*. On the evening of *Rob Roy*'s arrival in May of 1864, the *Bayou City* was serving as one of the Galveston Bay's lightly armed guard-ships.[22]

The other designated steamer serving as a guard-ship during this period was *Diana*. Like *Bayou City*, she was a side-wheel paddle steamer. *Diana* had arrived at Galveston Bay in December 1858 and had been in Confederate Army service since September 1861. Her captain and part-owner, John H. Sterrett had chartered *Diana*, along with the steamers *Bayou City*, and *Neptune No. 2* (with their crews) to the government at the rate of $7,500 per month, per boat. Although built at two different Northern shipyards, Commander William W. Hunter of the Confederate Navy described *Bayou City* and *Neptune No. 2* as being of the same "size, class, and power." Sterrett was a veteran captain who had operated steamboats on Galveston Bay and its tributaries since the days of the Texas Republic.[23]

Watson wrote that he arrived at Galveston "after a long passage of eighteen days" and that Captain Dave McClusky was already at the Brazos River "three days ago." As previously noted, McClusky and his schooner *Stingaree* arrived on May 23. Which meant that Watson would have arrived in Galveston on the 26th. Since *Rob Roy* sailed from Havana in company with Captain McClusky and his schooner *Stingaree* on May 11, 1864, Watson incorrectly remembered the details of his voyage. Contrary to the usual practice, Watson and McClusky left on the new moon and arrived off the coast of Texas when the moon was full.[24]

Confederate correspondence revealed another discrepancy with Watson's timeline and his stories of amiable relations with Texas officials. He said that he shared some of his coffee with a grateful crew from the guard ship, and welcomed the port health officer onboard *Rob Roy*. He said that another officer passed along General Magruder's invitation to join him at headquarters as soon as possible. After sharing breakfast onboard his schooner, Watson said the Confederate officials let him accompany them upon departure so that he could meet with the general. As usual, the literal truth did not match Watson's sea story.[25]

On June 1, 1864, the Chief of Galveston Harbor Police, Thomas Chubb, reported to the local District Commander, Brigadier General James M. Hawes that he had:

placed the Schooner *Rob Roy* in quarantine. The Health officer has not yet returned from his inspection of the vessel & crew. No communication with the vessel is permitted until the Health Officer makes his report at your head quarters and your permission obtained. A yellow flag is set on the schooner.[26]

Out of concern for the spread of deadly yellow fever, most southern ports routinely implemented quarantine procedures for all arriving vessels during the sickly summer months. It would not be until the early 1900s that there was an effective yellow fever vaccine. U.S. Army Major Walter Reed led the team that confirmed the theory of a Cuban doctor about the source of the yellow fever infection. The culprit was the female *Aedes Aegypti* mosquito, rather than sickly coastal vapors or other sanitation issues.[27]

When *Rob Roy* arrived in Galveston, the city was free of yellow fever, there were no reported cases in Havana, and the crew was healthy. Blockade runners simply had to anchor at a shallow area of the bay near Red Fish Bar. There, they expected a perfunctory examination and quick clearance from the medical officer. With the arrival of summer, conditions and procedures would change.

By early August 1864, the Confederates were using the former USS *Cavallo* as a guard and hospital ship off Red Fish bar in Galveston Bay. *Cavallo* had been captured along with *Harriet Lane* during the early morning hours of January 1, 1863, when General Magruder and Commodore Leon Smith chased the Yankee fleet out of Galveston Bay. As a hospital ship, *Cavallo*'s medical personnel could be more attentive to the needs of infected seamen, while keeping the disease and those exposed to it, safely offshore.[28]

In Galveston, the health officer was the German-born Gustavus Holland, Chief Surgeon, of the 1st Sub-District of Texas. He gladly accepted Watson's offer of

> some tea and coffee, two small cheeses, three kits of mackerel, a barrel of potatoes, a box of raisins, and other small articles; also, half-a-dozen bottles of brandy, a case of gin, and a dozen bottles of port. The liquor, of course, being a donation for the hospital.[29]

The doctor especially appreciated these edible gifts. His additional duty was as caterer for the general's mess and the general was "very partial" to pickled mackerel. Intoxicating spirits had long been banned from Galveston, but medicinal supplies were an exception.[30]

There was no official report of Holland's unremarkable visit to *Rob Roy*, but the doctor boarded the steamer *Susannah* the following day. As he did with *Rob Roy*, the doctor "cleared the vessel of quarantine." Holland also reported to the Sub-district commander, Brigadier General James M. Hawes, that "Capt. McConnell reports Havana healthy for the season of the year."[31]

Dr. Holland ran afoul of General Hawes in late July, during *Susannah*'s subsequent visit to Galveston. The doctor had again boarded the steamer and found her free of disease, but due to an outbreak of yellow fever in that city, Hawes had ordered all blockade runners to be placed in strict quarantine. The doctor obeyed those orders, but as he had with William Watson and *Rob Roy*, he again accepted gifts from the captain. In this case, Captain McConnell offered Dr. Holland "a few bunches of bananas and pineapples for distribution among the officers of these and

District Headquarters." This simple act enraged General Hawes who condemned Holland's "wanton and reckless disobedience of orders." Holland was shocked at the general's censure, assuring Hawes' aide that he had no such intent and that "fruits are utterly incapable of retaining or communicating infection."[32]

There was no deadly infection on board *Susannah*, but the good doctor's career did not survive his exposure to the wrath of General Hawes. A veteran of the U.S. Army with service in the Mexican War, Dr. Holland had already been court martialed earlier in 1864. His offense was disobedience to orders for sending reports directly to the Surgeon General in Richmond instead of addressing them to his immediate commander, Major General Magruder. By August, General Hawes had relieved Holland of his duties and on September 19, he accepted the doctor's resignation from the Army. None of this drama found its way into Watson's story.[33]

Since it was still early in the morning when Watson arrived in Galveston, the British Consulate was not open for business. Like most consuls, Arthur Lynn did not rely on his consular duties as his only source of income. He was also an independent businessman. In this case, he had been a Galveston cotton factor and general commission agent before the war in partnership with the 30-year-old John H. Williams. Their office was at the corner of Strand and 24th Street, but Lynn's consulate office was in his home on 23rd Street. Finding the consulate closed, Watson went instead to General Magruder's temporary headquarters while he was in Galveston. He did not cite the exact location, but he probably returned to one of the Hendley Buildings. Joseph and William Hendley's large, three-story red brick Greek revival mercantile buildings were on the Strand between 20th and 21st streets. Magruder had used one of the buildings as his headquarters during the Battle of Galveston. There was also an enclosed cupola at the top with a commanding view of the bay, its entrance, and the Gulf. This observatory functioned as a quasi-official lookout station during the war.[34]

Watson was told to go up to the General's room which must have been on the second floor. There, Magruder was struggling to slip on one of his boots. Despite his painful corns (callouses on the feet), the general was in good spirits. His aide had already opened one of *Rob Roy*'s bottles of gin and was preparing a morning gin cocktail. The general acknowledged the gift and assured Watson that the medical department valued spirituous liquors that were otherwise prohibited on Galveston Island. Not coincidentally, Magruder assured Watson that both he and his aide were on the sick list that morning.[35]

Watson made note of General Magruder's "slight lisp or stutter in his speech." The general's speech impairment was well known but rarely mentioned in contemporary reports. For "the gay, dashing, and festive Magruder," the lisp was not an impediment. Standing over six feet tall, he talked incessantly in social settings and was said to have been "the wittiest man in the old army." He could fight all day and dance all night. During the Mexican War, he had been a great favorite of General Winfield Scott's. He was brevetted to major on April 18, 1847, for "gallant and meritorious conduct" at the battle of Cerro Gordo. Five months later, he received a lieutenant colonel's brevet for his bravery in the storming of Chapultepec.[36]

When dressed "in full regimentals," contemporaries called him "the handsomest soldier in the Confederacy" and "One of the most soldierly looking men in the Corps." His fastidious attention to his appearance, earned him the nickname, "Prince John." But there was more to the man than appearances. The famous Texas Ranger and Confederate Colonel, John Salmon "Rip" Ford believed that "the advent of General Magruder was equal to the addition of 50,000 men to the forces of Texas." Even a Northern merchant and Union sympathizer admitted that the general was a man of action who "suited Texas."[37]

A story about Magruder's speech defect that was often retold first appeared in a 1906 book by Walter H. Taylor. The incident began when a Confederate soldier made an uninvited appearance at one of General Magruder's formal dinners at Yorktown, Virginia, in 1862.

> Turning sternly to the veteran, he asked, "Who are you thir?"
> The soldier promptly gave his name and command.
> "Well, thir, what are you doing here, thir?"
> The soldier replied that it was his purpose to get something to eat.
> 'Well, thir, and do you know with whom you propose to dine?'
> Promptly came the reply, "No, and I don't care a damn either. I used to be particular in such matters before the war, but it don't make a damned bit of difference now."
> Magruder was thunderstruck. Lost in admiration, and extending both arms toward the veteran, he exclaimed with his inimitable lisp, "Your impudenth ith thublime, thir; keep your theat, thir," and the dinner proceeded.[38]

Magruder had initial success commanding Confederate forces at Yorktown, Virginia. He cleverly deceived George B. McClellan about the strength of his forces, and delayed the Union offensive. However, his lack of aggressiveness during the Seven Days Battle earned him the disdain of General Robert E. Lee. The Confederate general ushered him off to command the District of Texas, New Mexico, and Arizona, where General Lee had been just prior to the Civil War. Magruder arrived in Texas on October 10, 1862, and assumed command seven weeks later. His predecessor, Brigadier General Paul O. Hébert, the former Governor of Louisiana, had surrendered Galveston to a small Union naval squadron and a single company of ground forces without a fight. Magruder promptly organized and led a successful attack against the Union fleet using a make-shift flotilla of cotton-clad riverboats loaded with "Horse Marines." His ground and naval forces had other successes at the Sabine River just a few weeks later. From his headquarters in Houston, Magruder traveled up and down the coast of Texas, administering the department with skill. His efforts garnered the appreciation and sometimes the adoration of Texas citizens.[39]

General Magruder's principal headquarters was in Houston, but he had come to Galveston to meet with his commanders there. He also played host to Santiago Vidaurri, Governor of the northern Mexican states of Nuevo León and Coahuila. Governor Vidaurri was an equally ill-fated ally of the French-backed Mexican Emperor Maximillian. In May of 1864, he was temporarily seeking refuge in Texas. Vidaurri was staying at the Washington Hotel on the corner of East Avenue and Tremont. It was one of the few hotels still open in Galveston and one of its finest.[40]

After enjoying his cocktail and slipping on his boots, Magruder turned his attention to William Watson. He was pleased with the armaments Watson had taken onboard from Major Helm in Havana and wanted them delivered as soon as possible. Since the Confederate customs house had moved its operations to Houston, offloading would have to wait until Watson could deliver his cargo manifest there. Subtly hinting that he would need a steamer to tow him up Buffalo Bayou to avoid a two to three-day delay, the general readily told his aide, Major William T. Carrington, to prepare an order to Commodore Leon Smith's Marine Department to that effect.

The general then had Major Carrington hand him a letter that Watson quoted verbatim:

"Headquarters, District Texas, Galveston
June 2nd, 1864.

Captain W., Schooner *Rob Roy*.

Captain, —I am directed by the Major General comdg. to say that you will take your vessel to Houston, and in the absence of the officer designated by General [E. Kirby] Smith, you will deliver the arms forwarded by Mr. Helm C.S. Agent, to Captain Scott, ordnance officer at that place. Conforming of course to the revenue laws.

I am, Captain,

Your most obedient servant,
Wm. S. Carrington [sic],
A.A.A.G.

You will hand the invoice to Captain Scott, ordnance officer."[41]

There was no copy of this special order found in the National Archives, indicating that Magruder did not intend it to be an official order. It was technically a military order given to a British citizen. Thanks in part to Watson's earlier complaints about the seizure of *Rob Roy*, British Consul Arthur Lynn had made the general sensitive to such overreach. However, given the precision of Watson's quote, it rang true. The timing was consistent with other events recorded in official documents and Watson's descriptions of the characters were reasonably correct. Major William T. Carrington (not William S. Carrington) was one of General Magruder's aides at the time and Captain Hugh T. Scott was the Confederate ordnance officer in charge of the Houston depot.[42]

In his haste to get *Rob Roy* unloaded, Watson turned down Magruder's invitation to share a second breakfast which included the highly prized coffee that he had given to Doctor Holland. Returning to *Rob Roy*, he brought his schooner alongside CSS *Island City*, the small transport steamer that General Magruder had said would tow him up to Houston. To his surprise and consternation, the captain of *Island City* (John Y. Lawless) had no orders regarding *Rob Roy*.[43]

This failure to communicate within the Confederate chain of command was not uncommon, but it sent Watson storming back to General Magruder's headquarters. The general had left to inspect the Island's forts and his staff expected him back in about an hour. On his way out of the building, Watson saw a group of civilians, mostly women and children standing in line holding plates. He discovered that Doctor Holland was distributing the food that he had gifted to General Magruder to the poor and hungry of the city.[44]

The doctor reported that the general made no effort to court favor or hide his faults, but he "would divide his last crust with these poor people"; and that "a kinder-hearted man was not in existence." This unpublicized show of generosity helped Watson form a higher opinion of Major General "Prince" John Bankhead Magruder. In view of Magruder's previous court martial action against him, Holland showed remarkable maturity and equanimity in his assessment of the general's character.⁴⁵

Soon after this revelation, General Magruder came rolling up in a "phaeton," a four-wheeled carriage with a bench for a driver in front, a covered seating area for two, and a small luggage space in the rear. When the general asked why he had not gotten away, Watson replied that *Island City*'s captain had no orders and the Marine Department said they had no authority to issue such orders. A frustrated Magruder asked for a pen and paper and scratched out another order directing *Island City* to tow *Rob Roy* up to Houston. Watson said it was addressed to "General Haines," but the commanding general told him to take it to Marine Headquarters.⁴⁶

"A Short History of General J.B. Magruder," from the *Histories of Generals* series (N114) issued by W. Duke, Sons & Co., 1888 (courtesy Duke University Libraries, Digital Collections, W. Duke, Sons & Co. Advertising Materials, 1880–1910).

Once again, there is no mention of this order in the logs that recorded Magruder's official special orders. Additionally, there was no "General Haines" in Texas. However, Watson's transcription of the hastily written and unrecorded letter was undoubtedly genuine. He commented on the difficulty of deciphering Magruder's barely legible scrawl and there were words that he simply could not make out. The "General Haines" that Watson referred to was the 40-year-old Brigadier General James Morrison Hawes. General Hawes was a U.S. Military Academy graduate (1845) from Kentucky who

Typical example of General Magruder's atrocious penmanship (letter from J.B. Magruder to S. Cooper, September 20, 1863, NARA RG: 109, Letters Sent, District of Texas, Chapter 2, Vol 130, p 71). Transcription: "The *Harriet Lane* & other vessels captured by troops & seamen under my command have been condemned by the Prize Court & were ordered to be sold. I urged an appraisement instead of a sale as the vessels were required for the public service & my request was assented to & the appraisement made."

had served with distinction in the Mexican War and at the Battle of Milliken's Bend, Louisiana, in the Confederate Army. After he was assigned to Major General Magruder's staff in February 1864, the general placed Hawes in charge of Galveston's defenses.[47]

When Watson took the order to Marine Department Headquarters, the major in charge also struggled with the barely legible writing. The day before *Rob Roy*'s arrival in Galveston Bay, General Magruder had ordered Commodore Leon Smith to Matagorda Bay where he was to supervise the parole of Captain Dave McClusky's prisoner, Acting Ensign Paul Borner of the U.S. Navy. Borner would play a significant role in McClusky's sea story that will be discussed in the following chapter. It was Borner's presence in Texas that accounted for Commodore Smith's absence. When the Marine Department's acting commander finally understood the intent of the general's scribbled pencil note, he issued an order for *Island City* to tow *Rob Roy* up Galveston Bay toward Houston.[48]

Watson reproduced the contents of the brief directive as follows:

"Galveston, June 2nd 1864,

The *Island City* will be ordered to take *Rob Roy* in tow for Harrisonburg as she goes up.

Robert Wagan, Major and
Chief Marine, 1st D.S."[49]

In addition to the lack of any official record of this order, there was no "Harrisonburg" in Texas, and there was no officer in Texas named Wagan, much less one assigned to the Marine Department. In June 1864, only Leon Smith had the authority to issue movement orders to a transport like *Island City*, but it was the commodore's duty to ensure that his steamers met the needs of the various district commanders, including General Hawes. In Leon Smith's absence, there would have been another officer acting in his place. Watson also cited Major Wagan as the "Chief Marine 1st D.S." This title was nonsensical, but he was probably referring to either Major John C. Stafford or Major Charles M. Mason.[50]

Major Stafford was briefly the quartermaster for the Texas Marine Department under Commodore Leon Smith in June 1864. His full title as the Chief of the Texas Marine Department's Quarter Master Department could have been abbreviated "Chief Marine Dept Q.M." In official orders, Stafford was sometimes referred to as "Q.M. C.S.P.A." or Quarter Master Confederate States Provisional Army.[51]

The other possible identity of Watson's non-existent Major Wagan was Major Charles M. Mason. He had been on General Magruder's staff, but in March 1863, Mason was placed in charge of artillery on the gunboats within General's Hawes' Eastern Sub-District. Of average height (five feet, six inches) with piercing blue eyes and dark hair, Mason had a history of filling in for Leon Smith during the Commodore's absence. His job titles with the Marine Department included "Chief of Marine Artillery" and "Adjutant General of the Fleet." In 1861, Charles Mason had been a member of Company D, First Regiment (also known as Cook's Regiment), Texas Heavy Artillery, abbreviated as "Co. D. 1st Tex. Arty." and "Co. D. 1st Regt. Heavy Arty." He would eventually return to the same company at the war's end. Major Mason's various titles and their abbreviations could account for some of Watson's transcription errors.[52]

The lack of a log entry for the order that "Major Wagan" wrote to *Island City* was understandable. There are scant records for any of the Texas Marine Department-issued orders. There was, however, a steamer named *Island City* performing similar duties in Galveston Bay during this period. Additionally, "Harrisonburg" was a common misspelling of "Harrisburg" which was adjacent Houston on Buffalo Bayou.[53]

Despite the bureaucratic delays, *Island City* was able to tow *Rob Roy* up to the mouth of Buffalo Bayou where it took on coal and lay overnight. After a good night's rest, the steamer continued to tow Watson's schooner upriver as far as "Harrisonburg." Watson was fortunate that he made it that far. Less than two weeks later, *Island City* would suffer a boiler casualty that kept it out of service for over six months.[54]

After bidding adieu to the crew of the steamer, Watson says his crew used their oars (sweeps) to power their way upriver to Houston. When they arrived there on June 3, "Mr. M." (Mills) greeted them. Watson does not say which "Mr. M." he was referring to. Robert Mills was at Havana, and his younger brother David was primarily involved with the management of their plantations and the 800 slaves who labored on them. This leaves their nephew John as the likely "Mr. M." who greeted him upon his arrival. John Robert Mills was the son of their older brother William and the company's managing partner based in Houston. Watson later referred to him as "J.M."[55]

Watson said that John Mills informed him that the blockading fleet had captured other Texas-bound schooners (*Sylvia*, *Lily*, and *Emily*) that had left Havana about the same time as *Rob Roy*. As previously noted, Watson had erroneously named the schooner *Amanda* as *Sylvia*. This was the schooner that the USS *Kanawha* captured near Corpus Christi Bay on May 14. The report about *Lily* was a bit closer to the mark. The USS *Owasco* captured the 61-ton schooner *Lilly* (often spelled *Lily*) on April 17, about 10 miles from Velasco and the Brazos River. It had cleared Havana customs for Belize on March 31 and departed for Texas on April 8, 1864, a full month before *Rob Roy*. However, the report of *Emily*'s capture was a bit more problematic.[56]

It was well known in Houston that *Emily* had sailed from Galveston the previous January for Vera Cruz. Rather than leaving from Havana, *Emily*'s port of departure for its return to Texas was from Tampico. As it approached the Brazos River, it ran up on the beach within range of the Velasco forts. It survived a bombardment from the U.S. Navy's blockading warship, thanks in part to artillery support from the forts. The local post commander reported that "the enemy fired four shots at the schooner *Emily*, wrecked below here. One shot came within 15 feet. Captain Saunders [William Saunders] was near the vessel with his company. No damage done."[57]

After removing its cargo and rigging, the resourceful Confederates were able to restore *Emily* and make her ready for sea. A few days before *Rob Roy*'s arrival, *Emily* was listed among six of Thomas W. House's schooners that were "under contract to bring in Gov't supplies." The USS *Mobile* did capture *Emily* off San Luis Pass, but that event would not occur for another four months, shortly after she finally ventured out of Galveston Bay in mid–October. The sum of the facts shows that Watson's recollection of the report from Mr. M. (John Mills) about *Emily* was incorrect.[58]

The other bit of news from John Mills was that Houston's large steam cotton press was under repair. This malfunction would impact Watson's plans. The compress was an essential piece of equipment for squeezing or "pressing" cotton into compact bales. Blockade runners especially needed these smaller compressed bales. Stevedores could more easily and efficiently stuff these bales into a vessel's hold and onto its deck. This potential delay was of no immediate concern to Watson. He was in no hurry to leave. The extended daylight hours and sultry winds of early summer offered no allure for captains of blockade-running schooners. They would rather wait for the promise of brisk winds and the longer nights of late summer before risking the ensnaring tentacles of the Union blockading fleet.[59]

10

Captain Dave's Exciting Sea Story

The Sequel

Soon after his arrival in Houston, Watson and Captain Dave McClusky enjoyed a reunion. They had both departed Havana on May 11, 1864. McClusky's *Stingaree* arrived at the Brazos three days before *Rob Roy* entered Galveston Bay. Watson never identified the schooner *Stingaree* by name, but contemporary references were plentiful. Unfortunately, they were silent about the particulars of *Stingaree*'s dimensions and the timing and circumstances of its arrival in Havana. There was ample documentation that McClusky and his schooner *Stingaree* arrived in the vicinity of the Brazos on May 22, 1864, two weeks after sailing from Havana. He was primed and ready to risk another attempt at running the blockade into Texas. Watson assured his readers that what followed was the tale of Captain Dave's second daring escapade. It was "true as it happened."[1]

In fairness to Watson, his sea story did closely match the historical records, with a few notable exceptions. Unlike McClusky's brazen escape in *Sarah*, this latest stain on the U.S. Navy's reputation received attention in both the Army and Navy official records. Perhaps this episode made it into more prominent historical records because McClusky captured several Yankee sailors and then turned them over to Confederate authorities. This embarrassing situation made the shameful affair impossible to ignore. Watson's account, along with contemporary newspaper and firsthand reports that appeared during and after the war, added colorful details.

Watson and McClusky had set sail from Havana in their schooners during the second week of May 1863. Captain Dave had a crew of four including the experienced sailor Fred Wolfean who was his mate, James Howe, an able-bodied seamen, plus John Gordon, another unnamed seaman, and a cook. The weather was magnificent for both sailors, and all went well as *Rob Roy* followed a more northerly course at a more deliberate pace. McClusky's *Stingaree* charged ahead on a west, northwesterly heading until the morning of the 22nd of May when they neared the mouth of the Brazos River.[2]

The Confederate lookouts at the Brazos River forts spotted an unidentified schooner in the distance, but so did the blockading gunboat. The forts stood helplessly by as the man-of-war chased the schooner to the southwest. Soon, they sailed over the horizon and beyond the view of the elevated forts. Shortly thereafter, the

USS *Kineo* (foreground) and USS *Hartford*, March 1863 (Library of Congress, Prints and Photographs Division, LC-DIG-stereo-1s0282).

warship returned with the schooner trailing behind. The capture occurred about 15 miles from shore. The steamer proved to be the USS *Kineo*, a sister ship to the 90-day gunboat *Aroostook*. The prize schooner was Captain Dave McClusky's *Stingaree*. McClusky and the captain of *Kineo* filled in the details about the cleverly audacious escape.[3]

Kineo had spotted *Stingaree* at daybreak on May 22 about five or six miles from Velasco. McClusky had obviously mistimed his arrival at the mouth of the Brazos River. He should have been in position to make a run in the dead of night. As Watson reported, Captain Dave was not a skilled navigator. He did not even carry a chronometer, which was essential for accurately calculating longitude. Dave would simply sail along the Cuban coast, cross the Yucatan Channel, and travel up the Mexican coast. He used a sextant (or octant) to determine his latitude and dead reckoning and soundings to estimate how close he was to land.[4]

It was 9 o'clock in the morning before *Kineo* closed the distance between the two vessels. The warship then fired a gun as a signal for the unidentified schooner to either "heave to" or risk destruction. The jig was up for McClusky, so he promptly complied. Captain John Watters of *Kineo* sent a boarding party led by Acting Ensign Paul Borner over to *Stingaree* to investigate.[5]

The ensign reported that the British schooner *Stingaree*'s papers appeared to be correct. She had cleared from Havana and was bound for Matamoros, Mexico, but had no bill of lading. Dave claimed that she was in ballast, with only a few bales of bagging and some coils of rope in her hold. Captain Watters was suspicious, given how far off course *Stingaree* was, if it was in fact heading for Matamoros. He decided to seize the schooner at least temporarily while he decided if McClusky's claims were true. Until then, he ordered Ensign Borner to take charge of her, giving him a boat and seven men to sail her.[6]

Stingaree's entire crew remained on board as prisoners while the prize crew followed *Kineo* as it returned to its anchorage off Velasco. Leaving boatswain's mate William Morgan in charge of the management of the schooner and the prize crew, Ensign Borner went below deck into the captain's cabin. He was searching for evidence that might support the schooner's condemnation as a blockade runner. When he came up on deck again, he found it entirely deserted except for one man at the helm (probably seaman John Smith). Boatswain William Morgan, along with seamen Charles Zimmerman, Daniel Hennessy, John Griffin, and Joseph Fernandez, had disappeared into the *Stingaree*'s cargo hold.[7]

Captain John Watters, USS *Kineo* (Naval History and Heritage Command, NH 119421).

While their officer had been in the captain's cabin, the Yankee sailors had been playfully taunting *Stingaree*'s crew. They said the men were sure to be put in prison; their vessel and cargo would be condemned and sold as a prize. Captain McClusky acknowledged the fact, and as a gesture of good will, invited the prize crew into the hold where he had a prominently placed a jar of rum. The prize crew reasoned that it would be confiscated along with everything else, so they might as well help themselves to it. And they did. Having whetted their taste for more, the prize crew broke into the hold to gain access to the rest of McClusky's stash of the intoxicating libation. There they stayed until Ensign Borner returned topside.[8]

The disgusted officer ordered his men back on deck, but to his surprise found that they were "so far gone as to be unable to get on deck without assistance." After staggering up from the hold, both boatswain Morgan and seaman Zimmerman lay prostrate on deck. "The rest were so drunk that they did not know what they were about." *Stingaree* was about three hundred yards from *Kineo* when Borner attempted to close the distance by tacking the schooner, but "in their drunken officiousness" his men "were baffled in their attempt."[9]

When the prize crew had first boarded *Stingaree*, McClusky left the retractable centerboard keel in the "up" position. This was a suitable configuration when in shallow water, but it made the schooner extremely difficult to manage against the wind and seas. While the ensign's attention was focused on making another attempt to turn up-wind, McClusky and his men saw their opportunity to strike.[10]

Not only was Ensign Borner the only sober member of the prize crew, he was also the only one who was armed with a revolver. Naturally, he was the first to fall. Captain McClusky held Borner's arms behind him while James Howe and the others wrestled away his pistol and cutlass. The other men had cutlases, but most of those had been placed in a rack that circled the main mast that was designed to hold belaying pins. Soon after McClusky disarmed Ensign Borner, the fight raged "all over the vessel man to man, with knives, blocks, hand-spikes, and other improvised implements of warfare." John Smith made the only attempt to aid the ensign. He picked up a handspike, but he was barely able to hold it much less use it as a weapon. Seaman Smith was soon disarmed. McClusky's first mate, Fred Wolfean, knocked down the man at the wheel and set *Stingaree*'s course for the beach, which was enticingly near at hand.[11]

Onboard the USS *Kineo*, Captain Watters noticed that "the schooner was very badly managed" by his prize crew and was steering too close to the shore. He ordered the gunboat about (i.e., to turn around) so that he could close the distance and take *Stingaree* under tow. When *Kineo* approached to within a mile, the schooner suddenly turned and ran straight for the shore. Watters then saw the men on the schooner cut away the small skiff from *Kineo* that still had seaman Edwards onboard. Edwards was the lone Union sailor remaining in the small boat which had been towing astern of *Stingaree* before being set adrift during the scuffle onboard *Stingaree*. Watters urgently ordered his engineers to bring his ship to full speed with the intent "to run her down." He also opened fire with his 20-pounder bow gun.[12]

The first shot went through *Stingaree*'s mainsail. The second almost knocked Wolfean from the wheel when it burst ahead of the schooner and threw up a plume of water that washed over the deck. The explosion and drenching also

Portrait of Paul Borner (courtesy Andy Hall and the Rosenberg Library, Galveston, Texas).

roused Boatswain Morgan from his drunken slumber. He tried to stand, but lost his balance and tumbled overboard with an assist from John Gordon of *Stingaree*'s crew. McClusky threw out a spar (life ring) to save him, if possible. Morgan escaped drowning when seaman Edwards managed to pick him up in the skiff.[13]

In the shock and confusion, Seaman Fernandez, "a West India negro," who was Portuguese, saw an opportunity to retaliate. He attacked Captain McClusky with a knife. McClusky fired two shots at the young sailor using Ensign Borner's revolver, but missed his target. Just as Fernandez had the knife to Captain Dave's throat, James Howe knocked it away. The desperate five foot, six-inch-tall Fernandez then rushed to the side of the schooner and made his escape in the schooner's yawl. The *Stingaree*'s crew cared little about the fleeing sailor, but they were incensed at the loss of the yawl. It contained their clothes and personal belongings. In Watson's version of this scene, he said that Captain Dave emptied his revolver at the man after he jumped into the boat and cut the tow rope.[14]

The crew had hastily thrown their personal belongings into two carpet bags along with some brandy and placed them in the yawl. The yawl had been a contingency measure. It was immediately available just in case they were unable to recapture the schooner or if *Kineo* was able to overtake them as the wind died down. If their attempt to recapture *Stingaree* failed, they planned to get away in the small boat. First mate Fred Wolfean reported that they allowed the man in the skiff to get away since, "We had no time to stop and fool with him."[15]

Their reason for haste was the presence of an ill-tempered U.S. Navy warship. *Kineo* was in hot pursuit and kept up a "furious shelling of the schooner," even though their own crewmen were on board. Four shots holed the *Stingaree*'s sails. Despite the heavy fire, McClusky pressed on. Captain Watters reported that as the fleeing schooner approached the shore, he "could pursue no farther without getting aground." He was "reluctantly obliged to desist, seeing her go, soon after, plump on the beach, which was soon lined with cavalry of the enemy, rendering it improper to send our boats."[16]

Contrary to Captain Watters' implied claim, he did send out two launches from *Kineo* in hopes of recapturing or burning the schooner. However, Lieutenant Colonel Henry Cayce, who commanded the post at Velasco, sortied Captain William Saunders' calvary company and 25 infantry to aid in the schooner's escape. Saunders "double quicked" his men two miles down the beach from the Brazos to a point opposite *Stingaree*. It was only when Captain Watters spotted the Confederate soldiers that he reluctantly abandoned his pursuit of the runaway schooner.[17]

Although Captain McClusky had advised his captors that *Stingaree* was sailing in ballast, with no cargo of value, such was not the case. The local newspaper reported that the "cargo was a very valuable one, consisting of iron, nails, bagging, rope, and some merchandise." Captain Saunders' men were able to salvage it all without damage or loss and returned the lot of it to Captain McClusky.[18]

While Captain Dave was collecting his cargo, Confederate soldiers were collecting his prisoners. They took charge of Ensign Borner and his drunken sailors, Felix Sellin, John Smith, Charles Zimmerman, Daniel Hennessy, and John Griffin. They were all marched to the Brazos where they spent the night in the guardhouse. A few hours after running aground on the beach and offloading its passengers and cargo, Captain Dave and his crew got *Stingaree* afloat and at once sailed into the Brazos River. Watson made no mention of *Stingaree*'s grounding, and his book was the only source that claimed some of the sailors were wounded and had to be sent to a Houston hospital.[19]

On *Kineo*, Captain Watters was able to surmise the cause of this "deplorable affair," when he questioned the three crew members who had escaped from *Stingaree*. The captain was unable to draw any conclusions from their incoherent reports of the affair. It was their condition that spoke volumes. They were "in a beastly state of intoxication, crazy drunk and howling," especially boatswain Morgan.[20]

Ensign Borner penned a letter to Captain Watters on the day of his capture. He handed it to Captain John Payne of the Confederate steamer *Mary Hill* in hopes that he would deliver his note to *Kineo* via the flag-of-truce boat. The letter detailed Borner's version of the affair. It was the ensign's "earnest desire to exonerate myself from the odious charge of having neglected my duty, and I hope that the following statement, ... will convince you and everybody else that no blame can be attached to me." Borner also requested Captain Watters to send a change of clothes for himself and his men. Captain Payne agreed to this request "on condition that the two carpet bags taken out of the schooner's boat are returned to him."[21]

When the flag-of-truce boat was sent out from the Brazos River, *Kineo* reciprocated. Captain Watters met the Confederate boat with one of his own. It was manned with a full crew, each armed with "a cutlass and two six-shooters." Watson claimed that McClusky accompanied the Confederates to parlay with the Union commanding officer. He hoped to recover his personal effects, especially the brandy. None of the other reports mentioned this unlikely scenario. It appeared to be another exaggeration intended to enhance Captain Dave's legacy for boldness. Watson also implied that Captain Watters was unaware that his sailors had gotten into McClusky's stash of liquor, which was the primary cause of *Stingaree*'s escape. That was clearly not the case, give their "beastly state" of inebriation that Watters reported on the day of *Stingaree*'s escape.[22]

Contemporary reports confirmed that Captain Watters agreed to send Ensign Borner's his clothes, but he refused to send the crewmen any of their personal effects. He reasoned that his men deserved to be without clothes and shoes as a penalty for getting drunk and losing a valuable prize schooner. Since the return of the two canvas bags belonging to *Stingaree*'s crew was a condition for delivering the letter from Ensign Borner, it is likely that Watters reluctantly turned them over. He did make the remark that if he had those "rebel pirates in my clutch, every one of them should dangle from the yard arm before the set of sun." Given his justified irritation, Captain Watters most likely did not return McClusky's brandy.[23]

At the Brazos, Confederate Colonel Joseph Bates did not share Watters' sentiments about the "pirates." He closed his report to General Magruder with a tribute to the "bold and patriotic heroism of Captain McCloskey [sic] and his crew in this affair. Such devotion to the interests which he represents and to the honor of his country should not go unrewarded." The local newspapers had similar praise for "Capt. McClusky and his men for the gallant manner in which they wrested the schooner and cargo from the enemy." The correspondent also confirmed that this was the second time "that Capt. McClusky has recaptured his vessel from the enemy."[24]

Another episode that Watson claimed resulted from the melee onboard *Stingaree* cannot be confirmed. He related McClusky's story about his collection of blockade runner CDVs that had been in his sea chest. These photographs allegedly included images of ship figureheads and portraits of blockade-running captains, including both McClusky and Watson. The CDVs were among Captain Dave's belongings that had been cast adrift in the schooner's dingy that was commandeered by one of the inebriated Yankee prize crewmen. They were now in the possession of the U.S. Navy.[25]

Watson reported that when Captain Dave went on board the USS *Kineo*, he asked the officer of the deck to return the CDVs. He reasoned that the Navy "ought not to keep them ... they don't belong to me, and these gentlemen will be annoyed." In response, the *Kineo*'s officer chided him saying, "...their *cartes* will be honored with a place in the 'Rogues Gallery' in New York."[26]

When Watson and McClusky met again in Galveston, McClusky brazenly asked Watson to give him "another one of your *cartes*" to replace the one he had lost. In the unlikely event that McClusky did indeed go on board *Kineo*, it would have been naïve to expect the Navy officers to surrender what would have been a significant intelligence coup. Although it was possible that the story about the missing CDV's was at least partially true, none of these images have ever appeared and there was no other mention of them in other contemporary sources or archives.[27]

On the other hand, there was confirmation from multiple sources that Ensign Borner did receive his personal effects from *Kineo* via the flag-of-truce-boat. After receiving these belongings, all the prisoners were transported upriver to the railhead at Columbia where they traveled via the Tap Railroad to Houston. Watson reported this event out of sequence. He claimed that the flag-of-truce-boat left Galveston several days after the prisoners had left the Brazos. That, however, was not the case. The exchange of personal effects occurred off the Brazos River prior to Borner's departure upriver. When the enlisted Union prisoners arrived in Houston, they were assigned to Camp Groce as prisoners of war. Their confinement came just three days after their capture.[28]

By May 30, Ensign Borner was given a parole of honor that allowed him to move about more freely than his incarcerated crew. The proviso was that he had to remain in the custody of the commanding officer of the Marine Department, Commodore Leon Smith. This privilege for paroled prisoners was not unusual for officers, and was documented in official District of Texas, New Mexico, and Arizona Special Orders. It would be another six and a half long months before the ensign was exchanged at Galveston. Borner's relative freedom gave credence to Watson's claim that the ensign (Watson said he was a lieutenant) had visited Watson on board *Rob Roy* while he was in Galveston. It also explained why Leon Smith was absent from Marine Department headquarters when Watson tried to get a tow up the Bay to Houston.[29]

Watson also said that Captain Dave wanted to get his schooner out of the Brazos and into Galveston Bay, which he did. However, Watson posited that *Stingaree* had to enter the Gulf to get there. According to Watson, McClusky safely got into Galveston Bay via San Luis Pass, but then had to traverse "a narrow channel, with nothing but a low, sandy point betwixt it and the sea." As a result, *Stingaree* was visible to the blockading fleet and within range of their big guns. It was difficult to accurately aim its fire, but the gunboat was undeterred from exacting revenge with shot and shell. Watson described the bombardment as lasting the entire day. The Navy allegedly threw so much lead in *Stingaree*'s direction that the sheer weight of it could have sunk the schooner. Watson said he personally observed the entire evolution which caused considerable damage to *Stingaree*, but it was still afloat.[30]

Once again, Watson embellished the truth to improve the drama of his sea story. The actual event took place one week after *Stingaree*'s arrival. Captain McClusky sailed his schooner through the canal that connected the Brazos to the west end of Galveston Bay. Even the daring Captain Dave would not have been so foolish as to attempt to run into the Gulf from the Brazos and back into Galveston Bay via San Luis Pass.[31]

There was no need for Captain Dave to take such a risk, and he did not. There was a better alternative, but even that safer route had its dangers. The canal was very shallow and *Stingaree*'s masts were visible to the Union gunboats, attracting unwanted attention. At about 11:00 a.m. on May 30, a newspaper correspondent reported that one of the blockading steamers had detected,

> the schooner *Stingaree* (Capt. McClusky's schooner) ... aground in the canal, and commenced shelling her firing about ten shots at her, one of which, I understand struck her bow, but did but little damage.[32]

The Union gunboat was probably the USS *Kineo*, but she was only able to inflict superficial damage to *Stingaree*. The bombardment carried away the cutwater (the forward part of the prow, which cuts through the water) and severed the topmast. These tales of *Stingaree*'s daring exploits preceded Captain McClusky and his crew's arrival at Galveston. Even without Watson's embellishments, the local citizenry greeted them as "heroes of the hour."[33]

Watson erroneously reported that the injury to *Stingaree* from the Union shelling was significant, but repairs were still necessary. Not surprisingly, the requisite materials were in short supply in wartime Texas. Contemporary records confirm that McClusky made his requirements known to the local military authorities. They endorsed his appeal to Commodore Leon Smith of the Marine Department for help on June 15, 1864. *Stingaree* needed 4 bars of iron, 10 gallons of coal tar, 50 pounds of oakum (tar-infused hemp used for caulking), and 150 feet of cypress lumber that could not be obtained from private sources. Commodore Smith replied that he too was unable to satisfy the requisition.[34]

To close out his story about *Stingaree*, Watson said that McClusky sold the schooner to another party who repaired and fitted it out with a load of cotton for Tampico. Once again, that is not quite what happened. When McClusky sailed into the Brazos River, he was merely the captain. The schooner's owner was the firm of William Clark & Company. William Clark owned a "Staple and Fancy

Dry Goods" store in Houston. Like many Texas merchants, he was dabbling in the blockade-running business. By September, Clark retained at least an interest in *Stingaree* when it cleared Galveston customs for Vera Cruz, Mexico. Clark owned 82 of the 195 bales onboard *Stingaree*. The others belonged to the Mills Brothers (25 bales), another 50 bales for a Houston merchant, Moses Reichman, with the rest belonging to the Confederate government.[35]

At this point, Captain Dave McClusky and *Stingaree* fade from Watson's story. But like William Watson and *Rob Roy*, their adventures in blockade running were not quite finished. *Stingaree* received her customs clearance on September 21, 1864, but had to delay her departure for almost a month. Blockade runners were having a challenging time getting military permits to pass the forts, courtesy of the ever-prickly General Hawes. Confederate authorities similarly detained the schooners *Flash* and *Lilly* (*Lily*) until mid–October due to the general's bureaucratic haggling.[36]

By the first week of September, the impatient Captain Dave McClusky was no longer captain of *Stingaree*. On September 1, his friend and fellow blockade runner, Captain James B. McConnell arrived in Galveston on the steamer *Susannah*. Dave lost no time gaining permission to go to sea onboard her, probably as a trusted pilot. Two weeks after she arrived, *Susannah* was on her way back to Havana. She safely arrived there on September 18 with 325 bales of cotton.[37]

As for Captain Dave's schooner *Stingaree*, it would successfully run the blockade to Tampico and back. Another of Watson's new-found blockade-running friends would be in command. Despite the interference of the ever-meddlesome General Hawes, Bill Flagg (or Fleigh) took *Stingaree* to sea with 195 bales of cotton in mid–October before returning to Texas by the end of the war. He cleared for Vera Cruz, but sailed for Tampico. Watson would introduce Flagg in a later chapter. *Stingaree* (*Stingray*) ended up back in the Federal Government's possession upon the surrender of Confederate forces in Texas.[38]

11

Preparing for Another Run Through the Blockade

Returning to his own story in mid–June 1864, Watson had several weeks to prepare *Rob Roy* for another run through the blockade. His first step was to perform basic maintenance that would improve his schooner's speed and sea keeping ability. He began by scraping her bottom to clean off barnacles, algae, and other muck. Rather than absorbing the expense of a drydock, he careened *Rob Roy* in the fresh water of Buffalo Bayou. Careening was a method of accessing the hull of a vessel by beaching it and using lines to haul it over on its port and starboard sides. Due to *Rob Roy*'s flat bottom, it was difficult to careen the schooner sufficiently to access the entire hull. After completing that arduous chore as best they could, his crew then busied themselves in repairing and replacing the rigging and "putting everything in good order."[1]

Toward the end of July 1864, Watson reported that yellow fever had arrived via one of the steamers from Havana and soon spread to Galveston and Houston. The anonymous culprit was James McConnell's *Susannah* (see Table 4). In addition to numerous deaths, another indirect victim of the virulent disease was Surgeon Gustavus Holland. Blaming him for insufficiently containing the disease, General James M. Hawes dismissed the doctor from his position as the port's health officer shortly thereafter. The fever would linger through the summer months and into the early fall. Military officials restricted travel and extended furloughs to control the spread.[2]

It was during this relatively serene, but unprofitable interlude, Watson impatiently awaited the repair of the cotton press and better blockade-running conditions. He naturally kept tabs on his fellow blockade runners. He observed that "one or two schooners got into Galveston Bay, but several others were captured in making the attempt." The first that got in, and the only one he specifically named, was *Mary Elizabeth*. Watson noted that she sailed under "Captain Shaeffer, who had sailed with us out of the Brazos River last trip." Watson reminded his readers that Captain George Shaeffer was the younger brother of Henry Shaeffer whom he had met during his previous stay at the Rio Grande. The 25-year-old George had coordinated his escape from the Brazos in *Mary Elizabeth* on the same February evening of 1864, as *Rob Roy*. Instead of heading for Havana with Watson, George went to Vera Cruz, Mexico.[3]

Once again, Watson's tale is a bit misleading while still having many truthful elements. As revealed earlier, *Mary Elizabeth*'s captain was George Scherffius, the younger brother of Henry. The unusual (for Americans) German surname was often misspelled in contemporary correspondence and official reports. The variations are too numerous to list, but "Shaeffer" was not a bad approximation of "Scherffius" for the time.[4]

A newspaper correspondent confirmed the presence of *Mary Elizabeth* at Vera Cruz where she was offloading her cargo of cotton on March 2. The American consul to Vera Cruz, Marquis de Lafayette Lane, also confirmed *Mary Elizabeth*'s arrival from Texas. He said that she had entered port at about the same time as the schooners *Charles Russell* and *Cora*. Each had a "cargo of about 75 bales of cotton." He noted that *Mary Elizabeth* had left Vera Cruz about April 11 while the other two schooners remained in port as of April 21, 1864.[5]

Consul Lane had just returned from the interior of Mexico where he was recovering from a bout with yellow fever. As a result, the consul's information was second-hand. He was mistaken about the date of *Mary Elizabeth*'s departure from Vera Cruz. The Confederate observatory at Bolivar Point had reported her arrival from "West Bay" late on the afternoon of April 6. For the schooner to have arrived in Galveston Bay in early April, it was more likely that *Mary Elizabeth* left Vera Cruz in early to mid–March and arrived in Texas later that month.[6]

Captain George Scherffius had run her into Galveston Bay either directly via San Luis Pass or the Brazos River and the connecting canal. Supporting this conclusion, General Magruder issued a special order specifically for *Mary Elizabeth* on April 26. It allowed the schooner "*Mary Elizabeth* Sheffies [George Scherffius] Master, … to pass all batteries and proceed to sea." In the 20 days since her arrival in Galveston Bay, she had completed loading one hundred bales of cotton. She had also received the "proper exemption from the Cotton Bureau."[7]

Despite having a Confederate customs clearance and the required military permit, *Mary Elizabeth* was not quite ready to depart. Four days after obtaining his clearance, Captain Scherffius' schooner was resting on the shallow bottom of Galveston Bay. The cause of her sinking was not given, but she had to be refloated. This unfortunate, but familiar circumstance kept the younger Scherffius and his schooner in Galveston Bay until late September 1864. This delay echoed the experience that *Rob Roy* endured at the Brazos the previous November. Taken together, the evidence confirms that *Mary Elizabeth* was at Galveston Bay well before Watson's arrival and refutes his claim that George Scherffius had run into Galveston Bay during the early summer of 1864.[8]

As for the other, unnamed schooners that Watson referenced, he was correct in saying that only a few made the attempt to enter or exit Galveston Bay while he was there. Curiously, Watson did not mention the schooner *Cora*. His friend, Henry Scherffius had been in Vera Cruz as captain of *Cora* at the same time as his brother George and *Mary Elizabeth*. Henry returned to Galveston Bay on the dark and cloudy evening of April 29. He evidently had been delayed in Vera Cruz for several weeks after *Mary Elizabeth*'s departure.[9]

Watson mentioned that George Scherffius was a newlywed, but he said nothing about his more recently married brother Henry. It is a puzzling omission. George had indeed just married the former Miss Catherina "Kate" Fox. The date of their marriage at Galveston was March 28, 1864, which helped confirm that he left Vera Cruz earlier that month and not in April as Consul Lane reported.[10]

The presence of a different Captain Scherffius who commanded *Cora* and not *Mary Elizabeth* probably confused Consul M.D.L. Lane's sources. Captain Henry Scherffius departed Vera Cruz on or about April 11. Henry had been so confident in his ability to sail *Cora* through the Texas blockading Fleet the previous February that he invited his friends to attend his wedding in Houston on May 5. Captain Scherffius fulfilled his boast to return to Texas from Vera Cruz with almost a week to spare. On the day of his wedding to the former Emily Branard, he made a grand appearance. He was toting a huge Mexican wedding cake that had somehow survived his voyage from Vera Cruz.[11]

In addition to *Rob Roy*, *Mary Elizabeth*, and *Cora*, there were at least three schooners in Galveston Bay awaiting favorable conditions to run the blockade in the summer of 1864. They were *W.D.S. Hyer*, *Velocity*, and *Emily*. Thomas W. House owned all three. All these vessels probably ran in during the spring, and one of them could have been the unidentified schooner that arrived on June 7. Despite Watson's claim of only one or two schooners running into Galveston Bay, no sailing vessels ran the blockade into the Bay during *Rob Roy*'s presence there. One explanation for this discrepancy may have been movements between Galveston Bay and the Brazos River via the connecting canal. The arrival of these schooners may have made it appear as if additional blockade runs into Galveston Bay were taking place.[12]

The blockading fleet did capture one sailing vessel as it tried to run the blockade in the vicinity of Galveston during this period. On July 12, USS *Penobscot* intercepted the 26-ton British-flagged schooner *James Williams* about 12 miles from the Brazos. It had departed from Tampico about two weeks earlier with a crew of four (three Swedes and a German), plus the schooner's Irish owner, C.W. Buckley.[13]

During the same period, Watson also said that two steamers entered, and one was captured trying to run into Galveston Bay. The actual count was four different steamers that made six successful inbound runs, and five outbound. The blockading fleet only managed to destroy, but not capture, the steamer *Carolina* after it left Galveston Bay as indicated in Table 4.

Table 4. Steam Blockade Runners at Galveston: Jun 1, 1864—Sep 12, 1864[14]

Steamer Name	Date Arrived	From	Date Departed	To
Susannah (Mail)	Jun 2	Havana	Jun 12	Havana
Carolina (Union, Rosita, Caroline)	Jun 9	Havana	Jun 11	Wrecked*
Susannah (Mail)	Jun 30	Havana	Jul 14	Havana
Matagorda (Alice)	Jul 6	Havana	Sep 6	Havana
Susannah (Mail)	Jul 29	Havana	Aug 12	Havana
Zephine (Frances, Francis, Marian, Zephyr, Neptune)	Sep 9	Havana	n/a†	Havana

* The U.S. Navy destroyed *Carolina* on the beach after she exited Galveston Bay.
† *Zephine* departed on Oct 10, 1864, for Havana where she changed her name to *Marian*.

When the cotton press was back in working order, Watson was anxious for a cargo of cotton and to be on his way. To avoid loading too many or too few bales of cotton, he needed the services of an expert stevedore. He had suffered the consequences of incompetent stevedores twice while at the Brazos. The first one overloaded *Rob Roy*, forcing open seams in her hull that caused her to sink. Another stevedore had improperly stowed the bales, which allowed the load to shift while underway, and created dangerous leaks. As a result of these near disasters, Watson decided to function as his own stevedore. Through a rare bit of good fortune, he discovered that one of the Irish seamen he had shipped in Havana had exactly the expertise and willing spirit that he needed.[15]

Watson marveled at Jim Hyland's skill in stowing his cargo of 198 bales of cotton. This was 52 more bales than he had on *Rob Roy*'s last run. More importantly, the schooner was not overloaded, and the cargo was appropriately distributed to avoid damaging its structural integrity while underway. Wondering why this talented man did not lend his skills to such a lucrative career, he discovered that Hyland had one serious flaw. Though normally quiet, industrious, and competent, he had a weakness for alcohol. It was not drinking, however, that laid him low in the summer of 1864. Hyland fell victim to the yellow fever epidemic. Fortunately, the symptoms did not appear until after he had loaded *Rob Roy*'s cargo. Though he only contracted a mild case, he had to remain ashore and would not be able to rejoin Watson's crew before his departure.[16]

Watson lingered several weeks in Galveston Bay, mostly in company with George Scherffius and *Mary Elizabeth*. Much of the time was spent "cruising about very much like exercising and amusement." Having scrubbed their hulls to the extent possible, Captain Scherffius schooled Watson in another inexpensive method of cleaning *Rob Roy*'s hull. When fully loaded, they would run their schooners onto the Bay's shallow banks of sand and shells at low tide. The crew then placed a kedge anchor in deeper water. As the high tide began to float the schooner, the men would set all sail, and crank *Rob Roy*'s windlass to "warp" their vessel over the shell bank and pull themselves into deeper water. As the hull slid across the bank, the shells effectively removed debris from the keel and other parts of the hull not cleaned by careening. The result was, "a marked difference in her sailing qualities."[17]

As he awaited favorable blockade-running conditions, Watson noted the presence of two steamers at the Galveston piers, probably *Matagorda* and *Susannah* (see Table 4). They were waiting for a load of compressed cotton bales to arrive from Houston. He also remarked that they were the first steamers to run the blockade into Galveston. He opined that Admiral David Glasgow Farragut's successful attack on Mobile Bay (August 5, 1864) would leave Galveston as the last viable port for blockade-running steamers. He was partially correct. Galveston would indeed become the primary blockade-running port of the Confederacy in the last few months of the war, but other steamships had already made successful runs into and out of Texas ports.[18]

As seen in Table 4, both *Susannah* and *Carolina* had entered and departed Galveston Bay in June 1864, shortly after *Rob Roy*'s arrival. As Watson lolled away the hours in Galveston Bay, *Susannah* made two round trips to Havana and was back in port for a third attempt. In addition to this recent activity, there had been other steamers that ran into and out of the Bay subsequent to the initial blockade of the Texas coast on July 2, 1861. One steamship, *Texas Ranger*, had run into Galveston Bay and three had run out, *Texas Ranger*, *General Rusk*, and *Union* (see Table 6). The steamers *General Rusk* (aka *Blanche*) and *Union* were already present in Galveston prior to the blockade.[19]

Table 5: Steam Blockade Runners at Galveston Bay, July 2, 1861–June 1, 1864

Name	Arrival	From	Departure	To	Remarks
Texas Ranger (*Ranger*)	07/07/1861	Berwick Bay	08/09/1862	Tampico	Wrecked[20]
General Rusk (*Blanche*)*	n/a	n/a	06/06/1862	Havana	Later returned to Matagorda Bay[21]
Union *	n/a	n/a	08/18/1862	Havana	Captured enroute[22]

* In port prior to the establishment of the blockade.

In late August, Watson said he got a message from his partners, the Mills Brothers. They confessed that they had been unable to sell a portion of the cargo to the government. They had to find another buyer. The letter was dated August 27, 1864, and Watson transcribed it in full for his readers. A copy of this letter does not appear in the national archives or other known university or private holdings of Mills brothers' correspondence, but it is probably authentic. According to Watson, the brothers penned a letter that said:

> Captain W., *Rob Roy*,—We have just seen Major Rhetts, of the Ordnance Department, and he refuses to purchase the cavalry swords and the Belgium muskets, so we must hold them over until some other opportunity.[23]

There were no other official records that document the claims of the Mills Brothers, but part of the letter's contents can be verified. Major Thomas G. Rhett was Chief of Ordnance and Artillery under the command of Lieutenant General E. Kirby Smith of the Trans-Mississippi Department at Shreveport, Louisiana. There is no record of Major Rhett ever being assigned to Texas, which suggests that the muskets and swords were rejected at departmental headquarters in Shreveport.[24]

Whenever the army in Texas had concerns about the viability of armaments for government use, the commanding general would organize a group of at least three qualified officers to form a Board of Survey. Their job was to assess the utility and value of the goods in question. In early 1865, General Magruder's replacement, Major General John George Walker formed a Board of Survey to evaluate a "certain lot of arms imported for the Govt. by Messrs. R.&D.G. Mills upon the Schr. *Rob Roy*." This Board of Survey did not convene until after Watson's reported second run into Galveston Bay. Although Watson did not specify the model of "Belgium muskets," some versions were better than others. They were used on both sides during the war. One of the better models was the Belgian 1842 short rifle, which suggested that Watson's particular lot of muskets was an inferior smooth-bore model.[25]

The Mills Brothers related this bit of unwelcome news about the armaments as a preface to even worse news, at least from Watson's perspective. They said that the net value of the cotton they had placed on board was $5,993.80. This total was supposedly over and above the amount they had received from the sale of the rest of *Rob Roy*'s cargo. Watson said that the balance did not take into account any sales of the inbound cargo. The Mills Brothers wanted Watson and his other partners to either pay half the amount or let them ship it all on their account. If he chose the latter option, they would merely pay freight charges and Watson would receive none of the profits. Something was not right, and Watson knew it.[26]

He directed his other partner's representative "Mr. P." (Ernest Parizot) to contact "Mr. H." [Thomas House]. Watson, like all blockade runners and businessmen in Texas, was very familiar with Thomas House. Several of Watson's friends had sailed in schooners either owned by or consigned to House & Company. Thomas W. House was a wealthy Houston businessman, owner of multiple blockade runners, and a former mayor of Houston. He had a large home in Galveston and had the confidence of General Magruder and his staff. Watson knew that he could trust Mr. House to give him good advice.[27]

House advised Ernest Parizot that "the whole thing was a right down swindle." Through his connections with the Confederate quartermaster department, he knew exactly how much money the government had paid for *Rob Roy*'s inbound cargo. Robert & David G. Mills, with the help of their business manager and nephew John Mills, were trying to take ownership of his entire load of 198 bales of cotton. The only way to cover Watson's half of this alleged financial obligation, was to sell additional ownership shares of his schooner. House advised that it was highly unlikely that *Rob Roy* would receive a permit to go to sea unless he acceded to all the Mills Brothers' demands.[28]

Watson had already gotten a customs clearance, but he had to have a military permit to pass the forts and depart Galveston Bay. The purpose of the permit was to ensure that customs duties had been paid and that there were no crew or passengers on board who were trying to avoid military service or prosecution. Watson could expect no help from his "friend" Major General John Bankhead Magruder. Almost all Texas residents, including Watson, were dismayed that Prince John was no longer in command of the Texas District. He had been ordered to Louisiana and departed Houston on August 17, 1864. This change in leadership returned Brigadier General Paul O. Hébert to temporary command until Major General John G. Walker arrived. General Walker would not take command until the day before *Rob Roy*'s departure.[29]

When Watson did not respond to the Mills Brothers' letter, he received a visit from their "manager and book-keeper, Mr. R." The Mills Brothers' emissary came onboard *Rob Roy* "with some hesitation, and seemed half ashamed of his mission." He asked Watson to pay a call on "J.M." (John Mills) in Houston. Watson refused and informed the clerk about the terms of his agreement with his bosses. The contract stipulated that R. & D.G. Mills had to provide an inbound cargo that was sufficient to cover the cost of an outbound cargo of cotton. If the cargo sale did not cover expenses, the Mills Brothers were supposed to assume ownership of the entire inbound cargo and forfeit all of their ownership interest in *Rob Roy*.[30]

Watson's "Mr. R." was Thomas Read, the bookkeeper and cashier for R. & D.G. Mills & Co. In 19th-century businesses, many bookkeepers had managerial responsibilities beyond just keeping accurate ledgers. Mr. Read had even been the nominal owner of the schooner *Eureka* (*Enriqueta*) on behalf of the Mills Brothers. This was the same schooner that fell victim to the blockading fleet when Watson's daring friend, Captain Francis Downs, sailed her out of the Brazos River in October 1863.[31]

After Thomas Read had left, Watson accelerated his timeline for departure. Jim Hyland, who was still recovering from yellow fever, sent another man to take his place with the crew. Watson got his clearance from the British consulate (Arthur Lynn). All was proceeding well, but as Thomas House had predicted, the Confederate Provost Marshal balked at giving him a permit for sea. The provost's manufactured reasons for refusal included a new requirement for having a consignee's certificate. Watson did not have the Mills Brothers' certificate and would not get one unless he agreed to their demands. The provost marshal also claimed that the government intended to press some schooners into government service to haul wood and water from the mainland to Galveston.[32]

All of these "requirements" were only required for the vessel named *Rob Roy*. Consignee certificates normally were not compulsory, and *Rob Roy* was already fully loaded. Watson's schooner was not a practical choice for Confederate logistic needs. These unnecessary bureaucratic obstacles confirmed Thomas House's prediction of permit problems due to the Mills Brothers' collusion with Confederate officials. "Captain Shaeffer" (George Scherffius) and his schooner (*Mary Elizabeth*) had already gotten a permit with no problems. Watson said that his fellow blockade runner captain and friend had gotten his "passport" the day before.[33] Once again, Watson's story did not precisely match the facts.[34]

Mary Elizabeth, the namesake of Thomas House's wife, had gotten its permit on August 16. This was 11 days prior to Watson's letter from the Mills Brothers. *Mary Elizabeth* was one of eight Thomas House-owned schooners that were preparing to run the blockade out of Texas. Five of these were in Galveston Bay (*Cora*, *W.D. Hyer*, *Velocity*, *Mary Elizabeth*, *Emily*), two were on the Brazos (*Lightfoot*, *Ann Giberson*), and one was at Sabine Pass (*Charles Russell*).[35]

Watson decided he would forego a permit and moved *Rob Roy* out of sight from the Mills Brothers' and their agents who might thwart his plan. For the past several weeks, he had been carefully surveying the wide entrance to Galveston Bay. He believed it would be relatively easy to slip past the Confederate forts even if he used the channel that hugged the coast nearest Galveston Island. He resolved to leave without full authorization on the first good breeze on a dark night. Watson never mentioned the inadvertent sinking of his friend's schooner, but said that Captain Scherffius agreed to take *Mary Elizabeth* out at the same time as Watson and *Rob Roy*. His friend had also visited Galveston and helped confirm that he wasn't being paranoid about R. & D.G. Mills & Company's spies. They were "inquiring very earnestly" concerning *Rob Roy*'s whereabouts and intentions. It was time to go.[36]

12

From Galveston to Tampico and Havana

In a rare instance of specificity, William Watson said it was September 12, 1864, when he was finally ready to run the blockade out of Galveston Bay. He had been there since June 1 awaiting the repair of the steam cotton press, the refitting of *Rob Roy*, and favorable sailing conditions. As the light of this late summer's day faded to dusk, the breeze was fresh, and he had made note of the positions of the blockading fleet. Watson had decided to take the narrow "south-west or Swash Channel" out of the bay. This shallow exit route would take him close to Galveston Island and the obscuring backdrop of land. He knew that even the low terrain would help mask *Rob Roy*'s silhouette from the watchful lookouts onboard the U.S. Navy warships lurking nearby, but in deeper water.[1]

The moon was waxing and about three-quarters full, but it must have been hidden by clouds, since Watson said that it was a dark night. *Rob Roy*'s sails were rigged in a double-reef configuration fore and aft, so that she sailed under low canvas to reduce her visual profile. Despite the proximity of both enemy gunboats and deadly breakers, *Rob Roy* and its crew bounded into the abyss. They would try their luck against this most life-threatening combination of man-made and natural hazards.[2]

As they entered the narrow channel devoid of any navigational aids, Watson spotted one and then another even larger Union gunboat through his "night-glass" telescope. The second warship was slowly maneuvering close to the breakers. To pass clear of the deadly reef, *Rob Roy* would also have to approach within a few yards of the large blockader. Watson had taken every precaution. He avoided using his binnacle compass for fear that the faint, shielded candlelight might reveal their position. He even worried about the sound of the water breaking over *Rob Roy*'s bow. At this point, there was no going back. The winds were favorable and "every breath was hushed." After a few interminable minutes, they were almost clear. The exhilaration and anxiety were palpable.[3]

Just then, "'Cock-a-leery-lou !' rang out in a loud and clear note from the hen-coop." The crew had taken aboard a "fine cock" as a pet to accompany some hens that would supply fresh eggs and poultry during their voyage. The men quickly captured the "poor chanticleer" and summarily executed and silenced the traitor. Similar humorous stories of a crowing cockerel were retold several times in blockade-running accounts. Each involved a startling surprise at the worse possible moment and a hasty execution, followed by a successful run through the blockade. Watson's familiar sea story may have had more feathers than chicken.[4]

To the crew's relief, *Rob Roy* remained undetected, and quickly vanished into the velvet folds of darkness. The adrenaline rush kept Watson awake until 0400 in the morning, when he finally retired for a brief nap. At daylight, the mate (James O'Hagan) sounded the alarm, and pointed out a large sailing vessel that was bearing down on them. For blockade runners, paranoia was a requisite for survival. The mate feared that the vessel was a Union sailing gunboat that Fred (Fred Jansen, the Swedish Cook) identified as *"John Anderson."* As previously discussed, Watson had again mis-identified the bark USS *William G. Anderson*. However, he was certain that the vessel was not a Union warship, but rather the schooner *Mary Elizabeth*. "Captain Shaeffer" (George Scherffius) had taken her out at the same night as *Rob Roy*, but she had been out of sight until the next morning.[5]

They had both passed well clear of the immediate warship threat, but the two blockade runners would not be safe until they reached Tampico. To avoid being sighted and potentially captured together, Watson maneuvered *Rob Roy* away from *Mary Elizabeth*. To pass the time, O'Hagan remarked that it was a good thing that "George" (seaman George Thompson) had not sailed with them. His superstitions would have paralyzed him. For not only was there a cat onboard, *Rob Roy* had also embarked a priest.[6]

Watson deduced that *Mary Elizabeth*'s crew had smuggled a cat aboard *Rob Roy* while both schooners were preparing to leave Galveston Bay. Watson noted that sailors believed that putting a cat ashore was sure to be followed by bad luck. Not wanting to tempt fate, the cat became a regular member of the crew. Contrary to seaman George Thompson's belief and Watson's story, most sailors considered cats to be good luck. In addition to their practical value in eliminating rodents, cats have a natural reaction to barometric pressure changes. This power led to a belief that they could predict or even control the weather. Seaman George's superstition about the cat probably had less to do with its presence than the dangerously unlucky consequences of losing the feline overboard.

The cat superstition was not the only one that was peculiar to George Thompson and *Rob Roy*'s crew. George would whistle long and loud to conger up a breeze whenever they were becalmed. This superstition had some nuances. Although a strong breeze was usually an ideal environment for a sailing vessel, unnecessary whistling might annoy King Neptune and bring on a storm. The expression "whistling for a wind" has come to mean to attempt a futile endeavor. Whistling was forbidden on many ships out of concern for coded communications among mutineers. Cooks were generally exempt from this prohibition. If the cook was whistling, he was not consuming more than his allotted share of the food.[7]

O'Hagan also commented on the presence of Father Ryan. The priest had boarded just before their departure and was bound for Havana. Watson knew that sailors believed that aboard ship, a clergyman was a "Jonah." But Father Ryan was a kind soul, willing to sleep on deck, and a paying customer to boot. Additionally, he was well known and liked by first mate O'Hagan who was once a member of Ryan's flock. Watson overcame his initial reticence and agreed to accommodate the elderly padre.[8]

The fear of having a bad luck "Jonah" on board was a long-established superstition among sailors. The belief originated with the Old Testament Biblical story about the prophet Jonah. The prophet had tried to run from God's call for him to go to the evil Kingdom of Nineveh. Instead, he sailed in the opposite direction. When a violent storm threatened to sink his boat, the sailors decided that Jonah was to blame. As soon as they threw him overboard, the sea became calm. For sailors, the theological point about the futility of opposing God's will, was of less importance than the consequences of having a Jonah onboard. Although anyone could be identified as a "Jonah," all clergymen were considered bad luck, as they were all thought to be of Jonah's ilk.[9]

Rather than a Jonah, Father Ryan ended up being a good luck charm for both William Watson and the crew of *Rob Roy*. Father Ryan privately informed Watson that O'Hagan was talking about himself and the rest of the crew when he raised the specter of George Thompson's superstitions. The sailors had gotten the notion that the devil had come on board in the form of a traitorous rooster. Even though the cock was now dead, it was an ominous omen for the rest of the voyage. Watson assured the priest that the cock had crowed just as *Rob Roy* passed over the reef and slammed into the large swells of the open Gulf. It was quite natural for the rooster to crow when it was rudely jostled awake from its roost. When the good padre explained the cause of the rooster's betrayal, the crewmen were all relieved and much amused with themselves.[10]

On about the eighth day out, Watson sighted *Mary Elizabeth* about eight miles to the east. Apparently, Captain George Scherffius did not share Watson's concern about sailing in proximity to another blockade runner. At midday, the crew made note of a large, purple-hewed circle around the sun. Rather than superstition, it was

"Crossing the Bar at Tampico in a Gale." William Watson, *Adventures of a Blockade Runner; or, Trade in Time of War*. London: Fisher Unwin, 1892, p. 220 (author's collection).

their experience that told them a heavy gale was in the offing. Even though the wind and seas were calm at that moment, they made ready for a storm. They secured all loose gear and closely reefed their sails. By 4 p.m., the sky to the north was "black as ink." In the furious storm that followed, *Rob Roy* proved to be a stout vessel. Watson vividly described how his schooner and crew narrowly averted disaster through a combination of luck and skill.[11]

As *Rob Roy* came to anchor off Tampico later that day, the crew saw nothing of George Scherffius and his schooner *Mary Elizabeth*. They were rightfully concerned about the fate of their sailing companion. Several weeks later, Watson learned from George's brother Henry that he had been lost at sea. The crew of *Rob Roy* had the last and only sighting of *Mary Elizabeth* after she departed Galveston Bay. It was presumed that she had foundered and sunk with all hands during the storm.[12]

In late October 1864, the American Consul Franklin Chase at Tampico reported the recent arrival of *Rob Roy* along with the Confederate-flagged schooner *Lilly*. Consul Chase did not immediately report *Rob Roy*'s presence to the State Department. Chase had few opportunities for timely reporting. There were no operational international underwater telegram cable connections in North America during the American Civil War. This lack of connectivity made overseas communications almost completely dependent upon seaborne postal carriers. As a result, consuls who were in relatively remote places like Tampico usually depended upon periodic mail steamer service. In this case, Franklin Chase waited until October 27, 1864, to pen his report to Assistant Secretary of State, Frederick W. Seward. He opened his

"Midnight in a Hurricane." William Watson, *Adventures of a Blockade Runner; or, Trade in Time of War*. London: Fisher Unwin, 1892, p. 211 (author's collection).

letter by summarizing political and military events related to Emperor Maximillian, the French, and the Mexican nationalists under Benito Juárez.[13]

Consul Chase then updated the blockade-running situation at Tampico:

> This port again displays a lively appearance of blockade runners. Some landing cotton, and others taking on cargoes of supplies for the coast of Texas. They sail under the Mexican, British, and Prussian flags from this port. Recently a secession vessel called the *Lily*[14] [sic], and a British vessel called the *Rob Roy*, arrived from the port of Galveston, and landed nearly 300 bales of cotton in this port for European Markets.
>
> Several vessels have lately left this port with supplies for the Texans, but I trust our ships of war will change their destination.[15]

The consul's report suggested that the Confederate-flagged *Lilly* and British-flagged *Rob Roy* were the two most recent blockade runners that had entered Tampico's port. Confederate official communications show that the 34-ton *Lilly* did not receive its permit to go to sea until October 13 and left Galveston Bay sometime before the 19th of October. However, a New Orleans correspondent reported that *Rob Roy* arrived at Tampico from Galveston on October 6 loaded with 160 bales of cotton. He also said that *Lilly* arrived at Tampico on October 21 with 115 bales. The consular and Confederate reporting confirm that *Mary Elizabeth* did not departure from Galveston Bay until the evening of September 25. These contemporary reports made it clear that Watson mis-remembered his sailing date, but correctly reported the duration of his voyage. Three other schooners had arrived at Tampico between late September and October 2 that Consul Chase did not mention. He only named the most recent arrivals that had run the blockade, *Rob Roy* and *Lilly* (see Table 6).[16]

When Watson arrived at Tampico, he reported that there were two schooners anchored off the bar awaiting entry into the port. One was from St. John, New Brunswick and the other was a larger vessel that seemed to be in ballast. She was riding high in the water and was anchored farther out. The Mexican pilots had said that they would take the larger schooner over the bar on the following morning tide. Watson figured they would have no problem with the smaller *Rob Roy*.

Regrettably for William Watson and his crew, with the new day, no pilots were in sight. It soon became apparent why. Large swells prevented the small pilot boats from making it across the bar. The heavy seas preceded another sudden storm. Watson had no choice but to ride the storm and scud into port. Like a surfer maneuvering through deadly reefs, *Rob Roy* survived a wild ride over and through the waves. The schooner from St. John was less fortunate. It escaped destruction but was dangerously grounded just before reaching the safety of the harbor. Watson said his crew helped rescue all the men from the other schooner. Its crew eventually worked the stranded vessel free after offloading some of her cargo of lumber.[17]

The Gulf of Mexico is particularly vulnerable to violent tropical depressions between late September and October. Much like the Rio Grande, the anchorage (or roadstead) off Tampico was unprotected from the elements. Contemporary sources confirmed that the area between the Rio Grande and Tampico had to endure such storms during the general period of Watson's story. On October 27, a newspaper correspondent at Bagdad on the Rio Grande reported,

The weather has been very stormy of late. On the 10th the schooner *Caroline*, Capt. Harking [sic: G.D. Hartney], from New Orleans, with an assorted cargo, while trying to cross the bar, was swept by the current on the Texas shore, and soon was a total loss.... On the 11th inst. [October 11, 1864] the brigantine *Dazzle*, Capt. Cook, just arrived from New Orleans, parted her cables [broke loose from her anchor chain] and went on the breakers and soon became a wreck.[18]

Similarly, the American captain of the U.S.-flagged *Ferdinand* belatedly reported the loss of his 5-ton coastal sloop on October 21, 1864. *Ferdinand* had arrived at Tampico in late August from the Rio Grande. At that time, U.S. forces had just withdrawn from their occupation of Brownsville. They retained a tiny toehold on a sandy spit of land between Brazos Santiago and the mouth of the Rio Grande known as Boca Chica. The sloop *Ferdinand* left Tampico on October 11, for Brazos Santiago, Texas. This intended port of call indicated that the sloop was under contract to the U.S. government to provide fresh provisions for the Army troops there. Consul Chase later learned that *Ferdinand* "beat about the Gulf, until the 21st of said month [October 1864], when she was wrecked about three miles north of Tampico Bar."[19]

When *Rob Roy* was safely at anchor on the Pánuco River that flows by the port city of Tampico, Watson took time to give thanks to the Almighty with Father Ryan. He also paused to rest his crew and treat everyone to a fine dinner in town. He then sold most of his cotton, but said he kept 25 bales of inferior quality cotton as ballast for the cruise to Havana. The early sale also served as a form of insurance. He wanted the assurance of having funds in his account in the event they encountered an overly zealous American warship captain on the way to Havana. The blockading fleet would be tempted to seize *Rob Roy* and himself as a habitual offender of the blockade. Despite Consul Chase's report, later events would cast doubt on this assertion about landing most of his cotton in Tampico.[20]

Things were going reasonably well in Tampico, until one of *Rob Roy*'s crewmembers got into a bit of a scrape. Watson had previously named his first mate (second in command) on this cruise as Hagan (James O'Hagan). But when he described the exploits of this slightly inebriated and considerably boisterous crewman in Tampico, he does not mention a name. He only describes him as the "mate." The mate had run afoul of the local authorities as he celebrated *Rob Roy*'s success with some French soldiers who were there in support of the ill-fated Emperor Maximillian. After a few libations, the mate started boasting of the prowess of his captain and crew in getting their schooner over the bar in a storm without the help of the timid, bureaucratic Mexican pilots. The pilots and local denizens in attendance naturally took offence and a general melee ensued, resulting in the mate's arrest.[21]

Watson said his consignees "Messrs G.," intervened on the mate's behalf and got him released. "Messrs. G." was probably a reference to George Oetling, of the large banking and commercial firm, Droege, Oetling & Co. Oetling was the Prussian vice consul in Matamoros. His company had offices in Tampico and was sometimes referred to as George Oetling & Co.[22]

The reason Watson did not mention the name of the mate may have been because *Rob Roy*'s mate was no longer James O'Hagan. In fact, O'Hagan was not

Bank's expedition, Sketch of Landing at Brazos [Santiago], Texas, Nov. 21, 1863 (The Miriam and Ira D. Wallach Division of Art, Prints and Photographs: Print Collection, The New York Public Library).

even a member of Watson's crew. Although he claimed that his passenger, Father Ryan and "All of my crew again joined the vessel" for their voyage from Tampico to Havana, one man did not. The missing crewman was one of his favorites, the 44-year-old Irishman, James O'Hagan. His former first mate had joined the crew of *Carrie Mair* as a cook. The shipping papers show that O'Hagan transferred from *Rob Roy* to *Carrie Mair* on October 15. He was a replacement for an unnamed man who had died. The appearance of O'Hagan's name on *Carrie Mair*'s shipping articles was not a clerical error. When the U.S. Navy captured *Carrie Mair* on November 30 for trying to run into Matagorda Bay, O'Hagan was onboard. His deposition was one of those submitted as evidence at the admiralty court in New Orleans.[23]

In addition to *Rob Roy* and *Carrie Mair*, at least eight other suspected blockade-running vessels were confirmed at Tampico from late September through October 1864 (see Table 6). Three of them had come from Montreal, Canada (British North America). None were registered at, or cleared from St. John, New Brunswick, but it was likely that the last port of call for at least one of them was at St. John. All three had cargos of lumber, but one arrived several days ahead of the other two. Since *Carrie Mair* left Havana for Tampico in early October, she was the most likely match for the Canadian schooner that rode the storm about the same time as *Rob Roy*. The two schooners were linked in one other important detail. James O'Hagan signed *Carrie Mair*'s shipping articles as a new crewmember on October 15, 1864. The articles showed that he had most recently served aboard *Rob Roy*. These key details place Watson's actual timeline for *Rob Roy*'s voyage to Tampico about two weeks later than he claimed.[24]

There were numerous other inconsistencies between Watson's story and the historical record concerning his departure from Galveston and arrival at Tampico. Once again, the gist of his sea story was true, but many of the particulars were not. He did leave Galveston Bay for Tampico in the latter part of 1864, and experienced a severe gale during a voyage of about nine days duration. The schooner *Mary Elizabeth* under George Scherffius departed Galveston during the same time frame, and was lost at sea. Watson was able to enter Tampico with a load of cotton the same day as a schooner from Canada and he stayed there for a few days before sailing to Havana. All this is true.

Just about everything else in his story was incorrect. Rather than leaving Galveston Bay about September 12, 1864, *Rob Roy* and *Mary Elizabeth* sailed about two weeks later. Watson arrived at Tampico on October 6, but the schooner *Carrie Mair* probably arrived a few days afterward, not at the same time as *Rob Roy*. She had originated from Montreal, Canada and made a brief stop at Havana, departing on October 3. A schooner simply could not make the trip from Havana to Tampico in only three or even four days. Additionally, *Carrie Mair*'s captain signed *Rob Roy*'s mate, James O'Hagan, to serve as a cook. Neither *Carrie Mair* nor the other two schooners from Canada were from St. John and James O'Hagan obviously did not rejoin Watson's crew in Tampico.[25]

Finally, Watson related a humorous story about his friend John Curry who stopped by to wish him *bon voyage* as *Rob Roy* was about to leave for Havana. Captain Curry had helped Watson get provisions for his crew, including perfectly good barrels of meat that profiteering U.S. Army officers had marked as "Condemned." Watson at first thought he was being swindled, but discovered that the only scoundrels in this transaction were the U.S. Army quartermasters. These supply officers were profiteering at the taxpayer's expense.[26]

Captain Curry was preparing for his own voyage into Texas when Watson first arrived at Tampico. He had already left the port when *Rob Roy* sailed. Curry sailed from Tampico on October 20 in the schooner *Lone* (previously *Cuca*) and by Watson's own timeline and the historical record, *Rob Roy* departed for Havana a month or two afterwards. Watson's story about Captain Curry wishing him well as *Rob Roy* began its voyage to Havana, could not have been true. By November 6, Captain John Curry was a prisoner of the U.S. Navy and on his way to the admiralty court at New Orleans.[27]

Table 6: Sailing Vessels at Tampico with *Rob Roy*, Late September–November 1864

Name	Type	Flag	Tons	Arr	From	Dep	To
Ferdinand[28]	Sloop	US	5	08/30	Brownsville	10/11	Brazos Santiago
Cuca (*Lone*)[29]	Schr	UK	35	09/10	Brazos River	10/20	Havana (Brazos)
Antoinetta (*Antoinette*)[30]	Schr	Mex	Unk	09/28	New Orleans	10/26	New Orleans
Anne Sophia[31] (*Anne Sheppard*)	Schr	UK	91	10/01	Brazos River	10/28	Havana
Pet[32] (*Phenix*, *Mary P. Burton*)	Schr	Prus	67	10/01	Havana	11/15	Galveston
Rob Roy[33]	Schr	UK	39	10/06	Galveston	11/05	Havana
Carrie Mair (*Carrie Muir*)[34]	Schr	UK	56	10/13	Montreal via Havana	11/10	Havana (Matagorda)
Lilly[35]	Schr	CSA	34	10/21	Galveston	12/21	Texas
Lady Hurley (*Lote Hurley*)[36]	Schr	UK	51	10/28	Montreal	11/15	Havana
A.C. Dana[37]	Schr	UK	69	10/28	Montreal	Unk	Matamoros

Watson's sojourn at Tampico was a brief one. When *Rob Roy* got underway in the first week of November, he set a course to the east northeast. Rather than hugging the coast of Mexico along the Yucatan Peninsula like he had on the previous voyage, Watson said that he headed toward the middle of the Gulf in hopes of avoiding capture. He succeeded in avoiding hostile warships, but found stormy weather instead. After five days at sea, he and his crew battled a squall. The gale lasted five days and deposited him about 40 miles northwest of Cape San Antonio, Cuba. From there, it was another three days to Havana.[38]

At the onset of the gale, Watson told another story about Father Ryan and James O'Hagan. The crew was terribly busy reefing sails and battening down the hatches. In the midst of frenetic preparations to weather the storm, Father Ryan was "offering his assistance, but on the whole, very much in the way." To make him feel useful while keeping him safely out of the way, O'Hagan handed the priest a rope with instructions to hold it taut until the sails were set "and everything got right." The story may have been true, but it could not have happened when Watson said it did. James O'Hagan was on board *Carrie Mair* at the time. He was not aboard *Rob Roy*.[39]

Contemporary sources do not give the exact date of *Rob Roy*'s arrival at the bustling Havana harbor, but according to Watson's sequence of events it would have been in mid–November. Having survived the travails of the Gulf, William Watson now had to deal with the land-sharks of the Cuban waterfront and prepare for another run through the blockading gauntlet.[40]

13

Phantom Voyages Part 1

From Havana to Texas

Watson's first order of business after setting *Rob Roy*'s anchor in the harbor was to consign his cargo of 25 bales of cotton. He called on "Messrs. A." who were his former consignees, Avendaño Brothers (Hermanos) & Co. They soon had his cargo of cotton offloaded onto lighters and taken to market. It is at this point that Watson's tale runs afoul of the historical record. A Havana newspaper dutifully reported *Rob Roy*'s arrival from Tampico with a full load of cotton. Watson, on the other hand, said that he sold most of the cotton at Tampico and only carried 25 bales of inferior quality, mostly to serve as ballast for the voyage. He had supposedly reshipped the other bales on the periodic mail steamer for the European market.[1]

During the year 1864, the 308-ton steamship *Barcelona* provided the only regularly scheduled steamship service to and from Tampico. It would typically leave Havana on the eighth of each month for Vera Cruz, Sisal, and Tampico and return three weeks later. During the October circuit, the Spanish-flagged *Barcelona* arrived at Havana on November 28 with a total of 57 bales of cotton, but none of that cotton originated from Tampico.[2]

Instead of reshipping most of his cotton and bobbing around the Gulf due to *Rob Roy*'s light load, it appears that he arrived in Havana with a full load of cotton. Havana's most prominent newspaper, *Diario de la Marina* (Marine Journal), had recorded *Rob Roy*'s cargo that had arrived from Tampico on December 14, 1864. The British-flagged schooner had a full load of 200 bales of cotton. Although *Rob Roy*'s arrival date was not listed, it would have been on December 12 or 13th. This glaring contradiction could be most generously explained if Watson simply mis-remembered the details of this voyage to Havana. He had also included James O'Hagan as part of his crew. However, the historical record proved that Watson's favorite Irishman Hagan (James O'Hagan) was onboard *Carrie Mair* out of Tampico. He was no longer a member of *Rob Roy*'s crew. It made sense that Watson also transposed colorful elements of earlier adventures into this portion of a vaguely remembered voyage. The reason for this apparent confusion was not poor memory on his part as will become clear in a later chapter.[3]

Some of the particulars of his journey did not occur as told; much of his story is true. There was no doubt that Watson arrived at Havana from Tampico in the latter part of 1864 with a cargo of cotton onboard his British schooner *Rob Roy*. Another reassuring event occurred in Cuba that affirmed one of Watson's more offhand comments about the tragic demise of the disappearance of George Scherffius and the entire crew of *Mary Elizabeth*. He said that Henry Scherffius, "afterwards called upon me in Havana to get the last and only information" about the fate of his brother.[4]

Henry Scherffius and his wife Kate ("Enrique Scherffius et senora") had arrived at Havana on November 29, 1864, on the steamer *Barcelona* from Vera Cruz, Mexico. The steamer may have touched at Tampico, but there was no opportunity during this brief stop to meet with William Watson. Since Father Ryan traveled to Havana as a passenger onboard *Rob Roy* instead of the more commodious passenger steamer, weather probably prevented passengers from boarding or disembarking from the mail steamer at Tampico. The timing of Henry Scherffius' arrival at Havana corroborated Watson's claim that Henry called upon him there. Scherffius' first priority was to uncover information about his brother George, but that was not the only reason he was in Havana. In January 1865, Scherffius assumed command of the new blockade-running steamer *Lark* and made multiple successful runs from Havana to Galveston and back. He reappeared later on as "Captain S." in William Watson's sea story as the true captain of the blockade runner *Pelican*.[5]

Watson had other reunions in Havana. The one he enjoyed least was his meeting with his partner "R.M." (Robert Mills). To his surprise, Robert told Watson that he had no knowledge of the underhanded maneuverings of his brother David or nephew John. He vowed to uphold his original agreement of a 50–50 split. He also provided a full invoice of cargo for another run through the blockade. Watson also agreed to allot some space at no charge to the Confederate agent Major Charles Helm for military supplies. With the addition of some seed potatoes for Texas farmers, Mills and Watson agreed to continue their partnership.[6]

Although Watson backed off his initial demand to buy back the Mills Brothers' interest in *Rob Roy*, he insisted on consigning the goods to another firm. Watson at first suggested "Mr. H. in Galveston (Thomas House), but Robert Mills balked at that idea. The Mills Brothers were 'not very friendly' with this specific competitor. Instead, they settled on 'a Mr. C. in Galveston.'" This was a reference to Matthias Dayton Conklin of M.D. Conklin & Co. who had successfully managed *Rob Roy*'s cargo in the past.[7]

When asked, Watson said that he needed to get his schooner out of the water to clean and paint the hull, make a few repairs, and obtain a new foresail. He estimated that he would be ready for sea in about two weeks. He noted that all the Confederacy's Atlantic ports were either "captured or closely invested," and that Mobile had been captured as well. These Union successes left Galveston as the "chief available port for 'blockade-running enterprise.'"[8]

As an example of this increased use of Galveston, Watson mentioned that two steamers had recently arrived with cargos of cotton. A third was captured. He was probably referring to *Luna* and *Maria*. Both steamers arrived at Havana with cotton from Galveston on November 5. The captured steamer was most likely *Susannah* (November 27, 1864). She had departed Galveston for Havana earlier that month, but took the circuitous route along the coast before being caught just north of the Yucatan Peninsula, not far from Cuban waters.[9]

Watson said these changing circumstances led to a debate among blockade-running speculators about which type of vessel was the better investment: schooners or steamers. Schooners cost less and had lower individual risk of ruinous loss, but they could not carry as many cotton bales, were slower, and more vulnerable to the elements. Steamers were faster and carried larger loads. On the other hand, they were much more expensive to buy and operate and therefore were a higher risk investment, despite the potentially higher rewards. Another drawback to sending steamers to Galveston was the lack of coal in Texas. Runners had to carry enough coal for a round trip which limited cargo space. Lack of sufficient coal often required the captain to divert to Mexican ports before proceeding to Havana.[10]

In addition to his important business concerns related to blockade running, Watson took time to observe and comment on the social condition of the Cuban people and their Spanish colonial overlords. His discourse helped explain the counterintuitive popularity of the pro-slavery Southern cause. This affinity was true for the island's business class and general population alike. The favoritism among the businessmen of Havana was easy to understand. As a major entrepot for blockade running, the port city's economy was booming. The affections of the lower classes also hinged on smaller scale finances.

Watson made note of how the government strictly controlled and regulated street panhandlers. The only day they could solicit for money was on Saturday and each had a separate area that they could exclusively stake out as their own. One elderly lady said that she had been at the same station for 11 years. Since blockade running had commenced out of Havana, her daily take had doubled. Due to the kindness of the blockade runners, "she prayed for their success."[11]

Another example of grass roots support for the Confederates came from the "able-bodied poor" who got licenses to act as *"Bilaterias"* to sell lottery tickets. To illustrate the situation, Watson cited the example of a fellow Texas blockade runner named Bill Flagg. According to Watson, Captain Bill had assumed command of Dave McClusky's former schooner (*Stingaree*) and sailed it into Tampico about two days after *Rob Roy* had departed from that port. After delivering *Stingaree* to Tampico, Watson said Flagg caught a steamer to Havana.[12]

Captain Bill Flagg's real name was William H. Fleigh. Captain Fleigh received his permit to proceed to sea with *Stingaree* on September 30, 1864. That was the same day as the schooners *Flash* and the previously mentioned *Lilly*. The 34-ton *Lilly* finally received its permit to leave Galveston Bay for Tampico on October 13 and *Stingaree* received hers the next evening.[13]

Flagg was skeptical at first, but discovered that he had won a prize of $500. That money was soon spent, but not before the blockade runner remembered the person who had sold him the ticket. Instead of the normal one-dollar gratuity, Flagg gave the man two ounces of gold. The man was "astonished and overwhelmed with gratitude" and gushed about how generous the "Americanos" were.[14]

One of Watson's unidentified crewmen who had joined the crew at Tampico invested his wages in lottery tickets. He too was a lucky winner. But he may not have been as generous as Captain Bill Flagg, for the crewman's luck was short-lived. According to Watson, the man bought a part interest in a blockade runner and was onboard the schooner when it was captured shortly after leaving port. There were four schooners captured between late–1864 and early–1865 that were candidates for Watson's story. However, the historical record does not provide enough detail to indicate which of them might have been owned, at least in part, by the sailor of Watson's tale.[15]

Other than this temporarily lucky seaman and "Fred the Swede" (Frederick Jansen), Watson said the rest of his crew reshipped for another voyage to Galveston. Jansen had been *Rob Roy*'s cook and steward. He had saved enough money to return to his home in Sweden where he intended to open a restaurant.[16]

Watson then used five pages to describe the plight of former crewman, Jim Hyland and his wife in considerable detail. Hyland had remained in Galveston to recover from a bout with yellow fever and was no longer a member of *Rob Roy*'s crew. An Irish woman had been loitering about Havana's wharves watching Watson's every move and following him around the city at a distance. His crew informed him that the woman was Jim Hyland's wife. She was seeking a portion of the sailor's back pay that she knew was due to him. She hoped to confront her husband when he contacted Watson for his pay. She wanted to lay her hands on some of it before Hyland either spent it all on alcohol or wasted it on a band of "land-sharks and sea-lawyers." These instigators were Hyland's constant companions.[17]

Jim Hyland had made his way back to his new home in Cuba on another blockade runner. He and Mrs. Hyland had fled to the island soon after U.S. forces occupied New Orleans. The couple had taken up residence in Havana. Hyland eventually staggered onto *Rob Roy* seeking his back pay and bonus. He was in an advanced state of inebriation, but the law and protocol required Watson to hand over the entire amount to the sailor. He was unable to directly assist Hyland's neglected spouse. Watson did allow the woman to come on board *Rob Roy*, which gave her the opportunity to snatch some of the money away from her drunken husband. After chasing her around the deck, Hyland was aghast when she circled around the raised cabin to capture even more coins that had been laid on its roof. After this bit of sport and nautical justice, the couple vanished bickering down the city streets. Watson confidently made preparations for getting underway.[18]

It was early December and blockade-running conditions were ideal. The nights were long and dark, the winds were steady, and *Rob Roy* had a full crew. Watson identified one of the replacements for his two missing crewmen as "Charlie." He was experienced hand at blockade running who had been in the U.S. Navy with the blockading fleet.[19]

Rob Roy was shipshape; the mail and cargo were onboard and stowed away. Watson then went into considerable detail about his cargo that was in great demand in wartime Texas. The schooner was deeply laden with about 25 tons of bar iron, an assortment of ironmongery, several crates of earthenware, general goods such as stationary, tea, coffee, groceries, and about 40 barrels of potatoes for seed. Major Charles Helm had provided "about thirty bales of army blankets, tent cloth, and army clothing," for the Confederate government. Watson opined that there were "one or two kegs of powder packed in the heart of each bale of blankets that were not listed on the bills of lading." He also had a "lot of furnace bars for the transport steamers." Steamships had to frequently replace the furnace bars (or firebars) in their boilers. These metal bars were closely spaced like grates to support lumps of hot coals and allowed the spent ash to pass through to the bottom.[20]

Contemporary archival sources were silent about the date of *Rob Roy*'s departure from Havana. Watson only said that he cleared for Matamoros in the first days of December. There were a few gaps in the newspaper reporting of the comings and goings of vessels at Havana in the second week of December. However, Havana's *Diario de la Marina* newspaper archives for the last week of November and first week of the December 1864, are complete and there was no mention of *Rob Roy* in the usual columns showing outbound maritime cargos, clearances, and departures.[21]

As the Cuban shore faded from view, Watson said he set his course for 20 miles east of Galveston, as he had done before. He sighted nothing until the sixth day out when he was already near the near the coast of Texas. The lookout spotted a sail about four miles distant to the eastward.[22] She was larger than *Rob Roy* and some of the crew supposed her to be the schooner *Emma*. Watson said that she had left Havana about two days before *Rob Roy*. She was a new vessel on her first blockade-running attempt. Watson, of course, did not like to be near other blockade runners. He reasoned that she might be a prize headed to New Orleans. Since she was under full sail, he thought it more likely that the schooner was running from a gunboat. She was. The warship was seven miles away when *Roy Roy*'s crew sighted her.[23]

Watson said the gunboat soon altered its course to give chase to *Rob Roy*. Watson again mentioned James Hagan (O'Hagan) as his crew set the topmast staysail to gain more speed. However, his alleged conversation with O'Hagan was not possible. O'Hagan had not been aboard *Rob Roy* since October 15, 1864, when he joined the crew of *Carrie Mair* as her cook. By December, O'Hagan was in New Orleans giving his deposition to an admiralty court judge. He had been aboard *Carrie Mair* when she was captured trying to run into Matagorda Bay from Tampico while *Rob Roy* was still in Havana.[24]

Another problem with Watson's sea story was that there is no record of a schooner or any other vessel at Havana during the last two months of 1864, with a name or part of a name that approximated "*Emma*." Nor were there any good candidates among the schooners captured in the Western Gulf of Mexico during the latter part of 1864. The U.S. blockading fleet did, however, intercept two schooners off the coast of Texas that departed Havana just prior to *Rob Roy*. Either one could have been headed for New Orleans from the vicinity of Galveston under control of Union prize crews during the time of Watson's story.

One was the British-flagged *Alabama*. The schooner had been built at Brooklyn, New York, in 1859, and arrived at Havana from Nassau in April 1864. She cleared for Matamoros and sailed from Havana on November 30. Her true destination was Galveston Bay. She was making her first attempt to run the blockade and was slightly larger than *Rob Roy*. The difference in their respective tonnage would not have been perceptible at a distance (*Rob Roy*: 48 tons; *Alabama*: 52-tons). *Alabama*'s maiden attempt to run the blockade ended in failure when the U.S.S. *Chocura* captured her on December 7, 1864, just off San Luis Pass. A prize crew took charge of her and headed for New Orleans on the same evening as her capture.[25]

Another candidate was the British-flagged schooner *Julia*. She originated from New York and sailed out of Havana on Nov 28th. Like the schooner *Alabama*, she cleared for Matamoros, only to be captured by the gunboat *Chocura* seven days later when 43 miles from Velasco. *Julia*'s captain pleaded that he had been driven off course by foul weather to no avail. Also, like *Alabama*, *Julia* was sent to New Orleans on the same day as her capture and the admiralty court quickly condemned them both. She measured 73 tons and fit Watson's description of being larger than *Rob Roy*. She was also making her first blockade-running attempt.[26]

Julia, however, did not fit Watson's description as a new vessel. The schooner was built in Maryland, and sailed under the name *Hewlett* for about seven years until September 1864, when she was sold and renamed *Julia*. Given their circumstances, locations, and timing, either *Alabama* or *Julia* could have been Watson's "*Emma*." However, the lack of documented evidence and several contradictions suggest that the whole story was a fabrication.

Watson noted that there was "no moon" on the evening of their sixth day out from Havana. If he had truly sailed on the 1st or 2nd of December, he would have been referring to the evening of the 7th or 8th. In another blow to Watson's credibility during this voyage, the new moon phase in December 1864 did not occur until two days after Christmas. The December moon was full on the 13th and nearly so from the 9th through the 16th. According to Watson's timeline, the moon was at about the first quarter and waxing, making for a relatively bright evening. Watson said the night was clear, adding more doubt about the already dubious story of his second voyage to Galveston.[27]

Two days after his escape from the gunboat, Watson said he ran into Galveston Bay using the same tactics as before, but with less dramatic tension. He observed that there had been "several steamers in Galveston in the past month or two, but we brought the latest news by ten days." For this statement to be true, there should have been no arrivals at Galveston prior to May 9 that left Havana after November 20, 1864.[28]

As Watson claimed, there were several steamers that ran into Galveston from Havana in November and early December of 1864. Those arrivals could have affirmed some of Watson's story. The best candidates were *Zephine*, *Maria*, and *Luna*. The steamer *Zephine* (sometimes identified as *Frances*, *Zephyr*, *Francis Marion*, or *Neptune*) cleared for Belize on November 23 and arrived at Galveston six days later. *Zephine* had departed Havana about eight days prior to Watson and was tied up to a Galveston pier before *Rob Roy*'s departure from Havana.[29]

The next steamer to leave Havana for Galveston in late November 1864, was *Maria*, the former passenger steamship operating between Newport and Providence, Rhode Island, as *Montpelier* (*Maria*). She cleared for Belize on November 25 and like *Zephine*, probably departed for Galveston the same day. Five days later she was at Galveston on about the same day that *Rob Roy* supposedly departed Havana.[30]

The final steamer that fits within Watson's story timeline was *Luna* (sometimes reported as "*Lunar*"). According to the U.S. Consul at Havana and newspaper accounts, *Luna* cleared for Belize, but headed for Galveston on December 1 or 2nd. Unlike *Zephine* and *Maria*, the Havana paper reported *Luna*'s sailing date.[31]

Given the omissions in the newspaper accounts for *Zephine* and *Maria*, it was possible that the reporter also neglected to report *Rob Roy*'s departure. However, each of the three steamers (*Luna*, *Zephine*, and *Maria*) were mentioned numerous times as loading and preparing to sail in both the Havana newspapers and consular reports. *Rob Roy* was not mentioned at all, which adds further doubt about this voyage of Watson and *Rob Roy*. Additionally, each of the three steamer blockade runners left within a 10-day interval prior to Watson's departure and all arrived at Galveston prior to *Rob Roy*. These inconvenient facts refute Watson's claim that he arrived with "the latest news by ten days."[32]

Another clearly false claim was Watson's statement that he spoke directly to "Commodore Smith" at Galveston. A Marine Department steamer under Leon Smith's command had reportedly approached too close to *Rob Roy*. It carelessly snapped the schooner's boom (the spar or pole along the bottom of the sail that attached to the mainmast). Watson needed a replacement. Commodore Leon Smith allegedly spoke to Watson and gave him a requisition for a replacement boom from the Transportation Department's stores. The part had been stripped from the captured USS *Harriet Lane*. Earlier in the year, this former U.S. Navy gunboat had been converted into a blockade runner and renamed *Lavinia*. Watson had noted its arrival at Havana back in May 1864, where it stayed for the duration of the war.[33]

It certainly was true that the Texas Marine Department was repurposing equipment salvaged from *Harriet Lane*, but it was not possible for Leon Smith to have issued the order. The former Governor's brother, Henry S. Lubbock, had relieved Leon Smith as commander of the Texas Marine Department in August 1864. Commodore Smith was no longer at Galveston in December of 1864.[34]

In 1863, Leon Smith had concocted a secret "scheme" to acquire a warship that could prey on Union commerce. Charles Stillman, Richard King, José San Román, and four others had signed an agreement to support the effort in South Texas. Mifflin Kenedy was Smith's "authorized agent" in Brownsville and got financial subscriptions from sympathetic citizens in the area. By late summer of 1864, Leon Smith was back in Matamoros. He was on his way to Havana, and perhaps to Liverpool. It was time to put the plan into motion. Smith's orders were to buy and take command of a blockade runner or gunboat.[35]

After leaving his position with the Marine Department, Commodore Smith was at the Rio Grande until early November 1864. He was busy creating mischief among Union transport steamers sailing out of Matamoros. He organized and funded a series of audacious captures of Union merchant vessels as they left the Rio Grande. Having set those plans in motion, Leon Smith was ready to execute his own operation. Leon Smith arrived at Havana with his wife in early November 1864. The misfortunes of war short-circuited his more ambitious plans. Smith ended up staying in Havana and signing on as a pilot for the new steam blockade runner *Wren*. He would make three runs into Galveston onboard *Wren*. The first departed Havana on the last day of January 1865. Her third and final blockade run to Galveston began from

Havana on April 29. Leon Smith was onboard once again as a passenger/pilot, but was accompanied by his wife. Commodore Smith was still very active, but his absence from Galveston and the Texas Marine Department in December 1864, meant that Watson's claim about meeting him there was not true.[36]

While at Galveston, Watson reported that he took the usual steps of contacting the British Consul, offloading his cargo, and acquiring another load of cotton. Due to the number of steamers now running into Galveston, the supply of steam-compressed bales was limited. He was wary of another long delay if he waited for optimal-sized, 500-pound bales. Watson had to accept bales that had been mechanically compressed. They were about twice the size of those compacted by the steam press. As a result of their increased size, Watson said he was only able to take on board 145 full bales and a few half bales of cotton.[37]

Commodore Leon Smith (courtesy Rosenberg Library, Galveston, Texas).

Watson said, "General Magruder was not in Galveston at the time." While this statement is true, it is also a bit misleading. The general's absence from Galveston was common since Magruder's base of operations was in Houston. He was rarely in Galveston for any length of time. In this case, not only was John Bankhead Magruder not in town, he was not even in Texas. He was no longer in command of the district. Major General John G. Walker had taken his place in mid–August 1864, when Magruder received orders to take over the Arkansas District. General Magruder would not return to Texas for another seven months.[38]

There was only one historical reference to *Rob Roy* being in Texas between late 1864 and early 1865, in the Texas letters, orders, and newspapers of the period. On January 3, 1865, Major General Walker ordered the formation of a board of survey to determine

> whether or not a certain lot of arms [that were] imported for the Govt. by Messrs. R.&D.G. Mills upon the Schr. *Rob Roy* are serviceable. If found so and to the interest of the Govt. to purchase; an estimate of their value will be made and accompany the report.[39]

Despite the timing of this order, *Rob Roy*'s cargo of arms had nothing to do with Watson's claim that he ran into Galveston in December of 1864. By his own account, he carried no guns on the December voyage. The guns that General Walker referenced were the "Belgian muskets" that were part of his cargo delivered to the Confederate Army in June 1864. They were also the same guns that the Mills Brothers had been unable to sell. Watson had delivered those guns to the local ordnance officer, Captain Hugh Scott. Now, six months later, Captain Scott was one of three officers appointed to assess the utility and value of the same muskets that officials in Shreveport had rejected.[40]

There were other incidents and events that Watson said occurred in Galveston while he was there that cannot be verified. Among them was his claim that his partner and consignee, "Mr. C.," was in Galveston. Two months after Watson had run the blockade out of the Brazos, his partner M.D. Conklin departed Galveston on the steamer *Alice* (aka *Matagorda*). To maximize its chances of escape, *Alice* left at the same time as *Lavinia* (formerly *Harriet Lane*) and *Isabel*. Despite this tactic, the USS *Huntsville* greeted them with an iron hailstorm of 109 cannon balls. To increase her speed, *Alice* had to jettison 300 to 350 bales of cotton as the captain increased speed by pushing her boiler to the limit. Under cover of darkness, they managed to limp into Vermillion Bay, Louisiana, to repair their boiler. Despite running out of fuel, Conklin and *Alice* made it safely to Havana in early May. Conklin and his friends found lodging at the luxurious Hotel de Inglaterra where they lived in "grand style." Watson had noted the arrival of *Matagorda* (*Alice*), but made no mention of his partner Conklin. There was no record of when, or if, Conklin returned to Galveston before December 1864.[41]

Another event that contemporary records cannot confirm was the presence of the blockade runner captain Bill Flagg (or Bill Fleigh) and the practical joke he played on Watson. Flagg was supposed to have told Watson that he could get a new boom for *Rob Roy* from Captain Bricktop at the Transport office. It turned out that the red-haired captain's name was not "Bricktop" and he detested the mocking nick-name. Watson's narrative did not disclose the man's real name, only identifying him as "Captain B."[42]

There were several officers who were involved with managing transport steamers, but only one had a surname beginning with the letter "B." The Chief Quartermaster for the District of Texas had been Major Benjamin Bloomfield, but Watson had met him before. He would have known that his name was not "Bricktop." By mid–November 1864, the Major had been relieved of his duties and had gone to Havana. The 39-year-old Bloomfield probably returned to Galveston in December 1864. He came back to retrieve his wife and six young children and return to Havana where he stayed until after the war ended.[43]

Until this chapter of Watson's story, contemporary sources had confirmed every one of his seven voyages on *Rob Roy*. There were omissions, exaggerations, and other lapses that could be chalked up to incomplete records, a faulty memory, or hubris. The late 1864 voyage from Havana to Galveston was the only one, up to this point, that contemporary sources did not verify. In fact, the evidence that does exist contradicts this part of his story. People like James O'Hagan and Leon Smith simply were not present at the places and times Watson claimed. His descriptions of the moon phases and associated arrival dates, and the other vessels he encountered were contradictory and inaccurate.

On the surface, William Watson's account of this voyage appears to be a figment of his vivid imagination and skill as storyteller. If this chapter was, indeed, just an entertaining work of fiction, the historical record should and does reveal enough of the truth to sort out what really happened to William Watson and *Rob Roy* in these last chaotic months of the Civil War. He had more adventurous tales to tell. Having gone off on a fictional tangent, he had to bring his story back to a logical, but believable ending.

14

Phantom Voyages
Part 2

Galveston to Vera Cruz and Havana

As usual, Watson was eager to run the blockade when conditions were ideal. He did not say when he left Galveston, but he did leave a clue. After loading his cargo of cotton, and securing *Rob Roy*'s customs clearance and permission to pass the forts, a favorable breeze began to blow during a dark and cloudy night. He said that it was just a "few days after the new moon." This phase of the moon placed Watson's intended date of departure close to New Year's Eve, December 31, 1864.[1]

Confederate records and all other archival sources make no mention of *Rob Roy* receiving a clearance or permit for sea during this general timeframe. The frustratingly incomplete Confederate records could be the reason for this omission, but there is a simpler explanation. Despite William Watson's claims, *Rob Roy* was probably not in Texas at all in the late fall and early winter of 1864. The Trans-Mississippi Department's Foreign Cotton Bureau ledgers show six different schooners as having cleared Galveston loaded with cotton for Havana in December 1864, and January 1865. *Rob Roy* was not one of them. For example, the schooner *Josephine* ran out of Galveston from San Luis Pass on December 28, but the U.S. blockading fleet captured her soon afterwards.[2]

If Watson had been at Galveston as claimed, he almost certainly would have mentioned the case of the schooner *Belle* (formerly *Gipsey* and *Zouave*). She had been preparing to run the blockade with a load of cotton after obtaining 91 pressed bales of cotton. When the fog lifted on the morning of December 28, she was ashore about four miles from Bolivar Point. The captain was not aboard at the time. He was ashore making final arrangements to make a run. There was some speculation in Galveston about whether her five-man crew had deserted or had fallen victim to a U.S. Navy cutting out expedition. The Captain of the USS *Virginia* after confirmed his role in planning and executing the capture of *Belle* from under the noses of the Confederate forts and guard ships. If Watson had truly been preparing to depart at the time and location as he claimed, *Rob Roy* just as easily could have been the target of the Union expedition.[3]

Watson said he cleared for Vera Cruz rather than for Havana at the request of his partners. He set his course out of the Bay by way of the "Swash Channel," the route that ran closest to Galveston Island. A heavy gale was blowing, and the sound of the breakers muffled any noises emanating from *Rob Roy*. As they approached the mouth of the channel, the clouds parted. The crew could see several gunboats of the blockading fleet in the distance. Worse, one warship was close by on the port bow.[4]

Quoting Lord Byron (and the lyrics of a Scottish Halloween dance tune), Watson said, "The Devil's in the moon for mischief." Just then, there was a flash and the ominous sound of a cannon firing. *Rob Roy* was the target. The cannon ball "whizzed across our bows, which was immediately followed by a second." Things could have been worse and soon were. *Rob Roy* ran aground on the windward side of the channel. Though the tide was rising, the enemy warship's small boat and its armed boarding party were nearby. The expression on the faces of the *Rob Roy*'s crew reflected their desperate situation, "Captured at last, we must just submit to it."[5]

Rob Roy was in a perilous situation and not just from the enemy. The heavy wind and seas, combined with the boarding party's attempt to come alongside using a boat hook, placed both crews in mortal danger. After much loud shouting in the excitement of the moment, the force of the wind and the rising tide jerked *Rob Roy* free from the sand bar. Suddenly released from the grip of the sand, the schooner shot forward. Watson's large schooner pushed the small boat full of frightened Navy sailors ahead of it. The Union officer in charge had to quickly decide what to do. Should he give the order to cast off, continue to hold on and risk being swamped, or try to jump onboard the blockade runner in a plunging sea. Watson made the decision for him. He "seized the hatchet and severed the rope" connecting them to the small boat. *Rob Roy* was off again with a bound. The wet and cold sailors were left behind in the darkness. Their only recourse was to fire angry, but futile volleys of pistol shots into the shadowy mist.[6]

"Chase of a Blockade Runner." *Harper's Weekly*, November 26, 1864, pp. 760–761 (Library of Congress Prints and Photographs Division, LC-USZ62-15554).

This specific incident with the Union gunboat cannot be confirmed. It may have occurred when *Rob Roy* made its first exit from Galveston, but not in the winter of 1864–1865. Watson was correct about there being a norther sometime around New Year's Eve. The captain of the USS *Seminole* reported that several navy gunboats had to head out to sea from the Rio Grande to avoid being blown ashore on the last day of the year. Watson's reference to the moon and improved visibility when the clouds parted also showed that the encounter had to have taken place sometime before or after the new moon of December 28, 1864.[7]

Official records described a similar incident involving a confrontation between a gunboat and a small, unnamed blockade runner off Galveston. During the early morning hours of January 4, 1865, the USS *Gertrude* detected the "strange sail." She gave chase, and fired two shots without effect. As the water began to shoal, the captain broke off the chase. There were two major differences between this episode and Watson's story. First, the gunboat did not try to launch a boarding party, and second, the vessel was running into Galveston Bay and not out.[8]

After his alleged harrowing escape from the enemy, Watson said he sailed along the shore for about 12 miles before shifting his course. He knew that the fleet would be on the alert. He returned to his tried-and-true tactic of taking down the sails at daybreak and keeping a bow-on perspective toward any vessel that steamed nearby. Unfortunately for his credibility, Watson persisted in describing his interactions with his mate "Hagan" during this voyage. Even with a speedy release, it was not possible for James O'Hagan to have rejoined *Rob Roy* so quickly after having been captured running the blockade onboard *Carrie Mair* and then taken to New Orleans as a prisoner. It seems likely that Watson was spreading out the tales of his adventures afloat by creating a second blockade-running voyage out of Galveston. The incidents on this voyage probably occurred on his previous run.[9]

Watson said he made it to Vera Cruz in six days. As *Rob Roy* approached the anchorage and awaited a pilot, his crew feared that they had been spotted by one of the ships of the U.S. blockading fleet. They were contemplating risking a direct run into port without benefit of a pilot. Watson finally realized that their pursuer was just the harmless Spanish mail steamer *Barcelona*.[10]

The steamer departed Havana on January 9, 1865, on its regular circuit. On this trip, *Barcelona* made brief stops at Tuxpan, Sisal, and finally, Vera Cruz, Mexico. Both the U.S. Consul and the Havana newspaper agreed that *Barcelona* began her three-day transit from Vera Cruz to Havana on January 28. This itinerary would have placed *Barcelona*'s arrival at Vera Cruz sometime in late January. If *Rob Roy* arrived at the same time, Watson's timeline was off by at least two weeks.[11]

When he arrived at Vera Cruz, Watson said he landed his cargo of cotton. The half that belonged to Robert Mills he turned over to the consignees. That left him with 73 bales to either take with him to Havana or sell. To reduce his risk in case of capture, Watson said that he sold 45 bales at a bargain price and retained the rest as ballast.[12]

Watson mentioned that there were "two or three small schooners" at Vera Cruz that had run out of Texas with cotton. He also reported that another "two schooners had recently sailed from Vera Cruz for Havana with part of their cargo of cotton on board and had been captured on the neutral passage." If true, there were a total of four to five blockade-running schooners that had gone into Vera Cruz in late 1864 and early 1865, in addition to *Rob Roy*. If Watson was correct, two of them should have appeared in official records as having been captured.[13]

Another, potentially more reliable source of Vera Cruz blockade-running information, was the American Consulate. Consul M.D.L. Lane had taken a leave of absence in the United States earlier in the year. He was back at his station in late November 1864 and throughout the timeframe of Watson's reported visit there through February 1865. Compared to the more prominent consuls, Lane was not a frequent correspondent with his boss, Secretary of State William H. Seward. For example, the Civil War consuls at Havana would typically write multiple letters each week. The level of blockade-running activity at the port had a lot to do with the frequency of consular letters. However, the more relevant factor was the number of regularly scheduled mail steamers that had connections that terminated at New York. Places like Vera Cruz did not have regular, weekly international mail services.[14]

From the date of his return to Vera Cruz in November through February 1865, Consul Lane wrote only nine dispatches to the State Department. His primary topics were the geopolitical situation with the French, the Mexican Civil War, consular administrative issues, and blockade-running activity. He did not mention *Rob Roy* in any of his sequentially numbered messages.

After his return to Vera Cruz, Lane's first dispatch naturally included an update on recent blockade-running activity.

> There are now in port three Confederate blockade runners from Texas. Two left here yesterday [November 22, 1864]. They came laden with cotton consigned to the House of H. d'Olure [*sic*], the Prussian Consul. During last month, a small steamer from Galveston Texas, arrived here laden with cotton. I learn that she has been sold to a Mexican; that he is now repairing her for the coasting trade.[15]

Although Consul Lane did not specifically identify the Texas blockade runners, they had three things in common: they arrived from Texas, were loaded with cotton, and d'Oleire and Company was the consignee. The three schooners that fit these criteria were *W.D.S. Hyer* and *Velocity* (*Chaos, Nellie Blair, Vigilant, Fairy*), and *Charles Russell*. Thomas W. House of Houston owned all three, and the Prussian Consul to Vera Cruz, doing business as Henry d'Oleire & Co., was the consignee (see Table 7).[16]

When Watson said that he arrived at Vera Cruz in late January or early February 1865, there were "two or three small schooners lying there which had run out from Texas with cargoes of cotton." One of them had taken cotton to Tampico but had to sail to Vera Cruz in ballast in search of a profitable return cargo. Watson did not name the schooners, but said that the one that sailed via Tampico had "Captain E." in command. If he had truly been at Vera Cruz, he should have mentioned the small steamer from Galveston and two other steam-powered blockade runners that were in port in January of 1865 (see Table 7).[17]

As for the schooner that Watson said had sailed under "Captain E.," there were at least five unnamed schooners anchored outside the Tampico bar in late November 1864. Unfortunately, the American Consul at Tampico, Franklin Chase, did not name any of them. Not all of them were necessarily blockade runners, but Consul Chase was not diligent in naming any of the vessels at Tampico unless they were steamers. It was possible, but unlikely, that one of these unidentified schooners continued to Vera Cruz under a "Captain E." There was no confirmation of a schooner having arrived at Vera Cruz from Tampico during *Roy Roy*'s visit, but other sources identified Consul Lane's three Texas schooners at Vera Cruz as well their captains. None of them had a "Captain E."[18]

The familiar Thomas W. House-owned schooner *W.D.S. Hyer* along with *Velocity*, departed Galveston for Vera Cruz in the early morning hours of Halloween 1864. They were two of the schooners that Consul Marquis de Lafayette Lane saw at Vera Cruz. Both schooners

Franklin Chase, U.S. Consul at Tampico, Mexico (courtesy Chase Family Papers, Special Collections, The University of Texas at Arlington Libraries).

cleared from Vera Cruz on December 1. The 100-ton *W.D.S. Hyer* sailed to Havana and arrived on December 22 under Captain Yawbes. The *W.D.S. Hyer*'s sailing consort was the 63-ton schooner *Velocity*.[19]

While at Vera Cruz with *W.D.S. Hyer*, *Velocity* acquired the more appropriate name of *Chaos*. After leaving Vera Cruz, *Chaos* may have made an undocumented stop at Havana, but she next appeared in the historical record at Kingston, Jamaica on February 1, 1865. Her captain, Joseph Davidson, had signed a crew of six men for her next voyage to Galveston. Most of them had been with him in Vera Cruz. The U.S. Navy finally caught up the former U.S. Navy warship and long-time blockade runner again in April 1865. The USS *Cornubia* captured *Chaos* on its run out of Galveston with 170 bales of cotton.[20]

Consul Lane eventually identified one of the schooners at Vera Cruz. Named after a Confederate Army quartermaster and cotton agent, *Charles Russell* sailed from Sabine Pass for Vera Cruz in mid–August 1864.[21] It probably arrived shortly thereafter. This Thomas W. House-owned schooner was under the command of its former first mate William Bayly (Baily). *Charles Russell* cleared from Vera Cruz to Havana in December, and was back in Texas by January 1865. It was the only schooner known to have been at Vera Cruz at the same time as *Rob Roy* was supposed to have been there. None of the three blockade-running Captains were candidates for Watson's "Captain E.," nor were any of them the owners of their schooners as Watson had claimed. Thomas House owned *W.D.S Hyer* and *Velocity/Chaos* as well as *Charles Russell*.[22]

Yet another of Watson's statements does not stand up to scrutiny. He said that the U.S. fleet had made recent captures along the Campeche coastal route that took outbound blockade runners along the Mexican coast and away from the contrary flow of the Gulf Stream current.[23]

The blockading fleet captured 20 vessels in the Western Gulf of Mexico Between November 1864, and January 1865. Only two of them originated from Vera Cruz. Both vessels, *John A. Hazard* (the former blockade runner *Gino*) and *Sea Witch* (*Pizarro*), were near Galveston when captured. The admiralty court condemned *John A. Hazard* as a valid prize. The judge released *Sea Witch* because it was on a legitimate voyage to New Orleans. The only vessel captured while trying to cross the Bay of Campeche by hugging the coast of the Yucatan Peninsula was the steamer *Susannah* (*Mail*) (see Table 7). It had sailed from Galveston.

Table 7: Western Gulf of Mexico Blockade Runners Captured November 1864–January 1865

Date	Type	Captain	Date	Sailed Fm	Capture Location
John A. Hazard (Gino)[24]	Schr	Henry Meyers	11/05	Vera Cruz	50 mi. off Galveston
Cuca (Lone)[25]	Schr	John Curry	11/06	Tampico	Off Brazos River, TX
Neptune[26]	Schr	Charles Berndt	11/19	Velasco	Near Brazos Santiago, TX
Sybil (Eagle)[27]	Schr	William E. Askins	11/20	Matamoros	Off NC for NY released
Flash[28]	Schr	Robert Vaughn	11/27	Galveston	Off Rio Grande; for Tampico
Susannah (Mail)[29]	Stmr	Charles W. Austin	11/27	Galveston	Off Campeche; for Havana
Carrie Mair[30]	Schr	Thomas McNamara	11/30	Tampico	14 mi. off Pass Cavallo, TX
Geziena Hilligonda[31]	Brig	Bernardus P. Jansen	12/04	Liverpool	Off Brazos Santiago, TX
Julia[32]	Schr	Richard Ross	12/05	Havana	43 mi. off Brazos River
Lowood (Witchie)[33]	Schr	Edward Ward	12/05	Brazos	65 mi. SE of Brazos River
Lady Hurley (Lote Hurley)[34]	Schr	P.C. Blanchet	12/06	Tampico	31 mi. SE of Brazos River
Alabama[35]	Schr	J.H. Davis	12/07	Havana	Off San Luis Pass, TX
Mary Ann[36]	Sloop	Unknown	12/08	Galveston	Ashore off Pass Cavallo
Cora (Snow Drift)[37]	Schr	John Greenough	12/19	Belize	6 mi. ESE of Galveston
Morris[38]	Schr	Jesse F. Potter	12/19	Matamoros	40 mi. fm SW Pass, LA
Belle (Gipsey, Zouave)[39]	Schr	James Brown	12/27	Galveston	Galveston Bay
Sea Witch (Pizarro)[40]	Schr	Pierre Jaureguiberry	12/31	Vera Cruz	76 mi. SSE of Galveston
Mary Ellen[41]	Schr	William S. Cooper	01/03	Matamoros	5 mi. off Brazos River
Lilly[42]	Schr	James H. Davison	01/06	Tampico	20 mi. east of Brazos River
Josephine[43]	Schr	Samuel L. Townsend	01/14	Galveston	4 mi. off Brazos Santiago

Watson also made no mention of Consul Lane's small steamer that had sailed from Galveston in October and was present at Vera Cruz until early December. She was the former USS *Sachem* that sailed under the command of Watson's old friend Henry Scherffius who renamed her *Clarinda*. Scherffius would have been in Galveston at the same time as Watson. This inconvenient fact contradicts Watson's claim that he had not seen Henry Scherffius after his brother George's death until Henry joined Watson in Havana. George Scherffius departed Galveston in September 1864, on his schooner *Mary Elizabeth*, but disappeared during his voyage to Tampico.[44]

Confederate forces had captured the U.S. Navy's *Sachem* along with the USS *Clifton* during the disastrous Union attempt to invade Texas via the Sabine River, in September 1863. The Texas Marine Department repaired the warships and briefly contemplated using them to attack the blockading fleet. In the meantime, they were employed for the defense of Sabine Pass. Thinking better of those plans, they sold the steamers to Thomas W. House who converted them into quasi-civilian blockade runners.[45]

Clifton was the first to make the attempt in March 1864, but she ran aground coming out of Sabine Pass. Her veteran captain Charles W. Austin had no interest in being captured again as he had onboard the SS *Union* in August 1862. He quickly assessed the situation and saw that there was "no hope of her escape, set the steamer on fire and then skeedaddled." Captain Austin found employment on the steamer *Susannah*, but was captured in late November (see Table 7).[46]

The former USS *Sachem* waited several months before making her attempt. Renamed *Clarinda*, she was an old 197-ton screw steamer, built in 1844 at New York City. The U.S. Navy had purchased her from the U.S. Coast Survey in 1861. Capt. Henry Scherffius successfully ran *Clarinda* through the blockade to Vera Cruz with 500 bales of cotton in October 1864.[47]

After selling *Clarinda* in Vera Cruz, Scherffius went to Havana and traveled as a passenger with his wife on the steamer *Barcelona* in November. As discussed in a previous chapter, he met William Watson in Havana in hopes of gathering information about his brother George. Soon thereafter,

Thomas W. House (courtesy Rosenberg Library, Galveston, Texas).

Scherffius took command of the new blockade-running steamer, *Lark*. *Clarinda* followed Scherffius to Havana in early December under a new captain. The steamer was in Havana prior to Watson's reported arrival. She ended the war engaged in commercial shipping between Havana and Mexico as the SS *Vera Cruz* and sailed under the Mexican flag.[48]

Of the seven blockade runners known to be at Vera Cruz between December 1864 and January 1865, three of them were the previously named schooners *Velocity/Chaos*, *Charles Russell*, and *W.D.S. Hyer*. In addition to the former USS *Sachem* and a Mexican-flagged brigantine named *Eco* (*Echo*), the other two schooners, were *Triton* and *Will 'o the Wisp* (see Table 8). *Triton* was probably present at the time of *Rob Roy*'s supposed arrival, but her departure date from Vera Cruz was not reported. In late 1864 and early 1865, blockade-running steamers were not at all common at Vera Cruz and would have been worthy of mention if Watson had been there.[49]

Charles William Austin (courtesy Edith Smith of East Bernard, Texas, from the Vincent Eastman Smith, Jr., Family Collection).

The only blockade runners at Vera Cruz by January 1865, were the steamer *Will o' the Wisp* and the schooner *Charles Russell*. The steamer was on its second and final visit to Vera Cruz. She had first called there in mid–December when her captain could not find any coal at Tampico. *Will o' the Wisp* had departed Vera Cruz on Christmas Eve for Galveston and returned on January 15 with 500 bales of cotton despite jettisoning 100 bales overboard during a gale. On February 1, 1865, Consul Lane reported the departure of the steamer *Will o' the Wisp* for Galveston with its mate in command. Her Captain had left separately as a passenger on *Barcelona*, supposedly to return to his home in Boston.[50]

The other blockade runner at Vera Cruz at the same time as *Rob Roy*'s reported visit was also a repeat visitor. On January 28, the schooner *Charles Russell* arrived from Galveston with 240 bales of cotton. Captain William Bayly remained in command. The brig *Eco* was present but had not attempted a blockade run.

Table 8: Blockade Runners at Vera Cruz, December 1864–January 1865

Name	Type	Captain	From	Arr	Dep	Comments
Charles Russell[51]	Schr	William Bayly	Sabine Pass	09/02	12/02	Seized at Galveston Jun 1865
Eco (Echo)[52]	Brig	Lorenzo Lena	Tampico	09/01	02/11	Arrived via Chiltapec; captured off Galveston 02/19
Sachem (Clarinda, Vera Cruz)[53]	Stmr	Henry Scherffius	Galveston	10/30	12/02	Arrived as Clarinda, to Havana as Vera Cruz under Mexican Captain Pares
Velocity (Chaos, Fairy, Nellie Blair)[54]	Schr	Joseph Davidson	Galveston	11/15	12/02	To Jamaica & Galveston as Chaos; captured Apr 21, 1865, off Galveston
W.D.S. Hyer[55]	Schr	William R. Tucker	Galveston	11/15	12/02	To Havana
Triton[56]	Stmr	Joseph C. Barnard	Galveston	12/06	unk	Probably reflagged and renamed in 1865.
Will o' the Wisp[57]	Stmr	Abner M. Godfrey	Tampico	12/18	12/24	Loaded coal for Galveston
Will o' the Wisp[58]	Stmr	Abner M. Godfrey	Galveston	01/16	01/31	Sailed from Vera Cruz with a new captain. Wrecked off Galveston 02/03
Charles Russell[59]	Schr	William Bayly	Galveston	01/28	02/23	Sailed for Galveston, turned over to U.S. forces 06/65

Watson said that he was able to retain all of his crewmembers that had sailed with him from Galveston. He also had 28 bales of cotton for ballast. After loading additional stores for the voyage, he was ready to sail to Havana. He stated that he departed Vera Cruz in early February 1865. To reduce his risk of capture, he took the eastward route to Havana away from the Mexican coastline. He enjoyed favorable winds and did not see any of the blockading fleet. He regretted selling part of his cargo at a reduced price when he arrived at Havana just eight days after departing Vera Cruz. He said that the "Spanish mail steamer" had reported Rob Roy's destination, which alerted Richard Mills of his pending arrival.[60]

There were more problems with Watson's claims about departing Vera Cruz and arriving at Havana in February 1865. Although Consul Lane only authored two reports between February 1 and 23 (Vera Cruz consular letters numbered 56 and 57), he continued his silence about Rob Roy's presence.[61]

More damning was the absence of any documentation confirming Rob Roy's arrival at Havana. The Havana maritime journal made no mention of Rob Roy until February 16. Fortunately for historians, the accessible archival copies of that newspaper (Diario de la Marina) are complete for the month of February 1865. It would have been a rare occurrence for that particular newspaper to omit reports about the movements of blockade runners and their cotton imports. To make matters worse for Watson's credibility, the newspaper report of February 16 that mentioned Rob Roy and William Watson was in reference to their clearance for another port, not their arrival.[62]

15

Phantom Voyages Part 3

Running the Gauntlet in Steamships

In Havana, Watson once again had to deal with the most disagreeable part of the blockade-running business. He could easily understand and manage the hazards of the sea and enemy warships, but the manipulations of unscrupulous cotton brokers on shore continued to try his patience. His old partner, Richard Mills, pressed him to consign his remaining cotton to one of the Mills Brothers' firms. His more trustworthy partner's representative, Mr. P (Parizot) was also in Havana. Parizot warned Watson that Mills was going to attempt another swindle. He would be better served to deal with his former consignees, Messrs. A. and Co. (Avendaño Brothers & Co.).[1]

When Watson met with Mr. Mills, his suspicions were confirmed. Robert Mills began by questioning him about why he did not carry as many cotton bales as before. When Watson described the problems with the steam cotton press at Houston, Mills protested that "the *Dahlia* and the *Catherine* got compressed bales, and why could not you." Watson explained that those two schooners got in before the steamers arrived and the cotton press broke down. "By the by [he added sarcastically], where are those vessels now?" Watson said that he knew that both vessels had been captured … or had they?[2]

The U.S. Navy did not capture any blockade runners named *Dahlia* or *Catherine* in late 1864 or in 1865. There were no blockade runners by those names even operating in the Gulf of Mexico during the timeframe of Watson's story. The closest matches were the schooners *Delia* and *Eliza Catharine*. *Delia* last departed Galveston in late September 1864, with 193 bales of cotton. She sailed from Havana on February 11, 1865, but the blockading fleet captured her trying to run into Bayport, Florida, six days later. *Eliza Catharine* was also at the Brazos and Galveston in September 1864. She wrecked departing the Brazos on April 6, 1865, resulting in the loss of all six crew members. She was never captured, and her loss occurred after Watson met with Robert Mills.[3]

Rather than prolonging this unreliable relationship, Robert Mills and William Watson mutually agreed to sell *Rob Roy* at auction. Unfortunately, the Havana newspaper did not contain any advertisement regarding *Rob Roy* among the many vessels that were offered for sale during this time. Watson said he attempted to purchase

Rob Roy, but a young British man outbid him. The youth was acting as a surrogate for Robert Mills. Watson then turned his attention to the larger steam-powered blockade runners that were collecting at Havana. Several of them would benefit from Watson's knowledge and experience on the Texas coast. He specifically remembered the steamers *Lark*, *Owl*, *Lizzie*, and *Denbigh*. As seen in Table 9, these four steamers made numerous runs into Texas between July 1864, and May 1865. All four were never in port at the same time, but Watson did not claim to have any personal contact with them. An exception was the steamer *Phoenix*.

Unlike the side-wheel steamers, *Lark*, *Owl*, *Denbigh*, and *Lizzie*, Watson's information about *Phoenix* was allegedly from his firsthand knowledge. He said it was a new twin-screw steamer, recently arrived from London. The unidentified captain who sailed her into Havana was not willing to risk running the blockade into Texas. However, one of her passengers had an ownership interest in the vessel and was qualified as a master mariner. This man, "Captain R.," decided to take command himself. The new captain had no experience sailing the open ocean or blockade running and neither he nor his first or second mates were trained in celestial navigation. In fact, of the 20 *Phoenix* crew members, only two had ever run the blockade. This is where William Watson's skills were needed.[4]

Although he had never commanded a steamer, Watson was experienced in blockade running in Texas waters and was an accomplished navigator. He said that *Phoenix* was broad abeam, with a flat bottom and good carrying capacity. She was schooner-rigged and had a fully loaded draft of just over seven feet. Her unnamed engineer was a former military man who had trained at Greenock, Scotland. Watson said his personal role was as the steamer's pilot and sailing master.[5]

Watson also left several clues about the timing of *Phoenix*'s arrival and departure from Havana and arrival at Galveston. After getting underway, Watson

"Blockade Runner *Lizzie*." *Illustrated London News*, August 6, 1864, p. 136 (author's collection).

complained that she was only making just over 10 knots after reaching 13 knots on her passage from London. The steamer had been at Havana for about six weeks, and due to lack of funds, was not able to enter drydock to clean her hull. As a result, her bottom was foul with marine growth which reduced her speed. Watson specifically said that *Phoenix* sailed out of Havana about the 1st day of March and then arrived off Galveston on the 4th day. They came to anchor without incident at 2 a.m. on the fifth day. Later that same day, they sailed up to the wharves and Watson noted that there were five or six steamers loading there. Two of those steamers would have been *Lark* and *Denbigh* (see Table 9).[6]

After they docked safely at Galveston, the vessel and cargo were consigned to Mister "H." This was a clear reference to the well-respected merchant Thomas W. House. A few days after *Phoenix*'s arrival, Watson said that Thomas House presented him with a proposition to take command of a different steamer. According to Watson, "Capt. S." of *Jeannette* lived in Houston and had some family members who were seriously ill. Thomas House said that he did not want to ask Captain S. to leave his family in their hour of need. Despite his troubles, the dedicated captain was willing to depart immediately, in part because of some idle talk about his unwillingness to place duty above personal concerns. Mr. House respected his captain and wanted to let him spend more time in port. Watson said that Captain S. and *Jeannette* had departed Galveston with his family, about the same time that *Phoenix* arrived. The voyage was a short one when she had to put back into port due to boiler-tube mechanical issues. It was important for her to get underway as soon as possible. Mr. House reported that "Captain R." who commanded *Phoenix* agreed to let Capt. S. take Watson's place as sailing master so that he could remain in port for a few days longer.[7]

Despite having reservations about taking command of a steamer for the first time, much less one with a defective boiler, Watson agreed. He would receive an extra $100 over his previous arrangement as sailing master. That agreement called for an advance of $500, plus $150 per month from the beginning to the end of the trip, and another bonus of $500 upon completion of a successful voyage. Temporary repairs to the boiler were sufficient until the boiler tubes could be replaced. Mr. House had arranged for new boiler tubes to be delivered from Havana to Tampico where *Jeannette* could enter drydock. Havana would have been a more desirable destination, but *Jeannette* could not carry enough coal to reach Havana, and there was little to be had in Galveston.[8]

Watson described *Jeannette* as a paddlewheel steamer. When he first saw her, he was impressed. "I found her to be a sharp little steamer drawing a little over five feet of water when loaded." She had been built on the River Clyde in Scotland and had originally run between Glasgow and Rothesay as a commercial steamer under the name *Eagle*. After being sold and converted into a blockade runner. She made several successful runs before the blockading fleet captured her. The admiralty court in New York promptly condemned her as a prize. After being sold at auction, the new owners renamed her *Josie*, and sent her to Havana. There, Andrew Jackson "Jack" Moore, one of Watson's newfound friends, took over as captain. Captain Moore renamed her *Jeannette* as she prepared to resume her blockade-running career (as

"A United States Gunboat." William Watson, *Adventures of a Blockade Runner; or, Trade in Time of War*. London: Fisher Unwin, 1892, p. 45 (author's collection).

discussed in a previous chapter). Archival records confirmed that all of Watson's claims about *Jeannette* were true up to this point.[9]

However, Watson then continued his sea story about *Jeannette* by telling tales that were mostly untrue. He said that the steamer was on her second or third trip between Havana and Galveston. Upon taking command, Watson said that he got underway at 8 p.m. It was a dark night, "near the end of the moon," which would have been about March 29. Watson said he spotted two warships on his way out of the channel, but *Jeanette* was able to slip away without detection. Due to the lack of coal, Watson steamed directly to Tampico at a rate of about 12 knots. The next day, he sighted a federal propeller cruiser that chased *Jeannette* throughout the day. Although the gunboat kept up a steady fire of cannon balls, only one inflicted superficial damage. Watson managed to lose his nemesis during the night and came to anchor off Tampico the following evening. Watson said the day was "now the equinox," which was March 20, about nine days before his supposed departure from Galveston.[10]

Table 9: Texas blockade runs: *Lark, Owl, Denbigh, & Lizzie*, Jul 1864–May 1865

Ship Name	Captain	Mexico		Havana		Galveston		Lavaca	
		Arr	Dep	Arr	Dep	Arr	Dep	Arr	Dep
Lark[11]	T. Griffiths/ H. Scherffius	----	----	1/09*	1/16	1/19	2/03	----	----
Lark[12]	Scherffius/ S. Marcy	----	----	2/05	2/17	2/20	3/23†	----	----

Ship Name	Captain	Mexico		Havana		Galveston		Lavaca	
		Arr	Dep	Arr	Dep	Arr	Dep	Arr	Dep
Lark[13]	S. Marcy	----	----	3/26	4/01	4/05	5/04	----	----
Lark[14]	S. Marcy / G. Blakely	----	----	5/07	5/18	5/21	5/24†	----	----
Owl/Foam[15]	J.N. Maffitt	----	----	3/30	4/02	4/04	5/05	----	----
Owl/Foam[16]	J.N. Maffitt	----	----	5/09	7/07	----	----	----	----
Denbigh[17]	A.M. Godfrey	----	----	7/30	8/26	8/29	9/10	----	----
Denbigh[18]	A.M. Godfrey	----	----	9/15	9/23	9/28	10/22	----	----
Denbigh[19]	LaBlache	----	----	10/27	11/07	11/11	12/09	----	----
Denbigh[20]	LaBlache	----	----	12/14	1/17	1/21	2/01	----	----
Denbigh[21]	LaBlache	----	----	2/05	2/22	2/27	3/19	----	----
Denbigh[22]	LaBlache	----	----	3/24	4/01	4/05	4/27	----	----
Denbigh[23]	A.M. Godfrey	----	----	5/01	5/18	5/23	n/a	----	----
Lizzie[24]	Lang/S. Marcy	----	----	10/16	10/28	----	----	11/02	1/11
Lizzie[25]	S. Marcy	1/20§	3/03§	----	----	----	----	3/07	4/26
Lizzie[26]	Lang	5/01**	5/16**	5/20	unk	----	----	----	----

* Capt. Scherffius took command of *Lark* for her first run into Galveston and remained with *Lark* until Mar 1865.

† Capt. Marcy was in command of *Lark* when she departed Galveston on March 23. He turned *Lark* over to George Blakely for her final run out of Galveston in May 1865.

§ At Tampico with 450 bales cotton consigned to Stewart (Stuart) L. Jolly & Co.

** At Vera Cruz with 422 bales cotton with customs clearance from LaSalle, Texas, located in Matagorda Bay.

Most historians have accepted Watson's accounts of his adventures onboard *Phoenix* and *Jeannette* as historical fact, at least for the most part. While there was a *Jeannette*, there was never a Western Gulf blockade runner named *Phoenix*. Knowledgeable analysts have speculated that Watson used *Phoenix* as an alias for the propeller-driven steamer *Pelican*. Watson's inspiration for selecting *Phoenix* as an alias for *Pelican* may have been the Phoenix Fire and Pelican Life Insurance Company of London. The Pelican Life Insurance Company was founded in 1797 as a sister company of the Phoenix Fire Office.[27]

Pelican arrived at Havana from London on January 17 via Dover, South Hampton, and Plymouth, England and Madeira, a small island and Portuguese colony located between the Azores and Canary Islands (see Table 11). *Pelican* was one of many blockade runners that ran into Galveston in 1865, but was the only one that was propeller-driven. Although she was only a single-propeller vessel and not double, she was a new-construction steamer. Built in 1863, *Pelican*'s owner had advertised her for sale at London in late 1864.[28]

Despite *Pelican*'s resemblance to *Phoenix*, the only vessel at Havana in early 1865 that matched Watson's description of a "double propeller" steamship was *Louisa Ann Fanny*. Commander James D. Bulloch, the secret agent of the Confederate Navy in Liverpool, had ordered the construction of *Louisa Ann Fanny* and her incomplete sister ship, *Mary Augusta*, for the purpose of escorting blockade runners. Both steamers were named after the wives of Bulloch's financial supporters, John and Algernon Gilliat, but *Mary Augusta* was not completed prior to the end of the Civil War. The steamers were intended to run the blockade into Wilmington,

North Carolina, where they would be converted into gunboats. They would then conduct night attacks against the blockading fleet.[29]

Louisa Ann Fanny completed her sea trials on the Thames in late January and arrived at Havana on the Ides of March 1865. She had first stopped at Spain to deliver an engineer to the Confederate ironclad CSS *Stonewall* that was on her way to the Confederate States. Her next port of call was Bermuda where she picked up the Confederate Agent Major Norman Walker and then made a brief stop at Nassau before continuing to Havana. Although under the nominal command of William G. Pinchon, Confederate Navy Lieutenant William Fitzhugh Carter was her *de facto* commanding officer.[30]

With Wilmington in Federal hands, Galveston was the only viable port available to the Confederates as of March 1865. After *Louisa Ann Fanny* arrived at Havana, she backtracked to Bermuda rather than running into Galveston as expected. In Bermuda, rumors of her impending conversion into an armed cruiser found their way into consular dispatches and newspaper reports. Although *Louisa Ann Fanny* had the same type of propulsion as Watson's *Phoenix*, and was a newly constructed vessel from London, her activities were far-removed from Watson's story. She never ran the blockade and returned to the United Kingdom via Bermuda with Major Walker and his family in May 1865. Lieutenant William F. Carter retained command and had no need for a civilian sailing master like William Watson among his crew.[31]

Watson's muddled description of *Phoenix*'s captain and the swap of her sailing master for *Jeannette*'s captain does not stand up to scrutiny. Watson's novice "Captain R." was probably a reference to Confederate Army Captain Robert B. Scott. He had purchased a half ownership interest in *Pelican* while in London on behalf of the Confederate government. Thomas W. House owned the other half of the vessel, as well as its cargo. The money to finance the purchase of *Pelican* had come from the sale of cotton run out on the captured USS *Harriet Lane* (renamed *Lavinia*). Captain R.B. Scott, acting on behalf of the Confederate Government, still owed Mr. House $32,000 to cover the cost of the government portion of the cargo.[32]

Captain Scott was sometimes listed as the commanding officer of *Pelican*, even though he was not. In fact, it was not Scott who took command of *Pelican* when it departed Havana. Her new commander was Watson's old friend, Henry Scherffius. Scherffius had recently sailed the captured USS *Sachem* out of Sabine Pass and sold her at Vera Cruz, Mexico under the name of *Clarina*. In late November 1864, he and his wife sailed to Havana as passengers on the Spanish Steamer *Barcelona*. After arriving in Havana, Scherffius took command of *Lark* on her first voyage to Galveston. He returned to Havana in time to take charge of *Pelican* on her first blockade run as well (see Tables 9 and 10).[33]

Other than Watson's story, there was no evidence that any "Captain S." or William Watson ever had command of *Jeannette* out of either Havana or Galveston. The blockade runner *Lark* was at Galveston upon the arrival of *Pelican* and not *Jeannette*. It was *Lark*'s presence that coincided with Watson's timeline for Captain Scherffius to have taken command of *Pelican*. Henry Scherffius was *Lark*'s captain when she arrived at Galveston on February 20, but when *Lark* departed on March 23, Samuel Marcy was in command. Just like Watson's "Captain S.," Henry Scherffius's family resided in Houston, and he relinquished command of a blockade-running steamer in Galveston. However, Scherffius had been in command of *Lark*, not *Jeannette*. Rather than lingering in Galveston onboard *Lark* to be with his family, Scherffius left his command early to hasten his departure, but not because he wanted to remain in Houston. Mr. House needed him back in Havana, and he could not wait for *Lark* to be loaded with cotton.[34]

Not only were Scherffius's skills urgently needed in Havana, his wife was probably there as well. She may have been ill as Watson inferred, but it was more likely that she was in Cuba at the time, rather than in Houston. Scherffius' return trip to Havana from Galveston to take command of *Pelican* was not recorded. But he had to travel back to Havana sometime after his arrival at Galveston on February 20 onboard *Lark* and his departure from Havana on March 25 as captain of *Pelican*. He probably took passage on another blockade runner. The most likely candidate was *Wren*, a sister ship of *Lark*. *Wren* departed Galveston about March 7 and arrived at Havana four days later. Henry Scherffius next appeared in the historical record as Captain of *Pelican* when she departed from Havana on March 25. This departure was over three weeks later than Watson's timeline for his fictional *Phoenix*. It was also after the Spring equinox, which is when Watson was supposed to have anchored *Jeannette* off Tampico.[35]

The most important discrepancy between Watson's story and the historical record was the presence of Henry Scherffius. He was one of the most experienced men to ever run the Texas blockade in both sailing craft and steamers, plus he was an accomplished navigator. There was simply no need for William Watson's skills on *Pelican*. Not surprisingly, there are no records to suggest that he ever was. Captain R.B. Scott remained onboard *Pelican* for its run into Galveston, but he was not a naval officer, nor was he in command. Scott did, however, exercise a degree of control over the vessel as the government representative.

Union and Confederate sources failed to specifically mention the date of *Pelican*'s arrival at Galveston, but there was one official report about a successful run which matched her timeline. On April 2, 1865, the captain of the blockading fleet off Galveston sent Rear Admiral H.K. Thatcher a request for light draft vessels. He was frustrated by his inability to intercept or prevent fast, shallow-draft steamers from running past his fleet. He complained that his warships had made a futile attempt to stop an unnamed blockade runner as it ran past a gauntlet of five gunboats. Even worse, this humiliating failure occurred, "in broad daylight." Despite "considerable damage from some of the many shots fired, the shot holes plainly visible in her side," the steamer succeeded in getting into port. If this report referred to *Pelican*'s run into Galveston, it was another contradiction to Watson's claim that she arrived in the middle of the night.[36]

When *Pelican* did arrive at Galveston, Major General Magruder had just returned to Texas after his assignment to Arkansas and Louisiana. The general acted quickly to help Captain Robert Scott settle his accounts with Thomas House. He also ordered three Texas Army and Marine Department men to join *Pelican*'s crew. One was a ship's carpenter, the next was the former mate from the CSS *Sachem* and the third was a musician belonging to a regimental band. The transfer of the mate, James G. Timmins, was probably a personal request from Henry Scherffius. Scherffius had been commanding officer of *Sachem* (later *Clarinda*) during her run from Sabine Pass to Vera Cruz.[37] Captain Scherffius also must have had known that the musician William Leopold had hidden talents as a mechanic. His orders assigned him as *Pelican*'s assistant engineer.[38]

Watson's story about *Phoenix/Pelican* and *Jeannette* was completely out of sequence. He had the *Phoenix/Pelican* arriving prior to *Jeannette*, but just the opposite was true. *Pelican* did not sail into Galveston until April 1865, long after *Jeannette* had already departed for the last time. *Jeannette* had arrived in Havana from New York after being sold at auction in late September 1864. After spending two weeks loading supplies, she was ready to rejoin the blockade-running business. *Jeannette* travelled to Galveston two separate times, in October and December 1864. Her commanding officer for all her voyages was another one of Watson's blockade-running acquaintances, Captain Andrew Jackson "Jack" Moore. He had been captain of the schooner *John* when Watson and *Rob Roy* were detained at the Brazos in the fall of 1864 through February 1864. As seen in Table 10, *Jeannette* did make two blockade runs into Galveston, but only one of those originated from or terminated in Havana. Her last run to Tampico took place in February, a month prior to Watson's reported departure from Havana.[39]

Jeannette's final cargo of cotton (Shipment number 17) was listed in the 1865 Galveston Customs records. She paid export duties and cotton press charges on January 25, and February 1, 1865, respectively. She also purchased 10 tons of coal from the blockade runner *Lark* on January 31. These were the only entries for *Jeannette* (or any of her other aliases) in 1865. The final Galveston Customs entries were for May 3, 1865, when *Owl* paid its cotton export duties for shipments number 48 and 49. This accounting shows that *Jeannette* did not export any cotton out of Galveston after February 1865, and probably did not return to that port afterwards. There was a gap in U.S. and Confederate reporting about *Jennette* between her departure from Galveston in February and a report from Consul Franklin Chase from Tampico in late June. However, there is no evidence to support the truth of Watson's story that he had command of *Jeannette*.[40]

While it is possible that *Jeannette* could have made an unrecorded round trip between Tampico and Galveston sometime in February–April 1865, it is not likely. Galveston's Custom's records are complete for that period, and they only list *Jeannette* as having made one voyage out of Galveston in 1865, as reflected in Table 10. When she arrived at Tampico, several months elapsed before *Jeannette* finally got her boiler tubes repaired. *Jeannette* eventually reappeared at Havana on July 7, 1865, after a five-day voyage from Tampico. Captain Jack Moore remained in command.[41]

Table 10. Watson's Blockade Runners, *Phoenix/Pelican* and *Jeannette* (Dec 1864–Jul 1865 & 1867)

Ship Name	Captain	Mexico		Havana		Galveston	
		Arr	Dep	Arr	Dep	Arr	Dep
Phoenix / Pelican[42]	Peters / Henry Scherffius	----	----	1/17	3/25	4/01	4/27
Phoenix / Pelican[43]	Henry Scherffius / Clark	----	----	5/01	1867*	----	----
Jeannette[44]	Thompson / Jack Moore	----	----	9/23	10/11	10/27	11/30
Jeannette[45]	Jack Moore	12/02†	12/13†	----	----	12/15	2/01
Jeannette[46]	Jack Moore	2/06§	7/02§	7/07	unk	----	----

* Refitting for voyage to U.S. with *Harriet Lane*, Jan 19, 1867, under supervision of Capt. Faunce, U.S. Revenue Service.
† Matamoros
§ Tampico

Watson said that when *Jeannette* arrived in Tampico, he had little to do. He paid off the crew, but retained one or two men to maintain the vessel. The boiler tubes and a supply of coal had already arrived. The workers to install the tubes appeared a few days later. Watson continued to grouse about double-dealing agents, buyers, sellers, speculators, and other middlemen. The public seemed to believe that those scoundrels were engaged in a "lawful and honourable business." Whereas reckless and lawless blockade runners like himself were conducting "an unholy trade and considered, subject to be shot or drowned for their tricks."[47]

He then went to see "Messrs. G. & Co." (George Oetling & Co.) about the cotton he had brought out in *Rob Roy*. The firm had insured the cotton for far more than it was worth. This approach to insurance would yield a handsome profit for everyone if the cargo was lost, but guaranteed a heathy fee to the consignees if it was not. Watson said he would make very little money when the cotton sold at market after he paid all commissions and fees.[48]

Watson said that there was a smallpox epidemic at Tampico when he arrived. He visited one of his stricken men at hospital. Shortly thereafter, he received instructions to leave *Jeannette* in charge of the repairmen and to take the next mail steamer to Havana. Instead of acting on those orders immediately, he took up temporary residence in Tampico. He was not feeling well and soon realized he too was suffering from smallpox. It turned out to be a mild case, but he was quarantined for three weeks. When he came out of isolation, he discovered that General Robert E. Lee had surrendered, and President Lincoln had been assassinated. Lee surrendered his Army of Northern Virginia at Appomattox Courthouse on April 9 and John Wilkes Booth shot Abraham Lincoln on April 15. Allowing for at least a week for the news to reach Tampico, this would have placed Watson in Tampico in late April or early May 1865.[49]

While at Tampico, Watson acknowledged the likelihood that his career as a blockade runner was ending. But there were lingering doubts. He observed that Yankees were zealous to preserve the Union, but that did not constrain their "individual proclivities for trade." He had often witnessed the spread of false rumors that were intended to manipulate money and commodity markets. Some speculators and patriots who were heavily invested in the southern Confederacy still held out hope. One possibility was the development of a new political and military front. There was a serious possibility that Texas might once again declare its independence and then form an alliance with Emperor Maximillian of Mexico.[50]

When he was fully recovered, Watson said he took passage in the mail steamer to Havana. He arrived at the same time as a large American flotilla of warships that anchored in the harbor. The cause of the excitement that motivated the fleet to congregate at Havana was the Confederate Ironclad CSS *Stonewall*. The Confederate master of legerdemain, James Dunwoody Bulloch, had managed to get this monster of the deep out of the clutches of his enemies and under the Confederate flag. She arrived at Havana on May 11 after departing from Denmark, with stops at the Netherlands, France, Spain, Portugal, and Nassau. She was the first American ironclad to cross an ocean, and struck fear in all who cast their eyes on this "invulnerable" leviathan. The U.S. Navy warships that tailed her across Europe and the Atlantic repeatedly refused to engage her in combat. Their only hope was that the Confederacy would collapse before they would have to face the beast. The gods of war granted their wish. A week after *Stonewall*'s arrival at Havana, Captain Thomas Jefferson Page surrendered his formidable ironclad to Spanish authorities.[51]

Unfortunately, the Havana passenger lists do not confirm William Watson's claim that he arrived onboard one of the mail steamers from Mexico. It was possible that he did, but there was no confirmation. Watson said nothing more about his employment or how he managed to return to his home in the United Kingdom. The question lingers about the truth of his last days, weeks, and months as a blockade runner. If William Watson did not make a second run into Texas with *Rob Roy* and never served onboard the steamers *Phoenix/Pelican* and *Jeannette*, what *did* he do? The historical record offers a surprising, though incomplete, alternative ending to his adventures as a blockade runner.

16

The Demise of *Rob Roy,* Blockade Running, and the Confederacy

The previous three chapters have addressed Watson's phantom voyages on board *Rob Roy*, *Phoenix/Pelican*, and *Jeannette*. As those chapters have shown, the historical record has no affirmation of Watson's claims about running the blockade on these vessels into and out of Galveston between December 1864, and the end of the war. There were also numerous other inconsistencies between Watson's memoir and credible contemporary sources. Even if Watson had been on these vessels during the period of his story, there were serious errors in his descriptions of events, places, sequencing, and personnel. The contemporary references that mention either *Rob Roy* or William Watson during this period are scarce. But they all point to a radically different ending to Watson's blockade-running career and the demise of his schooner *Rob Roy*.

The divergence between Watson's story about his adventures as a blockade runner and reliable archival sources begin with his departure from Tampico, Mexico. In his story, Watson said that he departed in *Rob Roy* about the end of October 1864, and arrived at Havana about two weeks later. He also said that he split his cargo to reduce his risk of loss in the event he was captured. As previously discussed, a single entry in a Havana newspaper dated December 14, 1864, refuted all those claims. Under the Overseas Import ("Importacion Ultramar") column was an entry for the British Schooner *Rob Roy*. The paper reported that it had imported 200 bales of cotton ("200 pacas algodon") from Tampico. This report shows that Watson had been detained at Tampico for an additional month before he was able to depart for Havana. He also did not split his cargo as he had claimed, since all 200 bales had arrived onboard *Rob Roy*.[1]

The next contradiction to Watson's tale about running into Galveston a second time is found in a series of three newspaper items that all describe the same pending voyage. On February 16, 19, and 25, 1865, the Havana newspaper, *Diario de la Marina*, detailed *Rob Roy*'s progress in departing Havana. On February 16, the paper listed *Rob Roy* and Captain Watson, under the heading, "Buques que han Abierto Registro," which translates to "Vessels that have Opened Registration." *Rob Roy* and Captain Watson were preparing to depart Havana. They were bound for Nassau and with a cargo consigned to "C.L. Beisner" [*sic*], a Texan and associate of R. & D.G. Mills who set up business in Havana.[2]

Three days later, *Rob Roy* and Captain Watson appeared in the "Buques que se han Despachado" column. Havana customs officials had cleared the British Schooner and her captain to depart Havana with 24 packages of goods consigned to C.L. Beissner that were bound for Nassau. The British schooner *Rob Roy* and Captain Watson appeared one last time in the February 25 edition of the same newspaper. Under the heading "Puerto de la Habana.... Salidas," the paper reported that the British schooner *Rob Roy* and Captain Watson sailed for Nassau on February 22, 1865. The schooner's cargo was still consigned to C.L. Beissner. These three entries refute all of Watson's claims about making a second run into Galveston, selling *Rob Roy*, stepping down as her captain, joining the crew of *Phoenix/Pelican* as sailing master, and taking command of *Jeannette* from Galveston to Tampico.[3]

Watson had said that *Rob Roy* met its final destiny when a new, but unidentified captain sailed his former schooner to Florida. Instead, the available evidence suggests that it was William Watson who remained in command when *Rob Roy* joined the denizens of Davy Jones' locker. Watson said that he learned of *Rob Roy*'s fate through one of the men that Captain Curry had recommended to him on his first run into Tampico. His name was George a "younger man, and exceedingly sober and faithful, and an excellent seaman." He had remained with *Rob Roy* "out of a veneration he had for the vessel, regarding her as a lucky vessel." Watson repeated George's story about sailing from Havana which was about 10 days after he had supposedly sold his schooner. *Rob Roy* was headed for the mouth of the Suwanee, a meandering river that empties into the Gulf of Mexico above Tampa Bay. According to Watson, the new captain made the coast in three days, but could not find the proper river entrance. While sailing along the coast, the U.S. Navy gunboat *Fox* chased them onto a beach. The crew set fire to the schooner to keep her out of the enemy's hands. The men landed safely, but to George's "sorrow, he saw his good old craft, as he called her, burned to the water's edge."[4]

Official records and contemporary newspaper reports confirm the portion of William Watson's story about the chase and burning of *Rob Roy*. They also add a few interesting details. The schooner *Fox* was operating as a tender to the steamer USS *Stars and Stripes*. Navy gunboat captains often deployed smaller sailing vessels to track down equally small blockade runners in the shallow waters of the Gulf coast. *Fox* had been lying at anchor in Deadman's Bay on March 2, 1865. The bay is found off Florida's Steinhatchee River, located north of the Suwanee River and due west of Gainesville. It was there that *Fox*'s crew, "discovered a strange schooner at anchor on the south side of the bay near the shore."[5]

The *Fox*'s captain, Acting Master Francis Burgess, immediately launched an armed boat to capture the unidentified schooner. *Rob Roy*'s crew tried to escape, but the U.S. Navy sailors cut her off. *Rob Roy*'s crew had no choice but to run their faithful vessel ashore and set her afire to prevent capture. "The flames spread with such rapidity and had obtained such a control by the time the boat's crew got alongside that it was found impossible to extinguish them. She proved to be the *Rob Roy*, of Belize, Honduras." The Navy sailors managed to salvage "a lot of cavalry sabers and farming and mechanical implements" in a damaged condition. The captain of the USS *Stars and Stripes* sent these articles to the "prize court at Key West for

16 . The Demise of Rob Roy, Blockade Running, and the Confederacy

adjudication." There, the admiralty court condemned the cargo as a valid prize valued at $528.43. After expenses of $98.36, the crew shared half the net total of $430.07.[6]

Watson recalled that George related his tale about *Rob Roy*'s final voyage after he made his way back to Havana. According to Watson, the two men reunited about two months after Watson and Robert Mills had sold the schooner at auction. Adding up the days between *Rob Roy*'s sale and its capture on March 2 provides context for the true ending for *Rob Roy*'s story. William Watson said he was at Havana in mid–April 1865. If Watson had been telling the truth about sailing onboard both *Phoenix*/*Pelican* and *Jeannette*, and his subsequent bout of smallpox at Tampico, it was not possible for him to have been at Havana in mid–April. The best explanation for his being at Havana in mid–April 1865, was that he did not detach from *Rob Roy* and had remained captain of his schooner, just as the newspapers had reported.

After burning *Rob Roy*, Watson and his crew probably made their way a few miles along the coast up to St. Marks, a small inland port south of Tallahassee, Florida. The schooner *Florida* was the most likely candidate for transporting Watson to Havana. She sailed from St. Marks on March 28 and arrived at Havana on April 3. The steamer *Owl*, under Captain John Newland Maffitt, had briefly lingered off the coast of St. Marks on March 24 to drop off Assistant Surgeon David S. Watson and Assistant Engineer Edward R. Archer of the Confederate Navy. However, it was unlikely that Captain Maffitt was able to organize transportation out of Florida for any sailors needing a ride to Havana. Other than these two vessels, no other blockade runners were known to have sailed from the western coast of Florida to Havana during the period William Watson and *Rob Roy*'s crew would have been there.[7]

There are no readily available records that provide clues about when William Watson might have returned to the United Kingdom. He offered no hints about when or how he got back to his homeland in Scotland. One possibility was via the twin-screw steamer *Louisa Ann Fanny*. She departed Havana for the last time on April 26, and arrived at Liverpool on May 14 after a quick 10-day run from Bermuda. If he had been a passenger, it might account for Watson's familiarity with such a vessel that he identified as *Phoenix*, even though he probably did not have any duties as part of her crew.[8]

The historical record supports Watson's claims to have sailed out of New Orleans, Belize, the Rio Grande, Brazos River, Tampico, Havana, and Galveston, during the Civil War. There are no records, other than his own account, which confirm Watson's presence onboard any blockade runner other than his own *Rob Roy* (the former *Francis Marquez, Jr.* and *James Cartey*). It also does not appear that he made a second run from Havana into Galveston onboard *Rob Roy* as he claimed. Instead, existing records show that he captained his schooner on its final run that ended in a conflagration on an isolated beach on Florida's west coast. Watson was probably back at in Havana in mid–April 1865, when his story returned to the realm of plausibility.

After his final return to Havana, Watson's trail went cold. He closed out his tale by summarizing the collapse of the Confederacy and the blockade-running business. When he totaled his profits and expenses for the voyages of *Rob Roy*, Watson found that he had barely broken even. Most of his earnings had come from wages and bonuses as a blockade runner captain. The primary benefit from his "rather enjoyable occupation" was the satisfaction of "some successful elusion of the enemy, a chase and escape, or other adventure, [more] than any other emolument."[9]

Rather than barely breaking even, Watson's financial situation could not have been as bad as he claimed. When he returned to Scotland in 1865, he built a house in Glasgow at 127 Argyle Street. In April 1871, just prior to his 45th birthday, he married Helen Milligan, the 32-year-old daughter of a local baker. After the wedding, William built two houses in his boyhood village of Skelmorlie that he named after two of his Civil War battles: Oakhill and Pea Ridge. These homes were completed by 1875, but he would rent them out while still residing on Argyle Street in Glasgow. In 1878, he took over the Ladyburn Boiler Works at Greenock. He proved to be an astute businessman. In 1882, his firm launched the 160-ton iron screw steamer *Talisman*. When railroad construction crews damaged his property, he sued and won a judgement that was equivalent to almost $2 million in today's dollars.[10]

William settled in Skelmorlie at his Pea Ridge villa where he was a trustee of the Parish Church. While living the life of a retired civil engineer, Watson began writing his two Civil War memoirs. The books describe his American Civil War adventures and impressions of life in the southern states. He first shared his experiences as a Confederate soldier in a memoir titled *Life in the Confederate Army Being the Observations and Experiences of an Alien in the South During the American Civil War*. The book appeared in the United Kingdom in 1887, and Scribner & Welford published the U.S. edition the following year. The *Boston Sunday Herald* proclaimed Watson's book as, "The Best Story of the Southern Side Yet Written."[11]

William Watson was the only Scottish ship captain who wrote his memoirs as a blockade runner. After Fisher Unwin released his blockade-running adventure book in 1892, most critics again gave Watson's tale a positive reception. The book reviews for *Civil War Adventures of a Blockade Runner; or, Trade in Time of War* (full title from the title page) typically ran along the following lines.[12]

> The narrative moves along with a fine free sweep, and, if it does not affect the graces of literary art, it has what is in many respects, better, the freshness that comes of immediate personal knowledge and takes one, besides, a strong interest from the adventurous nature of is subject ... while its first address is to those in search of a story of stirring incidents, it has some value as a historical picture of a state of things that is not likely again to be revived. Overall, the work forms a noteworthy addition to the series in which it appears, and deserves a hearty welcome.[13]

Another reported:

> Mr. Watson's book is so pleasant and useful just because it is concerned with nothing of which the writer was not an eyewitness. It is a live book; it gives us a vivid picture of phases of the great war which have been too much lost sight of in the more imposing spectacles of operations on land.... The blockade-running schooner *Rob Roy*, the feats of which are narrated in this volume, should henceforth be famous in the history of war.[14]

Despite the claim of the reviewer from *The Echo*, Watson made a subtle distinction between the two books in his prefaces. In *Life in the Confederate Army*, Watson said, "I claim no merit for the work beyond a plain, honest and truthful statement of what I actually saw and gathered." Watson was slightly less definitive in his truthfulness statement about *Adventures of a Blockade Runner*, "The writer … confines himself to a brief detail of his own acts and experience, and what came under his own observation." In both accounts, Watson left himself room to write about things that he observed as well as the acts he personally performed in Civil War memoirs. None of the columnists called into question the truth of any of Watson's claims in either volume.[15]

By 1895, William Watson was living at Beechgrove, a large mid–Victorian Tudor–style villa in Skelmorlie. Watson died in 1906, just before his 80th birthday. He was survived by his wife Helen and three children. They were Henry who worked for his father as a marine engineer in Greenock, and his daughters Agnes and Mary.[16]

While his blockade-running book may not qualify as a highly accurate historical account, it succeeds wonderfully as a stirring tale of adventure. More than a historical novel, Watson's book is ripe with vivid portrayals of people, places, and Civil War events that cannot be found anywhere else. His descriptions ring true and many can be verified in reliable contemporary sources. Watson's lively narrative adds invaluable flavor to often-bland official reports and shipping documents. Even his anecdotes that were not completely accurate in time and place, could very well have unfolded just as he said they did. Watson's exaggerations about his own skills and his errors regarding names, dates, and places, do not negate the validity of his descriptions of the events. Watson's account allows the reader to visualize very real Civil War blockade-running adventures. From cover to cover, Watson's book provides a true sense of what it was like to live the life of a Civil War blockade runner both at sea and ashore.

Appendix 1

Rob Roy and Henry Laverty, the Prequel

Henry Laverty was *Rob Roy*'s captain when William Watson bought the New Orleans schooner in May of 1863. Laverty had been captain of the former *Francis Marquez, Jr.* for three months. The 45-year-old Irishman was a veteran sea captain with 14 years of experience sailing in and out of New Orleans. *Rob Roy* was his second command since the outbreak of the Civil War. The first was a 109-ton schooner, *C.P. Knapp*.[1]

Laverty's first wartime voyage on the *C.P. Knapp* was shortly after the U.S. Navy established a blockade off the approaches to the Mississippi River in late May 1861. As a precaution, the owner of the schooner obtained a British registry. The change of registry reduced the risk of immediate condemnation if the vessel was captured by a Union or Confederate Navy warship. Her Britannic Majesty's consul at New Orleans, William Mure, signed the provisional register on May 21, 1861. Seven days later, Laverty cleared Confederate Customs at New Orleans bound for Matamoros. He was carrying a large cargo of flour, lard, sugar, candles, oil, and tobacco.[2]

After offloading her cargo at the Rio Grande, *C.P. Knapp* cleared Matamoros customs on June 24, having declared for Havana. However, her logbook revealed that Captain Laverty took a detour. After leaving Matamoras, he steered directly for Brashear, Louisiana, now known as Morgan City, on the Atchafalaya River. Laverty successfully eluded the blockading fleet, dry-docked his schooner, and discharged the crew.[3]

Laverty and *C.P. Knapp* were not out of action for long. In late July or early August, they got underway for Havana. Captain Henry Laverty sailed with nine crewmen, and two passengers. On August 8, about halfway to their destination, *C.P. Knapp* encountered the 62-gun sailing frigate USS *Santee*. The lumbering *Santee* was on its way from Hampton Roads, Virginia, to join the Gulf blockading fleet. Captain Henry Eagle's boarding party discovered the schooner's sailing log that detailed its run into Louisiana from the Rio Grande. Captain Eagle seized the schooner as a prize of war. He then towed *C.P. Knapp* and her crew to Pensacola and sailed her to the U.S. admiralty court at Key West, Florida. Two months later, *Santee* would relieve USS *South Carolina* on blockade duty off Galveston.[4]

Laverty and *C.P. Knapp* remained in Key West for several weeks as they awaited their day in court. Much to the bemusement of Yankee journalists and the U.S. Navy, the admiralty judge ordered the release of the schooner, her cargo, and crew on September 16, 1861. Twelve days later, the U.S. attorney withdrew his appeal after the judge agreed that there had been probable cause for the seizure. This decision meant that *C.P. Knapp*'s owners would not receive any restitution for their time and trouble, but it also meant that Henry Laverty was back in command of his schooner. On September 30, 53 days after their capture, *C.P. Knapp* and its crew cleared from Key West for Havana with a load of rice.[5]

The surviving official court records are silent about the reasons for *C.P. Knapp*'s release. Laverty had obviously run his schooner into and out of Louisiana in violation of the Union's declared blockade. Fortunately, a newspaper correspondent for the *New York Times* was on hand to provide a cynical commentary about the proceedings. The judge's ruling was based on a technicality, one that most of the admiralty courts and most certainly, the U.S. Navy usually ignored. For a blockade of a specific port to be legal, the Navy had to properly announce the blockade to port authorities, enforce it with a credible deterrent, and continuously maintain it at each port. An element of the announcement requirement was to inform each vessel in port of the initial establishment of the blockade as it entered port. Any neutral vessels in port at the commencement of the blockade had to have an opportunity to depart. Notification of the blockade was a minor detail that had been ignored in the bayous of Louisiana.[6]

The Key West correspondent gathered his information from a sheet of paper found tacked to a tree. He was not happy with the decision, and called the judge "His Sapiency," and a "lynx-eyed … very kind friend" of the South. Captain Laverty's did not reveal his own reaction, but he must have been surprised and relieved. After less than a day at sea, he finally arrived at Havana on October 1, 1861. It would be several weeks until he set sail again.[7]

Henry Laverty finally sailed the *C.P. Knapp* to the Rio Grande in January 1862 and loaded her with 150 bales of cotton bound for Havana. Over the next nine months, Laverty made several round trips between Havana and Matamoros as captain of the *C.P. Knapp*. By February of 1863, Laverty signed on as the captain of the schooner *Francis Marquez, Jr.* and was back in Matamoros. It was not a coincidence that Henry Laverty succeeded P.A. Fronty (Fronti) as the captain of the *Francis Marquez, Jr*. Fronty had also been the captain of the *C.P. Knapp* prior to Laverty's tenure in command. Captain Laverty sailed the smaller, 48-ton *Francis Marquez, Jr.* to the Rio Grande late that winter and returned to his home in New Orleans with 23 bales of cotton on April 4, 1863. A month later, Henry Laverty's schooner had a new owner and a new name: William Watson and *Rob Roy*.[8]

Appendix 2

Blockade Running or Smuggling

Before a vessel could depart a blockaded Texas port, the ships' captains first had to pay the appropriate customs fees and obtain health and military permits. Except for the extra military requirement, the process was the same as in peacetime. The same customs and permitting processes applied to overland trade when merchants exported goods across the Rio Grande and into Mexico. Maritime commerce in the presence of a blockade was difficult and dangerous, but the government still collected import and export fees.

If the U.S. Navy successfully captured a blockade runner, there would be significant financial consequences for the owners of the vessel and its cargo, but not because the sailors were breaking U.S. law by engaging in smuggling. The United States could not legally charge the crew or owners of a vessel (or its cargo) with smuggling if they had paid the requisite customs duties at the vessel's port of origin and destination. Blockade runners to and from Confederate ports usually paid all these fees, and they had the appropriately stamped customs clearance forms to prove it.

President Lincoln issued declarations about the blockade, and both the U.S and Confederate Congresses passed laws against trading with the enemy. These laws were often ignored or easily bypassed. The Union blockade of the Confederate states, on the other hand, was an act of war. Only a sovereign nation can declare a blockade against another country (or belligerent state). It is not a form of law enforcement that a nation can use against its own citizens. Therefore, when President Lincoln declared a blockade against the South, the international community automatically recognized it as a declaration of war against the Confederate States and acknowledged the confederation of southern states as a belligerent nation-state. The contemporary rhetoric from Union authorities, however, refused to officially acknowledge the "so-called" Confederate States. In the eyes of Union officials, the insurrectionary states were in rebellion. The U.S. maintained the official and diplomatic position that there was no civil war, and the Confederacy was not a legitimate country. These government officials knew better, but reality of the Civil War did not serve the Union's political purposes by publicly acknowledging the fact.[1]

The contemporary narrative regarding blockade running has muddled modern understandings of the distinction between blockade running and smuggling. The term "smuggling" refers to the illegal movement of goods into or out of a country. Blockade running is an act of defiance against a barrier maintained by force of arms. If a neutral vessel attempted to pass through the blockade without a permit, it was breaking no law, foreign or domestic. The United States' blockade of the Southern states was simply one aspect of a war between two belligerents. Contemporary international law stipulated three basic requirements for a blockade to be legitimate. The aggressor nation, i.e., the United States, had to properly announce the blockade, enforce it with a credible deterrent of armed forces (usually warships), and continuously maintain it at the relevant ports.[2]

While blockade running was not smuggling, there were legal and financial consequences for vessels, their cargos and crews, but only if the U.S. blockading fleet captured them in the process of running the blockade. A captured vessel and members of its crew that U.S. Navy officials suspected of running the blockade were brought before an admiralty court for adjudication. Whenever the court ruled that a captured vessel was guilty of attempting to violate the blockade, the result was condemnation. If the admiralty court condemned the vessel and cargo, the government would temporarily confine its neutral crew members. For a vessel or cargo belonging to Confederate entities, condemnation was guaranteed. The local U.S. marshal would then seize both the vessel and its cargo and sell them at public auction on behalf of the government. There were variations and degrees of condemnation when the court condemned only a portion of the cargo. The courts would sometimes release a vessel and its cargo, but refuse to pay the owners any reparations for extra expenses. In these cases, the evidence had convinced the judge that the blockading fleet had a legitimate justification for seizing the vessel, but insufficient evidence to condemn it.[3]

Captured sailors who were citizens of the Confederate States could be imprisoned or exchanged as belligerents, while U.S. citizens could be tried as traitors, insurrectionists, or for trading with the enemy. Blockade-running crewmen and shipowners were not, however, guilty of smuggling. The courts typically released neutral crew members as soon as they completed their testimony. While there were numerous instances of smuggling into and out of both the Union and Confederacy, most of the cotton trade out of Texas and the rest of the South did not constitute smuggling.[4]

If a vessel successfully evaded the blockade, its owners and their agents were free to conduct business in any neutral port. They also were not technically subject to future seizure or prosecution due to past blockade-running activities. However, if a vessel or ship captain were known to be a blockade runner by habit or reputation, the U.S. Navy would often detain them anyway. To avoid legal problems for trading directly with the enemy, American ship owners and merchants had to use intermediaries. If the vessel's papers certified that the owners of the vessel and its cargo were citizens of neutral countries, there would be no violation of the laws of the United States. For an admiralty court to uphold a seizure, there had to be sufficient evidence of enemy ownership of the vessel or cargo or that it had originated from or was bound to a Confederate port or buyer. Neutral vessels, crews, shipping agents, and ports provided an artificial, but technically lawful conduit for trade between the North and South. This indirect and surreptitious process added layers of cost and obscured the true nature of the transaction. But as a result, most of the Confederate cotton that departed Texas and landed at a United States port, did so quite legally.[5]

APPENDIX 3

Blockade Runs of the SS *Alice* (aka *Matagorda*)

Stephen Wise's normally reliable *Lifeline of the Confederacy* credits the *Alice/Matagorda* with a total of 25 successful runs: 14 at Mobile (7 in and 7 out) and 11 at Texas ports (six in and five out). On the following page, the table on the left consolidates the steamer's movements that Wise spread out over four different tables over several pages (265–269, 272, 274). This compilation highlights obvious errors in the entries for the blockade-running steamer *Alice* (*Matagorda*) blockade-running entries found in Wise's tables. The table on the right shows the actual movements of *Alice* (*Matagorda*) and is spaced for easy comparison with the movements extracted from Wise's tables. The *Alice* (*Matagorda*) made a total of 16 successful blockade runs, one out of New Orleans, eight at Mobile (4 in and 4 out), two each at Sabine Pass and the Brazos River (in and out), and three at Galveston Bay (2 in and 1 out). Wise omits the run out of Louisiana and into the Sabine.

Other than the initial trip between New Orleans and Sabine Pass, and the subsequent transit directly from the Brazos River to Galveston Bay, *Alice/Matagorda*'s blockade-running hub was Havana.

Blockade Runs of the steamer *Alice*
(aka *Matagorda*), a Comparison

Lifeline of the Confederacy *Runs*			*Actual Blockade Runs*		
Port	In	Out	Port	In	Out
			New Orleans	n/a*	Mar 13, 1862
			Sabine Pass	Mar 15, 1862	Apr 15, 1862
Mobile	Jul 22, 1862	Sep 29, 1862	Mobile	Aug 21, 1862	Sep 29, 1862
			Mobile	Dec 28, 1862	Feb 14, 1863
Mobile	Apr 1863	Apr 16, 1863	Mobile	Mar 25, 1863	Apr 16, 1863
Galveston	Apr 1863	Apr 30, 1863			
Mobile	May 23, 1863	May 1863	Mobile	May 23, 1863,	Jul 7, 1863
Mobile	Jun 23, 1863	Jul 7, 1863			
Brazos River†	Feb 1864	Apr 1864	Brazos River†	Feb 13, 1864	Apr 6, 1864
Mobile	Apr, 1864	Apr 16, 1864			
Galveston	Apr 1864	Apr 30, 1864	Galveston	Apr 7, 1864	Apr 30, 1864
Mobile	May 23, 1864	Jun, 1864			
Galveston	May 1864	May 31, 1864			
Galveston	Jun 1864	Jul 1864			
Mobile	Jun 23, 1864	Jul 7, 1864			
Galveston	Aug 1864	Sep 10, 1864	Galveston	Jul 5, 1864	Sep 6, 1864§

* Confederate authorities in Louisiana seized SS *Matagorda* on Jan 15, 1862.
† *Alice* was unable to run into Galveston in Feb 1864 and had to divert into the Brazos River.
§ *Alice* departed Galveston Bay on Sep 6th, but was captured on Sep 10th.

Appendix 4

Cast of Characters

Archer, Edward Richard (1834–1918). Former U.S. Navy engineer onboard the USS *Powhatan*, appointed as first assistant engineer in the Confederate Navy. Traveled to the west coast of Florida on board the blockade runner *Owl*.

Ashby (Ashbey), Joseph Henry (1827–1874). Originally from New York, he was captain of the blockade runner *Exchange* (also owned and commanded *Andromeda*). As captain of the Louisiana schooner *West Florida* (aka *Cephise* & *Hanover*), he used a Butler pass to run the blockade.

Askins, William E. Captain of the blockade runner *Sybil* (*Eagle*) captured off the coast of North Carolina out of Matamoros.

Austin, Charles William (1833–1889). Captain of the blockade-running schooner *Jane* and the steamers *Union*, CSS *Harriet Lane* (while in Galveston), CSS *Clifton*, and *Susannah* (*Mail*). He was first mate of the ironclad ram CSS *Manassas* at New Orleans.

Avendaño, José Maria (aka Luis María de Avendaño y López) (1833–?). A managing partner of Avendaño Hermanos & Company that Watson identified as "A. & Co." José Maria managed the business in Havana during the war. His other brothers Francisco (known as Peregrino), Miguel, and Teodomiro managed the office in New Orleans. Despite their long-term residence in New Orleans, the brothers remained citizens of Spain. The residents of his native Liendo, Spain erected a statue in his honor and hold an annual fiesta on May 1 to celebrate his generosity to the region.

Barnard, Joseph C. (1813–1877). Captain of the blockade-running schooner *Chaos* (*Velocity*, *Fairy*, *Nellie Blair*) before turning it over to Joseph Davidson and taking command of the steamer *Triton*. Originally from New York, he briefly commanded the *Harriet Lane* (*Lavinia*) during its run out of Galveston. After the war, he remained in Texas and became the U.S. Inspector of Hulls at Galveston.

Barrios, Appolonaria (Polly). Young crewman onboard *Rob Roy* from Chile.

Bates, Joseph. (1805–1888). Confederate colonel in charge at the Brazos who Watson identified as Colonel Evans. Former Alabama legislator, major general in the Alabama militia, Mayor of Galveston, plantation owner, and U.S. Marshal for Eastern Texas.

Bayly (Baily), William. Captain of the blockade-running schooner *Charles Russell*.

Beauregard, Pierre Gustave Toutant (1818–1893). West Point graduate and pre-war customer of William Watson at his sugar cane plantation in Louisiana. He was the Confederate general who initiated the attack on Fort Sumter in Charleston harbor and was the victorious commander at the First Battle of Bull Run (Manassas). He later fell out of favor with Jefferson Davis and commanded the defenses of Charleston and Petersburg. After the war, he returned to Louisiana.

Bee, Hamilton Prioleau (1822–1897). A Confederate brigadier general, veteran of the Mexican War, former Texas state legislator (1849–1859), and speaker of the house (1855–1857) from

Laredo. He was the Confederate general in command of the lower Rio Grande district prior to General Magruder. Nicknamed "General Wasp," he was an effective political general, but failed as a combat leader during the Red River campaign. After the war, he briefly worked in Havana, but moved to Mexico until returning to Texas in 1876. He managed a farm for what is now Texas A&M University, practiced law in San Antonio, and was a state agency commissioner in Austin. The City of Beeville, Texas, was named in his father's honor.

Beissner, Charles Ludwig (1839–1912). A German-born merchant and banker whose father owned a hotel in Galveston. Charles worked for R. & D.G. Mills, eventually becoming their chief clerk. He then formed C.L. Beissner & Co., shipping agents, and opened a branch in Havana, probably in association with the Mills Brothers. After the war, he was the owner of Rosenberg Bank with his brother, and was a lifelong resident of Galveston, Texas.

Bell, George Panton. British merchant and blockade runner owner doing business in Havana.

Berndt, Charles. Prussian-born captain, owner, and builder of the Confederate schooner *Neptune*.

Blakely, George (1831–1913). Relieved Samuel Marcy as captain of the blockade runner *Lark*; he was captured while captain of *Cumberland* as it attempted to run into Mobile, but managed to escape confinement. He was on furlough from Her Britannic Majesty's Royal Navy.

Blanchet, Pierre Constant (1830–1901). French-born Texan who was captain of the blockade-running schooners *Emily* and *Lady Hurley*. He remained in Galveston after the war and is buried there.

Bloomfield, Benjamin Seton (1824–1903). A major in the Confederate quartermaster corps; was originally a New Orleans book printer, ledger, and stationery shop co-owner. Although he opposed secession, he accepted a commission with the 2nd Louisiana Infantry; then joined General Magruder's staff in Virginia. In 1862, he transferred to Texas with the general as his chief quartermaster. He moved to Havana by Nov 1864, later joined by his wife and six children. By the end of the war, he was in New York where he cooperated with U.S. officials.

Booth, John Wilkes (1838–1865). Stage actor and President Abraham Lincoln's assassin.

Borner, Paul (1835–1911). Acting U.S. Navy Ensign on board USS *Kineo*. He commanded the prize crew for the blockade runner *Stingaree* when Captain Dave McClusky's crew recaptured the schooner and ran her into the Brazos River. Confederates officially paroled him on Dec 12, 1864, and exchanged him at Galveston seven days later.

Bragg, Braxton (1817–1876). Originally from North Carolina, he was one of only seven full Confederate generals. He had resigned from the U.S. Army in 1855 to settle onto a sugar plantation with his Louisiana wife near Thibodaux and was a pre-war customer of William Watson. The state appointed him brigadier general to train its militia. He enjoyed initial success training troops and in battle at Shiloh. President Davis later relieved him from duty when he had repeated combat failures. He died in Galveston and is buried in Mobile. He was the original namesake of Fort Bragg, North Carolina.

Brown, James W. Scottish-born captain of the schooner *Belle* (*Gipsey*, *Zouave*) that a cutting out crew from the USS *Virginia* captured in Galveston Bay while Captain Brown was ashore.

Buchel, August Carl (1813–1864). German-born (Hesse) Confederate colonel, originally commissioned into the Hesse-Darmstadt army, served as a lieutenant in the French Foreign Legion, decorated and knighted for his bravery by the Queen of Spain, an instructor in the Turkish army, sailed to Indianola with the Adelsverein in 1845. He raised a company during the Mexican War and was aide-de-camp for Gen. Zachary Taylor. After the war, he was customs collector at Port Lavaca and organized the Indianola Volunteers to combat Mexican bandits under Juan N. Cortina. During the Civil War, he joined the Texas militia in 1861 and served in South Texas. Promoted to colonel of the First Texas Cavalry in 1863, he was in command on the Texas Gulf Coast when the schooner *Sarah* appeared. Having been appointed a brigadier general, he transferred to Louisiana to counter a Union Army invasion. Mortally wounded at Pleasant Hill, Louisiana, on April 9, 1864, he was buried at the State Cemetery in Austin. He never married and spoke seven languages.

Buckley, Cornelius W. (1837–1869). Irish-born owner of the British-flagged blockade-running schooner *James Williams* who was captured a few miles from the Brazos River. He was a clerk for Captain Dick Dowling who led the successful defense of Sabine Pass.

Bulloch, James Dunwoody (1823–1901). Born into a prominent Georgia family, he joined the U.S. Navy at the age of 16 and became a well-known merchant sea captain. Siding with his state during the Civil War, he was appointed as a commander in the Confederate Navy and served in Liverpool as a secret agent in charge of procuring ships and supplies for the Confederacy. His nephew, Theodore Roosevelt, became the 26th President of the United States.

Burgess, Francis (1828–1899). An acting master in the U.S. Navy and captain of the USS *Beauregard* prior to taking command of the USS *Fox* off the west coast of Florida. His crew chased *Rob Roy* ashore and reached it in time to recover part of its cargo as it burned to the waterline.

Butler, Benjamin Franklin (1818–1893). A politically-appointed major general who commanded Union forces in New Orleans (May–Dec 1862) where he became known as "Beast Butler" for his harsh treatment of local citizens, corruption, and petty looting.

Byron, Lord (George Gordon Noel) (1788–1824). Flamboyant, notorious, and immensely popular British Romantic poet who was the son of an impoverished Scots heiress and a fortune-hunting widower.

Campbell, Andrew Donaldson (1777–1854). Former West Indies sugar planter and owner of Ashcraig estate in Skelmorlie, Scotland, the childhood home of William Watson.

Campbell, Janet Maria (1777–1855). Wife of Andrew Campbell.

Carrington, William Thornton (1833–1875). Virginia-born Confederate officer who was living in Texas prior to the war. Served as an aide to Major General Magruder.

Carter, William Fitzhugh (1815–1869). Confederate Navy lieutenant and de facto captain of the blockade runner *Louisa Ann Fanny*.

Cayce, Henry Petty (1819–1875). Confederate lieutenant colonel who commanded the post at Velasco consisting of the 13th Regiment, Texas Infantry.

Celda, Francis. Matamoros-born Mexican businessman and nominal captain of the schooner *Alma*.

Chase, Franklin (1806–1890). Merchant and U.S. Consul to Tampico (1837–1870). Met and married his wife Anna there in 1838.

Chubb, Thomas Beaverstock (1811–1890). He came to Texas during its war for independence as master of a sailing vessel. A lifelong mariner, he served as commodore of the Galveston Harbor Police during the Civil War, was captured in November 1861 but exchanged and returned to duty in March 1862. He served as harbormaster in Galveston from 1882 until his death at his summer home in Vermont. His 1859 Greek Revival home is in Galveston where he is buried at the Evergreen Cemetery.

Clark, Edward (1815–1880). Texas Lieutenant Governor in 1859; elevated to Governor in Spring 1861 when Governor Sam Houston resigned. He lost a close election to Francis R. Lubbock in the autumn of 1861.

Clark, William (1819–1872 ca). Owner of a "Staple and Fancy Dry Goods" store in Houston who had an interest in Captain McClusky's schooner *Stingaree* and the schooner *Flash*.

Conklin, Matthias Dayton (1810–1889). Principal owner of Houston-based M.D. Conklin & Co. and a consignee of *Rob Roy*'s cargo whom Watson referred to as "Mr. C."

Cooper, William S. (1826–?). Member of the Ancient Order of J.O.L.O. providing lookout services at Galveston in the early months of the war. Was captain of the blockade-running schooners *Lilly*, *Mary Ellen*, and *William* whom Watson described as "Captain C. of the L." He was captured on his return trip from Belize to the Brazos River on *Mary Ellen* and was identified as the former "notorious captain" of *Lilly*.

Cross, Abraham (1837–1905). The Confederate Army lieutenant and engineer on the Brazos River who seized *Rob Roy* to install obstructions in the river.

Curry (Currie), John M. (1812–?) British citizen who lived in Tampico with his wife and sisters. Owned and captained several blockade-running schooners including *Alma*, *Sylphide*, *Richard H. Vermilyea*, and *Lone* (*Cuca*).

Davidson, Joseph. Captain of the blockade-running schooners *Chaos* (*Velocity*, *Fairy*, *Nellie Blair*) and *Sam Houston*.

Davis, J.H. Captain who abandoned his blockade-running schooner *Alabama* just before the blockading fleet captured it off San Luis Pass.

Davison, James H. (1828–?). British captain of the 34-ton blockade-running schooner *Lilly*, captured off the Brazos River in January 1865. Previously served onboard SS *Susannah*. Originally from Liverpool, his wife resided in Texas when he was captured.

Debray, Xavier Blanchard (1818–1895). Naturalized Frenchman and Confederate Army colonel. He was promoted to brigadier general in April 1864, but was never confirmed.

Dowling, Richard "Dick" William (1838–1867). Confederate Army captain who led the brilliant defense of Sabine Pass on September 8, 1863. Dowling's small artillery company defeated a Union invasion fleet and captured the gunboats USS *Clifton* and USS *Granite City* during the assault.

Downs, J. Francis (1830–?). Born in British North America (modern Canada), he was captain of blockade-running schooners *Eureka* and *John* who befriended William Watson. He was a widower with one daughter.

Ennis, Cornelius (1813–1899). Former mayor of Houston (1857), Galveston merchant, and owner of the blockade-running schooners *Corelia*, *Foam*, *Richard O. Bryan*, and the steamer *Jeannette* that he named for his wife, the former Jeannette Ingals Kimball (1822–1898).

Fernandez, Joseph (1842–?). An illiterate U.S. Navy seaman and a member of *Stingaree*'s prize crew from the USS *Kineo*. Although Dave McClusky identified him as a West India Negro, he emigrated from Portugal in 1859 and enlisted in the Navy in 1861. He escaped capture when he jumped into *Stingaree*'s yawl and made his way back to his ship.

Fleigh, William Henry (1833–1923). Captain of the blockade-running schooners *Flash* and *Stingaree* (relieved Dave McClusky). Watson identified him as "Bill Flagg."

Fly, George Washington Lafayette (1836–1905). Confederate major who spoke up on behalf of William Watson in Galveston. Captured with Watson at the Battle of Corinth while with the 2nd Texas Infantry Regiment. Reported as killed in action, he only had a minor leg wound, was later exchanged, and rejoined his command. He returned to Texas in November 1863 and served under Col. John S. "Rip" Ford in South Texas.

Ford, John Salmon "Rip" (1815–1897). Colonel in command of Confederate operational forces at the Rio Grande (1861–1862 & 1864–1865). A former newspaper editor, State senator, and Texas Ranger. He acquired his nickname during the Mexican American War, when he closed his many condolence letters with "Rest in peace," later abbreviated to form his nickname "Rip."

Fremantle, Sir Arthur James Lyon (1835–1901). British Army lieutenant colonel who entered the Confederacy at the Rio Grande. He made his way North and witnessed the Battle of Gettysburg and the New York City draft riots. His diary documenting his observations of the

American Civil War was published in London shortly before Christmas 1863, as *Three Months in the Southern States: April–June 1863*. It was reprinted in both New York and Mobile in 1864. After his return to England in July 1864, he fought in the Afghan wars, was Governor of Malta, and retired as a lieutenant general.

French, Alonzo Frank (1834–1899). A supercargo identified as "Mr. F." onboard *Rob Roy* working on behalf of R. & D.G. Mills & Co. After the war, he remained in Galveston as a bookkeeper for W.B. Sorley and Ball, Hutchins, & Co., and a banker with Hutchins, Sealy, & Co.

Gilliat, Algernon (1837–1925). A junior partner with his brother John in the British merchant banking company founded by his father, John K. Gilliat, and financial supporter of the Confederacy. *Mary Augusta* (sister ship of *Louisa Ann Fanny*) was named in honor of his wife Lady Mary Augusta Georgiana Moore (1836–1903).

Gilliat, John Saunders (1829–1912). As head of J.K. Gilliat & Co. and director and then governor of the Bank of England, he was a financial supporter of James D. Bulloch and the Confederacy. He was later a Member of Parliament. The blockade runner, *Louisa Ann Fanny* (sister ship of the *Mary Augusta*), was named in honor of his wife, Louisa Ann Frances (1835–1914).

Godfrey, Abner Melchior (1825–1869). Captain of the blockade-running steamers *Denbigh* and *Will o' the Wisp*. After the war, he was the proprietor of the historic Battle House Hotel in Mobile, Alabama.

Gordon, John. An able-bodied seaman who helped recapture the schooner *Stingaree* from a U.S. Navy prize crew from the USS *Kineo*.

Greeley, Horace (1811–1872). The founder and editor of the *New York Tribune* who had a close, but complicated relationship President Lincoln.

Greenough, John. A Canadian from New Brunswick, living in Belize, he followed Henry Scherffius as captain of the blockade-running schooner *Cora*.

Gregory, William Henry (1816–1892). Pro-Confederate member of the British Parliament representing County Galway, Ireland (1857–1872). Visited the U.S. and Canada before the war and called on President James Buchanan and Vice President John Breckenridge.

Griffin, John (?–1864). A U.S. Navy landsman who was captured as one of the drunken prize crewmen from the USS *Kineo* on board the blockade-running schooner *Stingaree*. Subsequently incarcerated at prisoner of war prison at Camp Groce, Texas, until November 1864, later declared dead.

Griffiths, Thomas. British captain of *Lark* who delivered the steamer to Havana from Liverpool on behalf of John Laird for Fraser Trenholm to use as a Confederate blockade runner.

Hawes, James Morrison (1824–1889). A West Point graduate, he was promoted in the Mexican War for "gallant and meritorious conduct." After two-years at the French cavalry school, he joined the Confederate army and rose quickly to brigadier general, commanded cavalry West of the Mississippi, and fought at Shiloh. After stints in Arkansas and Louisiana, he took charge of the fortifications and garrison of Galveston Island under Major General Magruder in February 1864. After the war, he was in the hardware business in Kentucky.

Haynes, Samuel Barker (1815–1868). Self-professed blockade runner who worked as a U.S. secret agent in Havana under the name "Barker," and known to the consul as "Agent H."

Hébert, Paul Octave (1818–1880). Graduated first in his class at West Point and served in the Mexican War. Former Governor of Louisiana (1853–1856), he commanded Confederate troops in Texas (1861–1862), until he was relieved by Major General Magruder. He was also the interim commander after Magruder left for Arkansas and Major General John G. Walker arrived. After the war, he returned to Louisiana and served as the State's engineer.

Helm, Charles John (1817–1868). U.S. Consul (1858–1861) and then Confederate major and chief agent in Havana throughout the war. Served in the Mexican War and as a Kentucky State Congressman (1851–1853). After the war, he lived in Canada.

Hendley, Joseph J. (1807–1887). Connecticut-born ship captain, entrepreneur, and co-owner of Galveston's historic three-story Hendley Building, that served as a lookout station, and periodic headquarters for General Magruder during the Civil War. His father was also a sailor who was lost at sea; his older brother William was his Galveston business partner. During the Civil War, he was a founding member of volunteer lookouts posted at the top of his mercantile building and held the title of Grand Commander, J.O.L.O. (presumed to abbreviate "Jolly Order of Look Outs.")

Hendley, William (1798–1873). Ship owner, businessman, older brother of Joseph, and co-owner of the Hendley Row of office buildings on Galveston's Strand.

Hennessy, Daniel. A U.S. Navy landsman who was captured as one of the drunken prize crewmen from the USS *Kineo* on board the blockade-running schooner *Stingaree*. Subsequently incarcerated as a prisoner of war prison at Camp Groce, Texas.

Holland, Gustavus (or Gustave) Aldolphus (1819–1888). Born in Germany and served in the U.S. Army during the Mexican War. He was Chief Surgeon of the 1st Sub-District of Texas. Confederate General Hawes relieved him of his duties in July 1864 for not strictly enforcing a quarantine order regarding the blockade runner *Susannah*. After the war, he moved to San Francisco where he was a prominent member of the Board of Health. He then moved to El Paso where he died of cancer.

House, Thomas William (1814–1880). Originally from England, House moved to Houston in 1838 as a baker and confectioner. He then became a successful dry goods and grocery merchant and worked to improve river transportation. His position led to his ownership of several blockade runners (including *Velocity*, *Mary Sorley*, SS *Cora*, and the former U.S. warships *Sachem/Clarinda*, *Clifton*, and *Harriet Lane*) during the Civil War. He was a Houston mayor (1862), banker, railroad owner, and a major investor in the city's utility and transportation infrastructure.

Howe, James. An able-bodied seaman who helped recapture the schooner *Stinagree* from a U.S. Navy prize crew.

Hubbard, George N. Captain of the blockade runner *Agnes*.

Huke, Emile Alvin (1837–1864). A Confederate sergeant with Company "C" in Woods' Regiment of Texas Cavalry Volunteers at San Antonio. He resigned to become a Confederate agent and supercargo of the schooners *Sarah Jordan*, and *Ann Giberson*. He died in Galveston of yellow fever leaving his bride and one-year-old son to mourn his loss.

Hulburt, John E. Captain of *Cora* (*Snow Drift*) after Henry Scherffius.

Hutchins, William J. (1813–1884). Principal partner of Ball, Hutchins, & Co. A merchant, banker, steamboat owner, and railroad developer who came to Houston, Texas, in 1838 via New York and Florida. During the War, he was mayor of Houston and owner of a cotton compress company. Lt. Gen. E. Kirby Smith appointed him chief of the Texas Cotton Bureau in December 1863 with the rank of Lt. Col. The war reduced his fortune, but he retained extensive real estate holdings.

Hyland, Jim. Crewman of William Watson's *Rob Roy* who was a skilled stevedore, but suffered from both yellow fever and alcoholism, and left the crew in Galveston.

Jansen, Bernardas Peter. Dutch captain of the 180-ton brigantine *Geziena Hilligonda* that the U.S. Navy captured at the Rio Grande as a blockade runner. Jansen presented his case at the New Orleans admiralty court which ruled in his favor, releasing his brig without paying damages.

Jansen, Frederick. *Rob Roy*'s Swedish-born cook who saved his money to open a restaurant in Sweden.

Jauréguiberry (Tauréguiberry), Pierre (1824–?). French-born, Mexican citizen who was captain of the blockade-running schooner *Sea Witch* (*Pizarro*).

Johnson, Augustus A. (1839–?). Prussian-born Texan who commanded the *Schooner Sarah Jordan*.

Jolly, David Leitch (1833–1882). Scottish merchant with his older brothers Stewart and William in Jolly, Steward & Co. at Tampico, Mexico and the nominal owner of several schooners including *Lilly*, *Sarah*, *Henrietta* (*Cosmopolite*), and *Mary P. Burton*.

Jonah (eighth-century BCE). A Biblical prophet whom God called to the evil kingdom at Nineveh in the east. Instead, Jonah booked passage on a ship heading west. The crew tossed him overboard to quell a storm brought on because of God's displeasure. A large fish swallowed Jonah but took him back toward Israel and spit him out three days later. Superstitious sailors believed that a cursed person, especially a clergyman, was a Jonah, and sure to bring bad luck.

Joseph, Ferdinand Maximilian (1832–1867). Mainly referred to as Maximilian, he was archduke of Austria and installed by the French as emperor of Mexico from 1864 to 1867. Mexican loyalists executed him along with his wife Carlota in 1867.

Juárez, Benito (1806–1872). A national hero and president of Mexico (1861–1872), who for three years (1864–67) fought against foreign occupation under the emperor Maximilian and who sought constitutional reforms to create a democratic federal republic.

Kenedy, Mifflin (1818–1895). Rio Grande steamboat captain, entrepreneur, and senior partner in the firm of M. Kenedy & Co. with Richard King and Charles Stillman. As he had during the Mexican War, he was adept and gaining government contracts and investing in land and cattle during the Civil War and afterwards.

Kenney, Joseph Allen (1830–1905). New England-born captain of the blockade- running schooner *John Douglas*.

King, Richard (1825–1885). Steamboat captain and entrepreneur, land holder, and founder of the King Ranch who came to the Rio Grande at Mifflin Kenedy's invitation. His rancho at Santa Gertrudis became a staging depot for the cotton trade. He and his M. Kenedy & Co. partners enlarged their fortunes during and after the war.

Kuhn, Jacob Conrad (1809–?). A cotton trader and merchant originally from St. Gall, Switzerland, he opened his store in Galveston while Texas was still a Republic. The land-locked Swiss Confederation (the official name for the nation of Switzerland) appointed him as their consul to the State of Texas in 1846. He received permission to depart Texas via Mexico in May 1864.

Lane, Marquis de Lafayette (1825–1872). American consul to Vera Cruz.

Laverty, Henry (1818–1865). Irish immigrant out of New Orleans who was captain of the schooners *C.P. Knapp* (May 1861–Oct 1862) and *Francis Marquez, Jr.* (*Rob Roy*) (Jan–Jul 1863). He sailed *Francis Marquez, Jr.* to the Rio Grande (Jan-Mar 1863); remained as captain when William Watson purchased and renamed the schooner *Rob Roy*. Sailed to Belize and Matamoros, but did not want to risk running the blockade into Texas. Continued as captain of several different schooners until his death in Nov 1865.

Lawless, John Y. (1815–1877). Captain of *Island City* and the steamer *John F. Carr* during the Battle of Galveston.

Lee, Robert Edward (1807–1870). Served with the U.S. Second Cavalry regiment in Texas (Mar 1856–Oct 1857, and Feb 1860–Feb 1861), before General Winfield Scott offered Lee command of the Union Army. Although opposed to secession, he was unwilling to fight against his fellow southerners, and became General of the Army of Northern Virginia.

Lee, William. British pilot, navigator and acting captain of the Mexican flagged schooner *Alma*.

Leopold, Wilhelm (William) Edward (1839–1893). A musician who played the coronet with the

1st Texas Heavy Artillery's regimental band. The army detailed him as a foundry mechanic before he joined Henry Scherffius on the blockade runner *Pelican* as its assistant engineer.

Lincoln, Abraham (1809–1865). 16th President of the United States during the Civil War, whose assassination shocked the nation.

Little, George W. Captain of the blockade-running schooner *Stingray* (*Sting Ray*).

Lubbock, Francis Richard (1815–1905). Former comptroller of the Republic of Texas and Texas Governor (Nov 1861–Nov 1863); he then served in the army as a lieutenant colonel. After the war, he was a tax collector, and Texas State Treasurer. His brother, Henry, later commanded the Texas Marine Department. Another brother, Thomas, was a Texas Ranger and namesake of the City of Lubbock.

Lubbock, Henry Schultz (1823–1908). The South Carolina–born Confederate Army captain commanded *Bayou City* during the Battle of Galveston. He took command of the Texas Marine Department from Leon Smith. He moved to California with the steamship business after the war.

Luckett, Philip Noland (1824–1869). Served in the Mexican War as a surgeon for Rip Ford's Texas Rangers. Assumed Ford's command at the Rio Grande during the Civil War before taking over from William Scurry as an acting Brigadier General and commander of the Eastern Sub-District of Texas.

Lynn, Arthur Thomas (1812–1888). British Consul in Galveston (1846–1882) who had frequent interactions with William Watson and Major General J.B. Magruder.

Lyon, Samuel C. (ca 1811–1884). British-born pilot at the Brazos River who served in the Mexican War; was captured during the Meir Expedition and later released.

MacGregor, Rob Roy (1671–1734). Rebellious Scottish outlaw, folk hero, and namesake of Watson's schooner *Rob Roy*.

Maffitt, Caroline Matilda (Johnson) (1827–1855). Sister of John N. Maffitt, Jr., and wife of Judge Robert D. Johnson of Galveston.

Maffitt, Henrietta (Lamar) (1827–1891). Sister of John N. Maffitt, Jr., and second wife of former Republic of Texas President Mirabeau B. Lamar. Operated a boarding house in Galveston.

Maffitt, John Newland, Jr. (1819–1886). Son of a famous Methodist minister, Captain of the commerce raider CSS *Florida*, the ironclad CSS *Albemarle*, and the steam blockade runner *Owl*. Ran into Galveston where he met his sisters.

Magruder, John Bankhead (1807–1871). West Point graduate and Confederate major general who excelled early in the war but was ordered to Texas when he fell into disfavor with General Robert E. Lee. Known as "Prince John" for his fastidiously handsome appearance, he quickly attacked and repelled Union forces from Galveston Bay. He remained in command of the District of Texas, Arizona, and New Mexico until August 17, 1864, when Jefferson Davis sent him to command the Department of Arkansas. On March 31, 1865, Confederate president Jefferson Davis returned Magruder to command the District of Texas, New Mexico, and Arizona, but only in time to witness Gen. Edmund Kirby Smith's surrender of the Trans-Mississippi Department at Galveston on June 2, 1865. After the war, Magruder offered his sword to the Emperor Maximilian of Mexico, but after the collapse of the imperial forces he returned to Texas to make his home in Houston, where he died on February 19, 1871.

Mallory, Stephen Russell (1812–1873). Former South Carolina Senator and Secretary of the Confederate Navy.

Marcy, Samuel. Relieved Henry Scherffius as captain of the blockade-running steamer *Lark* before taking command of the steamer *Lizzie*. His father had been a shipwright in New Orleans.

Marmion, James Roger (1830–1895) Confederate Army captain who commanded Marine Department forces at Matagorda Bay.

Marquez, Francis, Jr. Louisiana owner of his namesake schooner that William Watson bought and renamed *Rob Roy*.

Marsden, Charles Poole (1828–1900). Captain of the blockade-running schooner *W.D.S. Hyer* from New York.

Mason, Charles M. (1834–1894). Confederate artillery major on General Magruder's staff until March 1863, when he became Chief of Marine Artillery and Adjutant General of the Fleet. He would sometimes take charge of the Texas Marine Department during Leon Smith's absence, but returned to his army artillery unit at the end of the war.

Mason, James Murray (1798–1871). Confederate commissioner to the United Kingdom and former U.S. senator from Virginia. Captain Charles Wilkes of the USS *San Jacinto* captured him and his counterpart to France, John Slidell, as they travelled to England on board HMS *Trent*. The incident brought the U.S. and the British to the brink of war.

Mason, Thomas E. (1835–?). Originally from Alabama, Watson described him as "Lt. Tom M." with the 3rd Louisiana Infantry. The lieutenant had been captured at the Battle of Pea Ridge, Arkansas, but had joined a Texas unit after he was exchanged.

Matthews, Asa Carrington (1833–1908). Major with the 99th Illinois Volunteer Infantry Regiment who commanded the Cavalry and Couriers on Matagorda who attempted to capture the schooner *Amanda*.

Maximilian. See **Joseph, Ferdinand Maximilian**

McBurney, Alex. Schooner captain who Watson identified as "Captain B." who tried to illegally sell *Eliza Catharine* to a Mr. "L." (probably E. De Launey who was *Eliza Catharine*'s consignee). He later was first mate of the steamer *Ike Davis*. Six Confederates posed as passengers who captured the steamer off the Rio Grande and ran it into Matagorda Bay where it was condemned and sold at auction. McBurney was first mate of the crew that ran *Ike Davis* through the blockade, and among 10 crewmembers rescued when it sank off the Rio Grande during a storm.

McClellan, George Brinton (1826–1885). Union general nicknamed "Young Napoleon" and "Little Mac," he was popular with the troops, but his skills were organization and training. His lack of battlefield aggressiveness earned him President Lincoln's disfavor. In 1864, he ran as the democratic challenger to the president as a peace candidate.

McClusky (McCluskey), David (1829–1877). Pilot of the steamer *Josiah H. Bell* at the start of the war; blockade-running captain of schooners *Magnolia*, *Sarah* and *Stingaree*. Watson identified him as "Dave McLusky."

McConnell, James Britton (1812–1868). Captain of blockade runner *Susannah* (*Susanna*).

McNamara, Thomas (1832–1898). Canadian captain of the blockade runner *Carrie Mair*.

Meyers, Henry. Captain of the blockade runner *John A. Hazard*.

Mills, David Graham (1811–1885). Formed R. & D.G. Mills cotton growing and brokerage company with his brother Robert. He managed the plantations while his brother Robert managed the brokerage business. After the war, the brothers struggled to maintain their cotton business, finally going bankrupt in 1873 when the cotton market collapsed.

Mills, John Robert (1829–1895). Born in Vicksburg, Mississippi, the son of Robert and David Mills' eldest brother. Graduated from Yale, engaged in mercantile pursuits in New York City, and then went to Galveston where he was employed with R. and D.G. Mills.

Mills, Robert (1809–1888). After Andrew Mills' death in 1836, he took over his father's mercantile firm with his younger brother, David G. Mills. Robert also had merchandising businesses with partners in Matagorda and Jackson Counties.

Mills, William (1800–1872). Older brother of R. & D.G. Mills and father of John Robert Mills.

Moore, Andrew Jackson "Jack" (1829–1884). Watson met this blockade-running Texan in Havana and identified him as "Captain M." Before the war, the North Carolina–born Moore commanded the Lighthouse Service schooner *Essayons*. His wartime commands were the schooners *William R. King* (*Isabel*, *Adela*), *Mary Ella* (*Mary Ellen*, *Orion*), and *John*, and the steamer *Jeannette*.

Moore, Thomas Overton (1804–1876). Louisiana governor (1856–1864) and pre-war customer of William Watson as a sugar plantation owner in Rapides Parish near Alexandria.

Morgan, Charles (1795–1878). Wealthy New York–based railroad and shipping magnate and founder of the Southern Steamship Company. Morgan's transfer of the company's assets to his New Orleans–based son-in-law did not deter the State of Texas from seizing *General Rusk*. The State of Louisiana then seized five other steamers in his fleet, forcing the son to sell them to private Southern interests.

Morgan, William (1841–?). A U.S. Navy boatswain's (bo'sun's) mate and member of *Stingaree*'s prize crew from the USS *Kineo*. Originally from England, he escaped capture when he fell overboard in a drunken stupor, but then had to face a court martial for drunkenness, scandalous conduct, and desertion.

Oaksmith, Appleton (1827–1887). Captain of the blockade runner *Carolina* (*Caroline*, *Union*, *Rosita*) using the alias, John McDonald. He was a convicted slave trader, unscrupulous grifter, and philanderer. But he was also a sensitive poet, accomplished seaman and a daring leader. After running *Carolina* ashore on Galveston Island to prevent capture, he led six other men in the capture of SS *Sonora* as it sailed from the Rio Grande for New Orleans. After having the steamer condemned as a prize at a Confederate admiralty court in Texas, he renamed her *Helena* and ran a load of cotton to Tampico. After the war, he received a pardon from President Grant and won a seat with the North Carolina legislature as a Republican.

Oetling, George Gottlieb (1828–1895). Principal partner with fellow German William Droege in the banking and commercial firm, Droege, Oetling & Co. with offices in Bremen, Hamburg, Manchester, Havana, Tampico, and Matamoros (through 1868), where Oetling was the Prussian vice consul.

O'Hagan, James (1840–?). Irish-born mate aboard *Rob Roy* and cook aboard *Carrie Mair*.

O'Sullivan, John. The brother-in-law of the British merchant John Maloney of Matamoros. O'Sullivan was also an agent for Confederate General Hamilton P. Bee who sent him to Havana. O'Sullivan's mission was to recover Confederate arms and ammunition that the French had taken from Mexico to Cuba.

Page, Thomas Jefferson (1808–1899). A former U.S. Navy officer who joined the Confederate Army before being appointed as a captain in the Confederate Navy and commanding officer of the CSS *Stonewall*, the first ironclad warship to cross an ocean.

Parizot, Ernest. A partner in the firm of Wegmann & Parizot & Co. until December 1, 1865. Parizot was also in partnership with Bernard (Barney) Tiernan (1835–1915) of Tiernan and Parizot & Co.

Payne, John W. (1834–1874). Irish-born Texan who was captain of the Confederate steamer *Mary Hill*, and commanded the Texas Marine Department forces at Velasco. Earlier he commanded the steamers *Roebuck*, *Belle Sulphur*, and the captured U.S. steamer *Clifton*. Remained a Galveston steamboat pilot until shortly before his death.

Pinchon, William Glenford (1825–1894). British master in nominal command of the blockade runner *Louisa Ann Fanny*.

Potter, Jesse F. (1822–1870). Massachusetts-born captain of the schooner *Morris* that the U.S. Navy seized as a blockade runner, but the New Orleans admiralty court released him. After the war, he was the Boston City Liquor Agent until his untimely death.

Price, Marcus Wesley (1894–1982). A director and chief archivist at the National Archives in Washington, D.C.; also, the author of "Ships That Tested the Blockade of the Gulf Ports: 1861–1865," that appeared in four consecutive issues of *The American Neptune* (Oct 1851–Oct 1852).

Purdie, William A. (1837–1900). Acting Ensign on board USS *Kanawha* and the prize schooner *Amanda*'s prize master; post-war clerk for U.S. Customs in New York City.

Read, Thomas (1838–1903). A bookkeeper and cashier for R. & D.G. Mills & Company. After the war he was a bank cashier and a director on the board of an insurance company.

Reed, Walter (1851–1902). The son of a Methodist minister, he was a U.S. Army Medical Corps Major. In 1901, he confirmed that female *Aedes Aegypti* mosquitoes were the source of yellow fever infection. After his return from Havana to Washington, Reed died following an operation for appendicitis.

Renshaw, William Bainbridge (1816–1863). Commodore in charge of the fleet occupying Galveston Harbor (Nov–Dec 1863). To prevent capture, he blew up his grounded flagship USS *Westfield* and accidentally killed himself and several crewmen in the delayed explosion.

Rhett, Thomas Grimke (1821–1878). A Confederate Army major who was Chief of Ordnance and Artillery for the Trans-Mississippi Department at Shreveport, Louisiana.

Rodriguez, José. Spanish citizen, born in Peru and residing in Havana with his family, he was Captain of the Mexican schooner *Amanda* when captured near Corpus Christi.

Ross, Richard. Irish Captain of the blockade-running schooner *Julia* who was from New Jersey.

San Román, José (1822–1895). A Spanish citizen who was a shrewd, but honest merchant, banker, and shipping agent in Matamoros and Brownsville. He arrived in Matamoros from Spain via New Orleans in 1846 and was one of the richest men in South Texas. He was both a partner and competitor with King, Kenedy, and Stillman in the steamboat and shipping business. After the war, he continued to do business on the Rio Grande, but returned to Spain in 1878.

Saunders, William (1836–?). Confederate Army captain with Brown's Calvary Regiment whose men helped salvage the cargo from Dave McClusky's *Stingaree* near Velasco.

Scherffius, Catherina "Kate" Fox (1845–1896). Married George Scherffius in Galveston shortly before he was lost at sea while running the blockade in 1864.

Scherffius, Emily Branard (1847–1889). Married Henry Scherffius at Houston in May 1864, shortly after he ran the blockade from Vera Cruz.

Scherffius, Georgius "George" (1840–1864). Newlywed younger brother of Henry who died at sea when his blockade-running schooner *Mary Elizabeth* was lost in a storm.

Scherffius, Henricus "Henry" Ervin (1838–1894). German-born blockade-running Texan. Watson identified him as "Captain Shaeffer," the older brother of George. Perhaps the most active of all Texas blockade runners, he commanded the schooners *Cora* and *Deer*, the former Union gunboat, USS *Sachem* (*Clarinda*, *Vera Cruz*), and the steam blockade runners *Lark* and *Pelican*. After the war, he was the Harris County Treasurer for 14 years and Mayor of Houston (1890–1892).

Scott, Hugh Trann (1838–1867). Confederate ordnance officer in charge of the Houston depot. After the war, he died in Houston after contracting yellow fever.

Scott, Robert B. Confederate Army captain identified as a novice "Captain R." He travelled to London to buy a half interest in the blockade runner *Pelican* with profits from the sale of cotton from *Harriet Lane*.

Scott, Winfield (1786–1866). Acclaimed hero of the Mexican War (1846–1848), he was an unsuccessful Whig Party candidate for U.S. president in 1852. Known as "Old Fuss and Feathers" for his equal love of discipline and pomp, he was commanding general of the United States Army from 1841 to the start of the Civil War.

Scrimgeour, William (1836–1919). Son of a Scottish immigrant who had come to Galveston from New York in 1857. Career sailor, steamboat man, and harbor master who lived in Galveston during and after the war. Was the first mate on the Confederate steam gunboat *General Rusk* under Leon Smith in March 1861 and captain of the steam blockade runner *Matagorda* (*Alice*) (Jun–Sep 1864). Watson identified him as "Captain S."

Scurry, William Read (1821–1864). Confederate Army officer who was a Tennessee-born lawyer and district attorney who arrived in Texas in 1839 and served in the Mexican War. Excelled in battle during the failed New Mexico expedition in March 1862 and earned a promotion to brigadier general in September. He met Watson just after Philip Luckett relieved him as commander of the Eastern Sub District of Texas.

Sellin, Felix. U.S. Navy officer steward who was captured as one of the drunken prize crewmen from the USS *Kineo* on board the blockade-running schooner *Stingaree*. Subsequently incarcerated at prisoner of war prison at Camp Groce, Texas.

Semmes, Raphael (1809–1877). Captain of the Confederate commerce raider CSS *Alabama*, who engaged and sank the USS *Hatteras* off the coast of Galveston. He was later promoted to Rear Admiral and then Brigadier General in the Confederate Army and returned to the Confederacy via Matamoros and Texas in the final months of the war.

Seward, Frederick William (1830–1915). Assistant Secretary of State for his father William.

Seward, William Henry (1801–1872). Secretary of State (1861–1869) for Presidents Abraham Lincoln and Andrew Johnson. He was seriously wounded as part of the conspiracy to assassinate President Lincoln and his war cabinet. He survived and became the motivating political figure behind the unsuccessful impeachment of President Johnson.

Seyburn, Isaac Declar (1824–1895). Welsh-born captain of the sailing schooner USS *Kittatinny* who intercepted and boarded *Rob Roy* near the Brazos River.

Sherrill, John (1834–1901). A former commercial sea captain from New York, he achieved the rank of acting volunteer lieutenant with the U.S. Navy. During the Civil War, he was captain of the USS *Stars and Stripes* after having commanded the USS *Roebuck*. He forwarded the cargo salvaged from *Rob Roy* to the admiralty court at Key West.

Slaughter, James Edwin (1827–1901). Confederate brigadier general from Virginia who fought in the Mexican War and at Shiloh. He served as General Magruder's chief of artillery, Eastern Sub-district of Texas commander, and chief of staff.

Smith, Edmund Kirby (1824–1893). Confederate lieutenant general in command of the of the Trans-Mississippi Department headquartered at Shreveport, Louisiana.

Smith, George Levin (1842–1926). Massachusetts-born able-bodied seaman onboard the USS *Virginia*. After the war, "Captain Smith" moved to Houston where he was a bookkeeper for the Southern Pacific Railroad.

Smith, John. A U.S. Navy ordinary seaman who was captured as one of the drunken prize crewmen from the USS *Kineo* on board the blockade-running schooner *Stingaree*. Subsequently incarcerated at prisoner of war prison at Camp Groce, Texas, but escaped and deserted before September 1864.

Smith, Leon (1820–1889). Steamboat captain that General Magruder promoted to Confederate Army major and placed in charge of the Texas Marine Department with the honorary title of "commodore." He commanded most of the transports and gunboats in Texas and led several successful attacks against U.S. naval forces. After the war, he worked for a telegraph company in New Orleans and San Francisco before being murdered at a trading post in Alaska.

Smith, Ralph Julius (1840–1913). Confederate Private with Company K of the 2nd Texas Infantry, and author of *Reminiscences of the Civil War, and Other Sketches*.

Stafford, John C. Confederate Major who was briefly the quartermaster for the Texas Marine Department under Commodore Leon Smith in June 1864.

Sterrett, John H. (1815–1879). Galveston captain and part-owner of the SS *Diana*, he chartered her along with the steamers *Bayou City*, and *Neptune No. 2* and their crews for service with the Texas Marine Department at the rate of $7,500 per month, per boat.

Sulakowski, Valery (1827–1873). Polish-born Confederate colonel, engineer, and designer of coastal fortifications in Texas.

Taylor, George (alias A. Brotherton). As the first mate on *Rob Roy*, Taylor had allegedly entered Texas on a blockade runner, but then joined the Texas Marine Department. He later had a falling out with Commodore Smith. He may have been F.K.A. Taylor (aka Fred Taylor) of the Marine Department. General Magruder levied charges and specifications against this man and filed them with the Confederate Judge Advocate on Mar 3, 1864. This was a few weeks after Watson said that the Confederates had removed "George Taylor" from *Rob Roy*. In mid–March, a sailor named Fred Taylor attempted to depart the Brazos as captain of Thomas House's schooner *John*.

Taylor, Walter Herron (1838–1916). Adjutant to Robert E. Lee and post-war merchant, banker, and author of books containing personal observations that defended the reputation of the Confederate general.

Thompson (or Thomson), George. First mate on the *Rob Roy* with an alcohol problem.

Thorpe, Thomas Bangs (1815–1878). U.S. Customs officer and prize commissioner at New Orleans. Later became a well-known humorist author and painter in New York.

Timmins, James Gregory (1835–1922). Former mate from the CSS *Sachem* who joined Henry Scherffius in the same position on the blockade runner *Pelican*.

Townsend, Samuel L. (1830–1905). Captain of the small coastal schooner *Night Hawk*. He was also the builder, owner, and captain of the blockade-running schooner *Josephine* that the USS *Seminole* captured about four miles off Brazos Santiago with 157 bales of cotton onboard. He was born on Long Island, New York, and lived in Refugio, Texas.

Tucker, William Rogers. Captain of the blockade-running schooners *Camita*, *Emily*, and *John* (for two months prior to being relieved by Captain Francis Downs).

Turbert, August. A French citizen who departed Texas in January 1864, in the schooner *Eliza Catharine* that he purchased at Havana in November 1862.

Turner, Edmund Pendelton (1836–1907). Virginia-born Confederate Captain and assistant adjutant on General Magruder's staff. He settled in Texas after the war.

Vaughn, Robert. British captain of the blockade-running schooner *Flash* who was captured in Nov 1864, off the Mexican coast with 41 bales of Texas cotton.

Vidaurri, Santiago (1809–1867). A powerful Mexican governor who had opposed Santa Anna and formed the combined state of Nuevo León y Coahuila. He initially supported Benito Juárez, but ran afoul of the revolutionary leader when he retained all income from the Rio Grande custom houses. At the outbreak of the American Civil War, he encouraged trade with Texas and cooperated with Southern officials. When the army of Napoleon III invaded Mexico and installed Maximilian on the throne, Vidaurri sided with the imperialists and fled to Texas where he met with General Magruder in Galveston. He later returned to Monterrey and joined Emperor Maximilian's government. When the Empire collapsed in 1867, Mexican nationalists executed him without a trial as a traitor.

Walker, John George (1822–1893). Confederate major general who served with the U.S. Army in the Mexican War, on the Texas frontier (1854–1856), and New Mexico when the Civil War broke out. He was promoted after serving under Stonewall Jackson and leading a division at

Antietam in 1862. He commanded Walker's Texas Division during the Red River campaign of Mar–May 1864, but was wounded at the battle of Pleasant Hill, Louisiana. On Aug 4, 1864, Walker replaced John B. Magruder as commander of the District of Texas, New Mexico, and Arizona. He remained in command until Magruder's return on Mar 31, 1865. After the war, he fled to Mexico and then Havana, but then moved to England. He was pardoned and returned to Texas in 1869 where he worked as an insurance agent. He then moved to New Orleans and Virginia, until becoming involved in the newspaper business in Austin and Dallas, as well as a railway agent. During Grover Cleveland's first term as president, Walker served as United States consul to Bogotá, Colombia (1885–1889).

Walker, Norman Stewart (1830–1923). A Confederate major and the Confederacy's principal commercial agent in Bermuda who traveled to the United Kingdom in the intended blockade runner *Louisa Ann Fanny* at the end of the war.

Walker, William (1824–1860). American physician, lawyer, journalist, and freelance mercenary general and filibuster who seized control of Nicaragua. The U.S. briefly recognized him as the country's president before indigenous forces ousted him, the British captured him, and the Honduran government executed him.

Ward, Edward. British Captain from New Orleans who commanded the blockade-running schooners *Lowood* and *The Allison*.

Watson, Agnes Milligan (1874–1941). The eldest daughter of Helen and William Watson

Watson, David Shelton (1830–1895). An assistant surgeon from Virginia who joined the Confederate Army and was one of the passengers onboard the blockade runner *Owl* who disembarked off St. Marks, Florida, in Mar 1864.

Watson, Helen Milligan (1839–1914). Scottish wife of William Watson.

Watson, Henry (1796–1875). Gardner for the Ashcraig Estate in Skelmorlie, Scotland, a grocer, and father of William Watson.

Watson, Henry (Harry) (1872–1943). The son of Helen and William Watson, employed as a marine engineer in his father's shipbuilding business.

Watson, Margaret Hamilton (1794–1828). Mother of William Watson who died when her son was only two years old.

Watson, Mary Milligan (1876–?). The youngest child of Helen and William Watson.

Watson, Robison Gilmour McLean (1812–1897). William Watson's stepmother.

Watson, William (1826–1906). Born at Skelmorlie, near Glasgow in Ayrshire, Scotland. His mother died shortly after giving birth to her fifth child. After serving in the Confederate Army and living an adventurous life as owner and captain of the blockade- running schooner *Rob Roy*, he returned to Scotland. He married and became a successful businessman and author of two books about his experiences in the American Civil War.

Watters, John (1828–1874). U.S. Navy commander of the USS *Kineo* who briefly captured Dave McClusky and his schooner *Stingaree*.

Williams, John Howell (1833–1883). Son of Henry Howell Williams who had financed six vessels for the Republic of Texas Navy in 1838–1839, and business partner of British Consul Arthur T. Lynn in Galveston.

Wolfean, Frederick Alexander (1834–1905). Born in Hannover, Germany, he moved to Galveston in 1854 as a ship captain. Wolfean served onboard the blockade runners *Flash* and *A.C. Shelton*, and was first mate on Dave McClusky's *Stingaree* when the crew recaptured the schooner from a U.S. Navy prize crew. Married three times, he sired several children, was active in post-war veterans' groups, and died of Bright's disease.

Zimmerman, Charles. A U.S. Navy seaman who was captured as one of the drunken prize crewmen from the USS *Kineo* on board the blockade-running schooner *Stingaree*. The Confederates subsequently incarcerated him as a prisoner of war at Camp Groce, Texas.

APPENDIX 5

Naval Order of Battle

This appendix provides brief summaries of prominent vessels mentioned in the text. The listed captains and ship's masters (when known) and the warship armaments reflect the relevant timeframe within the text. None of the individual entries are based on a single source. Each contains a fusion of the best available information from multiple sources. Most of the warship data comes from Paul Silverstone's *Civil War Navies, 1855–1883*, much of the steam blockade runner data is from Stephen Wise's *Lifeline of the Confederacy*, the primary source for vessels with New Orleans registries is from Work Projects Administration (WPA), *Ship Registers and Enrollments of New Orleans, Louisiana, Vol V, 1851–1860* and *Vol VI, 1861–1870*, other steamboats with Mississippi River basin connections are from Frederick Way's *Packet Directory, 1848–1994*. Other appropriate endnote citations are located within the text.

Notes about tonnage: There are many different methods of determining tonnage. Tons burden (sometimes spelled burthen) was a 19th-century measurement of a vessel's carrying capacity, but measuring formulas varied widely. In 1864, a standardized methodology appeared, but it was several years before its use became uniform. Other tonnage measurements include Deadweight (total weight a vessel can carry); Cargo (total cargo weight); Gross (weight of the vessel alone); Net (gross tonnage minus spaces for crew, engines, fuel, and ship operations); and variations of Displacement (weight of water displaced, loaded and unloaded). Tons displacement is more commonly used in the current era. For comparison, a vessel displacing 1335 tons might have a net tonnage of 400, gross tonnage of 600, and deadweight carrying capacity of 1000 tons. Varying usage of British and American measurements of tons (2,240 and 2,000 pounds) and dimensions (from outside and inside the beams) also account for variations in reporting of a vessel's tonnage.

When possible, the author uses the vessel's Gross Registered Tonnage (GRT) and rounds fractional amounts up or down for even numbers. GRT is the volume of space within the hull and enclosed spaces above the deck of a merchant ship that are available for cargo, stores, fuel, passengers and crew. GRT forms the basis for maritime manning regulations, safety rules and registration fees.

The formula for determining a vessel's cubic capacity or GRT during the Civil War was:

Tonnage = (Length−.6 × Beam × Beam × Draft) ÷ 95 [UK] or ÷ 94 [US].

Notes about naval guns: a 32-pounder (pdr) was a smooth-bore (unless labeled as "rifled") muzzle-loading cannon that fired a projectile weighing 32 pounds. Other common projectile weights were 100, 30, 24, 20 and 12 pounds. Some guns were measured by the diameter of the cannon bore in inches. Howitzers were lighter weight guns that often deployed aboard smaller vessels.

The following listing is organized by vessel name(s), and (when known): tonnage (usually GRT when known), flag (if non–U.S.), type (rig/propulsion), when and where built, dimensions (length, beam, depth of hold and/or draft), armament (warships only), captain or ship master's name, and a summary of significant events. (Consistent with standard 19th-century usage, the vessels are referred to using female pronouns rather than gender neutral or male pronouns.)

A.C. Dana, 69-ton Canadian schooner, built 1861 in the U.S., Captain Lawrence. She was at Tampico Oct–Nov 1864, and at the Rio Grande in Jan 1865, but there is no evidence of any blockade runs.

Agnes (*John Arthur*). 53-ton British schooner; Dimensions: 65'5" × 25'5" × 4'2" (3' draft); Captain George N. Hubbard. Watson may have misidentified her as *Hind*; captured departing the Brazos River on May 2, 1864, with 155 bales of cotton.

Alabama (*Ida Duvere*). 52-ton British schooner, Capt. J.H. Davis. From Havana captured Dec 1864, near San Luis Pass, but crew escaped ashore.

CSS *Alabama*. 1,050-ton bark-rigged screw steamer, built 1861 at Birkenhead, England by Laird Brothers'; Dimensions: 220' × 31'9" × 14', Armament: 1 × 110 pdr (rifled), 6 × 32 pdr, 1 × 68 pdr, Captain Raphael Semmes. The most successful of the Confederate commerce raiders took 60 prizes and sank the USS *Hatteras* off Galveston (Jan 11, 1863), before succumbing to the USS *Kearsarge* off Cherbourg (Jun 19, 1864).

Albert Edward (*Uncle Bill*). 53-ton British schooner, built 1844 at Portland, Connecticut; Dimensions: 61' × 19' × 4'8" (U.S. Standards) & 63'7" × 19'2" × 5' (UK standards); Capt. John Page. Captured on Halloween Day, 1864, heading out of Galveston for Vera Cruz with 150 bales of cotton.

SS *Alice* (*Matagorda*). 1250-ton side-paddlewheel steamer; built 1858 at Wilmington, Delaware; Dimensions: 220' × 30'× 10'6", Captain William Scrimgeour. Changed name from *Matagorda* to *Alice* in August 1862. See Appendix 3 for more about this steamer's blockade runs.

Alma. 20-ton Mexican schooner, Capt. Francis Celda (nominal), & William Lee (actual). Captured Apr 1864 enr Galveston from the Rio Grande.

Amanda. 60-ton Mexican schooner (3' draft), Captain José Rodriguez. Captured off Corpus Christi Bay in May 1864, but released by the New Orleans admiralty court.

Ann Giberson (*Anna Gibberson*). 99-ton British schooner, built 1856 at Toms River, New Jersey; Dimensions: 72 × 24'3" × 5'2"; Captains: John McCormick (Mar–Jul 1863), Stephen Clough (Aug 1863–Oct 1864).

Anne Sophia (*Annie Sophia*, *Anna Shepherd*), 91-ton British schooner, built 1859 at Nassau; Dimensions: 79'6" × 22'6" × 5'9"; Captain John Thompson. The U.S. consul in Havana erroneously referred to this vessel as *Anne Sheppard*; crews from the USS *Bienville* and *Princess Royal* captured her with 221 bales of cotton during a small boat expedition into Galveston Bay on Feb 7, 1865.

Antoinetta (*Antoinette*). Mexican commercial schooner, Captain Mattie, which was not involved in blockade running.

Arizona (*Caroline, Carolina,* USS *Arizona*). 670-ton British side-paddlewheel steamer, built 1858 at Wilmington, Delaware; Dimensions: 200' × 34' × 17'6" (8' draft); Armament (after U.S. Navy captured her on Oct 1862, and commissioned her on Mar 1863): 1 × 2pdr (rifled), 1 × 30pdr (rifled), 4 × 32pdr. Made four successful blockade runs early in the war, two at Brazos Santiago, Texas, and two at Berwick Bay, Louisiana.

USS *Aroostook*. 691-ton screw steamer, built 1861 at Kennebunk, Maine; Dimensions: 158'4" × 28' × 9'6"; Armament: 1 × 11' 2 × 24 pdr, 1 20 pdr (rifled), 2 × 12 pdr; LCDR Chester Hatfield. One of the 23 Unadilla-class 90-day gunboats; the steamer captured the schooner *Eureka* and Captain Downs on November 19, 1863.

Austin (*Donegal*). 603-ton British side-paddlewheel steamer, built 1860 at Wilmington, Delaware; Dimensions: 198' × 34' × 9'6"; Armament (after the Jun 1864 capture and U.S. Navy commissioning): 2 × 12pdr, 2 × 30pdr (rifled); Captains: Charles Fowler (Mar 1862–Dec 1863), William H. Smith (Jan 1864–Jun 1864). Wise in *Lifeline of the Confederacy* credits *Austin/Donegal* with nine successful blockade runs, but contemporary sources identify 12 probable runs between Jul 1861 and Jun 1864: Brazos Santiago (2), Louisiana (6), Mobile Bay (4), before being caught off Mobile Bay in June 1864.

Barcelona. 308-ton, Spanish mail, passenger, and cargo steamer, Capt. Iniesta. Made a regular, monthly circuit between Havana, Cuba and Sisal, Tampico, and Vera Cruz, Mexico.

Bayou City. 219-ton (calculated) Confederate side-paddlewheel steamer, built 1858 at Jeffersonville, Indiana; Dimensions: 165' × 28' × 5' (3'6" draft); Armament: 1 × 32pdr (Dec 1862–Sep 1863); Captains: John H. Sterrett (Oct 1861–Mar 1862), Henry S. Lubbock (Apr 1862–Sep 1863), J. McGarvey (Oct 1863–May 1864), J.Y. Lawless (Jun 1864. Arrived at Galveston Bay in Dec 1858 and chartered to the Texas Marine Department by Sep 1861).

Belle (*Gipsey, Zouave*). 45-ton British schooner, built 1860 at Mystic, Connecticut; Dimensions: 64'2" × 21' × 7'5"; Captain James Brown. Ran into Galveston from Havana (Nov 1864), but a U.S. Navy boat crew captured her in Galveston Bay.

Belle Sulphur. 127-ton Confederate side-paddlewheel steamer, built 1856 at Louisville, Kentucky; Dimensions: 111' × 25' × 4'4"; Capt. John Payne. Owned by Peel-Dumble & Co.; leased to the Confederate Army as a transport in Apr 1862; wrecked returning to Sabine Pass from Berwick Bay in May 1862.

USS *Bermuda*. 1,003-ton screw-steamer, built in 1861 at Stockton-on-Tees, England; Dimensions: 211' × 30'3" × 16'1"; Armament: 1 × 9", 2 × 30 pdr (rifled); Acting Master J.W. Smith. *Bermuda* was the first steamship to run the blockade; captured in Apr 1862, and taken into the U.S. Navy as an armed supply ship.

Black Joker (*C. Vanderbilt, Cornelius Vanderbilt*). 346-ton British side-paddlewheel steamer, built 1837 at New York, New York; Dimensions: 170'8" × 23'4" × 9'; Capt. Robert D. Smith. Renamed *Black Joker* Dec 1861. Made three successful blockade runs between Jul 1861, and Feb 1862 (New Orleans: 1 & Sabine Pass: 2). Wrecked out of Havana in Mar 1862.

California. 496-ton Confederate steamer, built 1847 at New York, New York; Dimensions: 200'6" × 29'7" × 8'6"; Captain Howard Porter. Ran out of New Orleans to Havana early in the war and then made round trip to and from Mobile before running into Matagorda Bay, Texas. Ran aground near Sisal, MX in Oct 1862 out of Matagorda, but salvaged 137 bales of cotton.

Carolina (*Caroline, Union, Rosita*). 149-ton British side-paddlewheel steamer, built 1859 at Philadelphia, Pennsylvania; Dimensions: 140' × 25' × 5'; Captain Appleton Oaksmith (aka John McDonald). During its brief life, the steamer was captured twice, had three different names, four different owners, six different captains, and successfully ran the blockade five times, but was sunk off the coast of Cuba on its 6th attempt in July 1864. This blockade runner is often confused with the screw steamer *Union* that also ran out of Galveston.

Caroline. 23-ton British schooner, built 1860 at Pass Manchac, Louisiana; Dimensions: 42'6" × 17' × 3'7"; Captain G.D. Hartney, owned by William R. Evans. Wrecked at the mouth of the Rio Grande during a storm on Oct 10, 1864, on its return trip to New Orleans.

Carrie Mair. 56-ton British schooner, built 1861 at Little Harbor, Wisconsin; Dimensions: 68'9" × 18'6" × 6'7"; Capt. Thomas McNamara. Captured Nov 1864, off the Brazos River from Tampico.

Catharine. See: *Eliza Catharine.*

USS/CSS *Cavallo* (*Henrietta*). 296-ton sailing bark, built 1856 at Mystic, Connecticut; Dimensions: 115' × 31'2" × 9'; Capt. Mayson. A U.S. Navy coal ship that was part of the occupying force at Galveston Bay in late 1862. The Confederates captured her on Jan 1, 1863; anchored off the Galveston bar and used as a naval stores ship before the Confederates converted her into a guard and hospital ship.

Chaos (*Velocity, Fairy, Nellie Blair*). 64-ton British schooner, built 1857 at Key West, Florida; Dimensions: 71'2" × 22'5" × 7'1"; Captains: Joseph C. Bernard (Apr 1863–Aug 1864), Joseph Davidson (Sep 1864–Mar 1865), Peter Anderson (Mar–Apr 1865). She successfully ran the blockade three times, but was also captured three times. USS *Kensington* first captured *Velocity* trying to enter Sabine Pass, Texas, in Sep 1862. The U.S. Navy converted her into an armed gunboat with the name USS *Fairy*. The Confederates recaptured *Fairy* off Sabine Pass on January 21, 1863 (along with the USS *Morning Light*). She then ran the blockade under several different captains as *Nellie Blair* and *Chaos* (captured April 1865).

Charles Russell (*Maria W. Lawson*). 64-ton British schooner, built 1858 at Baltimore, Maryland; Dimensions: 72' × 22' × 5' (4'6" draft); Captains: James Davidson (Oct 1863–Apr 1864), William Bayly (Apr 1864–Apr 1865). Renamed *Charles Russell* and registered in Kingston, Jamaica on Oct 31, 1863. Ran the blockade 10 times, twice each at the Brazos River and Sabine Pass and six times at Galveston. Turned over to U.S. forces upon the surrender of Galveston.

USS *Chocura*. 691-ton screw steamer, built 1861 at Boston, Massachusetts; Dimensions: 158'4" × 28' × 9'6"; Armament: 1 × 20 pdr (rifled), 4 × 24 pdr, 1 × 30 pdr (rifled), 1 × 100 pdr (rifled); LCDR Richard W. Meade, Jr. One of the 23 Unadilla-class 90-day gunboats, the steamer captured 13 blockade runners including the schooners *Julia* (Dec 5, 1864) and *Alabama* (Dec 7, 1864).

Clarinda (USS/CSS *Sachem, Vera Cruz*). 197-ton screw steamer, built 1844 at New York, New York; Dimensions: 121' × 23' 6" × 7'6" (5'4" draft); Armament: 1 ×

30pdr (rifled), 4 × 32pdr (USN, Sep 1863) & 4 × 32pdr, 2 × 24pdr (as Texas Marine Department gunboat, Oct 1863), Captains: Amos Johnson, USN, Henry Scherffius, CSA, & Pares (of Mexico). The U.S. Navy purchased her from the U.S. Coast Survey in 1861. The Confederates captured her at Sabine Pass with USS *Clifton* on Sep 8, 1863. Arrived in Vera Cruz (Oct 1864) as *Clarinda* and departed for Havana as *Vera Cruz* under Mexican Capt. Pares in Feb 1865.

USS/CSS Clifton. 892-ton side-paddlewheel steamship, built 1861 at Brooklyn, New York; Dimensions: 210' × 40' × 13'4"; U.S. armament as of 1863: 2 × 9", 2 × 30-pdr (rifled), 4 × 32-pdrs; CSA armament (Sep 1863): 2 × 9", 3 × 32-pdr; Captains: Acting Volunteer Lieutenant Frederick Crocker (Feb 1863–Sep 1863), John W. Payne (Sep 1863–Oct 1863), Charles W. Austin (Nov 1863–Mar 1864). Designed as a ferryboat, the U.S. Navy purchased the steamer in Dec 1861. Participated in the capture of New Orleans, attack at Vicksburg, and occupation of Galveston. Confederate forces captured the warship at Sabine Pass on Sep 8, 1863, and converted her into a blockade runner, but burned her when she ran aground on the first attempted run in Mar 1864.

Concordia. 69-ton British schooner, built 1850 at Fredericks, Maryland; Dimensions: 71' × 21'4" × 5'2"; Capt. Charles William Hurley. Ran into Calcasieu River in Louisiana in Oct 1863, chased ashore and burned.

Cora (*Snow Drift*). 70-ton U.S./British schooner, built 1858 at Essex, Massachusetts; Dimensions: 67' × 20' × 6'; Captains: Henry Scherffius (Sep 1863–Nov 1864), John Greenough (Nov 1864–Dec 1864). Henry Brastow sold her to Henry Scherffius at Matamoros. She made five successful runs from Texas to Belize and Vera Cruz with about 720 bales of cotton, until captured on Dec 19, 1864, out of Galveston with a new captain and 175 bales of cotton.

USS Cornubia. 411-ton side-paddlewheel steamer, built 1858 at Hayle, England; Dimensions: 210 × 24'6" × 10'; Armament: 2 × 12pdr (rifled), 2 × 24; 1 × 30pdr (rifled); Capt. John A. Johnstone. Captured the blockade runner *Chaos* (former *Velocity*, *Fairy*, and *Nellie Blair*) in April 1865, as the schooner ran out of Galveston.

C.P. Knapp. 109-ton British schooner, built 1859 at Pascagoula, Mississippi: Dimensions: 82'10" × 26'2" × 5'11"; captured off Pensacola in August 1861, taken to the Key West admiralty court and released with Captain Henry Laverty in command prior to taking charge of *Rob Roy*.

Cuca (*Lone*). 35-ton Mexican and British schooner, built 1856 at New Jersey; Dimensions: 51' × 17'4" × 4'7"; Captains: Pedro Rault (Jul 1863–Sep 1864), John Curry (Oct 1864–Nov 1864). Made four successful runs at the Brazos River, but was captured on the fifth attempt on Nov 6, 1864, out of Tampico.

Dazzle. 189-ton British brigantine, built 1855 at Bangor, Maine; Dimensions: 100' × 27'4" × 8'; Captain M. Cox (Cook). Ran aground during a storm Oct 11, 1864, off the Rio Grande.

Deer. 71-ton British schooner, built 1859 at New York, New York; Capt. Henry Scherffius. Ran ashore and wrecked Sep 22, 1863, near Caney Creek, about 22 miles from the Brazos.

Delia (*Dahlia*). 68-ton British schooner, Galveston blockade runner.

Denbigh. 162-ton British side-paddlewheel steamer, built 1860 at Birkenhead,

UK; Dimensions: 182' × 22' × 8'8"; Captains: McNevin (Nov 1863–Apr 1864), Abner M. Godfrey (Apr 1864–Sep 1864), Lablache (LeBlanch) (Oct 1864–May 1865). Ran aground and wrecked coming out of Galveston Bay on May 23, 1865.

CSS Diana. 225-ton Confederate side-paddlewheel steamer, built 1858 at West Brownsville, Pennsylvania; Dimensions: 171' × 28' × 3'2"; Armament: 2 × 12 pdr; captain and part-owner, John H. Sterrett. *Diana* arrived at Galveston Bay in Dec 1858 and began her Confederate Army service in Sep 1861.

Eco (*Echo*). 230-ton Mexican brig, built 1854 at Baltimore; Dimensions: 115' × 26' × 8'6"; Captain Lorenzo Lena. Captured on Feb 19, 1865, about seven miles from Galveston out of Vera Cruz.

Eliza Catharine. 87-ton British schooner, built 1855 at Louisbourg, Nova Scotia; Dimensions: 78' × 28' × 10'; Captain Alex MacBirney. Watson identified the schooner as *Catharine* when she arrived at the Brazos River from Havana under the ownership of August Turbert, a French citizen. Wrecked and sunk departing the Brazos on Apr 6, 1865.

Emily. 28-ton British 3-masted schooner; Dimensions: 54'8" × 14'4" × 3'3"; Captains: P.C. Blanchard (Sep 1863–Mar 1864), Henry Whiting (Mar 1864–Sep 1864), William Rogers Tucker (Sep 1864–Oct 1864). A Thomas W. House-owned schooner that Captain Whiting ran onto the beach near Velasco on Mar 20, 1864. The USS *Mobile* captured her when Capt. Tucker took her out of San Luis Pass on Oct 15, 1864.

Emma. William Watson's fictitious newly constructed schooner that was allegedly operating out of Havana in late 1864 and captured by the U.S. Navy.

Era No. 3. 144-ton stern-paddlewheel Confederate steamboat, built 1858 at Freedom, Pennsylvania; Dimensions: 129' × 28'4" × 4'4"; Captain William Jenkins. Owned by R. & D.G. Mills and leased to the Texas Marine Department as a logistics transport on the Brazos River.

Essayons. 40-ton (displacement) schooner; Dimensions: 42' × 14'6" × unk, Captain Andrew "Jack" Moore. The schooner's name is French for "Let Us Try." A U.S. Lighthouse Service schooner (1855–1859) serving the Gulf Coast lighthouses in Louisiana and Texas under direction of Lieutenant Thomas Holdup Stevens of the U.S. Navy and may have also performed coast survey duties.

Eureka (*Enriquita*). 19-ton British schooner; Dimensions: 42' × 17' × 3'4"; Captain Francis Downs (Oct 1863–Nov 1863). Captured Nov 22, 1863 when 3 days out of the Brazos.

Exchange. 87-ton British schooner, built 1856 at New Brunswick, New Jersey; Dimensions 63'3" × 22' × 7'6"; Captain Joseph H. Ashby. Captured on Christmas Eve, 1864, about 10 miles out of the Brazos from Vera Cruz.

Ferdinand. 5-ton sloop under U.S. Army contract, Captain S.W. Scott. Shipwrecked during a storm on Oct 21, 1864, near Tampico.

Flash. 29-ton British schooner; Dimensions: 42' × 13' × 4"; Captain Robert Vaughn. Departed Galveston to Tampico, but USS *Princess Royal* captured her 20 miles from the coast of Mexico with 46 bales of cotton on Nov 27, 1864.

CSS Florida. 410-ton Confederate Navy screw steamer, built 1862 at Liverpool, England; Dimensions: 191' × 27'3" × 13'; Armament: 1 × 12pdr howitzer, 6 × 6" (rifled), 2 × 7" (rifled); Captains: CDR John N. Maffitt (May 1862–Sep 1863), CDR Joseph N.

Barney (Sep 1863–Feb 1864), LT Charles M. Morris (Feb 1864–Sep 1864). The Confederate cruiser was responsible for capturing 31 vessels before the U.S. Navy illegally seized her during a Brazilian port call (Oct 1864). Deliberately sunk at Newport News, Virginia, the following month to prevent her return to Confederate custody.

USS *Fox* (*Alabama*). 80-ton sailing schooner, built 1859 at Baltimore, Maryland; Dimensions: unk × unk × 8'6"; Armament: 2 × 12pdr; Acting Master Alfred Weston. A former Confederate blockade runner named *Alabama*, captured Apr 1863. She chased *Rob Roy* onto a Florida beach where the crew set the blockade runner afire and burned to the waterline.

CSS *General Rusk* (*Blanche*). 418-ton Texas Marine Department side-paddlewheel steamer, built 1857 at Wilmington, Delaware; Dimensions: 200' × 25'3" × 8'6" (5'7" draft); Armament: 1 × 32 pdr, 2 × 6pdr, 20 muskets; Captains: Leon Smith (1860–May 1862), W.R. Davidson (May–Jul 1862), and Robert N. Smith (Aug–Oct 1862). William Scrimgoeur served as 1st mate. A Confederate armed steamer (Mar 1861–May 1862) that quartermaster Major T.S. Moïse illicitly leased to civilian owners for conversion into a British-flagged blockade runner. Renamed *Blanche*, she made two successful runs, one from Galveston to Havana with 583 bales of cotton in Jun 1862 and back to Matagorda Bay in Aug 1862. On her attempted return to Havana in Oct 1862, Capt. Hunter of the USS *Montgomery* captured and burned her in Cuban waters, sparking an international incident. The fire partially destroyed the cotton which sold for $30,000; both Major Moïse and Capt. Hunter were court martialed and convicted by their respective services.

CSS *Georgia*. 648-ton Confederate Navy screw steamer, built 1863 at Dumbarton, Scotland; Dimensions: 212' × 27' × 13'9": Armament: 2 × 100pdr, 2 × 24 pdr, 1 × 32pdr (rifled), CDR William L. Maury. The Confederate cruiser captured nine vessels, but was inefficient as a cruiser and sold in Jun 1864.

USS *Gertrude*. 283-ton screw steamer, built 1862 at Glasgow, Scotland; Dimensions: 156' × 21' × 10'5"; Armament: 2 × 12pdr (rifled), 6 × 24pdr howitzers; Acting Master Henry Clay Wade. She was on blockade duty off Galveston in Jan 1865.

***Geziena Hilligonda*.** 160-ton Dutch brig, built 1859 at Groningen, Holland (Netherlands); Dimensions: 96'6" × 21'6" × 10'6"; Capt. Bernardus P. Janson. The USS *Pembina* captured the brig off the Rio Grande on Dec 4, 1864, as it arrived from Liverpool. The U.S. Supreme Court ordered its release on Mar 5, 1865, with the vessel and cargo restored to the owners.

SS *Grampus No. 2*. 252-ton side-wheel steamer, built 1856 at McKeesport, Pennsylvania, Mifflin Kenedy was her initial captain and owner through Kenedy & Co. At the onset of the Civil War, it shuttled supplies between Brazos Santiago and the Rio Grande. They then sold the steamer to Chapple Dutton & Co. on behalf of Droege, Oetling & Co. who registered her in Mexico. Profits from the steamer's operations continued to flow into Kenedy & Co. accounts throughout the war. This is not the same *Grampus* that operated on the Mississippi River.

Harriet Lane (*Lavinia, Elliott Richie*). 750-ton side-paddlewheel steamer, belonging to the U.S. Revenue Service, the U.S. and Confederate Navies, and nominal Confederate civilian owners during the Civil War; built 1857 at New York, New York; Dimensions: 180' × 30' × 5'; Armament (when captured): 3 × 9", 1 × 12pdr (rifled), 1 × 30pdr (rifled); Captain John Faunce, USRCS, CDR Jonathan M. Wainwright, USN, Commodore Leon Smith, Texas Marine Dept., Joseph N. Barney, CSN, Joseph C. Bernard. Named after the bachelor President Buchanan's niece and White House hostess and first to be called "First Lady." She was the Revenue Service's first steamship before the U.S. Navy took her into the fleet. She fired the Navy's first shot of the Civil War and participated in the captures of Hatteras Inlet and New Orleans, before being captured at Galveston on Jan 1, 1863. Renamed *Lavinia* prior to running into Havana with a load of cotton. After the war, she reverted to Captain Faunce and the Revenue Service before having her engines removed and sold as a commercial sailing ship named *Elliott Richie*.

USS *Hatteras* (*St. Mary*'s). 1,126-ton side-paddlewheel steamer, built 1861 at Wilmington, Delaware; Dimensions: 210' × 34' × 18'; Armament: 1 × 20 pdr, 4 × 32pdr; Commander George F. Emmons. The U.S. Navy purchased her in 1861 as *St. Mary*'s. She captured seven blockade runners and detained, but released the SS *Indian No. 2* on Jul 19, 1862, off Berwick Bay. The CSS *Alabama* sank her on Jan 11, 1863, off Galveston Island.

Indian No. 2 (*Indian Queen No.* 2). 146-ton stern-paddlewheel steamer, built 1859 at Pittsburgh, Pennsylvania; Dimensions: 135' × 28' × 4'2"; Captain Eli H. Skaggs. Ran the blockade into and out of Sabine Pass in May 1862 using an illicit permit from U.S. Major General Ben Butler. Captain Skaggs used his "Butler Pass" to flummox Captain George F. Emmons of the USS *Hatteras* into letting him continue his voyage to Texas after taking a portion of the steamer's inbound cargo of bacon, lard, and flour as security. By 1863, *Indian No. 2* was back in Confederate service on the Red River.

SS *Isabel*: 286-ton British side-paddlewheel steamer, built at Brooklyn, New York; Capt. Edward P. Blake. Formerly Spanish-flagged, she escaped from Galveston with seven hundred bales of cotton on Apr 30, 1863, in company with the steamers *Harriet Lane* (*Lavinia*) and *Alice* (*Matagorda*). The USS *Admiral* captured her off Galveston on the return voyage from Havana on May 28, 1864, but she sank prior to reaching port in New Orleans.

CSS *Island City*. 245-ton Confederate side-paddlewheel steamer, built 1856 in Brownsville, Pennsylvania, Dimensions: 167' × 27' (at wheels; 44' max), × 5'9" (3' draft); Captain John Y. Lawless. Small Texas Marine Department supply and transport steamer in Galveston Bay. The 24-man crew included 13 slaves, under eight different owners, who served as 4th engineer (1), deck hands (6), firemen (4), cook (1), and cabin boy (1).

***James Williams*,** 27-ton British schooner, built 1854 in Texas; Dimensions: 45' × 17'3" × 4'3"; Capt. James D. French. Initially owned by the Swiss Consul to Galveston, Jacob Conrad Kuhn; USS *Penobscot* captured near the Brazos on Jul 12, 1864, from Tampico.

Jeannette (*Eagle, Josie, Jeanette*). 96-ton British iron-hulled, side-paddlewheel steamer, built 1852 at Dumbarton, Scotland; Dimensions: 169'11" × 16'9" × 8'4"; Captain Andrew Jackson "Jack" Moore (Oct 1864–Jul 1865), Cornelius Ennis owner. First captured in May 1863 on its seventh blockade run, sold at auction, renamed from *Eagle* to *Josie* for her voyage to Havana, and then renamed *Jeannette* in honor of the owner's wife (the former Jeannette Ingals Kimball). Made four successful runs at Galveston (2 in & 2 out).

John. 102-ton British schooner; Dimensions: 79'5" × 22'4" × 8'6"; Captains: Andrew Jackson "Jack" Moore (Jan 1863–Jul 1864), William Rogers Tucker (Jul 1864–Sep 1864), Francis Downs (Sep 1864). USS *Augusta Dinsmore* captured her with 81 bales of cotton on Sep 11, 1864.

John A. Hazard. 40-ton British schooner, built 1856 at South Milford, Delaware; Dimensions: 57'6" × 23' × 4'9"; Captain Henry Meyers (May–Nov 1864). USS *Fort Morgan* captured her 50 miles off Galveston Nov 5, 1865, from Vera Cruz to New Orleans; restored to owners in Jul 1865.

John Douglas (*Gino*). 57-ton British schooner, built 1860 at Fox River, Wisconsin; Dimensions: 61'5" × 20'8" × 5'6"; Captain Joseph Allen Kenney (Jun 1863–Feb 1864). Former blockade runner named *Gino* captured in Oct 1862 with 115 bales of cotton out of Berwick Bay, Louisiana. The British citizen John Douglas became the nominal owner in Feb 1863 and renamed the schooner in honor of himself. Ran into the Brazos from Matamoros, but was captured on Feb 29, 1864 with 125 bales of cotton, 12 miles from shore.

Josephine. 42-ton Confederate schooner, built 1864 at Buffalo Bayou, Texas; Dimensions: 75' × 13'5" × 4'5"; Captain Samuel L. Townsend (Oct 1864–Jan 1864). Captured with 157 bales of cotton four miles off Brazos Santiago, from Galveston to Matamoros.

Josiah H. Bell (*J.H. Bell*). 413-ton side-paddlewheel Texas Marine Dept. steamer, built 1852 at Jeffersonville, Indiana; Dimensions: 171' × 30' × 7'8"; Armament: 1 × 12pdr howitzer, 1 × 24pdr; Captains: David McClusky (mate & pilot), Charles Fowler, Peter Stockholm, John W. Payne, J.T. Cleveland. Before and during the early months of the Civil War the coastal steamer operated between Louisiana and Texas. Afterwards she served as a gunboat and logistics support vessel at Sabine Pass.

Julia (*Thomas R. Hughlett*). 73-ton British schooner, built 1856 at Talbot County, Maryland; Captain Richard Ross. Captured Dec 5, 1864, when 43 miles from Velasco heading for Matamoras.

USS *Kanawha*. 691-ton screw steamer, built 1861 at East Haddam, Connecticut; Dimensions: 158'4" × 28' × 9'6"; Armament: 1 × 9", 1 × 11", 2 × 24 pdr, 1 × 20 pdr (rifled); LCDR Bushrod B. Taylor. One of the 23 Unadilla-class 90-day gunboats, the steamer captured *Amanda* (May 14, 1864). With assistance from *Aroostook* and *Penguin*, she forced *Matagorda* aground on Galveston Island in Sep 1864.

USS *Kineo*. 691-ton screw steamer, built 1861 at East Haddam, Connecticut; Dimensions: 158'4" × 28' × 9'6"; Armament: 1 × 11", 1 × 20 pdr (rifled), 2 × 24 pdr, 2 × 32pdr; LCDR John Watters. One of the 23 Unadilla-class 90-day gunboats, she briefly captured the schooner *Stingaree*, but Capt. Dave McClusky recaptured his schooner and 5 U.S. Navy prize crew members.

USS *Kittatinny*. 421-ton 3-masted sailing schooner, purchased in 1861; Dimensions: 129' × 28' × 11'6"; Armament: 1 × 12pdr (rifled), 1 × 30pdr (rifled), 4 × 32pdr; Acting Master Isaac D. Seyburn. In Sep 1863, the captain sent a boarding party onboard *Rob Roy* to check Watson's papers. The Union sailors quickly retreated when they discovered that *Rob Roy*'s captain had contracted the dreaded yellow fever.

Lady Hurley (*Lote* or *Lottie Hurley*). 57-ton British schooner, built 1959 at Huron, Ohio; Dimensions: 68'6" × 19'7" × 5'9"; Captain P.C. Blanchet (Jul 1864–Dec 1865). Sailed out of Tampico with *Carrie Mair* and cleared for Havana, but USS *Chocura* captured her Dec 6, 1864, when 31 miles from the Brazos.

Lark. 267-ton side-paddlewheel steamer, built 1864 at Birkenhead, England; Dimensions: 210' × 23' × 10'3"; Captains: Henry Scherffius (3 runs, Jan–Mar 1865), Samuel Marcy (4 runs Mar–May 1865), & George Blakely (1 run, May 1865). Ran the blockade at Galveston 8 times (4 in, 4 out).

Laura Edwards. 387-ton British sailing bark (barque), built 1847 at East Boston, Massachusetts; Dimensions: 113'11" × 26'11" × 17'9"; Captain F. Olsen. *Laura Edwards* arrived at the Rio Grande from New Orleans in early August 1863 and then returned to Liverpool with 697 bales of cotton.

Lightfoot (*Light Foot*). 56-ton British schooner, built 1854 at Essex, Massachusetts. Ran the blockade from Galveston to Tampico in Aug–Sep 1864; was one of Thomas House's eight schooners with a government contract.

Lilly. 61-ton British schooner, built 1862; Dimensions: 70'6" × 22'5" × 4'5", Captain O. Raven. Captured with one hundred Enfield rifles and 120 muskets on Apr 17, 1864, about 10 miles from the Brazos from Havana.

Lilly (*Lily*). 34-ton Confederate schooner, built 1861; Dimensions: 61' × 17'4" × 4'; Captains: Frederick A. Pennefather (Aug–Oct 1864), James H. Davison (Oct 1864–Jan 1865). Shared the same name as several other Gulf schooners but was captured 20 miles east of the Brazos River.

Lilly (*Lily*, *Lilly No. 2*). 44-ton British schooner; Dimensions: 55' × 22'3" × 4'6"; Capt. William S. Cooper. Ran into the Brazos from Havana and Vera Cruz by Sep 1864. Arrived at Belize on Dec 14, 1863, but captured Feb 28, 1864, on the return trip when eight miles from the Brazos.

Lizzie. 153-ton, iron-hulled side-paddlewheel steamer, built 1864 at Renfrew West, Scotland; Dimensions: 230' × 22' × 9'; Captain Samuel Marcy. Ran the blockade four times at Matagorda Bay (2 in, 2 out) under Capt. Marcy who transferred from *Lark*.

Lone Star. 126-ton side-paddlewheel steamer for the Texas Marine Department, built 1854 at Louisville, Kentucky; Dimensions: 112' × 26' × 4'7", Captain Michael McCormick. Brazos River steamer with a draft shallow enough to pass through the canal to Galveston Bay.

Louisa Ann Fanny. 425-ton British-flagged twin screw steamer, built 1865 at London, England; Dimensions: 250' × 15'6" × 10'; Captains: William G. Pinchon (nominal), Confederate Navy Lieutenant William Fitzhugh Carter (actual). Named for the wife of CDR James D. Bulloch's financial supporter, Louisa Ann Frances "Fanny" Gilliat (1835–1914). She made it as far as Havana, but never ran the blockade, and was the likely inspiration for Watson's fictional blockade runner *Phoenix*.

Lowood (*Witchie*). 76-ton, 3-masted Confederate schooner, built 1860 at Calcasieu, Louisiana; Dimensions: 101' × 21' × 4', Captain John Henry Butler. Captured at sea on Dec 4, 1865, about 65 miles from the Brazos heading for Tampico.

Luna (*Lunar*). 163-ton side-paddlewheel steamer, built Apr 1864 at Greenwich, England; Dimensions: 170'1" × 24' × 8'6"; Captain James Britton McConnell.

Capt. McConnell also commanded the steam blockade runners *Calhoun* (*Cuba*) and *Susannah* (*Mail*). After the war, *Luna* made her way back to Liverpool before ending up in Australia.

Mack Canfield. 51-ton Swiss schooner, built 1853 at Essex, Massachusetts; Captain Heinrich (Henry) Schmidt. Owned by the Swiss Consul in Galveston, Jacob C. Kuhn, and captured Aug 25, 1863, with 133 bales of cotton off the Rio Grande by the USS *W.G. Anderson*. Condemned at New Orleans for a total of $33,445.11.

Maria (Montpelier). 406-ton British side-paddlewheel steamer, built 1863 in the US; Dimensions: 186' × 19' × 11'6" (derived from consular reports); Captains: Bill Johnson (died of a heart attack while in port Galveston in late Oct 1864), Jacobs (Nov 1864–Feb 1865). Made four successful runs between Galveston and Havana. *Montpelier* ran between Newport and Providence, Rhode Island, before changing flags and her name in Aug 1864 at St. John, New Brunswick.

Mary Ann. 9-ton Confederate sloop. On Dec 8, 1864, after clearing out of Galveston Bay, the USS *Itasca* chased her ashore at Cavallo Pass, salvaged 21 bales of cotton, and destroyed the vessel.

Mary Augusta. 829-ton British twin-screw steamer, built 1865 at London, UK (but not completed prior to the end of the Civil War); Dimensions: 250' × 15'6" × 10'. Named after Lady Mary Augusta Georgiana Moore (1836–1903), the wife of Algernon Gilliat, a financial supporter of Confederate Commander James D. Bulloch. Sister ship of the *Louisa Ann Fanny* and intended to be an armed blockade runner escort.

Mary Elizabeth (*Mary Eliza*). 33-ton British schooner; Captain George Scherffius (May 1863–Sep 1864). Named in honor of the wife of its owner, Thomas W. House. Made seven successful blockade runs (4 in; 3 out), but was lost with all hands in a storm on its 8th attempt.

Mary Ella (*Mary Ellen*, *Orion*). 173-ton British schooner, built at Montreal, Canada; Captain William S. Cooper. Captured 5 miles off the Brazos in ballast.

Mary Hill. 234-ton Confederate side-paddlewheel steamer, built 1859 at Smithfield, Texas; Dimensions: 147' × 30' × 5'10" (2–3' draft); Armament: 1 × 12 pdr howitzer, 1 × 24 pdr; Captains: John Y. Lawless; William H. Sangster; John McCormick. Built for the Trinity River and Galveston Bay trade, chartered to the Texas Marine Department in Nov 1861 and operated as a gunboat and transport in Galveston Bay, the Brazos River, and Matagorda Bay. When light-loaded her draft was only two feet.

Mary Louise (*Maria Louisa*). Thomas House-owned Confederate sloop that departed Galveston Bay, probably under Captain David McClusky and arrived at Tampico on Feb 16, 1864 with about 60 bales of cotton.

Mary P. Burton (*Phenix*, *Pet*), 67-ton Prussian- and British-flagged schooner; Dimensions: 72' × 22'7" × 4'11"; Captains: Edward T. Rich (Feb–Mar 1864), John Nagle (Sep–Nov 1864), Frederick A. Pennefather (Nov 1864–Feb 1865). Captured Mar 11, 1864, auctioned off and renamed *Phenix* with Prussian registry in Jul 1864; changed to British registry and renamed *Pet* at Tampico on Nov 5, 1864; captured with 256 bales of cotton in Galveston Bay on Feb 7, 1865. Made a total of three successful blockade runs (2 in; 1 out).

USS Mobile (*Tennessee*). 852-ton side-paddlewheel steamer, built 1853 at Baltimore, Maryland; Dimensions: 210' × 33'11" × 12' (19' draft); Armament: 1 × 12pdr (rifled), 1 × 30pdr (rifled), 2 × 32pdr; CDR William E. LeRoy. Renamed *Mobile* in Sep 1864; captured the schooner *Emily* off San Luis Pass in Oct 1864.

USS *Montgomery*. 787-ton screw steamer, built 1858 at New York, New York; Dimensions: 201'6" × 28'7" × 15'; Armament: 1 × 10", 1 × 32pdr (rifled), 4 × 32pdr; Captain Charles Hunter. The U.S. Navy purchased her in 1861. Her captain illegally boarded and burned the SS *Blanche* (former CSS *General Rusk*) on Oct 7, 1862, in Cuban waters causing an international incident.

Morris. 104-ton British schooner, built 1862 at Essex, Massachusetts; Captured Dec 19, 1864, 40 miles from the Southwest Pass of the Mississippi, but then released.

Neptune. 42-ton Confederate schooner, built 1863 at Port Lavaca, Texas; Captain, owner and builder: Charles Berndt. Captured Nov 19, 1864, 16 miles north-northeast of Brazos Santiago and then set adrift in a sinking condition.

Neptune No. 2. 257-ton side-wheel paddle steamer; Dimensions (approximate): 165' × 28' × 5'; Armament: 2 × 24pdr howitzers (Dec 1862); Captains: Charles Fowler, William H. Sangster. In Aug 1858, her captain and part-owner, John H. Sterrett disassembled the parts from the old 214-ton *Neptune* (built 1852 in Brownsville, Pennsylvania), and rebuilt *Neptune No. 2* on a new hull he had towed from New Orleans.

Nina. Small British schooner; Captain W.S. Flippen. She sailed from Galveston Bay and arrived at Tampico on Feb 16, 1864.

Owl (*Foam*). 330-ton, side-paddlewheel British steamer, built 1864 at Liverpool, England; Dimensions: 230'2" × 26'1" × 10'9"; Captain John N. Maffitt. Made six successful blockade runs including two at Galveston. Probably attempted another round trip in late May 1865 after the *de facto* Confederate surrender using the name *Foam* and then returned to Liverpool.

***Pelican*:** 445-ton screw steamer, built 1863 at Hull, England; Dimensions: 187'5" × 24' × 12'8", Capt. Henry Scherffius. Made one successful round trip between Havana and Galveston. Many authors have assumed that *Pelican* was the fictitious steamer *Phoenix* that Watson claimed to have commanded. However, multiple sources list Henry Scherffius as her captain for both blockade runs, plus she only had a single propeller, not two as Watson claimed for *Phoenix*.

USS *Penobscot*. 691-ton screw steamer, built 1861 at Belfast, Maine; Dimensions: 158'4" × 28' × 9'6"; Armament: 1 × 11", 2 × 12 pdr, 1 × 20 pdr (rifled), 2 × 24 pdr; LCDR Andrew E.K. Benham. One of the 23 Unadilla-class 90-day gunboats, the steamer captured the schooners *Lilly* (*Lily*) (Feb 28, 1864), *Stingray* (not Capt. McClusky's *Stingaree*), *John Douglas* (Feb 29, 1864), and *James Williams* (Jul 12, 1864).

Pet (*Phenix*). See: *Mary P. Burton*.

Phoenix. See: *Pelican*

Reserve. 65-ton British 3-masted schooner, built 1863 at Lynchburg, Texas; Dimensions: 80' × 18'2"x 4'8"; Captain William McPherson. Original owner was the Swiss Consul at Galveston, Jacob Conrad Kuhn. Sold to a surrogate British owner in Vera Cruz, but captured on her return trip to Galveston on Oct 25, 1863.

Richard H. Vermilyea (*R.H. Vermilyea*). 101-ton British schooner, built 1853 at Patchogue, New York; Dimensions: 76' × 22.5' × 6.75'; Captains: Albert H. DePass (Sep 1864–Jan 1865); John Curry (Feb–Mar 1865, also a part-owner). USS *Quaker City* captured her on Mar 12, 1865 from Tampico to Texas.

HBMS *Rinaldo*. 951-ton Royal Navy screw steamer, built 1860 at Portsmouth, England; Dimensions: 185' × 33' × 14'8"; Armament: 17 guns, CDR W.N.W. Hewett. Although smaller, the British sloop-of-war *Rinaldo* had an appearance similar to CSS *Alabama*, with three masts, and a single funnel aft of the forward mast. Commander Hewett had been awarded the Victoria Cross for bravery during the Crimean War and would retire as a Vice Admiral.

Rob Roy (*Francis Marquez, Jr., James Cartey*). 48-ton British top-sail schooner, rebuilt 1855 at Madisonville, Louisiana, using the keel of the *James Cartey* which had been built in 1849 at Bon Secours, Alabama; Dimensions: 58' × 22'4" × 4'7"; Captains: Henry Laverty (Jan–Jul 1863), Capt. J. (Aug–Nov 1863), and William Watson (Nov 1863–Mar 1865). Chased ashore and burned at Steinhatchee River, Florida (Mar 1865).

Sabine. Side-paddlewheel steamer, built 1860 at Pittsburg, Pennsylvania. Briefly operated as a transport between Sabine Pass and New Orleans, before running out of Sabine Pass, being chased ashore, and burned near Calcasieu on Mar 20, 1862.

USS *Sachem*. See: *Clarinda*.

Sarah. 22-ton British schooner, built about 1856 in Texas; Dimensions: 54' × 12'9" × 3'7"; Captain and original owner, Dave McClusky; nominal owner was Galveston's Swiss Consul Jacob Conrad Kuhn. The U.S. Navy briefly captured her, but McClusky's crew recaptured her and ran her aground on Dec 29, 1863, where she was wrecked 7 miles below Caney Creek.

Sarah Jordan. 41-ton Confederate schooner, built about 1857 in Texas; Captains: Caleb Letts (Mar–Jul 1862), Augustus A. Johnson (Aug 1862–Jan 1864). Levi Jordan built and owned the schooner, named in honor of his wife, Sarah; later leased and then sold to R. & D.G. Mills.

Sea Witch (*Pizarro*). 98-ton British schooner, built about 1855 at Baltimore, Maryland; Dimensions: 81'1" × 24'7" × 6'9"; Capt. Pierre Jauréguiberry. Captured on New Year's Eve 1864 from Vera Cruz to New Orleans, subsequently released.

SS *Sir William Peel* (*Don Pedro Segundo*). 1,238-ton twin-screw British steamer, built 1854 at Kent, UK; Dimensions: 249' × 32' × 16'4"; Captain Jesse Thornham. Captured off the Rio Grande with 904 bales of cotton Sep 11, 1863, but released without payment of any damages.

USS *South Carolina*. 1,165-ton screw steamship, built 1860 at Boston, Massachusetts; Dimensions: 219'10" × 33'2" × 13'8" (18' draft); Armament: 4 × 8", 1 × 32pdr, Commander James Alden. The U.S. Navy acquired her in 1861. She was the first U.S. Navy warship to blockade the Texas coast, arriving off Galveston on Jul 2, 1861.

Southern Flora. 63-ton stern-paddlewheel Confederate steamer, built 1859 at Wellsville, Ohio; Captain Alexander Cold. Served on the Arkansas and Mississippi Rivers prior to the Civil War.

USS *Stars and Stripes*. 407-ton screw-steamer, built 1861 at Mystic, Connecticut; Dimensions: 150'6" × 34'6" × 16'4" (9' draft); Armament: 1 × 12pdr, 1 × 20pdr (rifled), 4 × 8"; Volunteer Lieutenant John Sherrill. Its tender, USS *Fox*, ran *Rob Roy* ashore on a Florida beach.

Stingaree. 44-ton British schooner, Captains: A.D. Woodward (Mar–Apr 1864), Dave McClusky (May–Jul 1864), Bill Flagg (William H. Fleigh) (Jul 1864–Jul 1865).

Sailed from Mobile to Havana in Apr 1863 where Dave McClusky purchased her for his run into the Brazos.

Stingray (*Sting Ray*). 41-ton British schooner, built 1853 at Baltimore, Maryland; Dimensions: 65'5" × 18' × 4'3"; Captains: Joseph Z. (Zack) Sable (Apr 1861–Sep 1863), Robert Ergas (Sep–Dec 1863), George W. Little (Dec 1863–Feb 1864). The USS *Penobscot* captured her out of the Brazos River Feb 29, 1864, enroute to Jamaica with 82 bales of cotton.

CSS Stonewall. 1,390-ton Confederate twin-screw ironclad steamer, built 1864 at Bordeaux, France; Dimensions: 186'9" × 32'6" × 14'3"; Armament: 1 × 11", 2 × 5", Captain Thomas J. Page, CSN. Commander James D. Bulloch achieved a minor miracle in getting the ocean-going ironclad built, armed, manned, and into Confederate hands only for Capt. Page to surrender the warship to Spanish authorities a week after she arrived at Havana in May 1865. After the war, the Spanish turned her over to the U.S. Navy. The U.S. sold her to the Japanese who renamed the ironclad *Kotetsu* and then *Azuma* and was victorious at the Battle of Hakodate Bay in 1869, and served until 1888.

Susannah (*Mail, Susanna*). 350-ton British side-paddlewheel steamer, built 1860 at Glasgow Scotland; Dimensions: 179' × 18' × 7'; Captains: James B. McConnell (Apr–Oct 1864). Charles Austin (Oct–Nov 1864). The USS *Metacomet* captured her Nov 27, 1864, off Campeche after 11 successful runs between Galveston and Havana.

Sybil (*Eagle*). 210-ton British schooner, built 1862 at Camden, Maine; Dimensions: 91'4" × 24'2" × 8'6"; Captain William E. Askins. She changed her name (to *Sybil*) and registry (to British) at Nassau (Apr 1863) and made four voyages to Matamoros (Apr 1863–Dec 1864) carrying 1,230 bales of cotton to New York. Captured by the USS *Iosco* from Matamoros Nov 20, 1864; later released at New York.

Sylphide (*Sylfide, Selphide, Sylphyde*). 34-ton Prussian schooner; built 1838 at Bonfouca, Louisiana; Dimensions: 56'5" × 17'9" × 4'; Captains: John Curry (Jul 1863–Jan 1864), Richard Nugent (Feb–Mar 1864). Captured three miles from San Luis Pass, Texas, on Mar 9, 1864, out of Tampico.

Sylvia. 78-ton British schooner, built 1855 at Lunenberg, Nova Scotia; Dimensions: 64' × 19'5" × 7'6"; Captain Comstock. The schooner was a commercial trader that never ran the blockade, but found her way into Watson's narrative on several occasions.

Talisman. 160-ton British iron screw steamer, built 1882 at Greenock, Scotland; Dimensions: 112' × 19'1" × 8'5". One of the ships launched from William Watson's Ladyburn Boiler Works after the war.

Texas Ranger. 159-ton Confederate side-paddlewheel steamer, built 1852 at New Albany, Indiana; Dimensions: 136'6" × 22'4" × 5'6"; Captain John McPherson. Intended as a commercial steamer between Berwick Bay, Louisiana, and Galveston, the steamer ran into Galveston Bay the day after the U.S. Navy's blockade began. Ran out of fuel and wrecked in Aug 1862 while entering a Mexican port on an attempted voyage to Tampico. Only about 50 of the 450 bales of cotton were salvaged.

Triton. 217-ton screw steamer, built 1862 at Plymouth, England; Dimensions: 160' × 18' × 8'; Captain Joseph C. Barnard (Sep–Dec 1864). Arrived in Galveston in Sep 1864 from Liverpool via Spain, Portugal, Surinam, and Havana. Made two successful runs, inbound from Havana to Galveston and outbound from Galveston to Vera Cruz.

Union. 228-ton Confederate screw steamer; Dimensions: 128' × 23'11' × 8'6", Capt. Charles W. Austin. Made one unsuccessful blockade-running attempt in Aug 1862. Captured by USS *James S. Chambers* and taken to Key West where she was sold but proved to be unseaworthy.

Vera Cruz. See: *Clarinda* (USS *Sachem*).

Victoria. 487-ton side-paddlewheel steamer, built 1859 at Mystic Bridge, Connecticut; Dimensions: 180' × 29'6" × 9'8"; Captain Eugene Lambert. Made two successful blockade runs between Havana and Sabine Pass.

Wave. 92-ton British schooner, built at Wilmington, North Carolina; Dimensions: 68'9" × 22'2" × 7'1"; Captain Frederick Leyland. One of Swiss Consul Jacob Conrad Kuhn's schooners.

W.D.S. Hyer (*William D.S. Hyer*). 87-ton British schooner; built 1862 at Barnegat, New Jersey; Dimensions: 72' × 24' × 6'; Captains: C.P. Marsden (Mar–Nov 1863), Francis Downs (Nov 1863–Nov 1864). Made several trips to Havana and successfully ran the blockade into Galveston Bay (Dec 23, 1863) with a cargo of armaments and government gunpowder. She remained there for 10 months before running out for Vera Cruz in Oct 1864.

USS *Westfield*. 891-ton side-paddlewheel steamer, built 1861 at New York, New York; Dimensions: 215' × 35' × 13'6"; Armament: 4 × 8", 1 × 9", 1 × 100pdr (rifled); CDR William B. Renshaw. Commodore Renshaw destroyed his flagship (and himself) after running aground during the Battle of Galveston Bay.

Will o' the Wisp. 117-ton, side-paddlewheel steamer, built 1863, at Renfrow, Scotland; Dimensions: 209'6" × 23'3" × 9'8"; Captain Abner M. Godfrey. Arrived at Vera Cruz from Nassau when Capt. Godfrey could not find coal at Tampico. Made one successful run into Galveston (Dec 1864) and returned to Vera Cruz (Jan 1865) before running aground on Galveston Island (Feb 1865).

USS *William G. Anderson*. 593-ton sailing bark, built 1959 at East Boston, Massachusetts; Dimensions: 149'7" × 30'1" × 14'3"; Armament: 1 × 12pdr (rifled), 1 × 20pdr, 6 × 32pdr, Acting Volunteer Lieutenant Frederic Stanhope Hill. The U.S. Navy purchased the warship in 1861 and she captured five prizes plus the cotton salvaged from the wreck of the schooner *America*.

William R. King (*W.R. King, The Knight, Adela, Isabel*). 76-ton U.S. and Confederate schooner, built 1849 at Baltimore, Maryland; Dimensions: unknown (4' draft); Captains: Andrew Jackson (Jack) Moore (Mar–Nov 1861), C.P. Wilson (Dec 1861–Feb 1862), Acting Master's Mate Charles H. Post (Mar–Apr 1862), A.P. Laurent (May–Sep 1862), Oliver Thorpe (Oct 1862–Apr 1864). Launched in 1849 as *The Knight*, the U.S. Lighthouse Service, purchased, renamed, and refitted her as the Lighthouse Tender *William R. King* in 1853. The schooner's namesake was William Rufus King who died in April 1853, a few days after he had been sworn in as Franklin Pierce's Vice President. The Confederates seized her in 1861, but she remained part of the Confederate Lighthouse service with the same captain. Sold, converted into a blockade runner, and renamed *Adela* and then *Isabel*. The U.S. Navy captured her in Feb 1862, but the Confederates recaptured her on Apr 1, 1862, when she inadvertently sailed into Mobile Bay. She ran the blockade to Havana and probably continued her life as a merchantman running between Havana, Matamoros, and New Orleans.

Wren. 267-ton side-paddlewheel steamer, built 1864 at Birkenhead, England; Dimensions: 210'8" × 23'1" × 10'4"; Captains: William Raisbeck (Jan–Mar 1865), Moore (Mar–May 1865). Made six successful runs between Havana and Galveston, two with Capt. Raisbeck and four with Capt. Moore.

Zephine (*Frances, Francis, Marian, Zephyr, Neptune*). 679-ton side-paddlewheel steamer, built 1864 at Wilmington, Delaware; Dimensions: 225' × 32' × 10'; Captains John P. Smith (Sep 1864–Feb 1865) & Capt. Blakeley (Feb–Mar 1865). Made two successful roundtrips between Havana and Galveston under Capt. Smith, but on the third attempt, the steamer had to return to Havana after being chased.

APPENDIX 6

The Civil War Voyages of *Rob Roy*

Blockade runs in **bold** letters

Port	In	Out	Port	In	Out
New Orleans	n/a*	Jan 1863	Matamoros	Feb 1863	Mar 27, 1863
New Orleans	Apr 5, 1863	May 19, 1863†	Belize	Jun 1863	Jul 1863
Matamoros	Jul 1863	Sep 1863	**Brazos River**	**Sep 1863**	**Feb 1864**
Tampico	Feb 1864	Mar 6, 1864	Havana	Mar 21, 1864	May 11, 1864
Galveston	**Jun 1, 1864**	**Sep 12, 1864**	Tampico	Oct 6, 1864	Nov 1864
Havana	Dec 1864	Feb 23, 1865	**West Florida**	**Feb 1865**	n/a§

Total Voyages: 11; Total Blockade Runs: 5 (3 in; 2 out).

   * Operated on inland waters on Lake Ponchartrain using the name *Francis J. Marquez, Jr.*
   † Changed name to *Rob Roy* with William Watson as owner and Henry Laverty remaining as captain.
   § On Mar 2, 1865, U.S. Navy captured part of *Rob Roy*'s cargo after the crew abandoned ship and set the schooner afire at the Steinhatchee River, Florida.

Appendix 7

Nautical Tonnage and *Rob Roy* (Francis Marquez, Jr. and James Cartey)

William Watson obtained a permanent British registration for his schooner in Belize on Saturday June 13, 1863. Its official ship register number was "46416" and the schooner measured 37.92 tons using the Moorsom System for calculating vessel tonnage.[1]

The Moorsom System was a relatively new formulation that the British had begun using in 1849. This methodology first measured the vessel's gross internal volume, and then subtracted certain "exempted" spaces. These areas included crew berthing, food and water storage, navigation spaces, and other compartments that were not devoted to cargo or passengers. After deducting these non-revenue producing spaces, the surveyor then divided the total by 100 to determine the vessel's gross tonnage. Thus, the resulting figure such as the 37.92 calculation for *Rob Roy*, was typically much less than the total overall tonnage derived using other systems.[2]

Most U.S. and British surveyors preferred the more common gross registered tonnage (GRT) formula (see Appendix 4). This method used an approximate algebraic calculation to determine a ship's internal volume. GRT calculations compensated for the curved shape of the hull and then divided the total cubic volume by either 94 (British) or 95 (U.S.). Unfortunately, there were additional variations between the U.S. and British systems that make comparisons difficult. The British, for example, measured distances from the outside of the vessel's frames and the U.S. measured from the inside. As a result of these differences, the U.S. GRT measurement figure was usually slightly less that the British tonnage for the same vessel.[3]

According to William Watson, *Rob Roy* was a schooner with a retractable centerboard that measured 78 feet in length, 22 feet 6 inches abeam, with a loaded draft of 4 feet 9 inches and a hold that was 6 feet deep. Those dimensions yield a standard British gross tonnage figure of 92 60/94 tons. The American tonnage calculation for those measurements is 91 62/95 gross registered tons. The Moorsom figure for *Rob Roy* naturally would be lower than GRT, given the subtraction of non-revenue spaces. However, the official figure of 37.92 Moorsom tons is almost two and a half times less than the calculated GRT measurement. The tonnage differential is much greater than the norm as recorded for similar Belize-registered schooners. Schooners that were smaller than *Rob Roy* (as described by Watson) all had greater Moorsom tonnage figures.[4]

As shown in Table 1, something is clearly amiss with Watson's description of *Rob Roy*'s dimensions, particularly its length. Watson's numbers were in error, at least for the dimensions that surveyors used to determine tonnage. After establishing the fact that Watson purchased a schooner named *Francis Marquez, Jr.*, its antecedents and officially recorded dimensions and tonnage are relatively easy to trace. *Rob Roy* had been a 48-ton (GRT) schooner home ported in New Orleans under the command of Captain Laverty.[5]

Table 1. Registered Tonnage Comparison for Similar Civil War Era Schooners Schooners[6]

Name of Vessel	Dimensions			Gross Reg. Tonnage		Belize/ Moorsom
	Length	Beam	Depth	UK	US	
Rob Roy*	78'	22'6"	6'	92 60/94§	91 62/95§	37.92
Francis Marquez, Jr.	58'	22'4"	4'7"		48 4/95	37.92
James Cartey	58'	22'4"	4'7"		48 4/95	
Albert Edward (Uncle Bill)†	61'	19'	4'8"		47 20/95	
	63'7"	19'2"	5'	53 11/94		40.31
Cora (Snow Drift)	67'	20'	6'		69 45/95	47.5
John Douglas (Gino)	62'4"	21'	5'1"		60 75/95	40.64
Carrie Mair	68'9"	18'6"	6'7"		73 85/95	56.95
Concordia	71'	21'4"	5'2"		67 83/95§	53.47

* Dimensions for *Rob Roy* according to William Watson
† Dimensions using U.S and British measurement standards
§ GRT calculated from dimensions, all others from official U.S. and British records

For purposes of determining tonnage, the vessel's length was the distance between the forward and aft perpendicular frames of the hull. Watson's measurement of 78 feet might have been the overall length measured from the stern to the end of the bowsprit that extended beyond the forward length of the hull. The New Orleans surveyor registered *Francis Marquez, Jr.* at 48 4/95 Gross Registered Tons. This figure matches the GRT calculation that can be derived using the measured length of 58 feet. It also more closely matches the dimensions of similar Belize-registered schooners that had Moorsom tonnage totals similar to *Rob Roy*'s.

Chapter Notes

Introduction

1. William Watson, *Adventures of a Blockade Runner* (London: T. Fisher Unwin, 1892). The title from the title page is *The Adventures of a Blockade Runner; or, Trade in Time of War*. T. Fisher Unwin also printed an 1892 edition with a plain cover.
2. J. Barto Arnold III, Introduction to William Watson, *The Civil War Adventures of a Blockade Runner*, 1892 reprint (College Station: Texas A&M University Press, 2001), iii (quoted material). The author uses 19th-century place names.
3. Watson, *Adventures of a Blockade Runner*, cover, ii.

Chapter 1

1. Skelmorlie Villas skelmorlievillas.co.uk/people-of-local-interest/william-watson/ [accessed Jan 31, 2024]; Allan Mitchell, *William Watson, 1st Sergeant, 3rd Louisiana Infantry, Pelican Rifles* acwscots.co.uk/watson.htm [accessed Jan 31, 2024]; William Watson, *Life in the Confederate Army, Being the Observations and Experiences of an Alien in the South During the American Civil War* (London: Chapman and Hall, 1887, Baton Rouge: LSU Press, 1995) 2–3 (Introduction by Thomas W. Cutrer); Janet Maria Dunlop Campbell, Find a Grave in the UK and Ireland ancestry.com [accessed Feb 10, 2024].
2. "Board of Selectmen," Feb 16, 1859, *Daily Advocate* (Baton Rouge), p 2, col 4; Mitchell, *William Watson, 1st Sergeant, 3rd Louisiana Infantry, Pelican Rifles* acwscots.co.uk/watson.htm [accessed Jan 31, 2024]; Watson, *Life in the Confederate Army*, 2–3; Thomas O. Moore Papers Inventory, Mss 305, 893, 1094, Louisiana and Lower Mississippi Valley Collections Special Collections, Hill Memorial Library LSU Libraries, Baton Rouge; "Louisiana Governors," Louisiana Cemeteries la-cemeteries.com/Governors/ [accessed Apr 30, 2024]; "Engineers Licensed," Nov 1, 1859, *Daily Delta* (New Orleans), p 8, col 1.
3. U.S. Federal Census 1860, Baton Rouge, "William Watson."
4. Watson, *Life in the Confederate Army*, 4, 60 (quoted material); "List of the Officers and Members of the Pelican Rifles," Apr 30, 1861, *Daily Advocate* (Baton Rouge, LA), p 2, col 4; "Notice!" *Tri-Weekly Gazette and Comet* (Baton Rouge), May 11, 1861, p 5, col 5.
5. Watson, *Life in the Confederate Army*, 123, 140–141; Company Muster Roll, Mar 17, 1861, National Archives and Records Administration (cited hereafter as: NARA), Record Group: 109 (hereafter: RG: 109), Confederate Soldiers from Louisiana, William Watson.
6. Watson, *Life in the Confederate Army*, 213–231, 246–247; Company Muster Roll, Sept–Oct 1861, NARA, RG: 109, Confederate Soldiers from Louisiana, William Watson. The Battle of Oakhill was also known as Wilson's Creek or Oak Hills.
7. Watson, *Life in the Confederate Army*, 8–9, 285–310, 347–348; Discharge and pay account for William Watson, Jul 16, & 20, 1862, NARA, RG: 109, Confederate Soldiers from Louisiana, William Watson.
8. Discharge for William Watson, Jul 16, 1862 (quoted material), NARA, RG: 109, Confederate Soldiers from Louisiana, William Watson; Watson, *Life in the Confederate Army*, 9, 347–348, 447 (2nd quote).
9. Watson, *Life in the Confederate Army*, 9, 387–398.
10. Gen. McLellan's Retreat," *Daily Picayune* (New Orleans), Jul 15, 1862, p 2, col 3 (1st quote); *Ibid.*, 408, 409 (2nd quote), 410–412 (3rd quote), 413.
11. Walter E. Wilson, *Civil War Scoundrels and the Texas Cotton Trade* (Jefferson, NC: McFarland, 2020), 47, 151; Watson, *Life in the Confederate Army*, 411 (1st quote), 410 (2nd quote).
12. Watson, *Life in the Confederate Army*, 412 (1st quote), 413 (2nd quote), 416–419 (3rd quote).
13. Watson, *Life in the Confederate Army*, 420–421.
14. Watson, *Life in the Confederate Army*, 422–423, 447 (quoted material).
15. Charles Gardner (comp.). *Gardner's New Orleans Directory, 1861* (New Orleans: Charles Gardner, 1861), 447; Watson, *Life in the Confederate Army*, 22–25. In 1861, "Wm. Watson" was listed as an engineer living in New Orleans at 289 Calliope Street, a location near the river that is now the site of the Ernest N. Morral Convention Center.
16. *New-Orleans Price-Current and Commercial Intelligencer*, Jul 24, 1854; New Orleans *Times-Picayune*, Feb 12, 1856, & Mar 11, 1856, &

Jun 7, 1856, & May 21, 1859, & New Orleans *Crescent*, Feb 25, 1860; Schooner *F. Marquez* Manifest, Oct 9, 1862, Mss. 3923, Louisiana and Lower Mississippi Valley Collections, LSU Libraries, Baton Rouge, LA.

17. F.H. Hatch to J.C. Pemberton, Nov 3, 1862, *ORA* IV: 2, 169; WPA, *Ship Registers*, Vol VI, 1861–1870 (Baton Rouge: Louisiana State University, 1942), 496.

18. NARA RG: 36, Proofs of Citizenship Seamen's Protection Certificates Port of New Orleans, Louisiana, 1850–1851, Nov 15, 1850, Henry Laverty; *WPA Ship Registers*, Vol. V, No. 277.

19. NARA RG: 36, Proofs of Citizenship Seamen's Protection Certificates Port of New Orleans, Louisiana, 1850–1851, Nov 15, 1850, Henry Laverty; Watson, *Adventures of a Blockade Runner*, 17; Enrique Laverty Invoice for the *C.P. Knapp*; Jan 27, 1862, BCAH, José San Román Papers, Box 2G61; WPA, *Ship Registers*, Vol VI, No. 496; WPA, *Ship Registers*, Vol. V, No. 277; "Below Coming up," New Orleans *Times-Picayune*, Apr 1, 1863, p 4, col 3; "Marine News," New Orleans *Times-Picayune*, Apr 7, 1863, p 4, col 2.

20. Watson, *Adventures of a Blockade Runner*, 14.

21. George Walton Dalzell, *Flight from the Flag* (Chapel Hill: University of North Carolina Press, 1940), 241–248.

22. New Orleans Customs, Mar 31, 1862, Young-Sanders Center, NARA RG: 109, Confederate Vessel Papers: Papers Pertaining to Vessels Involved with the Confederate States of America, War Department Collection of Confederate Records, National Archives Building, Washington, DC. National Archives Microfilm Publication (hereafter: Confederate Vessel Papers), C-97, Roll: 7, *Calhoun*; U.S. vs. *Isabel*, Feb 28, 1862, NARA Ft. Worth RG: 21, M1360, Admiralty Papers, Roll: 0007, *Isabel*; New Orleans Customs, Jan 3, 1862, Dolph Briscoe Center for American History, University of Texas at Austin, TX (hereafter: BCAH), Ramsdell, Pickett Papers; Watson, *Adventures of a Blockade Runner*, 13.

23. Wilson, *Civil War Scoundrels*, 11–13, 22. The only natural outlet into the Gulf of Mexico as of 2024 are Pass Cavallo and the Rio Grande; the others have been dredged and altered. The San Bernard River and Caney Creek now take an indirect path to the Gulf through the Intracoastal Waterway and Matagorda Bay. Due to flood control and irrigation, the Rio Grande is less navigable at its mouth than it was during the Civil War.

24. Walter E. Wilson, "The Civil War Blockade Running Adventures of the Louisiana Schooner *William R. King*," *Louisiana History* 56 (Summer 2015): 303. A few small ports on Florida's Gulf coast enjoyed these same advantages, but lacked an international border.

25. Wilson, *Civil War Scoundrels*, 13–14.

26. *Ibid.*, 13–16.

27. "Belize, Honduras," *Times-Picayune* (New Orleans), May 8, 1863—May 19, 1863, p 3, col 3; "Marine News," *Times-Picayune* (New Orleans), May 20, 1863, p 4, col 1.

28. Watson, *Adventures of a Blockade Runner*, 11–12.

29. *Ibid.*, 6, 11, 12 (quoted material).

30. *Ibid.*, 9–11.

31. *Ibid.*, 11.

32. "From Fortress Monroe," *New York Tribune*, Jun 19, 1863, p 1, col 5; Charles M. Robinson III, *Shark of the Confederacy* (Annapolis: Naval Institute Press, 1995), 92–95; Chester G. Hearn, *Gray Raiders of the Sea, How Eight Confederate Warships Destroyed the Union's High Seas Commerce* (Camden, ME: International Marine Publishing, 1992), 94, 197, 242.

33. Lindsay W. Bristowe and Philip B. Wright, *Handbook of British Honduras, 1888–89* (William Blackwood and Sons, Edinburgh, 1888), 49; ShipIndex CLIP Appropriation Books, *Rob Roy*, Official Number 4641 crewlist.org.uk/ [accessed May 20, 2020]; Watson, *Adventures of a Blockade Runner*, 14.

34. Watson, *Adventures of a Blockade Runner*, 6, 14.

35. Watson, *Adventures of a Blockade Runner*, 14.

36. Watson, *Adventures of a Blockade Runner*, 17; "Marine News," *Times-Picayune* (New Orleans), May 20, 1863, p 4, col 1.

37. Henry Laverty to José San Román, Jul 13, 1863, BCAH, José San Román Papers, Box 2G65.

38. "Marine News," *Times-Picayune* (New Orleans), Apr 7, 1863, p 4, col 2; Work Projects Administration (WPA), *Ship Registers and Enrollments of New Orleans, Louisiana*, Vol. V, 1851–1860 (Baton Rouge: Louisiana State University, 1941), No. 466. & 617; Enrique Laverty Invoice for the *C.P. Knapp*; Jan 27, 1862, BCAH, José San Román Papers, Box 2G61.

39. WPA, *Ship Registers*, Vol. V, No. 466 & 617.

40. John J. Mayo (comp.), *Mercantile Navy List and Maritime Directory for 1872* (London: Sir William Mitchell, 1873), 403 (also 1880, 1890, 1900, 1910, & 1920 editions, pages 489, 577, 670, 866, & 949). See also Crew List Index Project crewlist.org.uk/data/viewimages?name=Rob+Roy&year=1872&steamsail=Sail&submit=Enter [accessed Feb 16, 2021]. Note: The Mercantile Navy List rounds all tonnage figures to the nearest whole number, e.g., *Rob Roy*'s Moorsom tonnage of 37.92 was rounded to 38 tons.

41. "Shipping Intelligence," *New-Orleans Daily Crescent*, Jan 7, 1856, p 3, col 5; "Marine News," *Times-Picayune* (New Orleans), Feb 12, 1856, p 8, col 5; & Mar 11, 1856, p 8, col 2; "Marine News," *Times-Picayune* (New Orleans), Jun 7, 1856, p 8, col 3; "Marine News," *Times-Picayune* (New Orleans), May 10, 1859, p 8, col 2; "Marine News," *Times-Picayune* (New Orleans), May 21, 1859, p 8, col 3; "Shipping Intelligence," *New Orleans Daily Crescent*, Feb 25, 1860, p 8, col 3; "Marine Intelligence," *Sunday Delta* (New Orleans), Apr 8, 1860, p 8, col 6; Schooner *F. Marquez* Manifest, Oct 9,

1862, Mss. 3923, Louisiana and Lower Mississippi Valley Collections, LSU Libraries, Baton Rouge, LA.

42. F.H. Hatch to J.C. Pemberton, Nov 3, 1862, *The War of the Rebellion: A Compilation of the Official Records of the Union and Confederate Armies* (here after cited as *ORA*) 4: 2, 169; WPA, *Ship Registers*, Vol. V, No. 277; WPA, *Ship Registers*, Vol. VI, No. 496; NARA RG: 36, Proofs of Citizenship Seamen's Protection Certificates Port of New Orleans, Louisiana, 1850–1851, Henry Laverty; "Marine News," *Times-Picayune* (New Orleans), Apr 7, 1863, p 4, col 2.

Chapter 2

1. *Ibid.*, 22–23 (1st quote), 24 (2nd & 3rd quotes), 25 (4th quote).
2. Watson, *Adventures of a Blockade Runner*, 25 (quoted material). In 1851, the city had repelled an attack by the revolutionary José María Jesús Carbajal who had recruited many of his troops from Texas. Today, the city is still officially known as Heroica Matamoros. Watson was not aware that the title of "Heroic Matamoros" had been bestowed upon the city in 1851.
3. Watson, *Adventures of a Blockade Runner*, 26–27.
4. Sir Arthur James Lyon Fremantle, Walter Lord (ed.), *The Fremantle Diary, Being the Journal of Lt. Col. Fremantle Coldstream Guard on his Three Months in the Southern States* (Boston: Little, Brown, 1954), 17–18; Wilson, *Civil War Scoundrels*, 153.
5. P.N. Luckett to E.P. Turner, Sep 27, 1863, *ORA* I: 26/2, 263; H. Laverty to José San Román, Jul 13, 1863, BCAH, José San Román Papers, Box 2G65; Watson, *Adventures of a Blockade Runner*, 31, 35; U.S. Government, *Compilation of Laws and Decisions of the Courts Relating to War Claims* (hereafter: *CLD*) (Washington, D.C.: Government Printing Office, 1908), 222; H.H. Bell to G. Welles, Sep 11, 1863, *Official Records of the Union and Confederate Navies in the War of the Rebellion* (hereafter cited as *ORN*), Series I: 20 (hereafter: I: 20) (Washington, DC: Government Printing Office, 1894–1922), 567; H. Rolando to G. Fox, Oct 3, 1863, *ORN* I: 20, 581; H.H. Bell to H. Rolando, Oct 2, 1863, *ORN* I: 20, 607; H. Rolando to H.H. Bell, Oct 13, 1863, *ORN* I: 20, 625; H.P. Bee to E.P. Turner, Sep 14, 1863, *ORA* I: 26/2, 229; H.P. Bee to E.P. Turner, Sep 18, 1863, *ORA* I: 26/2, 237; The *Sir William Peel*, 72 U.S. 517 (1866), Justia U.S. Supreme Court supreme.justia.com/us/72/517/ [accessed Jul 3, 2020]; *New York Times*, Oct 17, 1863; A&S Henry account with P. Milmo, Apr 14, 1863—May 31, 1867, BCAH, J.B. LaCoste Papers, 2E310; Watson, *Adventures of a Blockade Runner*, 31.
6. Pierre Fourier Parisot, *The Reminiscences of a Texas Missionary* (San Antonio: St. Mary's Church, 1899), 55–56 (1st quote); Semmes, *Memoirs of Service Afloat*, 792 (2nd quote); A. Wood to W.H. Seward, Feb 21, 1865, NARA RG: 59, Matamoros Consular Despatches, Vol. 8, pp 385–386; Watson, *Adventures of a Blockade Runner*, 22 (3rd quote), 26 (4th quote).
7. Watson, *Adventures of a Blockade Runner*, 31, 35.
8. *Ibid.*, 26 (2nd quote).
9. *Ibid.*, 20, 26.
10. *Ibid.*, 66–67.
11. P.N. Luckett to E.P. Turner, Sep 27, 1863, *ORA* I: 26/2, 263; H. Laverty to José San Román, Jul 13, 1863, BCAH, José San Román Papers, Box 2G65; Watson, *Adventures of a Blockade Runner*, 31, 35.
12. Watson, *Adventures of a Blockade Runner*, 31, 35, & 189 (quoted material); "Captain Henry Scherffius," *Galveston Daily News* (Houston), Nov 26, 1894, p 3, col 5; Find a Grave findagrave.com/memorial/18534762/henry-scherffius [accessed Dec 1, 2023]; Wilson, *Civil War Scoundrels*, 31 (quoted material), 74, 162. Note: *Civil War Scoundrels* erroneously lists Scherffius' mayoral term as 1892–1894 instead of 1890–1892.
13. Wilson, *Civil War Scoundrels*, 74, 176.
14. Watson, *Adventures of a Blockade Runner*, 31 (quoted material); "The *Telegraph* has a letter from Velasco," *Galveston Weekly News* (Houston), Sep 30, 1863, p 2, col 1.
15. Watson, *Adventures of a Blockade Runner*, 35.
16. J. Bates to E.P. Turner, Oct 11, 1863, NARA RG: 109, Confederate Vessel Papers, R-24, Roll: 25, *Rob Roy*; Watson, *Adventures of a Blockade Runner*, 35–38, 44–46; "Port of New Orleans," *Daily True Delta* (New Orleans), Aug 6, 1863, p 4, col 2; S. Langdon to José San Román Sep 6, 1863 and Consular Notes, Sep 9, 1863, BCAH, José San Román Papers, Box 2G 66; "For Sale," *Liverpool Mercury*, May 7, 1864, p 8, col 4. The British bark *Laura Edwards* cleared New Orleans for Matamoros on Aug 5, 1863, and was the only bark from New Orleans at the Rio Grande during this timeframe. There are two "mates" with possible Irish surnames beginning with "J" in the 1861 New Orleans directory: John Jacobs and Peter Johnson. The author was not able to further identify the man. See: Gardner, *Gardner's New Orleans Directory, 1861*, 237, 247.
17. Watson, *Adventures of a Blockade Runner*, 39, 41–42, 46; P.N. Luckett to E.P. Turner Sep 27, 1863, *ORA* I: 26/2, 263.
18. Paul H. Silverstone, *Civil War Navies, 1855–1883* (Annapolis: Naval Institute Press, 2001), 108; Watson, *Adventures of a Blockade Runner*, 39–41; H.H. Bell to J. P. Gillis, Sep 3, 1863, *ORN* I: 20, 506; H.H. Bell to C.H. Brown, Sep 24, 1864, *ORN* I: 20, 602.
19. Watson, *Adventures of a Blockade Runner*, 43–45.
20. *Ibid.*, 45–47; Kenneth E. Hendrickson Jr., "Brazos River," *Handbook of Texas Online* tshaonline.org/handbook/entries/brazos-river [accessed Sep 24, 2021].

21. P.N. Luckett to E.P. Turner Sep 27, 1863, *ORA* I: 26/2, 263–264; Watson, *Adventures of a Blockade Runner*, 46; Muster Reports, Nov 15, 1861—Feb 1863 "Confederate Soldiers from Texas, 13th Volunteers," S.C. Lyon to P.N. Luckett, Dec 27, 1863, "Citizens File," NARA RG: 109, Saml. C. Lyon; 7th & 8th Census for 1850 & 1860, Brazoria, Texas; T.J. Green, *Journal of the Texian Expedition Against Mier* (New York: Harper and Brothers, 1845) 71, 114–115, 127, 151, 156, 170, 318–319, 380, 440; "Condensed State Specials," *Galveston Weekly News* (Houston), May 6, 1886, p 5, col 5.

22. Watson, *Adventures of a Blockade Runner*, 31.

23. P.N. Luckett to E.P. Turner Sep 27, 1863, *ORA* I: 26/2, 263–264; "Galveston Weekly Customs Reports," NARA RG: 365 cited in Charles S. Davis (With additions by J. Barto Arnold III), *Colin J. McRae: Confederate Financial Agent, Blockade Running in the Trans-Mississippi South as Affected by the Confederate Government's Direct European Procurement of Goods* (College Station: Texas A&M Institute of Nautical Archaeology, 2008), 172; "Letter from Velasco," *Tri-Weekly Telegraph* (Houston), Sep 25, 1863, p 2, col 1; "The Galveston News," *Galveston Tri-Weekly News* (Houston), Sept 26 & Sep 29, 1863, p 2, col 1; "Saturday, Sept. 26, 1863," *Galveston Weekly News* (Houston), Sep 30, 1863, p 2, col 1; Watson, *Adventures of a Blockade Runner*, 31.

24. Isaac D. Seyburn log of the USS *Kittatinny*, Sep 22, 1863, *ORN* I: 20, 596; "Letter from Velasco," *Tri-Weekly Telegraph* (Houston), Sep 25, 1863, p 2, col 1; "The Galveston News," *Galveston Tri-Weekly News* (Houston), Sept 26 & Sep 29, 1863, p 2, col 1; "Saturday, Sept. 26, 1863," *Galveston Weekly News* (Houston), Sep 30, 1863, p 2, col 1; Watson, *Adventures of a Blockade Runner*, 31.

25. Watson, *Adventures of a Blockade Runner*, 47, 54, 56–57; A.C. Keaton to J. Bates, Oct 21, 1863, NARA RG: 109, Confederate Vessel Papers, R-24, Roll: 25, *Rob Roy*; S.D. Yancey to A.T. Lynn, Oct 21, 1863, *ORN* I: 20, 844.

26. E.P. Turner, Oct 11, 1863, NARA RG: 109, Confederate Vessel Papers, R-24, Roll: 25, *Rob Roy*; Watson, *Adventures of a Blockade Runner*, 48 (quoted material).

27. J. Bates to E.P. Turner, Oct 11, 1863, NARA RG: 109, Confederate Vessel Papers, R-24, Roll: 25, *Rob Roy*.

Chapter 3

1. Watson, *Adventures of a Blockade Runner*, 55, 59; W. Watson to R.S. Reid, Oct 13, 1863, NARA RG: 109, Confederate Vessel Papers, R-24, Roll: 25, *Rob Roy*.

2. Watson, *Adventures of a Blockade Runner*, 55–56, 59; *Handbook of Texas Online*, Alwyn Barr, "Sabine Pass, Battle of," *Handbook of Texas Online* tshaonline.org/handbook/online/articles/qes02 [accessed May 05, 2020].

3. J. Bates to E.P. Turner, Oct 11, 1863, NARA RG: 109, Confederate Vessel Papers, R-24, Roll: 25, *Rob Roy*; "Velasco, Feb 14th, 1865," *Tri-Weekly Telegraph* (Houston), Feb 20, 1865, p 2, col 5; Cooper K. Ragan, "Bates, Joseph," *Handbook of Texas Online* tshaonline.org/handbook/entries/bates-joseph [accessed Mar 22, 2021].

4. Ralph A. Wooster, "Clark, Edward," *Handbook of Texas Online* tshaonline.org/handbook/entries/clark-edward [accessed Mar 5, 2024]; Anne J. Bailey and Bruce Allardice, "Debray, Xavier Blanchard," *Handbook of Texas Online* tshaonline.org/handbook/entries/debray-xavier-blanchard {accessed March 22, 2021]; Special Order No. 94.1.2, Mar 8, 1863, NARA RG: 109, Military Departments—Special Orders, District of Texas, New Mexico and Arizona (hereafter: Special Orders, District of Texas), Chapter 2 (hereafter: Chap.), Vol. 111, p 172; J.A. Seddon to J. Bates, May 27, 1863 and J. Bates to J.B. Magruder, Dec 30, 1863, NARA RG: 109, Confederate Soldiers from Texas, Joseph Bates; Cooper K. Ragan, "Bates, Joseph," *Handbook of Texas Online* tshaonline.org/handbook/entries/bates-joseph [accessed Mar 22, 2021].

5. J.B. Magruder to W.R. Boggs, Sep 10, 1863, NARA RG: 109, Military Departments—Letters Sent, District of Texas, New Mexico and Arizona (hereafter: Letters Sent, District of Texas), Chap. 2, Vol. 132, p 306.

6. A. Cross to J. Bates, Sep 17, 1863, NARA RG: 109, Confederate Engineers, Abraham Cross.

7. Ibid.

8. Special Order 258.13, Sep 23, 1863, NARA RG: 109, Special Orders, District of Texas (quoted material), Chap. 2, Vol. 118, p 56.

9. Watson, *Adventures of a Blockade Runner*, 56 (quoted material).

10. Milledge L. Bonham, Jr., "The British Consuls in the Confederacy," *Studies in History, Economics and Public Law*, Vol. 43, No. 3 (1911), 184; "The City," *Galveston Weekly News* (Houston), Dec 11, 1888, p 8, col 1.

11. Watson, *Adventures of a Blockade Runner*, 56–57.

12. Ibid., 57–58; Watson, *Life in the Confederate Army*, 421–422; G.W.L. Fly, Oct 4, 1862, NARA RG: 109, Confederate Service Records, Texas Muster Rolls & Confederate Army Casualty Lists.

13. Watson, *Life in the Confederate Army*, 421–422; Watson, *Adventures of a Blockade Runner*, 58 (quoted material).

14. Betty D. Fly and Craig H. Roell, "Fly, George Washington Lafayette," *Handbook of Texas Online* tshaonline.org/handbook/entries/fly-george-washington-lafayette [accessed March 29, 2021]; G.W.L. Fly, Oct 4, 1862, NARA RG: 109, Confederate Service Records, Texas Muster Rolls & Confederate Army Casualty Lists.

15. Betty D. Fly and Craig H. Roell, "Fly, George Washington Lafayette," *Handbook of Texas Online* tshaonline.org/handbook/entries/fly-george-washington-lafayette [accessed March

29, 2021]; G.W.L. Fly, *Civil War Muster Rolls Index Cards (both Confederate and Union)*. Austin, Texas: Texas State Library and Archives Commission; Special Order No. 148.1, Nov 25, 1864, BCAH, Ashbel Smith Papers, Box 4L262. Note: By August 1864, G.W.L. Fly was commandant of the post at Galveston until the war's end.

16. Watson, *Adventures of a Blockade Runner*, 58; Clement A. Evans (ed.), *Confederate Military History*, Vol. 10: *A Library of Confederate States History* (Atlanta: Confederate Publishing Co., 1899), 352–353.

17. Evans, *Confederate Military History*, Vol. 10, 352–353; E.C. Wharton to E.P. Turner, Oct 16, 1863, NARA RG: 109, Confederate Officers & Enlisted Men, Edward C Wharton; Watson, *Adventures of a Blockade Runner*, 58; Evans, *Confederate Military History*, Vol. 10, 352–353; Thomas W. Cutrer, "Scurry, William Read," *Handbook of Texas Online* tshaonline.org/handbook/entries/scurry-william-read [accessed Mar 6, 2024].

18. Watson, *Adventures of a Blockade Runner*, 57–58.

19. E.P. Turner to J. Bates, Oct 8, 1863, NARA RG: 109, Letters Sent, District of Texas, Chap. 2, Vol. 131, p 14 (quoted material).

20. J. Bates to E.P. Turner, Oct 11, 1863, NARA RG: 109, Confederate Vessel Papers, R-24, Roll: 25, *Rob Roy*.

21. *Ibid*.

22. W. Watson to R.S. Reid, Oct 13, 1863, NARA RG: 109, Confederate Vessel Papers, R-24, Roll: 25, *Rob Roy*; J. Bates to R.S. Reid, Oct 16, 1863, NARA RG: 109, Confederate Soldiers from Texas, J. Bates; Watson, *Adventures of a Blockade Runner*, 59.

23. W. Watson to R.S. Reid, Oct 13, 1863, NARA RG: 109, Confederate Vessel Papers, R-24, Roll: 25, *Rob Roy*; Watson, *Adventures of a Blockade Runner*, 59–60.

24. *Ibid*.

25. P.N. Luckett to E.F. Gray, Mar 24, 1863, *ORA* 2: 5, 856; "Exciting Times at San Antonio," *The Ranchero* (Corpus Christi, TX), Feb 23, 1861, p 2, col 2; *Handbook of Texas Online*, Thomas W. Cutrer, "Luckett, Philip, Noland," *Handbook of Texas Online* tshaonline.org/handbook/online/articles/flu05 [accessed Apr 5, 2021]; Wilson, *Civil War Scoundrels*, 73, 158.

26. Wegmann & Parizot Partnership Agreement, Apr 28, 1860, Samuel Maas Papers, Series I GA-12 Folder 7, Special Collections, The University of Texas at Arlington Library; Henry Augustus Sand, *Crossing Antietam: The Civil War Letters of Captain Henry Augustus Sand, Company A, 103rd New York Volunteers*, Peter H. Sand and John F. McLaughlin (eds.) (Jefferson, NC: McFarland & Co., 2015), 87; "Dissolution," *Flake's Daily Bulletin* (Galveston), Dec 10, 1865, p 2, col 3; Watson, *Adventures of a Blockade Runner*, 60; "From Galveston," *Galveston Tri-Weekly News* (Houston), Jun 2, 1863, p 1, col 2; "G. Pauvert & Son," *Weekly Telegraph* (Houston), Feb 19, 1862, p 2, col 10. Parizot had formed his partnership with Louis Edward Wegmann (1814–1895) in 1860 along with an infusion of cash from a silent partner.

27. Watson, *Adventures of a Blockade Runner*, 60 (quoted material).

28. *Ibid.*, 60–61.

29. *Ibid.*, 61–62; 3rd Louisiana Infantry Roll of Prisoners of War, Mar 31, 1862, NARA RG: 109, Confederate Service Records, Louisiana, Thomas E. Mason, p 2; Roster Co. M, 27th Cavalry Texas, Nov 12, 1861, and Prisoners of War taken at Pea Ridge confined at Camp Chase, Apr 1, 1862, and T.E. Mason to W.H. Jackson, Jan 28, 1864, and Headquarters Demopolis, AL, Special Order No. 63, Mar 3, 1864, NARA RG: 109, Confederate Service Records, Texas, Thomas E. Mason, pp 8, 9, 22–23, & 21.

30. Watson, *Adventures of a Blockade Runner*, 61–64.

31. W. Watson to R.S. Reid, Oct 13, 1863, NARA RG: 109, Confederate Vessel Papers, R-24, Roll: 25, *Rob Roy*. Note: the schooner's bulwarks were an extension of its sides above the level of the deck.

32. *Ibid*.

33. E.P. Turner to J. Bates, Oct 20, 1863, NARA RG: 109, Letters Sent, District of Texas, Chap. 2, Vol. 131, p 92.

34. A.C. Keaton to J. Bates, Oct 21, 1863, NARA RG: 109, Confederate Vessel Papers, R-24, Roll: 25, *Rob Roy*.

35. *Ibid*. Note: The engineers also agreed to make any repairs to the Schooner *Enrequita* which had been impressed for pile-driving duty along with *Rob Roy*.

36. A.T. Lynn to J.B. Magruder Oct 3, 1863, *ORN* I: 20, 843–844; S.D. Yancey to A.T. Lynn, October 21, 1863, *ORN* I: 20, 844–845.

37. A.T. Lynn to J. B. Magruder, Oct 3, 1863, *ORN* I: 20, 843–844.

38. S.D. Yancey to A.T. Lynn, Oct 21, 1863, *ORN* I: 20, 844–845.

39. *Ibid*.

40. J.B. Magruder to W.H. Gregory and J. Mason, Oct 22, 1863, NARA RG: 109, Letters Sent, District of Texas, Chap. 2, Vol. 131, 98 & 99; J.B. Magruder to J. Mason, Oct 22, 1863, *ORN* I: 20, 842; John D. Bennett, *The London Confederates* (Jefferson, NC: McFarland, 2008), 139–141; "Despatch of American Mails," & "The Court," *Daily News* (London), Sep 1, 1859, p 5, col 5 & Jan 5, 1860, p 4, col 6; Sir William Henry Gregory, *Sir William Gregory, K.C.M.G., Formerly Member of Parliament and Sometime Governor of Ceylon: an Autobiography*, 2nd ed. Lady Gregory (ed.) (London: John Murray, Albemarle St., 1894), 188 (quoted material).

41. Gregory, *Sir William Gregory*, 186–198, 199 (quoted material), 200–205; "The Court," *Daily News* (London), Jan 5, 1860, p 4, col 6.

42. Bennett, *The London Confederates*, 139–141, 148, 157. Gregory did join the Southern Independence Association of London in Dec 1863, and remained a Member of Parliament until 1871, when he was appointed Governor of Ceylon (now Sri Lanka).

43. J.B. Magruder to W.H. Gregory, Oct 22, 1863, NARA RG: 109, Letters Sent, District of Texas, Chap. 2, Vol. 131, 98.

44. Edward T. Cotham, Jr. *Sabine Pass: The Confederacy's Thermopylae* (Austin: University of Texas Press, 2004), 36, 39; Ralph A. Wooster (ed.), *Lone Star Blue and Gray, Essays on Texas in the Civil War* (Austin: Texas State Historical Association, 1995), 177–210; James R. Ward, "Dowling, Richard William," *Handbook of Texas Online* tshaonline.org/handbook/entries/dowling-richard-william [accessed Mar 5, 1865].

45. J.B. Magruder to W.H. Gregory, Oct 22, 1863, NARA RG: 109, Letters Sent, District of Texas, Chap. 2, Vol. 131, 98. The Navy's Official Records omitted Magruder's letter to Gregory, but included the one to James Mason.

46. J.B. Magruder to J. Mason, Oct 22, 1863, NARA RG: 109, Letters Sent, District of Texas, Chap. 2, Vol. 131, 99 & *ORN* I: 20, 842–843; Walter E. Wilson and Gary L. McKay, *James D. Bulloch, Secret Agent and Mastermind of the Confederate Navy* (Jefferson, NC: McFarland & Co., Inc, 2010), 62, 291; Milledge L. Bonham, Jr. *The British Consuls in the Confederacy* (New York: Columbian University, Longmans, Green & Co., agents, 1911), 184–193; Bennett, *The London Confederates*, 139–141, 148, 157; Find a Grave, Arthur T. Lynn findagrave.com/memorial/34174437/arthur-t-lynn [accessed Oct 4, 2021].

47. J. Bates to P.N. Luckett, Oct 22, 1863, NARA RG: 109, Confederate Vessel Papers, R-24, Roll: 25, *Rob Roy*; Watson, *Adventures of a Blockade Runner*, 64.

Chapter 4

1. Watson, *Adventures of a Blockade Runner*, 64–65; Galveston Customs Report, Oct–Dec 1863, "Records of the Customs Service, 1847–65," NARA RG: 365, cited in Davis, *Colin J. McRae*,167.

2. Watson, *Adventures of a Blockade Runner*, 65–66, 79.

3. *Ibid.*, 49, 53–54, 69–70, 73.

4. *Ibid.*, 54, 66.

5. *Ibid.*, 54, 66, 69, 72; R.W. Shufeldt to W.H. Seward, Dec 1, 1862, NARA RG: 59, Havana Consular Despatches, Vol. 44, No. 111, pp 550–551; Special Order No. 27.7, Jan 27, 1864, NARA RG: 109, Special Orders, District of Texas, Chap. 2, Vol. 108, p 41; "Records of the Customs Service, 1847–65," NARA RG: 365, cited in Davis, *Colin J. McRae*, 173. Alexander McBurney's surname was sometimes spelled MacBirney.

6. Galveston Quarterly Customs Report, Jan–Mar 1864, NARA RG: 365, cited in Davis, *Colin J. McRae*, 173; Watson, *Adventures of a Blockade Runner*, 54, 66, 69, 72.

7. Watson, *Adventures of a Blockade Runner*, 66–68.

8. *Eureka* Crew List, Oct 25, 1863, and Provisional Register, Nov 3, 1863, NARA Ft. Worth RG: 21, New Orleans Admiralty Case No. 7790, U.S. vs *Eureka*; Galveston Customs, Oct–Dec 1863, NARA RG: 365, cited in Davis, *Colin J. McRae*, 167. A man from Louisiana named Pascalis Roubien had run afoul of Confederate authorities for sailing his Mexican-flagged schooner *Enriquita* (aka *Henrietta*) to Texas from New Orleans in Jul 1863.

9. *Eureka* Crew List, Oct 25, 1863, NARA Ft. Worth RG: 21, New Orleans Admiralty Case No. 7790, U.S. vs *Eureka*; Special Order No. 243.6, Nov 11, 1863, NARA RG: 109, Special Orders, Eastern Sub-District of Texas, Chap. 2, Vol. 102, p 235; Galveston Customs, Oct–Dec 1863, NARA RG: 365, cited in Davis, *Colin J. McRae*, 167; Ancestry, "John Robert Mills," ancestry.com/familytree/person/tree/57324268/person/46022071073/facts [accessed Mar 8, 2024]; Yale Class Committee, *Biographical Record of the Class of 1850, of Yale College* (New Haven: Tuttle, Morehouse, & Taylor, Printers, 1877), 61.

10. Watson, *Adventures of a Blockade Runner*, 68.

11. Special Order No. 27.7, Jan 27, 1864, NARA RG: 109, Special Orders, District of Texas, Chap. 2, Vol. 108, p 42; Galveston Quarterly Customs Report, Jan–Mar 1864, NARA RG: 365, cited in Davis, *Colin J. McRae*, 173; Watson, *Adventures of a Blockade Runner*, 54, 69, 72; "Loss of the *Ike Davis*," *Tri-Weekly Telegraph* (Houston), Dec 26, 1864, p 2, col 1.

12. Watson, *Adventures of a Blockade Runner*, 68, 258 (quoted material); Galveston Quarterly Customs Report, Oct–Dec 1863, NARA RG: 365, cited in Davis, *Colin J. McRae*, 167; "Houston," *Weekly Telegraph* (Houston), Dec 18, 1860, p 1, col 3.

13. Watson, *Adventures of a Blockade Runner*, 68 (quoted material).

14. *Ibid.*, 69–71.

15. *Ibid.*, 71 & 94 (quoted material).

16. *Ibid.*, 72 (quoted material), 73.

17. *General Rusk* Presentation Pitcher on display at the Rosenberg Museum Library, Galveston, TX; F.J. Porter to B.H. Hill, Mar 13, 1861, *ORA* 1: 52/1, 132–133.

18. Wilson, *Civil War Scoundrels*, 29–30, 171; R.W. Shufeldt to W.H. Seward, Oct 13, 1862, NARA RG: 59, Havana Consular Dispatches, Vol. 44, Enclosure to No. 100 (Translation from Oct 14, 1862, *Diario de la Marina*), pp 500–507; "Burning of the Steamer *General Rusk*—Outrage on Spanish Soil—worse than the Trent Affair," *Galveston Weekly News* (Houston), Oct 29, 1862, p 2, col 6; "Another Federal Outrage," *Illustrated London News*, Nov 8, 1862, p 486, col 3; "The American Blockade," *The Times* (London), Nov 11, 1862; WPA *Ship Registers*, Vol. V, No. 487.

19. William S. Cheesman to Gideon Welles, Sep 10, 1864, *ORN* I: 17, 756; Thomas Savage to William H. Seward, Sep 23, 1864, NARA RG: 59, Havana Consular Despatches, Vol. 47, No. 208, p 640–642; E.A. Hitchcock to J.E. Mulford, Mar 23, 1865, *ORA* 2: 8, 407; Stephen R. Wise, *Lifeline*

of the Confederacy, Blockade Running During the Civil War (Columbia: University of South Carolina Press, 1988), 274; Watson, *Adventures of a Blockade Runner*, 72, 73 (quoted material).

20. Watson, *Adventures of a Blockade Runner*, 72–76.

21. Ibid., 77.

22. Ibid., 77–80.

23. Special Orders No. 218.7, Aug 5, 1864, NARA RG: 109, Special Orders, District of Texas, Chap. 2, Vol. 105, p 116; "More Old Water Front Memories," *Galveston Weekly News* (Houston), Jan 15, 1911, p 17, col 1; Chris Kneupper, "Chronological and Archaeological History of the Forts Velasco," Unpublished Manuscript, Jan 19, 2021; P.N. Luckett to E.P. Turner, Sep 27, 1863, *ORA* I: Vol. 26/2, 263–264.

24. Special Order No. 313.11, Nov 17, 1863, NARA RG: 109, Special Orders, District of Texas, Chap. 2 Vol. 110, p 80; Galveston Special Order No. 20, Dec 12, 1863, BCAH, Ashbel Smith Papers, Box 4L262.

25. Watson, *Adventures of a Blockade Runner*, 82; C. Hatfield to H.H. Bell, Nov 23, 1863, *ORN* I: 20, 696; U.S. Government, *CLD*, 205, 240.

26. H.R. Marks to R. & D.G. Mills & Co., Jul 31, 1863, NARA RG: 109, Confederate Vessel Papers, E-18, Roll: 10, *Era No. 3*; Leon Smith Report of Marine Dept. Gun Boats, Oct 27, 1963, NARA RG: 45, Operations of Naval Ships and Fleet Units; "Columbia, Brazoria, County, Dec 13th, 1863," *Galveston Tri-Weekly News*, Dec 18, 1863, p 1, col 3; WPA *Ship Registers*, Vol. V, No. 406.

27. J.H. Sterrett, to E.P. Turner, Oct 27, 1863, and J. Bates to E.P. Turner, Dec 5, 1863, *ORA* I: Vol. 26/2, 362–363 & 483; Watson, *Adventures of a Blockade Runner*, 82.

28. Watson, *Adventures of a Blockade Runner*, 83–84, 98.

29. *Handbook of Texas Online*, René Harris, "Mills, David Graham" and Marie Beth Jones, "Mills, Robert," *Handbook of Texas Online* tshaonline.org/handbook/online/articles/fmi64 [accessed Apr 20, 2021]; Wilson, *Civil War Scoundrels*, 138.

30. *Era No. 3* Crew List, Sep 30, 1863, NARA RG: 109, Confederate Vessel Papers, E-18, Roll: 10, *Era No. 3*; Naval History and Heritage Command, "*Era No. 3*," history.navy.mil/research/histories/ship-histories/confederate_ships/era-no-3.html [accessed May 26, 2024]; WPA, *Ship Registers*, Vol. V, No. 40.

31. Watson, *Life in the Confederate Army*, 22–44.

32. Watson, *Adventures of a Blockade Runner*, 87–88.

33. "A Letter from the President," *Daily National Intelligencer and Washington Express* (Washington, DC), Aug 23, 1862, p 3, col 1 (quoted material); Mr. Lincoln's White House, "Notable Visitors: Horace Greeley (1811–1872)," mrlincolnswhitehouse.org/residents-visitors/ [accessed April 16, 2024].

34. Galveston Quarterly Customs Report, Jan–Mar 1864, NARA RG: 365, cited in Davis, *Colin J. McRae*, 173–174.

35. Watson, *Adventures of a Blockade Runner*, 94–96.

36. Ibid., 95.

37. Galveston Special Order No. 32, Dec 18, 1863, BCAH, Ashbel Smith Papers, Box 4L262; Galveston Quarterly Customs Report, Oct–Dec 63, NARA RG: 365, from Davis, *Colin J. McRae*, 167; F. Chase to F.W. Seward, Feb 17 & Feb 23, 1864, NARA RG: 59, Tampico Consular Despatches, No. 8 & 10, Vol. 7, pp 199–200 & 203–205.

38. Watson, *Adventures of a Blockade Runner*, 95 (1st quotation), 96; Special Order No. 308.13, Nov 12, 1863, NARA RG: 109, Special Orders, District of Texas, Chap. 2, Vol. 110, p 60 (2nd quotation).

Chapter 5

1. Watson, *Adventures of a Blockade Runner*, 89; *Weekly Civilian and Gazette* (Galveston), Jul 16, 1861; "Funeral of David McClusky," *Galveston Daily News* (Houston), Apr 13, 1877 (quoted material), p 4, col 2. The various spellings of Captain Dave McClusky's surname include McCluskey, McCloskey, McClosky, and McLusky.

2. "Later from Sabine," *Weekly Civilian and Gazette* (Galveston), Jul 16, 1861, p 3, col 2; "Funeral of David McClusky," *Galveston Daily News* (Houston), Apr 13, 1877 (quoted material), p 4, col 2.

3. Watson, *Adventures of a Blockade Runner*, 89–90; U.S. Federal Census 1850, "David McClosky."

4. Ibid., 90–91.

5. Ibid., 92–93.

6. Ibid., 39–41.

7. WPA, *Ship Registers*, Vol. VI, No. 1248, *Sarah*; Special Order No. 232.1 & 232.2, Oct 28, 1863, NARA RG: 109, Special Orders, Eastern Sub-District of Texas, Chap. 2, Vol. 102, p 229; F. Chase to F.W. Seward, Nov 24, 1863, NARA RG: 59, Tampico Consular Despatches, No. 37, Vol. 7, 153–155.

8. F. Chase to F.W. Seward, Sep 14, 1863, NARA RG: 59, Tampico Consular Despatches, No. 28, Vol. 7, 124–126; F. Chase to G. Welles, September 19, 1863, *ORN* I: 20, 594–595; Special Order 147.2, Jul 27, 1863, NARA RG: 109, Special Orders, Eastern Sub-District of Texas, Chap. 2, Vol. 102, p 139 (quoted material).

9. F. Chase to F.W. Seward, Sep 14, 1863, NARA RG: 59, Tampico Consular Dispatches, No. 28, Vol. 7, pp 124–126 (quoted material); Albert B. Faust, *Guide to the Material for American History in Swiss and Austrian Archives* (Washington, D.C.: Carnegie Institution of Washington, 1916), 67.

10. Jacob De Cordova, *Texas: Her Resources and Her Public Men, A Companion for J. De Cordova's New and Correct Map of the State of Texas* (Waco,

Texas: Texian Press, 1858), 239; Galveston Weekly Customs Reports, Dec 1861–Mar 1863, NARA RG: 365, cited in Davis, *Colin J. McRae*, 168; Provisional Register, Oct 8, 1863 & McPherson Deposition, Nov 19, 1863, NARA Ft. Worth RG: 21, New Orleans Admiralty Case File No. 7777, U.S. vs *Reserve*; "Our Alexandria Correspondence," *Tri-Weekly Telegraph* (Houston), Oct 7, 1863, p 1, col 3; "The Galveston News," *Galveston Tri-Weekly News* (Houston), Sep 29, 1863, p 2, col 1; Great Britain, Foreign Office, *Correspondence on The Slave Trade with Foreign Powers: Parties to Treaties and Conventions, under which Captured Vessels are to be Tried by Tribunals of the Nation to which They Belong* (London: William Clowes and Sons for Her Majesty's Stationery Office, 1844), No. 449; J.E. Slaughter to W. Hyllested, May 5 1864, NARA RG 109, Letters Sent, District of Texas, Chap. 2, Vol. 124, p 56.

11. F. Chase to F.W. Seward, Sep 14, 1863, NARA RG: 59, Tampico Consular Dispatches, No. 28, Vol. 7, pp 124–126; F. Chase to G. Welles, September 19, 1863, *ORN* I: 20, pp 594–595; F. Chase to F.W. Seward, Sep 16, 1863, NARA RG: 59, Tampico Consular Despatches, No. 29, Vol. 7, pp 129–130; F. Chase to G. Welles, September 19, 1863, *ORN* I: 20, 594–595; Geneanet gw.geneanet.org/brynjulf?lang=en&n=jolly&oc=0&p=david [accessed Mar 9, 2024]; F. Chase to F.W. Seward, Nov 24, 1863, NARA RG: 59, Tampico Consular Despatches, No. 37, Vol. 7, pp 153–155 (quoted material).

12. F. Chase to G. Welles, September 19, 1863, *ORN* I: 20, 594–595.

13. E.P. Turner to W. Alston, Dec 30, 1863, NARA RG: 109, Military Departments—Letters Sent in the Field, District of Texas, New Mexico and Arizona (hereafter: Letters Sent in the Field, District of Texas), Chap. 2, Vol. 127, p 124 (also in *ORN* I: 20, 748–749).

14. *Ibid.* (quoted material); A. Buchel to E.P. Turner. Dec 31, 1863, NARA RG: 109, Confederate Soldiers from Texas, A. Buchel; "A Reminiscent Mariner," *Galveston Weekly News* (Houston), May 15, 1892, p 5, col 2; USS *Virginia* Muster Roll, Jun 30, 1864, NARA RG: 24, Muster Rolls of Naval Ships, p 38; "Mortuary," *Houston Post Dispatch*, Dec 27, 1926, p 13, col 6–7. Known as "Captain" Smith in Houston, he was an able-bodied seaman assigned to the USS *Virginia* at the time of McClusky's escape on board *Sarah*. In his 1892 interview, Smith mistakenly identified *Stingaree* as *Stingray* and thought the schooner had run directly into San Luis Pass.

15. Robert W. Stephens, "Buchel, Augustus Carl (1813–1864)," *Handbook of Texas Online* tshaonline.org/handbook/entries/buchel-augustus-carl [accessed Mar 12, 2024]; A. Buchel to E.P. Turner, Jan 1, 1864, NARA RG: 109, Confederate Vessel Papers, *Sarah* (quoted material); E.P. Turner to W. Alston, Dec 30, 1863, NARA RG: 109, Letters Sent in the Field, District of Texas, Chap. 2, Vol. 127, p 124 (also in *ORN* I: 20, 748–749).

16. *Ibid.*

17. "From the Front, … Camp Wharton, Dec, 31, 8 A.M., 1863," *Tri-Weekly Telegraph* (Houston), Jan 4, 1864, p 1, col 3; "Death of E.P. Turner," *Virginia Gazette* (Williamsburg), Aug 10, 1907, p 2, col 2.

18. A. Buchel to E.P. Turner. Dec 31, 1863, NARA RG: 109, Confederate Soldiers from Texas, A. A. Buchel; A. Buchel to E.P. Turner, Jan 1, 1864, NARA RG: 109, Confederate Vessel Papers, *Sarah*; E.P. Turner to J.E. Slaughter, Jan 5, 1864, NARA RG: 109, Letters Sent in the Field, District of Texas, Chap. 2, Vol. 127, p 148 (quoted material).

19. "From the Front, … Camp Wharton, Dec 31, 8 A.M., 1863," *Tri-Weekly Telegraph* (Houston), Jan 4, 1864, p 1, col 3.

20. Galveston Quarterly Customs Report, Jan–Mar 1864, NARA RG: 365, cited in Davis, *Colin J. McRae*, 173; Galveston Special Order No. 39, Feb 8, 1864, BCAH, Ashbel Smith Papers, Box 4L262; F. Chase to F.W. Seward, Feb 17 & Feb 23, 1864, NARA RG: 59, Tampico Consular Despatches, No. 8 & 10, Vol. 7, pp 199–200 & 203–205; Watson, *Adventures of a Blockade Runner*, 147.

Chapter 6

1. Watson, *Adventures of a Blockade Runner*, 86–97.

2. E.P. Turner to J.R. Marmion, Dec 24, 1863, NARA RG: 109, Letters Sent in the Field, District of Texas, Chap. 2, Vol. 127, p 43 (quoted material).

3. Watson, *Adventures of a Blockade Runner*, 100 (quoted material).

4. "The Ranger Lost," *Tri-Weekly Telegraph* (Houston), Aug 27, 1862, p 1, col 5; "Bombardment of Corpus Christi," *Galveston Tri-Weekly News* (Houston), Aug 30, 1862, p 1, col 5; L. Pierce to W.H. Seward, Aug 27, 1862, NARA RG: 59, Matamoros Consular Despatches, Vol. 7, No 14, pp 169–170; Wise, *Lifeline of the Confederacy*, 74; Marcus Price, "Ships That Tested the Blockade of the Gulf Ports, 1861–1865," *American Neptune* 11, No. 4 (Oct 1951), 288. Wise omits the *Texas Ranger*'s arrival at the Sabine from Berwick Bay.

5. "Two Days Later," *Galveston Weekly News* (Houston), Jul 9, 1861, p 2, col 2; "Latest from Sabine! Safety of the Steamer *Bell*," *Weekly Civilian and Gazette* (Galveston), Jul 16, 1861, p 2, col 4. Not listed in Wise or Price.

6. José San Román Account Sales, Jul 15, 1861, BCAH, José San Román Papers, Box 2G61. Not listed in either Wise or Price.

7. New Orleans Southern Steamship Co. to Butler Kleiber, freight on Steamship *Austin*, Sep 11, 1861, BCAH, José San Román Papers, Box 2G 61; Price, "Ships That Tested the Blockade of the Gulf Ports, 1861–1865," *American Neptune*, Vol. 11, No. 4 (Oct 1951), 280. Brazos Santiago was the port for Brownsville prior to the appearance of U.S. Navy blockaders. This well-documented run is not in Wise.

8. "Later from Brownsville," *Weekly Telegraph* (Houston), Oct 30, 1861, p 1, col 8; José San Román to S. Hernandez & Co., Oct 16, 1861, BCAH, José San Román Papers, Box 2G 120, Letter Press, Sep 10, 1861–May 29, 1862; Price, "Ships That Tested the Blockade of the Gulf Ports, 1861–1865," *American Neptune*, Vol. 11, No. 4 (Oct 1951), 280. Not in Wise.

9. Log of the CSS *Bayou City*, Oct 3, 1861, ORN I: 16, 861; *Royal Yacht* Journal, Aug 18, 1862, Rosenberg Library; H.R. Marks to C.M. Mason, Aug 18, 1862, NARA RG: 109, Confederate Officers, Henry R. Marks; "Captain H.R. Marks," *Tri-Weekly Telegraph* (Houston), Jun 17, 1863, p 2, col 1; D.F. Mosman to G. Welles, Aug 29, 1862, *ORN* I: 17, 304; Wise, *Lifeline of the Confederacy*, 272, 274. Price, "Ships That Tested the Blockade of the Gulf Ports, 1861–1865," *American Neptune* Vol. 12, No. 1 (Jan 1952), 59; Charles Fowler Log Entry, Sept 15, 1861, MSS 27-0701, J.O.L.O. Observatory Record Book, Rosenberg Library, Galveston, TX; P.F. Appel, Log of the C.S.S. *Bayou City*, Oct 3 & Oct 5 1861, ORN, I: 16, 861; T. Chubb Log Entry, Aug 3, 1862, & Aug 18, 1862, Rosenberg Library, Galveston, TX, Log of the *Royal Yacht*, 1862–1863: 53-0001. Wise erroneously shows *Union* arriving & departing in Aug 1862; Price only lists 1862.

10. G.L. Smith to Charles Stillman, Oct 5, 1861, Stillman business papers, MS Am 800.27, Houghton. Not in Wise or Price.

11. S.B. Davis to T.O Moore, Jan 1, 1862 & S.B. Davis to W. Creevy, Jan 17, 1862, NARA RG: 109, Letters Sent, Department of Texas, Chap. 2, Vol. 135, p 63, 68; S.B. Davis to C. Choisy and W.R. Buddendoff & S.B. Davis to Commanding Officer Sabine Pass, Jan 20, 1862, Letters Sent, Department of Texas, Chap. 2, Vol. 135, p 82; M. Lovell to J.P. Benjamin, Feb 27, 1862, *ORA* I: 6, Chap. 16, 832–834; "Key West, Feb. 27, 1862" *New York Daily Herald*, Mar 6, 1862, p 8, col 3–4; Wise, *Lifeline of the Confederacy*, 272, 274; Price, "Ships That Tested the Blockade of the Gulf Ports, 1861–1865," *American Neptune* Vol. 12, No. 1 (Jan 1952), 53. Wise lists "C. Vanderbilt" which had been renamed the *Black Joker* with a British registry by this time. Correctly listed as "*Black Joker* (*C. Vanderbilt*)" in Price.

12. P.O. Hébert to J. Payne, Feb 11, 1862, NARA RG: 109, Department of Texas, Letters Sent, Chap. 2, Vol. 135, p 127; "Houston, Thursday, May 15, 1862," *Galveston Weekly News* (Houston), May 21, 1862, p 1, col 1. Not in Wise or Price.

13. "Tuesday, Oct. 22, 1861," & "Another Naval Engagement," *Columbia Democrat and Planter*, Oct 22, 1861 p 1, col 1 & p 1, col 2; H. Eagle to D.G. Farragut, Feb 27, 1862, *ORN* I: 18, 41. Not in Wise or Price.

14. *Ibid.*

15. H. Eagle to D.G. Farragut, Feb 27, 1862, *ORN* I: 18, 41; A. Cold to P.O. Hébert, Jun 10, 1862, & N. Clements to P.O. Hébert, Jun 12, 1862, NARA RG: 109, Confederate Civilian Files, Alexander Cold. Not in Wise or Price.

16. "List of Vessels in Port Not Cleared," *New Orleans Daily Crescent*, Mar 3, 1862, p 2, col 2; C.J. Helm to W.M. Browne, *Mercantile Weekly Report of Havana*, May 6, 1862, *ORN* 2: 3, 411; Price, "Ships That Tested the Blockade of the Gulf Ports, 1861–1865," *American Neptune* Vol. 12, No. 1 (Jan 1952), 57; "Puerto de la Habana," *Diario de la Marina* (Havana), Apr 22, 1862, p 1, col 5. Not in Wise.

17. Ballinger Diary, Oct 21, 1861, p 23, BCAH, William Pitt Ballinger Papers, Box 2Q422; "Running of the *Sabine*," *Tri-Weekly Telegraph* (Houston), Mar 26, 1862, p 1, col 1. Not in Wise or Price.

18. Galveston Weekly Customs Reports, Dec 1861–Mar 1863, NARA RG: 365, cited in Davis, *Colin J. McRae*, 168–170; Wise, *Lifeline of the Confederacy*, 272, 274; Price, "Ships That Tested the Blockade of the Gulf Ports, 1861–1865," *American Neptune* Vol. 12, No. 1 (Jan 1952), 53. Wise omits this successful run from Galveston to Havana, but includes the run into Matagorda Bay and the departure when the steamer wrecked on the Cuban coast.

19. Eli H. Skaggs to P.O. Hébert, Jul 8, 1862, NARA RG: 109, Confederate Citizens File, E.H. Skaggs; Wm. W. Davis Sworn Statement, Jul 17, 1862, *ORN* I: 19, 79; "Houston, Wednesday, August 13, 1862," *Galveston Weekly News* (Houston), Aug 13, 1862, p 2, col 1; G.F. Emmons to G. Welles, Jul 19, 1862, *ORN* I: 19, 76–79; Wilson, *Civil War Scoundrels*, 48–49; WPA, *Ship Registers*, Vol. V, No. 589 & WPA, *Ship Registers*, Vol. VI, No. 673; Frederick Way, Jr. (comp.), *Way's Packet Directory, 1848–1994, Passenger Steamboats of the Mississippi River System Since the Advent of Photography in Mid-Continent America* (Athens: Ohio University Press, rev. ed. 1983), No. 2751. *Indian No. 2's* blockade run is not in Wise or Price.

20. B.F. McDonough to E.P. Turner, Jul 20, 1863, NARA RG: 109, Confederate Citizen Files, B.F. McDonough; G.F. Emmons to D.G. Farragut, Jul 25, 1862, *ORN* I: 19, 88, 89; J.W. Zacharie to C. Stillman, Jun 28, 1862, Stillman business papers, MS Am 800.27, Houghton Library, Harvard University, Cambridge, MA; Wise, *Lifeline of the Confederacy*, 272, 274, 325; Price, "Ships That Tested the Blockade of the Gulf Ports, 1861–1865," *American Neptune* Vol. 12, No. 1 (Jan 1952), 59. Wise erroneously lists *Victoria's* arrival as "September, 1862."

21. J.L. Macaulay to P.O. Hébert, Aug 25, 1862 & Sep 19, 1862, NARA RG: 109, Confederate Citizens File, J.L. Macanlay [sic]; T.S. Moïse to P.O. Hébert, Sep 20, 1862, NARA RG: 109, Confederate Officers, T.S. Moïse; *NYT*, Sep 06, 1862; R. Mills to J.L. Macaulay, Sep 2, 1862, BCAH, William Pitt Ballinger Papers Box 2A; J.B. Burke to C.M. Mason, Sep 22, 1862, NARA RG: 109, Miscellaneous Confederate Records, Jno Burke; "The American Blockade," *The Times* (London), Tue, Nov 11, 1862, p 19, col 5; Wise, *Lifeline of the Confederacy*, 272, 274; Price, "Ships That Tested the Blockade of the Gulf Ports, 1861–1865," *American Neptune* Vol. 12, No. 1 (Jan 1952), 55. The Confederate gunboat *General Rusk* was refitted and renamed as the commercial steamer *Blanche* sometime between June and

July 1862. Wise lists "August" as the arrival date vice Aug 24, 1862. *Blanche* cleared from Lavaca on Sep 7th, but delayed her departure.

22. "Lavaca, Dec. 5, 1862," *Tri-Weekly Telegraph* (Houston), Dec 15, 1862, p 1, col 5; T.S. Moïse to P.O. Hébert, Sep 20, 1862, NARA RG: 109, Confederate Officers, T.S. Moïse; W.M. Samuel to S.A. Arsenal, Feb 28, 1863, and D.M. Stapp Customs Certification for SS *California*, Mar 10, 1863, NARA RG: 109, Confederate Citizen Files Business, Fulton and Jacobs; "Late from Mexico," *New York Tribune*, Dec 11, 1862, p 8, col 1-2; "Articulos de Importacion," *El Lloyd Español* (Barcelona, SP), Jan 28, 1863, p 3, col 2. Not listed in Wise and Price omits this run into and out of Texas.

23. S. Simpson to José San Román, Apr 6, 1863 & Apr 21, 1863, BCAH, José San Román Papers, Box 2G64. Not in Wise or Price.

24. S. Thompson to José San Román, May 5, 1863, BCAH, José San Román Papers, Box 2G 64; Price, "Ships That Tested the Blockade of the Gulf Ports, 1861–1865," *American Neptune* Vol. 12, No. 3 (Jul 1952), 234. Not in Wise; Price only has 1865 capture.

25. Stephen Wise, *Lifeline of the Confederacy*, 272, 274). More than half of the Texas blockade runs from 1861 through 1863 listed in Wise have errors in the dates. The Texas listings have inaccurate data attributed to the steamer *Union* which arrived in Galveston on October 3, 1861, rather than August 1862. Additionally, there are two entries for the *Alice* (*Matagorda*) indicating it arrived in Galveston on Apr 30, 1863, but there is no entry for its corresponding departure from that port. The data should show that *Alice*, formerly known as *Matagorda*, arrived in Mobile rather than Galveston on April 30th.

26. Watson, *Adventures of a Blockade Runner*, 98.

27. *Ibid.*, 98, 140.

28. "Letter from Galveston," *Tri-Weekly Telegraph* (Houston), Jun 3, 1863, p 1, col 5; Special Order No. 8.13, Jan 8, 1864, NARA RG: 109, Special Orders, District of Texas, Chap. 2, Vol. 110, p 295; "Death of Alonzo F. French," *Dallas Morning News*, Feb 7, 1899, p 6, col 3; Crew List, Sep 30, 1863, NARA RG: 109, Confederate Vessel Papers, E-18, Roll: 10, *Era No. 3*.

29. *Ibid.*, 97, 109, 110; Frederick Jonson, Tampico consular shipping papers, Nov 15, 1864, and Deposition of James O'Hagan, Dec 13, 1864, NARA Ft. Worth RG: 21, New Orleans Admiralty Case No. 7943, U.S. vs Schooner *Carrie Mair*.

30. Watson, *Adventures of a Blockade Runner*, 97, 99 (quoted material); Wilson, *Civil War Scoundrels*, 163.

31. *Ibid.*, 97–100.

32. Special Order 141.1, May 27, 1863, NARA RG: 109, Special Orders, District of Texas, Chap. 2, Vol. 111, p 231; General Order No. 74.3 & 74.4, May 30, 1863, NARA RG: 109, General Orders, District of Texas, Chap. 2, Vol. 246, p 19.

33. E.P. Turner to J.D. Henry, Mar 3, 1864, NARA RG: 109, District of Texas, Letters Sent, Chap. 2, Vol. 122, No. 417, p 211; Watson, *Adventures of a Blockade Runner*, 98 (1st quote); E.P. Turner to T.W. House, Mar 15, 1864, NARA RG: 109, Letters Sent, District of Texas, Chap. 2, Vol. 122, No. 535, p 238 (2nd quote).

34. Galveston Quarterly Customs Reports, Oct–Dec 1863 & Jan–Mar 1864, NARA RG: 365, cited in Davis, *Colin J. McRae*, 167 & 173–174. The schooner *Rob Roy* received two clearances. The first was on Nov 14, 1863, for 150 bales of cotton weighing 67,145 pounds, with fees paid totaling $83.93. The second clearance was for 72 bales weighing 33,673 pounds, with $42.09 fees paid. This clearance had a note that the total was reduced to 146 bales, 74 of which had been reshipped and fees already paid.

35. Watson, *Adventures of a Blockade Runner*, 97 (quoted material); Galveston Quarterly Customs Report, Jan–Mar 1864, NARA RG: 365, cited in Davis, *Colin J. McRae*, 167, 173–174.

36. Watson, *Adventures of a Blockade Runner*, 100–101.

37. U.S. Government, *CLD*, 211, 244; C. Hatfield to H. Bell, Nov 23, 1863, *ORN* I: 20, 696.

38. Watson, *Adventures of a Blockade Runner*, 101 (quoted material).

39. *Ibid.*, 102–104.

40. U.S. Government, *CLD*, 211, 244; C. Hatfield to H. Bell, Nov 23, 1863, *ORN* I: 20, 696; Silverstone, *Civil War Navies*, 30.

41. Deposition of F. Downs, Dec 15, 1863, NARA Ft. Worth RG: 21, New Orleans Admiralty Case File No. 7790, U.S. vs *Eureka*.

42. Galveston Quarterly Customs Report, Oct-Dec 63, NARA RG: 365, cited in Davis, *Colin J. McRae*, 166; F. Chase to F.W. Seward, Nov 24, 1863, NARA RG: 59, Tampico Consular Despatches, No. 37, Vol. 7, 153–155; Deposition of J. Stewart, May 21, 1864, NARA Ft. Worth RG: 21, New Orleans Admiralty Case No. 7887, U.S. vs. *Agnes*; F. Downs to T. House, Sep 10, 1864 & Depositions of Downs & Delany, Oct 03, 1864, NARA Ft. Worth RG: 21, New Orleans Admiralty Case No. 7913, U.S. vs. *John*; U.S. Government, *CLD*, 205, 240; C. Hatfield to H. Bell, Nov 23, 1863, *ORN* I: 20, 696; Deposition of F. Downs, Dec 15, 1863, & Crew List Oct 25, 1863, NARA Ft. Worth RG: 21, New Orleans Admiralty Case No. 7790, U.S. vs *Eureka*; Watson, *Adventures of a Blockade Runner*, 101, 104.

43. Deposition of J. Stewart, May 21, 1864, NARA Ft. Worth RG: 21, New Orleans Admiralty Case No. 7887, U.S. vs. *Agnes*; F. Downs to T.W. House, Sep 10, 1864 (quoted material from captured letter) & Depositions of F. Downs & C. Delany, Oct 3, 1864, NARA Ft. Worth RG: 21, New Orleans Admiralty Case No. 7913, U.S. vs. *John*; M.B. Crowell to G. Welles, Sep 11, 1864, *ORN* I: 21, 638–639. When John finally cleared the Brazos, Watson and his men were on *Rob Roy* in Galveston Bay. The New Orleans admiralty court condemned the schooner *John* and its 81 bales of cotton that netted a total of $29,470.22 at auction. A jackstay is a rope or rod that runs vertically on the forward

side (head) of the mast and allows the wooden yard to move.

44. C.A. Leas to F.W. Seward, Dec 7, 1863, NARA RG: 59, Belize Consular Despatches Vol. 2, No. 93, pp 502–503; "River and Steamboat News," *New Albany* (IN) *Daily Ledger*, Feb 21, 1859, p 3, col 3; P.N. Luckett to L.G. Aldrich, Dec 20, 1863, NARA RG: 109, Confederate Officers, Phillip N. Luckett; E.P. Turner to W.G. Webb, Dec 21, 1863, NARA RG 109, Letters Sent in the Field, District of Texas, Chap. 2, Vol. 128, p 152, No. 171.F; W.A. Alston to W.J. Hutchins, Dec 21, 1863, NARA RG 109, Letters Sent in the Field, District of Texas, Chap. 2, Vol. 127, No. 196.F, p 25; Special Order No. 350.15 & 350.16, Dec 22, 1863, NARA RG: 109, Special Orders, District of Texas, Chap. 2, Vol. 110, p 251.

45. Special Orders No. 51.3, Feb 20, 1864, NARA RG: 109, Special Orders, District of Texas, Chap. 2, Vol. 108, p 180.

Chapter 7

1. Watson, *Adventures of a Blockade Runner*, 105.
2. Ibid.
3. Ibid., 105–107: E.P. Turner to Capt. of *Rob Roy*, Jan 3, 1864, NARA RG: 109, Letters Sent in the Field, District of Texas, Chap. II, Vol. 127, No. 14.F.
4. Watson, *Adventures of a Blockade Runner*, 106; J.B. Magruder to Helm, Dec 27, 1863, NARA RG: 109, Letters Sent in the Field, District of Texas Chap. 2, Vol. 122, No. 265.F (quoted material).
5. Wilson, *Civil War Scoundrels*, 58.
6. Paul A. Tenkottr and James C. Claypool (eds.), *The Encyclopedia of Northern Kentucky* (Lexington: University Press of Kentucky, 2009), 441; Charles Stuart Kennedy, *The American Consul: A History of the United States Consular Service 1776 –1924*, 2nd ed. (Washington, DC: New Academia Publishing, 2015), 153–155; "From Havana," *New York Times*, Dec 23, 1862, p 1, col 6; "Letter from Havana, Feb. 15, 1863," *Tri-Weekly Telegraph* (Houston), Mar 27, 1863, p 1, col 4 (quoted material); Samuel Bernard Thompson, *Confederate Purchasing Operations Abroad* (Chapel Hill: University of North Carolina Press, 1935), 8–9; H.H. Bell to D.G. Farragut, Feb 27, 1863, *ORN* I: 19, 636.
7. E.P. Turner to Capt. of *Rob Roy*, Jan 3, 1864, NARA RG: 109, Letters Sent in the Field, District of Texas, Chap. II, Vol. 127, No. 14.F, p 142; Watson, *Adventures of a Blockade Runner*, 106 (quoted material).
8. E.P. Turner to P.N. Luckett, Jan 2, 1864, NARA RG 109, Letters Sent in the Field, District of Texas, Chap. 2, Vol. 127, p 141.
9. W.J. Hutchins to E.P. Turner, Jan 11, 1864, NARA RG: 109, Confederate Officer Records, Wm. J. Hutchins.
10. F.H. Odlum. to E.P. Turner, Aug 2, 1863, Matamoros, NARA RG: 109, Confederate Citizen Papers, Augustus A. Johnson; Special Order No. 138.6, Jul 14, 1863, NARA RG: 109, Special Orders, Eastern Sub-District of Texas, Chap. 2, Vol. 102, p 132; Descriptive List and Account of Pay and Clothing of E. A. Huke, Jun 16, 1863, NARA RG: 109, Confederate Soldiers from Texas, E. Alvin Huke; E.A. Huke to E.P. Turner, Jul 27, 1863, NARA RG: 109, Confederate Citizens File, E.A. Huke.
11. Sallie McNeil, *The Uncompromising Diary of Sallie McNeil 1858–1867*. Ginny McNeill Raska and Mary Lynne Gasaway Hill (eds.) (College Station: Texas A&M University Press, 2009), 2–4.
12. J.O.L.O. Observatory record book, June 29, 1861, Rosenberg Library, Galveston Box, 27–0701; Levi Jordan, to R. & D.G. Mills, Mar 15, 1862 & Apr 15, 1862, BCAH, Ballinger Papers Box 2A186.
13. Levi Jordan, to R. & D.G. Mills, Mar 15, 1862 (quoted material), Apr 3, 1862, & Apr 15, 1862, BCAH, Ballinger Papers Box 2A186.
14. Levi Jordan to R. & D.G. Mills, Mar 15, 1862, Apr 15, 1862, & Jul 1, 1862 (quoted material), BCAH, Ballinger Papers Box 2A186.
15. G. Raymond to W.H. Seward, Aug 25, 1862, NARA RG: 59, Belize Consular Despatches, Vol. 1, No. 37, p 171.
16. B.F. McDonough to E.P. Turner, Jul 20, 1863, NARA RG: 109, Confederate Citizen Files, B.F. McDonough; F.H. Odlum. to E.P. Turner, Aug 2, 1863, NARA RG: 109, Confederate Citizen Papers, Augustus A. Johnson; Descriptive List and Account of Pay and Clothing, Jun 16, 1863, NARA RG: 109, Confederate Soldiers from Texas, E Alvin Huke; Special Order No. 162.4, Jun 16, 1863, NARA RG: 109, Special Orders, District of Texas, Chap. 2, Vol. 111, p 270.
17. Special Order No. 138.6, Jul 14, 1863, NARA RG: 109, Special Orders, Eastern Sub-District of Texas, Chap. 2, Vol. 102, p 132; Special Order No. 266.10, Oct 1, 1863, NARA RG: 109, Special Orders, Special Orders, District of Texas, Chap. 2, Vol. 118, p 95; E.A. Huke to E.P. Turner, Jul 27, 1863, NARA RG: 109, Confederate Citizens File, E.A. Huke; Special Order No. 208.2, Aug 4, 1863, NARA RG: 109, Special Orders, District of Texas, Chap. 2, Vol. 111, p 349.
18. Genaro del Regato to José San Román, Nov 3, 1863, BCAH, José San Román Papers, Box 2G66 & 2G67; W.J, Hutchins to E.P. Turner, Jan 11, 1864, NARA RG: 109, Confederate Officer Records, Wm. J. Hutchins; "Weekly Telegraph, Houston, Texas," *Weekly Telegraph* (Houston), Jan 5, 1864, p 2, col 3.
19. E.P. Turner to E.A. Huke Feb 2, 1864 (with four duplicate letters enclosed) & Feb 6, 1864 (quoted material), NARA RG: 109, Letters Sent, District of Texas, Chap. 2, Vol. 127, No. 101.H, p 101 & No. 157.H, p 136.
20. Galveston Quarterly Customs Report, Jan–Mar 1864, NARA RG: 365, cited in Davis, *Colin J. McRae*, 173–174; Watson, *Adventures of a Blockade Runner*, 98, 108–109.
21. Appraisers & Auctioneer's Report Jul 2, 1864, NARA Ft. Worth RG: 21, New Orleans Admiralty Case No. 7887, *Agnes*; Galveston

Quarterly Customs Report, Jan–Mar 1864, NARA RG: 365, cited in Davis, *Colin J. McRae*, 173; Julia Beazley, "House, Thomas William," *Handbook of Texas Online* tshaonline.org/handbook/entries/house-thomas-william [accessed Nov 26, 2021].

22. "Loss of the Schooner *Eliza Catherine* and Six Lives," *Galveston Daily News* (Houston), April 13, 1865, p 2, col 2; "Mouth of Old Caney," *Galveston Weekly News* (Houston), April 14, 1865," 18, 1865, p 1, col 2; "Post Velasco, Texas," *Galveston Daily News* (Houston), 27, 1865, p 1, col 3.

23. Galveston Quarterly Customs Report, Jan–Mar 1864, NARA RG: 365, cited in Davis, *Colin J. McRae*,174; Special Order No. 51.3, Feb 20, 1864, NARA RG: 109, Special Orders, District of Texas, Chap. 2, Vol. 108, p 182. Note: *Ann Giberson* carried 222 bales of cotton consigned to Thomas W. House.

24. J.B. Magruder to C. Helm, R. Semmes, and J.N. Maffitt, Dec 27, 1863, NARA RG: 109, Letters Sent in the Field, District of Texas, Chap. 2, Vol. 127, No. 265.F, p 90, & No. 267.F, p 94; Galveston Quarterly Customs Report, Jan–Mar 1864, NARA RG: 365, cited in Davis, *Colin J. McRae*, 173.

25. J.B. Magruder to C. Helm, R. Semmes, and J.N. Maffitt, Dec 27, 1863, NARA RG: 109, Letters Sent in the Field, District of Texas, Chap. 2, Vol. 127, No. 265.F, p 90, & No. 267.F, p 94.

26. D.G. Farragut to G. Welles, Jan 15, 1863, *ORN* I: 19, 506; D.G. Farragut to H.H. Bell, Jan 15, *ORN*, series 1, vol. 19, 525–526; Andrew W. Hall, *Civil War Blockade Running on the Texas Coast* (Charleston, SC: History Press, 2014), 44–45; *Houston Telegraph* excerpt from the *Josiah A. Bell*, Jan. 25, 1863, *ORN* I: 19, 570–574; "More of the Sabine Pass Victory!" *Tri-Weekly News* (Houston), Jan 26, 1863, p 2, col 2; Statistical Data of U.S. Ships, USS *Hatteras*, *ORN* 2: 1, 100.

27. H.P. Bee to E.P. Turner, Sep 4, 1863, NARA RG: 109, Confederate Vessel Papers, C-108, Roll: 7, *Caroline Goodyear*; "Letter from Mexico. Piedras Negras, Jan. 1, 1864," *Galveston Tri-Weekly News* (Houston), Jan 15, 1864. p 1, col 1; L. Pierce to H.H. Bell, Mar 28, 1863, *ORN* I: 20, 290; "General Banks in Brownsville," *Weekly National Intelligencer* (Washington, DC), Nov 26, 1863, p 2, col 6.

28. Watson, *Adventures of a Blockade Runner*, 133–135.

29. T. Savage to W.H. Seward, Jul 26, 1865, Havana Consular Dispatches, Vol. 48, No. 122, pp 122–125.

30. P.N. Luckett to L.G. Aldrich, Dec 20, 1863, NARA RG: 109, Confederate Officer Records, Phillip N. Luckett.

31. *Ibid*.

32. "Velasco, Dec 26th, 1863," *Galveston Tri-Weekly News* (Houston) Dec 30, 1863, p 2, col 2; "From the Front. Special to the Telegraph," *Weekly Telegraph* (Houston), Dec 30, 1863, p 1, col 2; P.N. Luckett to L.G. Aldrich, Dec 23, 1863, NARA RG: 109, Confederate Officer Records, Phillip N. Luckett; R.S. Reid to Col Rainey, Dec 24, 1863, NARA RG: 109, Confederate Officer Records, Robert S. Reid; Watson, *Adventures of a Blockade Runner*, 101–102; W.J. Hutchins to E.P. Turner, Jan 11, 1864, NARA RG: 109, Wm. J. Hutchins; United States, 48th Congress, 1st Session, 1883–1884, House Executive Document (Ex. Doc.) No. 103, *Mexican Claims, Feb 25, 1884* (Washington, D.C.: Government Printing Office, 1884), 235; "Charles Poole Marsden," *New York Tribune*, Jun 19, 1900, p 6, col 4.

33. L.G. Aldrich to Thomas, Jun 10, 1864, NARA RG: 109, Letters Sent, District of Texas, Chap. 2, Vol. 124, No. 1136, p 125; W.J. Hutchins to E.P. Turner, Jan 11, 1864, NARA RG: 109, Confederate Officer Records, Wm. J. Hutchins.

34. U.S. Government, *CLD*, 205, 241; A.L.B. Zerega to G. Welles, Dec 24, 1863, *ORN* I: 20, 734–735; Provisional Registry, Dec 7, 1863, NARA Ft. Worth RG: 21, New Orleans Admiralty Case No. 7803, U.S. vs *Exchange*.

35. E.P. Turner to W. Alston, Dec 30, 1863, NARA RG: 109, Letters Sent in the Field, District of Texas, Chap. 2, Vol. 127, p 124 (also in *ORN* I: 20, 748–749); A. Buchel to E.P. Turner, Dec 31, 1863, NARA RG: 109, Confederate Soldiers from Texas; A. Buchel to E.P. Turner, Jan 1, 1864, NARA RG: 109, Confederate Vessel Papers, S-66, Roll: 28, *Sarah*.

36. Crew list, Kingston, Jamaica, Dec 15, 1863, NARA Ft. Worth RG: 21, New Orleans Case No. 7842, U.S. vs *Stingray*.

37. Special Order 4.1 & 4.2, Jan 4, 1864, and 16.1, Jan 18, 1864, NARA RG: 109, Special Orders, Eastern Sub-District of Texas, Chap. 2, Vol. 102, p 270–271, and p 278; Bristowe, *Handbook of British Honduras, 1888–89*, 49.

38. C.A. Leas to F.W. Seward, Dec 24, 1863, NARA RG: 59, Belize Consular Despatches, Vol. 2, No. 104, pp 551–555; Clearance & manifest, Feb 5, 1864, NARA Ft. Worth RG: 21, New Orleans Admiralty Case No. 7844, U.S. vs *John Douglas*.

39. Ralph J. Smith, *Reminiscences of the Civil War, and other Sketches* (Waco: W.M. Morrison, 1962), 32; J. Bates to L.G. Aldrich, Apr 20, 1864, Columbus, NARA RG: 109, Confederate Soldiers from Texas, Joseph Bates.

40. E.P. Turner to W. Alston, Dec 30, 1863, NARA RG: 109, Letters Sent in the Field, District of Texas, Chap. 2, Vol. 127, p 124 (also in *ORN* I: 20, 748–749).

41. *Ibid*.; Robert W. Stephens, "Buchel, Augustus Carl (1813–1864)," *Handbook of Texas Online* tshaonline.org/handbook/entries/buchel-augustus-carl [accessed Mar 12, 2024]; A. Buchel to E.P. Turner, Jan 1, 1864, NARA RG: 109, Confederate Vessel Papers, S-66, Roll: 28, *Sarah*.

42. E.P. Turner to W. Alston, Dec 30, 1863, NARA RG: 109, Letters Sent in the Field, District of Texas, Chap. 2, Vol. 127, p 124 (also in *ORN* I: 20, 748–749); A. Buchel to E.P. Turner, Dec 31, 1863, NARA RG: 109, Confederate Soldiers from Texas; A. Buchel to E.P. Turner, Jan 1, 1864, NARA RG: 109, Confederate Vessel Papers, S-66, Roll: 28,

Sarah; "From the Front," *Tri-Weekly Telegraph* (Houston), Jan 4, 1864, p 1, col 3.

43. R.S. Reid to A. Buchel, Dec 24, 1863, NARA RG: 109, Confederate Officer Records, Robert S. Reid.

44. J.B. Magruder to E. Kirby Smith, Jan 6, 1864, *ORA* I: 34/2, 832–833; P.N. Luckett to L.G. Aldrich, Dec 20, 1863 & Dec 23, 1863, NARA RG: 109, Confederate Officer Service Records, Philip N, Luckett.

45. J. Bates to L.G. Aldrich, Apr 20, 1864, NARA RG: 109, Confederate Soldiers from Texas, Joseph Bates.

46. Smith, *Reminiscences of the Civil War, and other Sketches*, 32.

47. *Ibid.*, 33.

48. Raphael Semmes, *Memoirs of Service Afloat, during the War Between the States* (Baltimore: Kelly Piet & Co., 1869), 722–723; Robinson, *Shark of the Confederacy*, 120–122.

49. Frank Lawrence Owsley, Jr. *The C.S.S. Florida, Her Building and Operations* (Philadelphia: University of Pennsylvania Press, 1965) 76,98, 116–117; Export duties, Shipment No. 48, 49 per Steamer Owl to Havana, May 3, 1865, Henry Sampson Papers, Box 2, FF 10 Shipping Account Sheets, Rosenberg Library, Galveston, TX.

50. Robert Thorp, *Mersey Built, The Role of Merseyside in the American Civil War* (Wilmington, DE: Vernon Press, 2017), 361; "Galveston, April 16, 1865," *Galveston Weekly News* (Houston), Apr 19, 1865, p 2, col 3; "An Event of '65," *Galveston Weekly News* (Houston), May 6, 1901, p 8, col 4; Special Order No. 111.25, Apr 21, 1865, NARA RG: 109, Special Orders, District of Texas, Chap. 2, Vol. 103, p 125.

51. "Galveston, April 16, 1865," *Galveston Weekly News* (Houston), Apr 19, 1865, p 2, col 3; "Says Owl Was Not Sunk." *Houston Daily Post*, May 27, 1900, p 4, col 4 (quoted material); "An Event of '65," *Galveston Daily News* May 6, 1901, p 8, col 4; Emma Martin Maffitt, *The Life and Services and Services of John Newland Maffitt* (New York: Neale Publishing Co., 1906), 350; Royce Shingleton, *High Seas Confederate: The Life & Times of John Newland Maffitt* (Columbia: University of South Carolina Press, 1994), 97; Andrew W. Hall, *The Galveston-Houston Packet Steamboats on Buffalo Bayou* (Charleston, SC: The History Press, 2012), 82; Hall, *Civil War Blockade Running on the Texas Coast*, 99–101.

52. "Capt. J.N. Maffitt, C.S.N.," *Galveston Weekly News* (Houston), Apr 28, 1865, p 2, col 3–4; A. Smith to J.N. Maffitt, & A.S. Kittridge to J.C. Stafford, Apr 20, 1865, BCAH, Ashbel Smith Papers, Box 4L261; E.M. Maffitt, *The Life and Services and Services of John Newland Maffitt*, 28; Ancestry, "Find a Grave, Caroline Matilda Maffitt," ancestry.com and Ann Carnic Murry ancestry.com [accessed Mar 16, 2024].

53. "Galveston, April 15, 1865," *Galveston Weekly News* (Houston), Apr 15, 1865, p 2, col 2; "Gen. Magruder in Galveston," *Tri-Weekly Telegraph* (Houston), Apr 17, 1865 (quoted material), p 1, col 1; Galveston Special Order Nos. 95.2 & 92.3 & 92.6, May 4, 1865, and Galveston Special Order Nos. 96.8 & 96.9, May 5, 1865, BCAH, Ashbel Smith Papers, Box 4L262; T.M. Jack to A. Smith, May 5, 1865, NARA RG 109, Telegrams Sent, District of Texas, Chap. 2, Vol. 136, No. 298, p 13.

Chapter 8

1. Watson, *Adventures of a Blockade Runner*, 125.

2. *Ibid.*, 116–120; P.W. Dever to José San Román, Bill of Lading for *Morga*, Jan 10, 1863, BCAH, José San Román Papers Box 2G63 (quoted material); "Marine Disasters," *New York Evening Post*, Mar 25, 1864, p 4, col 3.

3. Wilson, *Civil War Scoundrels*, 123–125; ShipIndex CLIP Appropriation Books, *Sylvia*, Official Number 37581 crewlist.org.uk [accessed Nov 29, 2021]; "Ship—Ships ... for Matamoros," *Times-Picayune* (New Orleans), May 10, 1864, p 4, col 5; "Marine News," *Times-Picayune* (New Orleans), May 22, 1864, p 8, col 7; "American Ports," *New York Daily Herald*, May 19, 1864, p 8, col 4.

4. Watson, *Adventures of a Blockade Runner*, 127 (quoted material), 129–130, 157, 188, 286. Watson identified his crewmember George Thompson (or Thomson) as both his Scottish first mate out of the Brazos who went on a drunken bender, and the 35-year-old seaman whom John Currie had recommended to him out of Belize and who remained with *Rob Roy* from Tampico until its final voyage to Florida.

5. Watson, *Adventures of a Blockade Runner*, 129 (1st quote), 130 (2nd quote); Deposition of John Currie, Nov 11, 1864, NARA Ft. Worth RG: 21, New Orleans Admiralty Case No. 7930, U.S. vs *Lone*.

6. *Ibid.*

7. Bristowe, *Handbook of British Honduras, 1888–89*, 49; "The Blockade," *Times-Picayune* (New Orleans), Mar 27, 1863, p 2, col 5; C.H. Brown to G. Welles, Apr 19, 1864 & D.G. Farragut to G. Welles, Apr 25, 1864, *ORN* I: 21, 202; Deposition of John Bartel, Apr 27, 1864 & Deposition of Francis Celda, Apr 28, 1864, NARA Ft. Worth RG: 21, New Orleans Admiralty Case No. 7871, U.S. vs *Alma*; Watson, *Adventures of a Blockade Runner*, 129. Marcus Price does not record any successful blockade runs for the schooner *Sylphide*.

8. Joseph Kelley to José San Román, Feb 18, 1863, BCAH, José San Román Papers, Box 2G63; *Jenny* Crew List, May 29, 1863, NARA Ft. Worth RG: 21, New Orleans Admiralty Case File No. 7743, U.S. vs *Jenny*; Special Order No. 171.3, Aug 24, 1863, NARA RG: 109, Special Orders, Eastern Sub-District of Texas, Chap. 2, Vol. 102, p 162 (quoted material); Clearance & Crew List Feb 25, 1864, and Richard Nugent Deposition, Mar 21, 1864, NARA Ft. Worth RG: 21, New Orleans

Admiralty Case Files, No. 7848, U.S. vs. *Sylphyde* [sic].

9. Provisional Registry & Declaration of Ownership, Oct 4, 1864, NARA Ft. Worth RG: 21, New Orleans Admiralty Case No. 7930, U.S. vs *Lone*; D. Augustin to G. Welles, Nov 18, 1864, *ORN* I: 21, 732; W.B. Eaton to G. Welles, Nov 10, 1864, *ORN* I: 27, 635–636; F. Chase to F.W. Seward, Dec 5, 1864, NARA RG: 59, Tampico Consular Despatches, Vol. 7, No. 46, pp 342–333.

10. Manifest Customs Extract & Health Clearance & Invoice, Feb 18, 1865, NARA Ft. Worth RG: 21, New Orleans Admiralty Case No. 8017, U.S. vs *R.H. Vermilyea*; U.S. Government, *CLD*, 221, 250; W.F. Spicer to G. Welles, Mar 12, 1865, *ORN* I: 22, 103.

11. Watson, *Adventures of a Blockade Runner*, 137.

12. *Ibid.*, 138.

13. *Ibid.*, 138 (1st quote), 139 (2nd quote); "Arrivals and Havana and Other Cuban Ports," *Times-Picayune* (New Orleans), Mar 30, 1864, p 2, col 1; "Puerto de la Habana," and "Importacion de Ultramar," *Diario de la Marina* (Havana), Mar 22, 1864, p 1, col 2, & Mar 23, 1864, p 1, col 4, and Mar 31, 1864, p 1, col 5.

14. Clearance & Crew List Feb 25, 1864, and Richard Nugent Deposition, Mar 21, 1864, NARA Ft. Worth RG: 21, New Orleans Admiralty Case Files, No. 7848, U.S. vs. *Sylphyde* [sic].

15. Watson, *Adventures of a Blockade Runner*, 139, Wilson, *Civil War Scoundrels*, 51–52; Richard Henry Dana, *To Cuba and Back: A Vacation Voyage* (London: Smith, Elder & Co., 1859), 19–20 (quoted material).

16. Watson, *Adventures of a Blockade Runner*, 139.

17. *Ibid.*, 139 (1st quote), 140 (2nd quote), 281 & 282 (3rd quote); *Indian* Matamoros Consular Note, Feb 17, 1863, BCAH, José San Román Papers, Box 2G 66; *Caroline Heyman* Havana Consular Note No. 1, May 30, 1864, BCAH, José San Román Papers, Box 2G 69; "Notice—The Copartnership," *New-Orleans Commercial Bulletin*, Jul 3, 1871, p 1, col 7; B.F. Butler to E.M. Stanton, Oct 27, 1862, *ORA* 3: 2, 687–691; El Correo, "Una estatua a la deuda perpetua," elcorreo.com/vizcaya/20140202/mas-actualidad/sociedad/estatua-deuda-perpetua-201401251637.html [accessed Apr 23, 2024]. Francisco was more commonly referred to as Peregrino, but his full name was Francisco Pablo Peregrino De Avendaño Y López.

18. Watson, *Adventures of a Blockade Runner*, 140, 142 (quoted material).

19. *Ibid.*, 140–141 (quoted material).

20. *Ibid.*, 141, 142 (quoted material).

21. *Ibid.*, 142 (1st quote); Wise, *Lifeline of the Confederacy*, 146; Official regulations to carry into effect the act "to impose regulations upon the foreign commerce of the Confederate States to provide for the public defense." I. As to the Sea, Mar 5, 1864, *ORA* 4: 3, 187–189; Theodore Heermann to W.J. Hutchins, Jan 31, 1864, NARA RG: 109, Letters Sent, District of Texas, Chap. 2, Vol. 127, No. 107.H, p 105 (2nd quote).

22. Watson, *Adventures of a Blockade Runner*, 142 (quoted material), 144–145.

23. *Ibid.*, 141, 142 (1st quote), 143 (2nd quote).

24. "Passengers Arrived," *New York Times*, Sep 7, 1870, p 10, col 5; "Personal Intelligence," *New York Herald*, Aug 18, 1870, p 6, col 1; Personal Intelligence," *New York Herald*, Nov 1, 1870, p 4, col 1.

25. W.J. Hutchins to E.P. Turner, Jan 11, 1864, NARA RG: 109, Confederate Officer Records, Wm J. Hutchins; U.S. 38th Congress, 2nd Session, *Papers Relating to Foreign Affairs* (Washington, DC: GPO, 1865), 149; U.S., 48th Congress, 1st Session, House Ex. Doc. No. 103, *Mexican Claims, Feb 25, 1884*, 235; L. Pierce to José San Román, Oct 20, 1863, BCAH, José San Román Papers, Box 2G66; G.P. Bell to José San Román, Dec 15, 1862, BCAH, José San Román Papers, Box 2G 62; N.A. Blume and C.H. Brown to G.F. Emmons, Jan 11, 1865, *ORN* I: 21, 773; D.L. Braine to G. Welles, Apr 30, 1864, *ORN* I: 9, 711–712; W.F. Spicer to G. Welles, Mar 12, 1865, *ORN* I: 22, 103; B. Gheradi to G. Welles, May 3, 1864, *ORN* I: 21, 237, 239; J.A. Johnstone to G. Welles, Apr 2, 1965, *ORN* I: 22, 136–137; "Galveston, Dec. 27, 1864," *Tri-Weekly Telegraph* (Houston), Dec 28, 1864, p 1, col 3; "Galveston, Dec 28th, 1864," *Galveston Weekly News* (Houston), Jan 4, 1865, p 1, col 3; Depositions of Joseph Dixon & Harry Brayson [Henry Blessen], Jan 3, 1865, NARA Ft. Worth RG: 21, New Orleans Admiralty Case No. 7962, U.S. vs *Belle*; Philip Van Doren Stern. "The Unknown Conspirator," *American Heritage*, Feb 1957, Vol. 8, Issue 2, 54–59; Agreement for Foreign Going Ship, Sep 29, 1864, & Provisional Certificate of Registry, Sep 20, 1864, NARA Ft. Worth RG: 21, New Orleans, Admiralty Case No. 8017, U.S. vs Schooner *R.H. Vermilyea*; CLIP Appropriation Books, *Agnes*, Official No. 46989 crewlist.org.uk [accessed Dec 1, 2021]; P.N. Luckett to E.P. Turner, Sep 27, 1863, *ORA* I: 26/2,263; Bristowe *The Handbook of British Honduras, 1888–89*, 49; CLIP Appropriation Books, *Mary Elizabeth*, Official No. 46993 crewlist.org.uk/ [accessed Dec 1, 2021]; CLIP *Mercantile Navy List and Maritime Directory*, 1870, *Chaos*, Official No. 5080 crewlist.org.uk [accessed Dec 10, 2021]; H. d'Oleire & Co to T.W. House, Dec 1, 1864, BCAH,T.W. House Papers, Box 2R 43, Vol. 2; U.S. Government, *CLD*, 195, 196, 198, 202, 210, 221, 233, 234, 238, 250.

26. Watson, *Adventures of a Blockade Runner*, 148 (quoted material), 149.

27. Galveston Quarterly Customs Report, Jan–Mar 1864, NARA RG: 365, cited in Davis, *Colin J. McRae*, 173; Galveston Special Order No. 39, Feb 8, 1864, BCAH, Ashbel Smith Papers, Box 4L262; F. Chase to F.W. Seward, Feb 17 & Feb 23, 1864, NARA RG: 59, Tampico Consular Despatches, No. 8 & 10, Vol. 7, 199–200 & 203–205; "Capturing a Tartar," *Galveston Daily News* (Houston), Jan 20, 1878, p 4, col 2; Watson, *Adventures of a Blockade Runner*, 147, 170. Contemporary sources also

identify *Stingaree* as *Stingeree* or *Stingray*. This can create confusion since there was another blockade running schooner named *Stingray* (or *Sting Ray*) that was also active along the Texas coast during the Civil War. The text uses the name *Stingaree* for Dave McClusky's schooner for the sake of consistency and personal preference. The author attended Texas City High School, home of the "Fighting Stingarees," and was born in Victoria, Texas, another home for "Fighting Stingarees." Additionally, a friend and mentor's family nickname is Stinger, which is short for Stingaree.

28. Watson, *Adventures of a Blockade Runner*, 145–149, 150 (quoted material), 154. The vessel's dimensions were about 75 feet in length, 22 feet abeam, 6 feet depth of hold, and 3 feet draft.

29. *Ibid.*, 145–150, 154.

30. *Ibid.*, 152 (1st quote), 151 (2nd quote); Louis A. Pérez Jr., *Imitations of Modernity Civil Culture in Nineteenth-Century Cuba* (Chapel Hill: University of North Carolina Press, 2017), 50–51; Dick Cluster and Rafael Hernández, *The History of Havana* (New York: Palgrave Macmillan, 2008), 43 (3rd quote).

31. Cluster and Hernández, *The History of Havana*, 43 (1st quote); Watson, *Adventures of a Blockade Runner*, 151 (2nd quote), 152 (3rd quote).

32. Watson, *Adventures of a Blockade Runner*, 154 (1st quote), 151, 152 (2nd quote).

33. "Shipping News," *New York Daily Herald*, May 1, 1864, p 8, col 6; "Marine Journal," *Boston Daily Advertiser*, May 3, 1864, p 4, col 4; "Deposito Mercantil," *Diario de la Marina* (Havana), Apr 30, 1864, & May 1, 1864, p 1, col 5, & pg 1, col 6; C.J. Helm to J.B. Magruder, Apr 30, 1864, ORA I: 34/3, 798; "Havana," *Times-Picayune* (New Orleans), Jan 21, 1860, p 5, col 3; "For Havana Direct," *Times-Picayune* (New Orleans), Aug 29, 1860, p 4, col 5. Wise, in *Lifeline of the Confederacy*, 272, erroneously has *Susannah* arriving at Galveston about Apr 12, 1864.

34. Ancestry, "James B. McConnell passport application, May 14, 1866" ancestry.com [accessed Mar 24, 2024]; Discharge and pay account, Jul 16 and 20, 1862, NARA RG: 109, Confederate Soldiers from Louisiana, William Watson; Watson, *Adventures of a Blockade Runner*, 151 (quoted material).

35. Robert L. Scheina, *Latin America's Wars: The Age of the Caudillo: 1791–1899*, vol. 1 (Washington, DC: Brassey's, 2003), 225–231; Wilson & McKay, *James D. Bulloch*, 26, 293, 305 fn48; John J. TePaske, "Appleton Oaksmith, Filibuster Agent," *The North Carolina Historical Review* 35, No. 4 (Oct 1958), 427–447; Jonathan W. White, *Shipwrecked: A True Civil War Story of Mutinies, Jailbreaks, Blockade-Running, and the Slave Trade* (Lanham, MD: Rowman & Littlefield, 2023), p 171; "Affairs in Nicaragua," *New York Times*, Sep 2, 1856, p 2, col 2; "A Curious Slave Trade Case," *Boston Daily Advertiser*, Mar 13, 1865, p 2, col 2; T. Savage to W.H. Seward, Jun 22 and Jul 9, 1864, NARA RG: 59, Havana Consular Despatches, Nos. 170 & 180, Vol. 47, pp 478–479 and 493–504.

36. TePaske, "Appleton Oaksmith, Filibuster Agent," 427–447; White, *Shipwrecked*, 186; U.S. Government, *CLD*, 220; W.B. Hilton to G. Welles, Feb 8, 1864, ORN I: 2, 599; Price, "Ships That Tested the Blockade of the Gulf Ports, 1861–1865," *American Neptune* Vol. 12, No. 3 (Jul 1952), 229; "Capture of the Blockade Runner *Rosita*, of Havana," *New York Daily Herald*, Feb 4, 1864, p 2, col 1; T. Savage to W.H. Seward, Feb 3, 1864, NARA RG: 59, Havana Consular Despatches, Vol. 47, No. 37, 796–797; Walter E. Wilson, "Blockade Runner *Union* (Later *Rosita* and *Carolina*)," *Civil War Navy, The Magazine*, Spring 2024, 32–43; "U.S. Marshal's Sale," *New York Tribune*, Apr 21, 1864, p 7, col 4.

37. T. Savage to W.H. Seward, Jun 2, Jun 22, and Jul 9, 1864, NARA RG: 59, Havana Consular Despatches, Nos. 158, 170, & 180, Vol. 47, pp 457–458, 478–479, & 504–493; "Puerto de la Habana," *Diario de la Marina* (Havana), Jun 2, 1864, p 1, col 2; "Houston: Tuesday, June 7, 1864," *Galveston Weekly News* (Houston), Jun 15, 1864, p 1, col 1; Appleton Oaksmith, ca. 1865. From the Oaksmith Family Photograph Album, Appleton Oaksmith papers, 1840–1885, David M. Rubenstein Rare Book & Manuscript Library, Duke University; White, *Shipwrecked*, xiii–xiv, 47, 95, 109, 116, 196; TePaske, "Appleton Oaksmith, Filibuster Agent," 427–447.

38. Invoice & manifest Herrera to Burchard, Apr 10, 1863, NARA RG: 109, Confederate Vessel Papers, L-83, Roll: 20, *Lilly*; Logbook entries, Aug 30, 1861 & Sep 24, 1861, J.O.L.O. Observatory record book, 1861: 27-0701, Rosenberg Library, Galveston, Texas, p 160, 188; Watson, *Adventures of a Blockade Runner*, 151–152 (quoted material).

39. U.S. Government, *CLD*, 213, 245; A.E.K. Bennett to G. Welles, Feb 28, 1864, ORN I: 21, 118; D.G. Farragut to G. Welles, Mar 5, 1864, ORN I: 21, 126; C.A. Leas to F.W. Seward, NARA RG: 59, Apr 1, 1864, Belize Consular Despatches, Vol. 3, No. 140, pp 98–99; Deposition of Wm. S. Cooper, Mar 14, 1864, NARA Ft. Worth RG: 21, New Orleans Admiralty Case No. 7843, U.S. vs *Lilly*; B.B. Taylor to G.F. Emmons, Jan 7, 1865, ORN I: 22, 5; P.N. Luckett to E.P. Turner, Sep 27, 1863, ORA I: 2, 263–264; "The Situation," *Tri-Weekly Telegraph* (Houston), Sep 25, 1863, p 1, col 1; Ship register Jul 1, 1864, & Deposition of F. Downs, Oct 3, 1864, NARA Ft. Worth RG: 21, New Orleans Admiralty Case No. 7913, U.S. vs. *John*; Deposition of J. Stewart, May 21, 1864, NARA Ft. Worth RG: 21, New Orleans Admiralty Case No. 7887, U.S. vs. *Agnes*.

40. John Henry Brown, *Indian Wars and Pioneers of Texas* (Austin: L.E. Daniell, 1896), 326; "Death of Col. Ennis," *Shiner Gazette* (Shiner, TX), Feb 22, 1899, p 8, col 1; N. Collins to G. Welles May 22, 1863, ORN I: 2, 208; "New York, Oct 17," *New Orleans Times*, Oct 31, 1864, p 1, col 5; "Galveston, Oct. 28. 1864," *Galveston Weekly News* (Houston), Nov 2, 1864, p 2, col 5; H. Willke receipt to C. Ennis, Oct 31, 1865, NARA RG: 109, Confederate Citizen Files, Cornelius Ennis.

41. Watson, *Adventures of a Blockade Runner*, 151, 152. 154, 157, 179 (quoted material), and 186.

42. Andrew Moore Appointment as Port of Galveston Branch Pilot, Jun 16, 1846, and Application from Andrew J. Moore to Gov. J.W. Throckmorton for Pilot's commission, Dec 7, 1866, and Galveston Branch Pilot Oath of Office, Sep 10, 1870, *Texas, U.S., Bonds and Oaths of Office, 1846-1920* [database on-line], Secretary of State Bonds and Oaths of Office. Austin, Texas: Texas State Library and Archives Commission; "Vessels in Port of Galveston," *Galveston Commercial and Weekly Prices Current*, Jan 10, 1856, p 2, col 3; "Death of Captain Moore," *Galveston Weekly News* (Houston), Feb 8, 1884, p 4, col 3; "Stray Notes," *Galveston Weekly News* (Houston), Feb 10, 1884, p 4, col 3; U.S. Coast Guard, "*Essayons*, 1855," history.uscg.mil/ [accessed: Jun 6, 2024]; Wilson, "The Civil War Blockade Running Adventures of the Louisiana Schooner William R. King," 297; "That Oil Vessel," *Galveston News Tri-Weekly*, Apr 6, 1861, p 2, col 2. *Essayons* may have also performed coast survey duties.

43. Wilson, "The Civil War Blockade Running Adventures of the Louisiana Schooner William R. King," 297; J.M. Frailey to G. Welles, Jul 26, 1862, *ORN* I: 17, 292–293. U.S. Government, *CLD, Orion*, 217, 248; Ship register, Jan 3, 1863, NARA Ft. Worth RG: 21, New Orleans Admiralty Case No. 7913, U.S. vs. *John*.

44. "Death of Captain Moore," *Galveston Weekly News* (Houston), Feb 8, 1884, p 4, col 3; "Stray Notes," *Galveston Weekly News* (Houston), Feb 10, 1884, p 4, col 3.

45. Watson, *Adventures of a Blockade Runner*, 154 (quoted material), 155.

46. *Ibid.*, 98, 127, 129–130, 157, 188, 286; Galveston Quarterly Customs Report, Jan–Mar 1864, NARA RG: 365, cited in Davis, *Colin J. McRae*, 173; Shipping Articles Havana, Dec 4, 1864, NARA Ft. Worth RG: 21, New Orleans Admiralty Case No. 8000, U.S. vs Schooner *Annie Sophia*.

47. Watson, *Adventures of a Blockade Runner*, 149 (quoted material), 156, 157, 158, 171; "Beating a Yankee Trick," *Galveston Weekly News* (Houston), Jun 1, 1864, p 2, col 5.

48. *Ibid.*, 158, 159; "Capturing a Tartar," & "Blockade Running Stories," *Galveston Daily News* (Houston), Jan 20, 1878, p 4, col 2 & May 13, 1900, p 7, col 1–4; J. Watters to G. Welles, May 23, 1864, *ORN* I: 21, 293–294.

49. Watson, *Adventures of a Blockade Runner*, 146; Wise, *Lifeline of the Confederacy*, 26, 231, 312; J.A. Kennedy to W.H. Seward, Sep 15, 1861, *ORA* 2: Vol. 2, 67; Wilson, *Civil War Scoundrels*, 27–28, 140–141; James P. Baughman, "Morgan, Charles (1795–1878)," *Handbook of Texas Online* tshaonline.org/handbook/entries/morgan-charles [accessed Mar 17, 2024].

50. R.W. Shufeldt to J.L. Lardner, Aug 18, 1862, NARA RG: 59, Havana Consular Despatches, Vol. 45, No. 89 (enclosure), pp 376–378; Mary G. Fowler to Sister Lizzie, May 7, 1864, NARA Ft. Worth RG: 21, New Orleans Admiralty Case No. 7899, U.S. vs. SS *Isabel*; T. Savage to W.H. Seward, May 7, 1864, NARA RG: 59, Havana Consular Despatches, Vol. 47, No. 147, pp 418–419; "News from Key West. The Blockade Runners still Busy—The *Harriet Lane* at Havana, &c." *Nashville Daily Union*, May 21, 1864, p 4, col 2; "Chasing Blockade Runners," *The Guardian* (London), Jun 18, 1864, p 5, col 1; Special Order No. 100.21, Apr 9, 1864, Special Orders, District of Texas, Chap. 2, Vol. 106, p 36; Journal of J.B. Marchand, May 1, 1864, *ORN* I: 21, 813–814; Chief Signal Reports from Houston Observatory Relating to Meteorological Conditions and Enemy Vessels (hereafter: Houston Signal Reports), Apr 30, 1864, NARA RG: 109, District of Texas, Chap. 8, Vol. 7, p 278; M.G. Fowler to Sister Lizzie, May 7, 1864, and George Thebo to Miss Lou, May 11, 1864, and J.P. Smith to Alex MacCauley, May 14, 1864, NARA Ft. Worth RG: 21, New Orleans Admiralty Case No. 7899, U.S. vs. SS *Isabel*; "A Ultima Hora, Confederacion del Sur" & "Puerto de la Habana," *Diario de la Marina* (Havana), May 6, 1864, p 1, col 1 & p 1, col 7.

51. Watson, *Adventures of a Blockade Runner*, 146.

52. J. Sorely to J.B. Magruder, Apr 6, 1865, NARA RG: 109, Confederate Vessel Papers, L-120, Roll: 20, *Lavinia*.

53. "Headquarters in the Field, Jun 14, 1864," *Weekly State Gazette* (Austin), Jun 29, 1864, p 1, col 4; W.B. Eaton to G. Welles, May 29, 1864, & Jun 15, 1864, *ORN* I: 21, 306.

Chapter 9

1. Watson, *Adventures of a Blockade Runner*, 158–159; *Diario de la Marina* (Havana), May 7, 1864, p 1, col 3; "Beating a Yankee Trick," *Galveston Weekly News* (Houston), Jun 1, 1864, 2, col 5; "Capturing a Tartar," & "Blockade Running Stories," *Galveston Daily News* (Houston), Jan 20, 1878, p 4, col 2 & May 13, 1900, p 7, col 1–4; J. Watters to G. Welles, May 23, 1864, *ORN* I: 21, 293–294; "Puerto de la Habana," *Diario de la Marina* (Havana), May 12, 1864, p 1, col 3.

2. Watson, *Adventures of a Blockade Runner*, 159–160.

3. *Ibid.*, 161–163.

4. *Ibid.*, 162–163.

5. "Shipping News," *New York Daily Herald*, May 19, 1864, p 8, col 4; "Marine News," *Times-Picayune* (New Orleans), May 10, 1864, p 4, col 3; "Port of New Orleans," *Daily True Delta* (New Orleans), May 22, 1864, p 8, col 4.

6. "Puerto de la Habana," *Diario de la Marina* (Havana), May 7, 1864, p 1, col 3; Depositions of George Gemmies & John Raoul, Jun 4, 1864, NARA Ft. Worth RG: 21, New Orleans Admiralty Case No. 7889, U.S. vs. *Amanda*.

7. B.B. Taylor to Judge of the Eastern District Court of New Orleans, May 15, 1864, & A.C. Matthews to R. Skinner, May 14, 1864, NARA Ft. Worth RG: 21, New Orleans Admiralty Case No. 7889, U.S. vs. *Amanda*; J. McClernand to A.C.

Matthews, Mar 29, 1864, *ORA* I: 34/2, 771; "Col Asa Carrington Matthews," *Find a Grave* findagrave.com/memorial/35688945/asa-carrington-matthews [accessed Mar 17, 2024].

8. J.M. Avendaño to José San Román, Mar 10, 1863, BCAH, José San Román Papers, Box 2G64; Deposition of José Rodriguez, Jun 3, 1864, NARA Ft. Worth RG: 21, New Orleans Admiralty Case No. 7889, U.S. vs. *Amanda*; "Puerto de la Habana," *Diario de la Marina* (Havana), May 7, 1864, p 1, col 3.

9. Decree of Judge Edward H. Durell, Jul 8, 1864, NARA Ft. Worth RG: 21, New Orleans Admiralty Case No. 7889, U.S. vs *Amanda*; Abstract log of the USS *Bermuda*, May 20, 1864, *ORN* I: 27, 677.

10. Stanton Garner, "Thomas Bangs Thorpe in the Gilded Age: Shifty in a New Country," *The Mississippi Quarterly*, Vol. 36, No. 1 (Winter 1982–1983), 35–52; Chester G. Hearn, *When the Devil Came Down to Dixie: Ben Butler in New Orleans* (Baton Rouge: LSU Press, 2000), 182–185; Wm. A. Purdie deposition to T.B. Thorpe, Jun 3, 1864, & Decree of Judge Edward H. Durell, Jul 8, 1864, NARA Ft. Worth RG: 21, New Orleans Admiralty Case No. 7889, U.S. vs *Amanda*.

11. U.S. Government, *CLD*, 194–272.

12. Watson, *Adventures of a Blockade Runner*, 163.

13. *Ibid.*, 164 (1st quote), 155 (2nd & 3rd quotes).

14. Bruce Lockett, "The Last of the Mound Builders," *The Record* (Bridge City, TX), Dec 8, 2020 therecordlive.com/story/2020/12/09/local/last-of-the-mound-builders/29630.html [accessed Jun 20, 2022].

15. A. Pat Daniels, "High Island, TX," *Handbook of Texas Online* tshaonline.org/handbook/entries/high-island-tx [accessed June 20, 2022].

16. Watson, *Adventures of a Blockade Runner*, 164–165.

17. *Ibid.*, 165; A. Buchel to E.P. Turner, Nov 5, 1863, *ORA* I: 26/2, 391–392; X. B. (Xavier Blanchard) Debray, A sketch of the history of Debray's (26th) Regiment of Texas Cavalry (Austin: E. von Boeckmann, 1884), 15–19; Steven P. Salyer, "Twenty-Sixth Texas Cavalry," *Handbook of Texas Online* tshaonline.org/handbook/entries/twenty-sixth-texas-cavalry [accessed June 22, 2022].

18. O.M. Watkins to J. Bates, May 25, 1864, NARA RG: 109, Letters Sent, District of Texas, Chap. 2, Vol. 124, No. 1043, p 95 (quoted material); Watson, *Adventures of a Blockade Runner*, 165.

19. *Ibid.*, 166, 167, 168 (quoted material).

20. *Ibid.*, 169.

21. J.B. Magruder to S. Cooper, Feb 26, 1863, *ORA* I: 15, 212–220; *Houston Telegraph* excerpt from the *Josiah H. Bell*, Jan 25, 1863, *ORN* I: 19, 570–573; Hall, *Civil War Blockade Running on the Texas Coast*, 44–45; Donald S. Frazier, *Cottonclads! The Battle of Galveston and the Defense of the Texas Coast* (Abilene, TX: McWhitney Foundation Press, 1998), 65, 82–84. Pelican Spit was a small sand bar that has now joined with Pelican Island north of Galveston Harbor. See: Anonymous, "Pelican Island (Galveston County)," *Handbook of Texas Online* tshaonline.org/handbook/entries/pelican-island-galveston-county [accessed June 28, 2022].

22. E.P. Turner to L. Smith, Apr 11, 1864, NARA RG: 109, Letters Sent, District of Texas, Chap. 2, Vol. 122, No. 787, p 332; Frazier, *Cottonclads*, 48–51, 73–75, 122; G.E. Atwood to F.W. Emery, Jul 25, 1865, *ORA* I: 48 part 2, 1121.

23. *Ibid.*; B.A. Shepherd, F.W. Smith, and J.H. Sterrett Charter Agreement for the Houston Navigation Co. with the Confederate Government, September 23, 1861, *ORN* I: 16, 841; W.W. Hunter to P.O. Hébert, Nov 29, 1861, *ORN* I: 16, 853 (quoted material); Hall, *The Galveston-Houston Packet Steamboats on Buffalo Bayou*, 39–41, 67; Special Order No. 180.6, Jun 28, 1864, NARA RG: 109, Special Orders District of Texas, Chap. 2, Vol. 106.5, p 20; "Thursday, August 24, 1858," *Tri-Weekly Telegraph* (Houston), Aug 31, 1858, p 1, col 6; Wednesday, August 25, 1858," *Tri-Weekly Telegraph* (Houston), Aug 25, 1858, p 2, col 1; "Friday, August 27, 1858," *Tri-Weekly Telegraph* (Houston), Sep 1, 1858, p 1, col 5; "The Diana," *Cincinnati Commercial Tribune*, Nov 1, 1858, p 5, col 4; "Western Texas Items," *Texas State Gazette* (Austin, Tex.), Dec 18, 1858, p 2, col 5.

24. Watson, *Adventures of a Blockade Runner*, 170 (quoted material); "Buques que se ha Despachado," *Diario de la Marina* (Havana), May 7, 1864, p 1, col 3; "Puerto de la Habana," *Diario de la Marina* (Havana), May 12, 1864, p 1, col 4.

25. Watson, *Adventures of a Blockade Runner*, 170–171.

26. T. Chubb to J.M. Hawes, Jun 1, 1864, NARA RG: 109, Confederate Vessel Papers, R-24, Roll: 25, *Rob Roy*.

27. Patrick Feng, "Major Walter Reed and the Eradication of Yellow Fever," *National Museum United States Army* armyhistory.org/major-walter-reed-and-the-eradication-of-yellow-fever/ [accessed Apr 30, 2023].

28. Marine Department Special Order No. 221, Aug 1, 1864, NARA RG: 109, Confederate Vessel Papers, C-57 3/8, Roll: 7, *Cavallo*; Galveston Special Order No. 214, Aug 1, 1864, BCAH, Ashbel Smith Papers, Box 4L261.

29. Watson, *Adventures of a Blockade Runner*, 171.

30. *Ibid.*, 149. 171.

31. G. Holland to J.M. Hawes, Jun 2, 1864, NARA RG: 109, Confederate Officer Records, Gustave Holland.

32. G. Holland to C. McClarty, Jul 30, 1864, NARA RG: 109, Confederate Officer Records, Gustave Holland.

33. J.H. Hanson to S.P. Moore, Nov 23, 1864, NARA RG: 109, Civil War Service Records, Confederate Officers, Roll: 0130, Gustave Holland; J.H. Berrien to J.M. Hawes, Aug 10, 1864, NARA RG: 109, Civil War Service Records, Confederate Officers, Roll: 0023, James Hunter Berrien; "Gone to

Their Reward," *Las Vegas Daily Optic* (New Mexico), Dec 14, 1888, p 4, col 2.

34. "Business Cards," *Weekly Civilian and Gazette* (Galveston), Aug 14, 1860, p 4, col 2; W. & D. Richardson, *Galveston City Directory, 1859-1860* (Galveston News Book and Job Office, 1859), 19; Margaret S. Henson, "Williams, Henry Howell (1796–1873)," *Handbook of Texas Online* tshaonline.org/handbook/entries/williams-henry-howell [accessed Mar 21, 2024]; "Died" and "Death of Mr. John H. Williams," Dec 15, 1883, *Baltimore Sun*, p 2, col 2, and p 4, col 3; "A Biographical Sketch," Oct 5, 1887, *Galveston Weekly News* (Houston), p 9, col 2; "Death of William Hendley," *The Daily Constitution* (Middletown, CT), Sep 20, 1873, p 2, col 2; Historical Marker Database, "The Hendley Building," hmdb.org/m.asp?m=119196 [accessed Mar 22, 2024]; Historical Marker Database, "Hendley Row, 1859," hmdb.org/m.asp?m=119195 [accessed Mar 22, 2024]; S.B. Davis to J.J. Hendley, Nov 8, 1861, NARA RG: 109, Letters Sent, Department of Texas, Chap. 2, Vol. 129, p 75. A historical marker on the Hendley building shows that it became the first headquarters of the U.S. Army Corps of Engineers in 1880. Referred to as J.O.L.O., the observatory kept a formal log noting the comings and goings in Galveston Bay and positions of the Federal fleet. Captain Joseph J. Hendley was the Grand Commander of the lookouts and had printed cards that read "Hendley's Lookout." It is presumed that J.O.L.O. was a whimsical acronym for "Jolly Order of Look Outs."

35. Watson, *Adventures of a Blockade Runner*, 172–173.

36. *Ibid.*, 172 (1st quote); Thomas North, *Five Years in Texas; or, What You Did Not Hear During the War from January 1861 to January 1866. A Narrative of his Travels, Experiences, and Observations in Texas and Mexico* (Cincinnati: Elm Street Printing Co., 1871), 107–108 (2nd quote); Thomas W. Cutrer, "Magruder, John Bankhead," *Handbook of Texas Online* tshaonline.org/handbook/entries/magruder-john-bankhead [accessed June 10, 2022] (3rd quote); Encyclopedia Virginia, "Winfield Scott (1786–1866)." A "brevet" promotion was based on merit, but did not come with the corresponding increase in pay and was usually temporary.

37. John N. Edwards, *Shelby's Expedition to Mexico, an Unwritten Leaf of the War* (Kansas City, MO: Kansas City *Times* Steam Book and Job Printing House, 1872), 20 (1st and 2nd quotes); Thomas M. Settles, *John Bankhead Magruder, a Military Reappraisal* (Baton Rouge: Louisiana State University Press, 2009), 11 (3rd quote); John Salmon Ford, *Rip Ford's Texas* (Austin: University of Texas Press, 1963), 343 (4th & 5th quotes); North, *Five Years in Texas*, 107–108 (6th quote).

38. Walter Herron Taylor, *General Lee: His Campaigns in Virginia, 1861–1865, with Personal Reminiscences* (Brooklyn: Press of Braunworth & Co., 1906), 52–53 (quoted material); Encyclopedia Virginia, "Walter H. Taylor (1838–1916)," encyclopediavirginia.org/entries/taylor-walter-h-1838-1916/ [accessed Mar 22, 2024]. Note: Casdorph repeats but slightly misquotes this episode on page 2 of *Prince John Magruder*. Casdorph cites Mark Grimsley, "Inside a Beleaguered city: A Commander and Actor, Prince John Magruder," *Civil War Times Illustrated* 21 (Sep 1982), p 16 as his source.

39. Carl Coke Rister, "Lee, Robert Edward (1807–1870)," *Handbook of Texas Online* tshaonline.org/handbook/entries/lee-robert-edward [accessed Mar 23, 2024]; Thomas W. Cutrer, "Hébert, Paul Octave (1818–1880)," *Handbook of Texas Online* tshaonline.org/handbook/entries/hebert-paul-octave [accessed Mar 22, 2024]; Thomas W. Cutrer, "Magruder, John Bankhead," *Handbook of Texas Online* tshaonline.org/handbook/entries/magruder-john-bankhead [accessed June 10, 2022]; James M. Schmidt, *Galveston and the Civil War, an Island City in the Maelstrom* (Charleston, SC: The History Press, 2012), 54–55 (quoted material); American Battlefield Trust, "George B. McClellan," battlefields.org/learn/biographies/george-b-mcclellan [accessed Mar 22, 2024].

40. J.E. Slaughter to J.M. Hawes, May 23, 1864, NARA RG: 109, Telegrams Sent, District of Texas, Mar– Jul 1863, Chap. 2, Vol. 138, No. 230, p 89; Edward H. Moseley, "Vidaurri, Santiago (1809–1867)," *Handbook of Texas Online* tshaonline.org/handbook/entries/vidaurri-santiago [accessed Mar 23, 2024]; "Editorial Correspondence," *The Weekly State Gazette.* (Austin, TX), Apr 13, 1864, p 2, col 2.

41. Watson, *Adventures of a Blockade Runner*, 173–174.

42. Special Order No. 218.7, Aug 5, 1865, NARA RG: 109, Special Orders, District of Texas, Chap. 2, Vol. 105, p 116; "Houston Correspondence," Oct 11, 1867, *Galveston Weekly News* (Houston), p 2, col 5; Ancestry. "Hugh Trann Scott," ancestry.com [accessed Mar 26, 2024].

43. Watson, *Adventures of a Blockade Runner*, 174–175; "From Our Correspondent on the *Neptune*," Jan 5, 1863, *Tri-Weekly Telegraph* (Houston*)*, p 3, col 4; *Island City* Crew List for July 1863, Aug 31, 1863, NARA RG: 109, Confederate Vessel Papers, I-6. Roll: 15, *Island City*; "Houston Lyceum," *Weekly Telegraph* (Houston), Jan 7, 1856, p 1, col 2.

44. *Ibid.*, 175.

45. *Ibid.*

46. *Ibid.*, 176.

47. *Ibid.* (quoted material); Thomas W. Cutrer, "Hawes, James Morrison," *Handbook of Texas Online* tshaonline.org/handbook/entries/hawes-james-morrison [accessed July 21, 2023].

48. Special Order No. 151.17 & 25, May 30, 1864, NARA RG: 109, Special Orders, District of Texas, Chap. 2, Vol. 106, pp 226–227.

49. Watson, *Adventures of a Blockade Runner*, 174–177.

50. *Ibid.*, 177 (quoted material); Special Order

No. 151.33, May 30, 1864, NARA RG: 109, Special Orders, District of Texas, Chap. 2, Vol. 106, p 230.

51. Special Order No. 224.6, Aug 11, 1864, NARA RG: 109, Special Orders, District of Texas, Chap. 2, Vol. 105, p 130 (1st quote); Special Order No. 111.6, Apr 20, 1864, & No. 137.17, May 16, 1864, No. 151.10, May 30, 1864, & No. 181.23, Jun 29, 1863, NARA RG: 109, Special Orders, District of Texas, Chap. 2, Vol. 106, p 82, 183, 226, & 320. "Quartermaster" was also often abbreviated as "Q. Mr."

52. Eastern Sub-District of Texas, Special Order No. 16.1, Mar 4, 1863, NARA RG: 109, Confederate Officer Records, Charles M. Mason, p 57 & Special Orders, Eastern Sub-District of Texas, Feb 1863–Jan 1865, Chap. 2, Vol. 102, p 13; Loyalty Oath, Jul 12, 1865, NARA RG: 109, Confederate Soldiers from Texas, Charles M. Mason, p 44; Special Order Nos. 164.1 & 164.12 (1st & 2nd (quotes), Jun 18, 1863, NARA RG: 109, Special Orders, District of Texas, Chap. 2, Vol. 111, p 274, 274.5; Parole of Honor, Jun 3, 1865, NARA RG: 109, Confederate Officer Records, Charles M. Mason, p 47 (3rd quote); Muster Roll, Company D, 1st Texas Regiment Heavy Artillery, Nov 7, 1861, NARA RG: 109, List of the Adjutant General's Office for carded records of military organizations. (The Ainsworth List), 1765–1899, Roll: 0107, p 3 (4th quote). Charles M. Mason was sometimes referred to as a captain and at other times as a major, indicating that his rank of major may have been a local brevet appointment, not yet approved by the Confederate War Department.

53. Andrew F. Muir, "Harrisburg, TX (Harris County)," *Handbook of Texas Online* tshaonline.org/handbook/entries/harrisburg-tx-harris-county [accessed July 22, 2023]. Houston annexed Harrisburg in 1926.

54. J.B. Magruder to J.M. Hawes, NARA RG: 109, Telegrams Sent, District of Texas, Chap. 2, Vol. 138, p 112; Galveston Special Order No. 81.14, Nov 30, 1864, BCAH, Ashbel Smith Papers, Box 4L261 & NARA RG: 109, Special Orders, District of Texas, Chap. 2, Vol. 104, p 150.

55. Watson, *Adventures of a Blockade Runner*, 178, 194; René Harris, "Mills, David Graham" and Marie Beth Jones, "Mills, Robert," *Handbook of Texas Online* tshaonline.org/handbook/online/articles/fmi64 [accessed June 02, 2019].

56. WPA, *Ship Registers*, Vol. VI, No. 857; A.E.K. Benham to G. Welles, Feb 28, 1864, *ORN* I: 21, 118; "Puerto de la Habana," *Diario de la Marina* (Havana), Apr 9, 1864, p 1, col 3; Oscar Raven Deposition, Apr 27, 1864, NARA Ft. Worth RG: 21, New Orleans Admiralty Case No. 7418, U.S. vs *Lilly*.

57. W.S. Herndon to J. Bates, Mar 22, 1864, *ORN* I: 21, 151 & Mar 23, 1864, *ORN* I: 21, 883 & *ORA* I: 34/2, 1077 (quoted material).

58. *Ibid.*; O.M. Watkins to J.C. Thomas, May 26, 1864, NARA RG: 109, Letters Sent, District of Texas, Chap. 2, Vol. 124, p 97 (quoted material); Galveston Special Order. No. 121.1, Oct 15, 1864, BCAH, Ashbel Smith Papers, Box 4L262; William F. Le Roy to D.G. Farragut, Oct 20, *ORN* I: 21, 698.

59. Watson, *Adventures of a Blockade Runner*, 178.

Chapter 10

1. Watson, *Adventures of a Blockade Runner*, 170, 179 (quoted material); "Capturing a Tartar," *Galveston Daily News* (Houston), Jan 20, 1878, p 4, col 2.

2. "Beating a Yankee Trick," *Galveston Weekly News* (Houston), Jun 1, 1864, 2, col 5; Find a Grave, "Frederick Alexander Wolfean," findagrave.com/memorial/55173214/frederick-alexander-wolfean [accessed Apr 6, 2024] "Capturing a Tartar," & "Blockade Running Stories," *Galveston Daily News* (Houston), Jan 20, 1878, p 4, col 2 & May 13, 1900, p 7, col 1–4. The sailor identified as "Howe" may have been House.

3. J. Watters to G. Welles, May 23, 1864, *ORN* I: 21, 293–294; J. Bates to L.G. Aldrich, May 23, 1864, *ORA* I: 34/1, 943–944.

4. J. Watters to G. Welles, May 23, 1864, *ORN* I: 21, 293; Watson, *Adventures of a Blockade Runner*, 179.

5. "Capturing a Tartar," *Galveston Daily News* (Houston), Jan 20, 1878, p 4, col 2; J. Watters to G. Welles, May 23, 1864, *ORN* I: 21, 293.

6. *Ibid.*, 293–294.

7. "Capturing a Tartar," *Galveston Daily News* (Houston), Jan 20, 1878, p 4, col 2; John Watters to G. Welles, May 23, 1864, *ORN* I: 21, 293–294; P. Borner to J. Watters, May 23, 1864, *ORN* I: 21, 294–295.

8. "Capturing a Tartar," *Galveston Daily News* (Houston), Jan 20, 1878, p 4, col 2; Watson, *Adventures of a Blockade Runner*, 180–181; P. Borner to J. Watters, May 23, 1864, *ORN* I: 21, 294–295; J. Bates to L.G. Aldrich, May 23, 1864, *ORA* I: 34/1, 943–944.

9. P. Borner to J. Watters, May 23, 1864, *ORN* I: 21, 294–295 (1st & 2nd quotes); "Beating a Yankee Trick," *Galveston Weekly News* (Houston), Jun 1, 1864, p 2, col 5; "Capturing a Tartar," *Galveston Daily News* (Houston), Jan 20, 1878, p 4, col 2 (3rd quote).

10. Watson, *Adventures of a Blockade Runner*, 180; P. Borner to J. Watters, May 23, 1864, *ORN* I: 21, 294–295.

11. *Ibid.*; "Blockade Running Stories," *Galveston Daily News* (Houston), May 13, 1900, p 7, col 1–4; "Capturing a Tartar," *Galveston Daily News* (Houston), Jan 20, 1878, p 4, col 2 (quoted material).

12. "Capturing a Tartar," *Galveston Daily News* (Houston), Jan 20, 1878, p 4, col 2; J. Watters to G. Welles, May 23, 1864, *ORN* I: 21, 293–294 (quoted material).

13. P. Borner to J. Watters, May 23, 1864, *ORN* I: 21, 294–295; J. Watters to G. Welles, May 23, 1864, *ORN* I: 21, 293–294; "Capturing a Tartar," *Galveston Daily News* (Houston), Jan 20, 1878, p 4, col 2.

14. "Capturing a Tartar," *Galveston Daily News* (Houston), Jan 20, 1878, p 4, col 2; J. Watters to G. Welles, May 23, 1864, *ORN* I: 21, 293–294; Watson, *Adventures of a Blockade Runner*, 182.

15. P. Borner to J. Watters, May 23, 1864, *ORN* I: 21, 294–295; Watson, *Adventures of a Blockade Runner*, 180, 182; "Exciting Sea Scenes," *Galveston Daily News* (Houston), Dec 30, 1906, p 16, col 1–3.

16. "Velasco, May 23, 1864," *Houston Daily Telegraph*, May 25, 1864, p 2, col 4; "Beating a Yankee Trick," *Galveston Weekly News* (Houston), Jun 1, 1864, p 2, col 5 (1st quote); J. Watters to G. Welles, May 23, 1864, *ORN* I: 21, 293–294 (2nd & 3rd quotes).

17. "Beating a Yankee Trick," *Galveston Weekly News* (Houston), Jun 1, 1864, p 2, col 5 (quoted material); J. Bates to L.G. Aldrich, May 23, 1864, *ORA* I: 34/1, 943–944; "Exciting Sea Scenes," *Galveston Daily News* (Houston), Dec 30, 1906, p 16, col 1–3.

18. "Beating a Yankee Trick," *Galveston Weekly News* (Houston), Jun 1, 1864, p 2, col 5.

19. "Capturing a Tartar," *Galveston Daily News* (Houston), Jan 20, 1878, p 4, col 2; "The Schooner Stingray," *Galveston Daily News* (Houston), May 22, 1892, p 6, col 1–2; "Blockade Running Stories," *Galveston Daily News* (Houston), May 13, 1900, p 7, col 1–4; Watson, *Adventures of a Blockade Runner*, 183.

20. J. Watters to G. Welles, May 23, 1864, *ORN* I: 21, 293–294; Muster Rolls of USS. *Kineo*, Mar 31, 1864, 1862–1865, NARA RG 24: Records of the Bureau of Naval Personnel, p 77.

21. P. Borner to J. Watters, May 23, 1864, *ORN* I: 21, 294–295 (quoted material).

22. "Beating a Yankee Trick," *Galveston Weekly News* (Houston), Jun 1, 1864, p 2, col 5 (1st quote); Watson, *Adventures of a Blockade Runner*, 183–184; J. Watters to G. Welles, May 23, 1864, *ORN* I: 21, 293–294 (2nd quote).

23. "Capturing a Tartar," *Galveston Daily News* (Houston), Jan 20, 1878, p 4, col 2 (quoted material); "Beating a Yankee Trick," *Galveston Weekly News* (Houston), Jun 1, 1864, p 2, col 5; Watson, *Adventures of a Blockade Runner*, 185–186.

24. J. Bates to L.G. Aldrich, May 23, 1864, *ORA* I: 34/1, 943–944 (1st & 2nd quotes); "Beating a Yankee Trick," *Galveston Weekly News* (Houston), Jun 1, 1864, p 2, col 5 (3rd & 4th quotes).

25. Watson, *Adventures of a Blockade Runner*, 179 (quoted material).

26. *Ibid.*, 186. "Rogues Gallery" is a 19th-century term for police "Mug Shots."

27. *Ibid.* (quoted material); T. Savage to W.H. Seward, June 2, 1864 & Jun 22, 1864, NARA RG: 59, Havana Consular Despatches, Vol. 47, No. 158 & No. 170, pp 457–458 & pp 478–479; *Galveston Weekly News* (Houston), Jun 15, 1864.

28. P. Borner to J. Watters, May 23, 1864, *ORN* I: 21, 294–295; "Beating a Yankee Trick," *Galveston Weekly News* (Houston), Jun 1, 1864, p 2, col 5; "Capturing a Tartar," *Galveston Daily News* (Houston), Jan 20, 1878, p 4, col 2; Danial F. Lisarelli, *The Last Prison, The Untold Story of Camp Groce CSA* (Parkland, FL: Universal Publishers, 1999), 74, 167, 191.

29. U.S. Veteran Affairs Office, "Paul Borner," Find a Grave, findagrave.com/memorial/2585526/paul-borner [accessed Mar 24, 2024]; Special Order No. 151.10 & 151.17, May 30, 1864, NARA RG: 109, Special Orders, District of Texas, Chap. 2, Vol. 106, p 226, 227; Watson, *Adventures of a Blockade Runner*, 183.

30. Watson, *Adventures of a Blockade Runner*, 187 (quoted material).

31. "Mouth of Brazos River, May 30th, 1864," *Galveston Weekly News* (Houston), Jun 8, 1864, p 1, col 7.

32. "Mouth of Brazos River, May 30th, 1864," *Galveston Weekly News* (Houston), Jun 8, 1864, p 1, col 7 (quoted material).

33. "Exciting Sea Scenes," *Galveston Daily News* (Houston), Dec 30, 1906, p 16, col 1–3; "Blockade Running Stories," *Galveston Daily News* (Houston), May 13, 1900, p 7, col 1–4; "Mouth of Brazos River, May 30th, 1864," *Galveston Weekly News* (Houston), Jun 8, 1864, p 1, col 7; "Capturing a Tartar," *Galveston Daily News* (Houston), Jan 20, 1878, p 4, col 2 (quoted material).

34. W. Clark to A.C. Jones, Jun 15, 1864, NARA RG: 109, Confederate Vessel Papers, S-37 ½, Roll: 28, *Stingaree*.

35. *Ibid.*; "Wanted to hire," *Tri-Weekly Telegraph* (Houston), Nov 2, 1863, p 2, col 5; "New Advertisements," *Tri-Weekly Telegraph* (Houston), Dec 11, 1863, p 2, col 5; Anonymous, "The Houston of the Daring Plungers," *The Houston Review* 2, No. 2 (Summer 1980), 106 (quoted material); A.C. Jones to W. Clark, Aug 31, 1864, NARA RG 109, Telegrams Sent, District of Texas, Chap. 2, Vol. 137, p 33; Bill of Lading, Dec 20, 1864, NARA Ft. Worth RG: 21, New Orleans Admiralty Case No. 8001, U.S. vs Schooner *Pet*.

36. James. Sorley, Galveston Export Duty on Cotton, Sep 17–24, 1864, NARA RG: 109, Confederate Citizens File, James Sorley; "Wanted to Hire," *Tri-Weekly Telegraph* (Houston), Nov 2, 1863, p 2, col 5; "New Advertisements," *Tri-Weekly Telegraph* (Houston), Dec 11, 1863, p 2, col 5; Anonymous, "The Houston of the Daring Plungers," 106; A.C. Jones to W. Clark, Aug 31, 1864, NARA RG 109, Telegrams Sent, District of Texas, Chap. 2, Vol. 137, p 33; Bill of Lading, Dec 20, 1864, NARA Ft. Worth RG: 21, New Orleans Admiralty Case No. 8001, U.S. vs Schooner *Pet*.

James. Sorley, Galveston Export Duty on Cotton, Sep 17–24, 1864, NARA RG: 109, Confederate Citizens File, James Sorley; J.M. Hawes to W. Christian, Oct 6, 1864, BCAH, Ashbel Smith Papers, Box 4L261; Galveston Special Order No. 120.1, Oct 14, 1864, BCAH, Ashbel Smith Papers, Box 4L262; A. Smith to W.S. Smith Anderson, Oct 19, 1864, BCAH, Ashbel Smith Papers, Box 4L261.

37. Houston Signal Reports, Jul 7 & Jul 8, 1864, NARA RG: 109, District of Texas, Chap. 8, Vol. 7, pp 341–342; Special Order No. 251.11, Sep 7, 1864,

NARA RG: 109, Special Orders, District of Texas, Chap. 2, Vol. 105, p 193; T. Savage to W.H. Seward, Jul 19, 1864, NARA RG: 59, Havana Consular Despatches, No. 181, Vol. 47, pp 506–507.

38. Special Order No. 20.12, Sep 30, 1864, NARA RG: 109, Special Orders, District of Texas, Chap. 2, Vol. 104, p 55: Export Duty on Cotton collected for the week ending September 24th, 1864, NARA RG: 109, Confederate Citizens File, James Sorley; Watson, *Adventures of a Blockade Runner*, 240–241; G.E. Atwood to F.W. Emery, Jul 25, 1865, *ORA* I: 48/2, 1121.

Chapter 11

1. Watson, *Adventures of a Blockade Runner*, 187.
2. G. Holland to C. McClarty, Jul 30, 1864, NARA RG: 109, Confederate Officer Records, Gustave Holland; Special Order No. 46.5, Oct 26, 1864, NARA RG: 109, Special Orders, District of Texas, Chap. 2, Vol. 104, p 101.
3. Watson, *Adventures of a Blockade Runner*, 108–109, 187–188 (quoted material).
4. *Ibid.*, 31 & 189 (quoted material).
5. *Maine Historical Society*, Holly Hurd-Forsyth, "From the Collections: From Maine to Mexico and Back Again," mainehistory.wordpress.com/2013/09/26/from-the-collections-from-maine-to-mexico-and-back-again/ [accessed Aug 12, 2023]; M.D.L. Lane to W.H. Seward, Apr 21, 1864, NARA RG: 59, Vera Cruz Consular Despatches, No. 38, Vol. 9, pp 76–77 (quoted material). Signing his name "M.D.L. Lane," the American Consul to Vera Cruz was born on June 11, 1825, the same month that the famous Revolutionary War General Marquis de Lafayette visited his home state of Maine.
6. Houston Signal Reports, Apr 6, 1864, NARA RG: 109, District of Texas, Chap. 8, Vol. 7, p 254 (quoted material).
7. Special Order No. 117.5, Apr 26, 1864, NARA RG: 109, Special Orders, District of Texas, Chap. 2, Vol. 106, p 102 (quoted material).
8. J.E. Slaughter to J.M. Hawes, May 30, 1864, NARA RG: 109, Telegrams Sent, District of Texas, Chap. 2, Vol. 138, No. 234, p 94; Galveston Special Order No. 111.1, Sep 25, 1864, BCAH, Ashbel Smith Papers, Box 4L262; Special Order No. 117.5, Apr 26, 1864, NARA RG: 109, Special Orders, District of Texas, Chap. 2, Vol. 106, p 102.
9. Houston Signal Reports, Apr 29, 1864, NARA RG: 109, District of Texas, Chap. 8, Vol. 7, p 277; "Captain Henry Scherffius," *Galveston Daily News* (Houston), Nov 23, 1894, p 3, col 1 & Nov 26, 1894, p 2, col 5; John Greenough Deposition, Jan 2, 1865, NARA Ft. Worth RG: 21, New Orleans Admiralty Case No. 7961, U.S. vs Schooner *Cora*; Woolsey to G. Welles, Dec 20, 1864, *ORN* I: 21, 763–764; Ancestry, "Henry Scherffius," ancestry.com [accessed Mar 24, 2024].
10. Watson, *Adventures of a Blockade Runner*, 189.
11. "Mortuary Report," *Galveston Daily News* (Houston), May 13, 1894, p 3, col 4; Galveston Quarterly Customs Report, Jan–Mar 1864, NARA RG: 365, cited in Davis, *Colin J. McRae*, 173; Houston Signal Reports, Apr 29, 1864, NARA RG: 109, District of Texas, Chap. 8, Vol. 7, p 277; "Captain Henry Scherffius," *Galveston Daily News* (Houston), Nov 23, 1894, p 3, col 1 & Nov 26, 1894, p 2, col 5; John Greenough Deposition, Jan 2, 1865, New Orleans Admiralty Case #7961, NARA Ft. Worth RG: 21, U.S. vs Schooner *Cora*; Ancestry, "Texas, Marriage Collection, 1814–1909, Texas Department of State Health Services, Austin, TX, Henry Scherffius," ancestry.com [accessed Aug 16, 2023].
12. Houston Signal Reports, Jun 6, 1864, NARA RG: 109, District of Texas, Chap. 8, Vol. 7, p 316.
13. U.S. Government, *CLD*, 211, 244; D.G. Farragut to G. Welles, Jul 26, 1864, *ORN* I: 21, 370; Depositions of J.D. Funch, Aug 4, 1864, & C.W. Buckley, Aug 15, 1864, & Appraisers' Report, Aug 17, 1864, NARA Ft. Worth RG: 21, New Orleans Admiralty Case No. 7898, U.S. vs. schr *James Williams*; Ancestry, "Cornelius W. Buckley," ancestry.com [accessed April 12, 2024].
14. G. Holland to C. McClarty, Jun 2, 1864, NARA RG: 109, Confederate Officer Records, Gustave Holland; "Tuesday July 5, 1864.," *Galveston Weekly News* (Houston), Jul 6, 1864, p 2, col 2; Wise, *Lifeline of the Confederacy*, 272; Special Order No. 194.6, Jul 12, 1864, NARA RG: 109, Special Orders, District of Texas & Orders Received, Eastern Sub-District of Texas, Chap. 2, Vol. 106.5, p 40; "Galveston, July 14th, 1864," *Galveston Tri-Weekly News* (Houston), Jul 15, 1864, p 2, col 1; T. Savage to W.H. Seward, Jul 19, 1864, NARA RG: 59, Havana Consular Despatches, No. 181, Vol. 47, pp 506–507; J.B. Magruder to C.J. Helm, Jul 24, 1864, NARA RG: 109, Confidential Letters and Telegrams Sent, and Special Orders Issued, District of Texas, Chap. 2, Vol. 125, pp 71–72; G. Holland to C. McClarty, July 30, 1964, NARA RG: 109, Confederate Officer Records, Gustave Holland; Houston Signal Reports, Jun 1, Jun 11, Jun 30, Jul 5, Jul 7–8, Jul 29, Sep 9, & Aug 12, 1864, NARA RG: 109, District of Texas, Chap. 8, Vol. 7, pp 311, 322, 334, 346, 348–349, 370, 383, & 414; T. Savage to W.H. Seward, Jul 9, 1864, NARA RG: 59, Havana Consular Despatches, No. 180, Vol. 47, pp 504–506; "Buques que se han Despachado," & "Deposito Mercantil," & "Puerto de la Habana," *Diario de la Marina* (Havana), Jun 26, 1864, p 1, col 3, & July 2, 1864, p 1, col 6 & Jul 5, 1864, p 1, col 3; Wilson, "Blockade Runner *Union*," 39; B.B. Taylor to M.B. Woolsey, Jul 8, 1864, *ORN* I: 21, 364–365; "Camp Collins Galveston Island," *Galveston Weekly News* (Houston) Jul 20, 1864, pg 2, col 1; T. Savage to W.H. Seward Sep 7, 1864, NARA RG: 59, Havana Consular Despatches, Vol. 47, No. 202, pp 625–627; S.D. Yancey to C.J. Helm, Sep 17, 1864, NARA RG: 109, Letters Sent in the Field, District of Texas, Chap. 2, Vol. 123, No. 19.F, p 7; T. Savage to W.H. Seward, Sep 17, 1864, Havana Consular

Despatches, Vol. 47, No. 205, pp 635–639. Wise erroneously shows *Matagorda* departing Mobile on July 7th while it was in Galveston. See: Wise, *Lifeline of the Confederacy*, 268.

15. Watson, *Adventures of a Blockade Runner*, 188.

16. Ibid., 98, 189, 190, 195; Galveston Quarterly Customs Report, Jan–Mar 1864, NARA RG: 365, cited in Davis, *Colin J. McRae*, 173.

17. Watson, *Adventures of a Blockade Runner*, 190 (1st quote), 191 (2nd & 3rd quotes). The windlass was a large nautical winch mounted on the deck and used to hoist anchors.

18. Ibid., 191.

19. Wise in *Lifeline of the Confederacy* (272, 274) is only one day off on the departure date of *General Rusk* and ten days off for *Union*. He shows *Texas Ranger's* departure several weeks before her actual sailing and does not show *Texas Ranger's* arrival just five days after the establishment of the blockade. Similarly, Wise estimated that *Union* arrived at Galveston Bay in August 1862 even though she had been at Galveston Bay continuously since July 1861.

20. WPA, *Ship Registers*, Vol. VI, No. 159; Way (comp.), *Way's Packet Directory, 1848–1994*, no. 5350; J. Alden to W. Mervine, July 8, 1861, *ORN* I: 16, 576–577; "The Blockade Run Already!" *Galveston Weekly News* (Houston), Jul 9, 1861, p 2, col 1; "Port of Galveston, Arrived," *Weekly Civilian and Gazette* (Galveston), Jul 3, p 3, col 2, & Jul 9, 1861, p 1, col 1; J.O.L.O. Observatory record book, Jul 2, 1861 & J.O.L.O. to A.T. Lynn, Aug 7, 1861, Rosenberg Library, Galveston, Box 27-0701; "Galveston Blockade—Six Schooners Seized," *Daily Delta* (New Orleans), Jul 11, 1861, p 2, col 3; S.B. Davis to J McPherson, Dec 2, 1861, NARA RG: 109, Letters Sent, Department of Texas, Chap. 2, Vol. 135, p 13; L. Pierce to W.H. Seward, Aug 27, 1862, NARA RG: 59, Consular Matamoros Despatches, Vol. 7, No. 14, pp 169–170; Wise, *Lifeline of the Confederacy*, 274. The 159-ton stern-paddlewheel steamer *Texas Ranger* entered Galveston Bay through the very shallow north channel adjacent Bolivar Point and anchored at 0530 on the morning of Jul 3, 1861. The steamer cleared for the Brazos River on Dec 2, 1861, but it is unclear whether *Texas Ranger* made the attempt. Short of fuel, the steamer wrecked on Aug 4, 1862, trying to enter the Santana River about 75 miles north of Tampico. Texas observers had sighted *Texas Ranger* earlier that month as it passed by the mouth of the Rio Grande. Wise does not list *Texas Ranger's* arrival at Galveston, and erroneously shows its departure as approximately Jun 19, 1862.

21. Galveston Quarterly Customs Report, Dec 1861–Mar 1863, NARA RG: 365, cited in Davis, *Colin J. McRae*, 168, 170; "Houston, Tuesday, June 10, 1862," *Tri-Weekly News* (Houston, Jun 10), 1862, p 1, col 1. Confederate forces seized the steamer *General Rusk* prior to blockade implementation.

22. Log entries, Aug 3 and 18, 1862, T. Chubb MS53-0001—Log of the *Royal Yacht*, Rosenberg Library, Galveston, TX; H.R. Marks to C.M. Mason, Aug 3, 1862, NARA RG: 109, Confederate Officer Records, Henry R. Marks; "Captain H.R. Marks," *Tri-Weekly Telegraph* (Houston), Jun 17, 1863, p 2, col 1.

23. Watson, *Adventures of a Blockade Runner*, 192.

24. Thos. G. Rhett Service Record, Mar 16, 1861–Jan 8, 1865, NARA RG: 109, Confederate Officer Records, Thos. G. Rhett; J.B. Magruder to W.R. Boggs, Apr 7, 1864, NARA RG: 109, Telegrams Sent, District of Texas, Chap. 2, Vol. 137, No. 65, p 26; Robert E. L. Krick, *Staff Officers in Gray: A Biographical Register of the Staff Officers in the Army of Northern Virginia* (Chapel Hill: University of North Carolina Press, 2003), 253; John H. Eicher and David J. Eicher, *Civil War High Commands* (Stanford, CA: Stanford University Press, 2001), 424, 609.

25. Special Order No. 3.4, Jan 3, 1865, NARA RG: 109, Special Orders, District of Texas, Chap. 2, Vol. 104, p 203 (1st quote); David Miller (ed.), *The Illustrated Directory of Uniforms, Weapons, and Equipment of the Civil War* (London: Salamander Books Ltd., 2001), 302 (2nd quote).

26. Watson, *Adventures of a Blockade Runner*, 192–193.

27. Ibid., 193 (quoted material); Julia Beazley, "House, Thomas William," *The Handbook of Texas Online* tshaonline.org/handbook/online/articles/fho68 [accessed Sep 9, 2023].

28. Watson, *Civil War Adventures*, 193 (quoted material); Galveston Special Order No. 111, Sep 25, 1864, BCAH, Ashbel Smith Papers, Box 4L262; Thomas W. Cutrer, "Walker, John George (1822–1893)," *Handbook of Texas Online* tshaonline.org/handbook/entries/walker-john-george#: [accessed Jul 20, 2024].

29. Watson, *Civil War Adventures*, 193; Paul D. Casdorf, *Prince John Magruder, His Life and Campaigns* (New York: John Wiley & Sons, Inc, 1996), 282; Thomas W. Cutrer, "Magruder, John Bankhead," *Handbook of Texas Online* tshaonline.org/handbook/entries/magruder-john-bankhead [accessed June 10, 2022]; J.G. Walker to W.R. Boggs, Sep 11, 1864, NARA RG: 109, Letters Sent in the Field, District of Texas, Chap. 2, Vol. 123, p 1.

30. Watson, *Adventures of a Blockade Runner*, 194 (quoted material), 195.

31. W. Richardson (comp.), *Galveston City Directory, 1866–1867* (Galveston: W. Richardson & Co., 1866), 22; Provisional Register, Nov 7, 1863, Galveston, NARA Ft. Worth RG: 21, New Orleans Admiralty Case No. 7790, U.S. vs *Eureka*; C. Hatfield to H.H. Bell, Nov 23, 1863, *ORN* I: 20, 696. The 1866 *Galveston City Directory* listed Mr. Read as: "Read, Thos, cashier R & DG Mills."

32. Watson, *Adventures of a Blockade Runner*, 195, 196.

33. Ibid., 196 (quoted material).

34. Wilson, *Civil War Scoundrels*, 196.

35. Special Order No. 229.10, Aug 16, 1864,

NARA RG: 109, Special Orders, District of Texas, Chap. 2, Vol. 105, p 145.

36. Watson, *Adventures of a Blockade Runner*, 199 (quoted material).

Chapter 12

1. *Ibid.*, 200 (quoted material), 201.
2. *Ibid.*, 201.
3. *Ibid.*, 201 (1st quote), 202 (2nd quote). A night-glass was a telescope especially designed to improve vision at night. It was relatively short (about two feet in length), with a wide aperture object lens and relatively low magnification. See: Peter Reaveley, "Navigation and Logbooks in the Age of Sail," U.S. Naval Academy, Historic Shipwrecks: Science, History, and Engineering, Spring 2012 Syllabus (Jan 8, 2012) www.usna.edu/Users/oceano/pguth/website/shipwrecks/published_syllabus.htm [accessed Sep 8, 2023].
4. *Ibid.*, 202 (1st and 3rd quote), 201 (2nd quote); Wilson & McKay, *James D. Bulloch*, 57; James D. Bulloch, *Secret Service of the Confederate States in Europe*, Vol. 1 (New York: G. P. Putnam's Sons, 1884), 124; Edward C. Anderson, *Confederate Foreign Agent: The European Diary of Major Edward C. Anderson*, ed. William S. Hoole (Tuscaloosa, AL: Confederate Publishing, 1976), 96–97; James Sprunt, *Chronicles of the Cape Fear River, 1660–1916*, 2nd ed. (1916; reprint, Wilmington: Broadfoot Publishing Co., 1992), 448.
5. Watson, *Adventures of a Blockade Runner*, 116–120, 202, 203, 204 (quoted material).
6. *Ibid.*, 205 (quoted material), 206.
7. *Ibid.*, 114, 197; TMP Staff, "Why is it Bad Luck for Sailors to Whistle on a Ship?—The Superstitious Reasons," *The Maritime Post*, Sep 4, 2023 themaritimepost.com/2023/09/bad-luck-for-sailors-whistle-ship-superstitious/ [accessed Sep 9, 2023].
8. Watson, *Adventures of a Blockade Runner*, 197, 199.
9. Jonah 1: 1–17; Ryan White, "History: Cats in the Navy," *Naval Post*, Mar 1, 2021 navalpost.com/ship-cat-navy-history-simon-oscar-tiddles-blackie/ [accessed Sep 8, 2023].
10. Watson, *Adventures of a Blockade Runner*, 206–208.
11. *Ibid.*, 209 (quoted material), 213.
12. *Ibid.*, 215.
13. Walter V. Scholes, *Encyclopedia Britannica*, "Benito Juárez, president of Mexico," britannica.com/biography/Benito-Juarez [accessed Mar 23, 2024.
14. Shipping Agreement, Dec 19, 1864, NARA Ft. Worth RG: 21, New Orleans Admiralty Case No. 7766, U.S. vs Schr *Lilly*. Although Consul Chase identified the other schooner as "*Lily*," he was referring the to the 34-ton British flagged "*Lilly*."
15. F. Chase to F.W Seward, Oct 27, 1864, Tampico Consular Despatches, Vol. 7, pp 327–328. The NARA website only shows pages 1 and 4 of this letter; it omits pages 2 and 3. However, page 2 is faintly visible on page 1 and page 3 is visible on page 4 of the letter. The reverse images can be read by adjusting contrast and flipping the pages. See: catalog.archives.gov/id/211198943?objectPage=328 [accessed Sep 7, 2023].
16. J.T. Scott to W. Christian, Oct 6, 1864, BCAH, Ashbel Smith Papers, Box 4L261; J.G. Walker to Ashbel Smith, Oct 13, 1864, NARA RG: 109, Telegrams Sent, District of Texas, Chap. 2, Vol. 137, No. 65, p 65; A. Smith to W.S. Smith Oct 19, 1864, BCAH, Ashbel Smith Papers, Box 4L261; "Our New Orleans Correspondence," *New York Herald*, Nov 18, 1864, p 1, col 1; Tampico Customs Administrator & Accountant Certificate, Dec 21, 1864, NARA Ft. Worth RG: 21, New Orleans Admiralty Case No. 7766, U.S. vs Schr *Lilly*.
17. Watson, *Adventures of a Blockade Runner*, 215–221.
18. "Letter from Bagdad, Mexico," *New Orleans Times*, Nov 2, 1864, pg. 1, col 2; Wilson, *Civil War Scoundrels*, 169; Master Hartney Statement, Jun 27, 1864 & Judgement, Aug 5, 1864, NARA Ft. Worth RG: 21, New Orleans Admiralty Case No. 7891, U.S. vs *Caroline*; WPA, *Ship Registers*, Vol. VI, No. 221.
19. Wilson, *Civil War Scoundrels*, 16; F. Chase to F.W. Seward, Oct 12, 1864, NARA RG: 59, Tampico Consular Despatches, Vol. 7, No. 43, pp 324–326; F. Chase to F.W. Seward, Jan 28, 1865, NARA RG: 59, Tampico Consular Despatches, Vol. 8, No. 7, pp 382–383 (quoted material).
20. Watson, *Adventures of a Blockade Runner*, 225, 228.
21. *Ibid.*, 225–226.
22. *Ibid.*, 223 (quoted material), 224–226; Wilson, *Civil War Scoundrels*, 160; Charles Stillman to Capt. R. King, Mar 11, 1862, King Ranch Archives, Kingsville, TX; Petition of Droege, Oetling & Co., vs. E. H. Cushing & E.W. Cave, June 2–3, 1865, BCAH, William Pitt Ballinger Papers, Box 2A189; Patrick Gaul, "Trading in the Shadow of Neutrality: German-Speaking Europe's Commerce with Union and Confederacy during the American Civil War," *Bulletin of the German Historical Institute*, 67, Fall 2020 (41–70) 58–59.
23. Watson, *Adventures of a Blockade Runner*, 228 (quoted material), 229; Agreement for Foreign Going Ship, Aug 16, 1864, and William Ject, Dec 12, 1864, and Deposition of James O'Hagan, Dec 13, 1864, NARA Ft. Worth RG: 21, New Orleans Admiralty Case No. 7943, U.S. vs Schooner *Carrie Mair*; G. Brown to D.G. Farragut, Nov 30, 1864, *ORN* I: 21, 745.
24. F. Chase to F.W. Seward, Nov 15, 1864, NARA RG: 59, Tampico Consular Despatches, Vol. 7, No. 44, pp 331–333; "Puerto de la Marina," *Diario de la Marina* (Havana), Oct 4, 1864, p 1, col 2; Agreement for Foreign Going Ship, Aug 16, 1864, NARA Ft. Worth RG: 21, New Orleans Admiralty Case No. 7943, U.S. vs Schooner *Carrie Mair*.

25. "Puerto de la Marina," *Diario de la Marina* (Havana), Oct 4, 1864, p 1, col 2.
26. Watson, *Adventures of a Blockade Runner*, 228, 229 (quoted material).
27. Deposition of John Curry, Nov 11, 1864 & Deposition of Timothy Kelly, Nov 14, 1864, NARA Ft. Worth RG: 21, New Orleans Admiralty Case No. 7930, U.S. vs Schr *Lone*; "Importación de Ultramar," *Diario de la Marina* (Havana), Dec 14, 1864, p 1, col 4.
28. F. Chase to F.W. Seward, Jan 28, 1865, NARA RG: 59, Tampico Consular Despatches, Vol. 8, No. 7, pp 382–383.
29. Shipping Papers, Nov 16, 1864, NARA Ft. Worth RG: 21, New Orleans Admiralty Case No. 7964, U.S. vs Schr *Lady Hurley*; Provisional Registry & Declaration of Ownership, Oct 4, 1864, and Consular Clearance & Permit & Shipping Agreement, Oct 5, 1864, and Health Certificate, Oct 8, 1864, and Depositions of John Curry & of Timothy Kelly, Nov 14, 1864, NARA Ft. Worth RG: 21, New Orleans Admiralty Case No. 7930, U.S. vs Schr *Lone*; D. Augustin to G. Welles, Nov 18, 1864, *ORN* I: 21, 732.
30. "Marine News," *Times-Picayune* (New Orleans), Aug 9, 1864, p 8, col 5 and Nov 6, 1864, p 6, col 4; "Marine Intelligence," *Era* (New Orleans), Aug 6, 1864, p 4, col 1.
31. "Puerto de la Habana," *Diario de la Marina* (Havana), Nov 10, 1864, p 1, col 2; G.F. Emmons to J.S. Palmer, Nov 8, 1865, *ORN* I: 22, 29.
32. F. Chase to F.W. Seward, Nov 15, 1864, NARA RG: 59, Tampico Consular Despatches, Vol. 7, No. 44, pp 331–333; Customs Clearance & Provisional Registry, Nov 5, 1864 & Deposition of Frederick A. Pennefeather, Feb 18, 1865, NARA Ft. Worth RG: 21, New Orleans Admiralty Case No. 8001, U.S. vs Schooner *Pet*.
33. "Importación de Ultramar," *Diario de la Marina* (Havana), Dec 14, 1864, p 1, col 4.
34. Invoice, Nov 10, 1864 & Droege & Co. to T. McNamara, Nov 16, 1864, NARA Ft. Worth RG: 21, New Orleans Admiralty Case No. 7943, U.S. vs Schooner *Carrie Mair*; Crew List Index Project crewlist.org.uk/data/appropriation/46241 [accessed Sep 19, 2023]; G. Brown to G. Welles, Dec 8, 1864, *ORN* I: 21, 756.
35. Tampico Shipping Agreement, Dec 19, 1864 & Manifest, Dec 21, 1864, NARA Ft. Worth RG: 21, New Orleans Admiralty Case No. 7766, U.S. vs Schr *Lilly*.
36. Invoice, Nov 9, 1864, & Health Clearance, Nov 14, 1864, & Montreal Health Clearance, Nov 14, 1864, & Customs Clearances, Nov 15, 1864, & Droege & Co. to P.C. Blanchet & Shipping papers, Nov 16, 1864, & Prize Appraisers' Report, Jun 13, 1865, & Auctioneer's Report, Jun 15, 1865, NARA Ft. Worth RG: 21, New Orleans Admiralty Case No. 7964, U.S. vs Schr *Lady Hurley*; R.W. Meade, Jr., to G. Welles, Dec 6, 1864, *ORN* I: 21, 750.
37. ShipIndex CLIP Appropriation Books, *A.C. Dana*, Official Number 46237 crewlist.org.uk/ [accessed Sep 26, 2023]; F. Chase to F.W. Seward, Nov 15, 1864, NARA RG: 59, Tampico Consular Despatches, Vol. 7, No. 44, pp 331–333.
38. Watson, *Adventures of a Blockade Runner*, 230–231.
39. *Ibid.*, 230 (quoted material).
40. "Importación de Ultramar," *Diario de la Marina* (Havana), Dec 14, 1864, p 1, col 4; Watson, *Adventures of a Blockade Runner*, 231.

Chapter 13

1. Watson, *Adventures of a Blockade Runner*, 228, 232 (quoted material), 233.
2. "Importación de Ultramar," *Diario de la Marina* (Havana), Oct 30, 1864, p 1, col 5 and Dec 1, 1864, p 1, col 5.
3. "Importación de Ultramar," *Diario de la Marina* (Havana), Dec 14, 1864, p 1, col 4.
4. Watson, *Adventures of a Blockade Runner*, 215 (quoted material).
5. "Puerto de la Habana" & "Pasageros Llegados" (quoted material), *Diario de la Marina* (Havana), Nov 30, 1864, p 1, col 3–4; Wise, *Lifeline of the Confederacy*, 273–275; "Puerto de la Habana," *Diario de la Marina* (Havana), Jan 18, 1865, p 1, col) and Feb 7, 1865, p 1, col 33; W.T. Minor to W.H. Seward, Jan 19, 1865, NARA RG: 59, Havana Consular Despatches, 47, No. 31, pp 787–788.
6. Watson, *Adventures of a Blockade Runner*, 233 (quoted material), 234.
7. *Ibid.*, 235 (quoted material); Galveston Quarterly Customs Report, Oct–Dec 1863, NARA RG: 365, cited in Davis, *Colin J. McRae*, 167; "Houston," *Weekly Telegraph* (Houston), Dec 18, 1860, p 1, col 3.
8. Watson, *Adventures of a Blockade Runner*, 236 (quoted material); Walter E. Wilson, "'Sail Ho!': A Civil War Surgeon and the Texas Blockade," *Southwestern Historical Quarterly*, April 2021, Vol. CXXIV, No. 4, p 460.
9. Puerto de la Habana," *Diario de la Marina* (Havana), Sep 27, 1864, p 1, col 4 and Nov 11, 1864, p 1, col 2 & p 1, col 5; "Puerto de la Habana" & "Importacion de Ultramar," *Diario de la Marina* (Havana), Nov 6, 1864, p 1, col 2 & 4; B.R. Davis invoice to Ball, Hutchins & Co., Oct 15, 1864, NARA RG: 109, Confederate Civilian Files, Ball, Hutchins; "The blockade steamer," *The Countryman* (Bellville, TX), Oct 25, 1864, p 1, col 1; "Galveston, Oct. 28, 1864," *Galveston Weekly News* (Houston), Nov 2, 1864 , p 2, col 5; "Galveston Oct. 31, 1864," *Galveston News Tri-Weekly* (Houston), Nov 2, 1864, p 1, col 5; J.E. Jouett to D.G. Farragut, Dec 4, 1864, *ORN* I: 21, 740–741; D.G. Farragut to G. Welles, Dec 4, 1864, *ORN* I: 21, 740. Wise in *Lifeline of the Confederacy* does not mention the voyages of *Luna* or *Maria* (*Luna*: Departed Havana Oct 5, arrived at Galveston Oct 9th, departed Galveston Oct 30th, and arrived at Havana Nov 5, 1864; *Maria*: Departed Havana Sep 25th, arrived Galveston about Sep 30th, departed Galveston Oct 30th, and arrived at Havana Nov 5, 1864).
10. Watson, *Adventures of a Blockade Runner*,

236; T. Savage to W.H. Seward, Jul 9, 1864, NARA RG: 59, Havana Consular Despatches, No. 180, Vol. 47, 504-493.

11. Watson, *Adventures of a Blockade Runner*, 238 (quoted material).

12. Ibid., 238-241.

13. Special Order No. 20.12, Sep 30, 1864, NARA RG: 109, District of Texas, Chap. 2, Vol 104, p 54; Special Order No. 120.1, Oct 14, 1864, BCAH, Ashbel Smith Papers, Box 4L262.

14. Watson, *Adventures of a Blockade Runner*, 242, 243 (quoted material).

15. Ibid., 243-244.

16. Ibid.

17. Ibid., 244-246 (quoted material).

18. Ibid., 244, 247-248; Gardner, *Gardner's New Orleans Directory, 1861*, 235. In 1861, there were two men named James Hyland living in New Orleans. One was a cook and another was a laborer living at 296 New Levee Street which was near numerous docks and adjacent the river on its northern bank. See: Charles Gardner, "Map of the city of New Orleans, and the adjacent towns" Map, New Orleans: C. Gardner, 1861, Boston Public Library, *Norman B. Leventhal Map & Education Center* collections.leventhalmap.org/search/commonwealth:wd3764502 accessed Oct 13, 2023.

19. Watson, *Adventures of a Blockade Runner*, 249, 252 (quoted material).

20. Ibid., 249.

21. See: Title Set: *Diario de la Marina* (Havana), University of Florida George A. Smathers Libraries Digital Collections ufdc.ufl.edu/ [accessed Oct 14, 2023].

22. Watson, *Adventures of a Blockade Runner*, 250.

23. Ibid., 250-251.

24. Ibid., 252; G. Brown to G. Welles, Dec 8, 1864, ORN I: 21, 756; Deposition of James O'Hagan, Dec 13, 1864, NARA Ft. Worth RG: 21, New Orleans Admiralty Case No. 7943, U.S. vs Schooner *Carrie Mair*.

25. Puerto de la Habana," *Diario de la Marina* (Havana), Apr 5, 1864, pg. 1, col 2 and Dec 1, 1864, pg. 1, col 2; Price, "Ships That Tested the Blockade of the Gulf Ports, 1861-1865," *American Neptune* Vol. 12, No. 3 (Jul 1952), 229; T.S. Woolsey to G. Welles, Dec 7, 1864, ORN I: 21.

26. Puerto de la Habana," *Diario de la Marina* (Havana), Nov 29, 1864, p 1, col 3; R.W. Meade to G. Welles, Dec 5, 1864, ORN I: 21, 746. Registration, Nov 8, 1864 & Deposition of Richard Ross, Dec 19, 1864, NARA Ft. Worth RG: 21, New Orleans Admiralty Case No. 7944, U.S. vs Schr *Julia*; U.S. Government, *CLD*, 197, 211, 233, 244; Price, "Ships That Tested the Blockade of the Gulf Ports, 1861-1865, 1861-1865," *American Neptune* Vol. 12, No. 3 (Jul 1952), 231.

27. Watson, *Adventures of a Blockade Runner*, 252, 254.

28. Ibid., 257.

29. "Buques que se han Despachado," *Diario de la Marina* (Havana), Nov 27, 1864, p 1 col 3; T. Savage to C.K. Stribling, Dec 2, 1864, NARA RG: 59, Havana Consular Despatches, Vol. 47, No. 226 (attachment), pp 703-706; W.B. Sorley & A.B. Cammack to A.C. Hutchinson, Nov 30, 1864, NARA Ft. Worth RG: 21, New Orleans Admiralty Case No. 7962, U.S. vs Schooner *Belle*.

30. "Morning Boat for Newport," *The Evening Bulletin* (Providence, RI), May 10, 1864, p 2, col 5; "Marine Intelligence," *Providence* (RI) *Evening Press*, Aug 12, 1864, p 3, col 2; T. Savage to W.H. Seward, Sep 17, 1864, NARA RG: 59, Havana Consular Despatches, Vol. 47, No. 205, pp 635-639; "Buques que se han Despachado," *Diario de la Marina* (Havana), Nov 27, 1864, p 1, col 3; T. Savage to RADM C.K. Stribling, Dec 2, 1864, NARA RG: 59, Havana Consular Despatches, Vol. 47, No. 226 (attachment), pp 703-706; Shipping Account Sheets, Dec 1, 1864, BCAH, Henry Sampson Papers, Box 2, FF10. Wise in *Lifeline of the Confederacy* (273, 275, 328) erroneously credits *Zephine* with six successful runs; she only made four. Her final attempt ended in failure when she had to return to Havana in distress on Feb 24, 1865, after eight days at sea.

31. T. Savage to J.L. Palmer, Nov 22, 1864, NARA RG: 59, Havana Consular Despatches, Vol. 47, No. 225 (enclosure), pp 695-696; T. Savage to C.K. Stribling, Dec 2, 1864, NARA RG: 59, Havana Consular Despatches, Vol. 47, No. 226 (enclosure), pp 703-706; "Deposito Mercantil," *Diario de la Marina* (Havana), Nov 30, 1864, p 1, col 6, & Dec 1, 1864, p 1, col 6; "Deposito Mercantil" & "Buques que se han Despachado," *Diario de la Marina* (Havana), Dec 2, 1864, p 1, col 2; "Puerto de la Habana," *Diario de la Marina* (Havana), Dec 3, 1864, p 1, col 2; Crew List Index Project, "Melbourne, Main Register subsequent to Merchant Shipping Act 1854, Vol. 4, 1867-1872, Folio 45" crewlist.org.uk/data/vesselsnum?officialnumber=50060&submit=search [accessed Jun 8, 2024].

32. Watson, *Adventures of a Blockade Runner*, 257 (quoted material); James Q. Howard to F.W. Seward, Aug 26, 1864, NARA RG: 59, St John, NB Consular Despatches, Vol. 5, No. 81, p 414-415.

33. Watson, *Adventures of a Blockade Runner*, 146, 259 (quoted material).

34. Special Order No. 230.5, Aug 17, 1864 & No. 238.2, Aug 25, 1864, NARA RG: 109, Special Orders, District of Texas, Chap. 2, Vol. 105, p 150C & 167; Special Order No. 18.9, Sep 28, 1864, NARA RG: 109, Special Orders, District of Texas, Chap. 2, Vol. 104, p 50.

35. W.H. Seward to G. Welles, Oct 15, 1864, ORN I, Vol. 21, p. 684; L. Smith to M. Kenedy, April 25 & Jul 15, 1863, Mifflin Kenedy Papers, Box 2A, James C. Jernigan Library, The South Texas Archives & Special Collections, Texas A&M University Kingsville (1st quote); Leon Smith letter designating Mifflin Kenedy as his agent, Apr 28, 1863 (2nd quote), Box 2A, Kenedy Family Collection A 1995-045, James C. Jernigan Library, The South Texas Archives & Special Collections, Texas A&M University Kingsville; Wilson, *Civil War*

Scoundrels, 162; J.B. Magruder to J.E. Slaughter, Aug 14, 1864, NARA RG: 109, Letters Sent, District of Texas, Chap. 2, Vol. 124, No. 1398, p 213.

36. Walter E. Wilson, "Captain King's Cotton, The Civil War Blockade-Running Adventures of Richard King and Mifflin Kenedy," in *Supplementary Studies in Rio Grande Valley History*, 15, ed. Milo Kearney et al., 91–130 (Edinburgh, TX: The University of Texas Rio Grande Valley, 2017), 108–109; T. Savage to W.H. Seward, Nov 14, 1864, NARA RG: 59, Havana Consular Despatches, No. 180, Vol. 47, No. 221, pp 686–689; "Puerto de la Habana," *Diario de la Marina* (Havana), Feb 2, 1865, p 1, col 3; W.T. Minor to W.H. Seward, Feb 3, 1865, NARA RG: 59, Havana Consular Despatches, Vol. 47, No. 37, 796–797; W.T. Minor to W.H. Seward, May 1, 1865, NARA RG: 59, Havana Consular Despatches, Vol. 47, No. 76, pp 861–862; Wise, *Lifeline of the Confederacy*, 273, 275; Douglas French Forrest, William N. Still, Jr. (ed.), *Odyssey in Gray: A Diary of Confederate Service, 1863–1865* (Richmond: Virginia State Library, 1979), 301.

37. Watson, *Adventures of a Blockade Runner*, 258–260, 263–265.

38. *Ibid.*, 259 (quoted material); J.G. Walker to W.R. Boggs, Sep 11, 1864, NARA RG: 109, Letters Sent in the Field, District of Texas, Chap. 2, Vol. 123, No. 1, p 1; J.B. Magruder to J.A. Seddon, Sep 29, 1864, *ORA* I, Vol. 41/3, pp 963–964; Settles, *John Bankhead Magruder*, 278–279.

39. Special Order No. 3.4, Jan 3, 1865, NARA RG: 109, Special Orders, District of Texas, Chap. 2, Vol. 104, p 203.

40. *Ibid.*, Watson, *Adventures of a Blockade Runner*, 173–174, 192; T. Chubb to J.M. Hawes, Jun 1, 1864, NARA RG: 109, Confederate Vessel Papers, R-24, Roll: 25, *Rob Roy*.

41. G. Thebo to Miss Lou, May 11, 1864, NARA Ft. Worth RG: 21, Admiralty Case File No. 7899, U.S. vs SS *Isabel*; Watson, *Adventures of a Blockade Runner*, 146.

42. Watson, *Adventures of a Blockade Runner*, 260–262.

43. T. Savage to W.H. Seward, Nov 14, 1864, NARA RG: 59, Havana Consular Despatches, No. 221, Vol. 47, pp 686–689; Special Order No. 107.9, Dec 26, 1864, NARA RG: 109, District of Texas, Chap. 2, Vol. 104, p 186.

Chapter 14

1. Watson, *Adventures of a Blockade Runner*, 266 (quoted material).

2. Letter-press books of Capt. William C. Black, Museum of the Confederacy, Richmond, VA, NARA RG: 365, cited in Davis, *Colin J. McRae*, 122–123; Depositions of Samuel L. Townsend & Peter O'Meare, Jan 30, 1865, NARA Ft. Worth RG: 21, New Orleans Admiralty Case No. 7985, U.S. vs Schr. *Josephine*.

3. N.A. Blume to C.H. Brown to Jan 11, 1865, *ORN* I: 21, 773; "Galveston, Dec. 27, 1864," *Tri-Weekly Telegraph* (Houston), Dec 28, 1864, p 1, col 3.

4. Watson, *Adventures of a Blockade Runner*, 265, 266 (quoted material), 267.

5. *Ibid.*, 267 (quoted material), 268; Lord George Gordon Byron, *Don Juan: in Sixteen Cantos, with Notes* (London: H.G. Bohn, 1849), 25; Poetry Foundation, Poems & Poets, "Lord Byron (George Gordon) poetryfoundation.org/poets/lord-byron [accessed April 15, 2024].

6. Watson, *Adventures of a Blockade Runner*, 268–271 (quoted material), 272.

7. A.G. Clary to G.F. Emmons, Jan 4, 1865, *ORN* I: 22, 6.

8. *Ibid.* (1st quote); H.C. Wade to M.B. Woolsey (2nd quote), Jan 4, 1865, *ORN* I: 22, 6.

9. Watson, *Adventures of a Blockade Runner*, 270, 272–275.

10. *Ibid.*, 276.

11. M.D.L. Lane to W.H. Seward, Feb 1, 1865, NARA RG: 59, Vera Cruz Consular Despatches, Vol. 9, No. 56, pp 136–137; "Puerto de la Habana," *Diario de la Marina* (Havana), Jan 10, 1865, p 1, col 3 & Feb 1, 1865, p 1, col 2.

12. Watson, *Adventures of a Blockade Runner*, 277–279.

13. *Ibid.*, 278,

14. M.D.L. Lane to W.H. Seward, Nov 22, 1864, NARA RG: 59, Vera Cruz Consular Despatches, Vol. 9, No. 49, pp 117–118; Wilson, *Civil War Scoundrels*, 162–163.

15. M.D.L. Lane to W.H. Seward, Nov 22, 1864, NARA RG: 59, Vera Cruz Consular Despatches, Vol. 9, No. 49, pp 117–118.

16. H. d'Oleire & Co to T.W. House, Dec 1, 1864, BCAH, T.W. House Papers, Box 2R 43, Vol. 2.

17. Watson, *Adventures of a Blockade Runner*, 278.

18. F. Chase to F.W. Seward, Nov 21, 1864, NARA RG: 59, Tampico Consular Despatches, Vol. 7, pp 335–336.

19. "Galveston Oct. 31, 1864," *Galveston News Tri-Weekly* (Houston), Nov 2, 1864, p 1, col 5; H. d'Oleire & Co to T.W. House, Houston via Havana, Dec 1, 1864, BCAH, T.W. House Papers, Box 2R 43, Vol. 2 "Puerto de la Habana," *Diario de la Marina* (Havana), Dec 23, 1864, p 1, col 1.

20. H. d'Oleire & Co to T.W. House, Dec 1, 1864, BCAH, T.W. House Papers, Box 2R 43, Vol. 2; Shipping Articles, Feb 8, 1865, NARA Ft. Worth RG: 21, New Orleans Admiralty Case No. 8035, U.S. vs Schooner *Chaos*; J.A. Johnstone to G. Welles, Apr 22, 1965, *ORN* I: 22, 136. H. d'Oleire routed his letter to Houston via Havana.

21. Special Order No. 229.10, Aug 16, 1864, NARA RG: 109, Special Orders, District of Texas, Chap. 2, Vol. 105, p 145; H. d'Oleire & Co to T.W. House, Dec 1, 1864, BCAH, T.W. House Papers, Box 2R 43, Vol. 2.

22. A. Buchel to L.G. Aldrich, May 4, 1864, NARA RG: 109, Confederate Vessel Papers, C-122, Roll: 7, *Charles Russell*; Medical Discharge

for George Hendrickson, Feb 5, 1864, NARA Ft. Worth RG: 21, New Orleans Admiralty Case No. 7958, U.S. vs Schooner *Flash*; Special Order No. 88.1, Mar 29, 1865, NARA RG: 109, Special Orders, District of Texas, Chap. 2, Vol. 103, p 59; H.C. Philips to J. Speed, Sep 14, 1865, NARA RG:94, Amnesty Papers Roll: 0053, Thomas W. House; H. d'Oleire & Co to T.W. House, Dec 1, 1864, BCAH, T.W. House Papers, Box 2R 43, Vol. 2; P.N. Luckett to L.G. Aldrich, Dec 20, 1863, NARA RG: 109, Confederate Officers, Phillip N. Luckett; Special Order No. 229.10, Aug 16, 1864, NARA RG: 109, Military Departments, District of Texas, Chap. 2, Vol. 105, p 145; Watson, *Adventures of a Blockade Runner*, 278 (quoted material).

23. Watson, *Adventures of a Blockade Runner*, 278–279.

24. U.S. Government, *CLD*, 211; D. Augustin to G. Welles, Nov 18, 1864, *ORN* I: 21, 732; H. d'Oleire & Co to T.W. House, Dec 1, 1864, BCAH, T.W. House Papers, Box 2R 43, Vol. 2; Deposition of Henry Myers, Nov 29, 1864 & Deposition of John Morgan, Jan 16, 1865, NARA Ft. Worth RG: 21, New Orleans Admiralty Case No. 7931, U.S. vs Schr *John A. Hazard*.

25. D. Augustin to G. Welles, Nov 18, 1864, *ORN* I: 21, 732; Tampico Custom's Permit, Oct 5, 1864 & Deposition of John Curry, Nov 11, 1864, NARA Ft. Worth RG: 21, New Orleans Admiralty Case No. 7930, U.S. vs Schr *Lone*.

26. U.S. Government, *CLD*, 217; M.B. Woolsey to G. Welles, Nov 28, 1864, *ORN* I: 21, 733; "Boca del Rio, Mexico," *Tri-Weekly Telegraph* (Houston), Dec 12, 1864, p 2, col 3; Depositions of W. E. Cannon, C. Berndt, J. Baker & C. Reynolds, Dec 1, 1864, NARA Ft. Worth RG: 21, New Orleans Admiralty Case No. 7933, U.S. vs Schooner *Neptune*.

27. Samuel Blatchford, *Reports of Cases in Prize, Argued and Determined in the Circuit and District Courts of the United States, for the Southern District of New York. 1861–65* (Washington, DC: Government Printing Office, 1866), 615–618; U.S. Government, *CLD*, 223; "Marine Intelligence," *New York Times*, Dec 2, 1864, p 8, col 5.

28. U.S. Government, *CLD*, 207, 245; M.B. Woolsey to G. Welles, *ORN* I: 21, 739; Appraiser's Report, Feb 22, 1865, NARA Ft. Worth RG: 21, New Orleans Admiralty Case No. 7958, U.S. vs Schooner *Flash*.

29. J.E. Jouett to D.G. Farragut, Nov 27, 1864, *ORN* I: 21, 740.

30. Agreement for Foreign Going Ship, Aug 16, 1864, NARA Ft. Worth RG: 21, New Orleans Admiralty Case No. 7943, U.S. vs Schooner *Carrie Mair*; G. Brown to D.G. Farragut, Nov 30, 1864, *ORN* I: 21, 745.

31. J.G. Maxwell to G.F. Emmons, Dec 4, 1864, *ORN* I: 746-7; D. Augustin to G. Welles, Dec 24, 1864, *ORN* I: 769; G.F. Emmons to G. Welles, Dec 29, 1864, *ORN* I: 777; Deposition of Roeld Hendrik Dinkela, Jan 18, 1865, & Prize Appraisers' Report, Jun 8, 1865, NARA Ft. Worth RG: 21, New Orleans Admiralty Case No. 7945, U.S. vs Brig *Geziena Hilligonda*.

32. Depositions of Richard Ross & Henry M. Ehrenwerth, Dec 19, 1864 & Richard Ross Statement, Dec 22, 1864, NARA Ft. Worth RG: 21, New Orleans Admiralty Case No. 7944, U.S. vs Schr *Julia*.

33. Appraisers' Report, Feb 16, 1865, & Auctioneer's Report, Feb 20, 1865, & Deposition of John H. Butler, Dec 23, 1864, NARA Ft. Worth RG: 21, New Orleans Admiralty Case No. 7946, U.S. vs Schr *Lowood*; WPA, *Ship Registers*, Vol. VI, No. 1471.

34. Invoice, Nov 9, 1864, & Health Clearance, Nov 14, 1864, & Montreal Health Clearance, Nov 14, 1864, & Customs Clearances, Nov 15, 1864, & Droege & Co. to P.C. Blanchet & Shipping papers, Nov 16, 1864, & Prize Appraisers' Report, Jun 13, 1865, & Auctioneer's Report, Jun 15, 1865, NARA Ft. Worth RG: 21, New Orleans Admiralty Case No. 7964, U.S. vs Schr *Lady Hurley*; R.W. Meade, Jr., to G. Welles, Dec 6, 1864, *ORN* I: 21, 750.

35. T.S. Woolsey to G. Welles, Dec 7, 1864, *ORN* I: 21, 751–752; D. Augustin to G. Welles, Dec 24, 1864, *ORN* I: 769; G.F. Emmons to G. Welles, Dec 29, 1864, *ORN* I: 777; CLIP "Official No. 48320, *Alabama*," Mercantile Navy List, 1873, p 101 crewlist. org.uk/data/viewimages? [accessed Jun 15, 1865].

36. G. Brown to G. Welles, Dec 8, 1864, *ORN* I: 21, 756; G.F. Emmons to G. Welles, Dec 29, 1864, *ORN* I: 21, 777; C. Bullitt to R. Waples, Feb 6, 1865, NARA Ft. Worth RG: 21, New Orleans Admiralty Case No. 7946, U.S. vs Schr *Lowood*.

37. J.S. Palmer to G. Welles, Jan 18, 1865, *ORN* I: 21, 772; N.A. Blume to C.H. Brown to Jan 11, 1865, *ORN* I: 21, 773; D. Augustin to G. Welles, Dec 27, 1864, *ORN* I: 21, 773–774; G.F. Emmons to G. Welles, Dec 29, 1864, *ORN* I: 21, 777–778; Depositions Joseph Dixon & Harry Brayson (Henry Blessen), Jan 3, 1865, NARA Ft. Worth RG: 21, New Orleans Admiralty Case No. 7962, U.S. vs Schooner *Belle*.

38. Depositions of Jesse F. Potter & Joseph W. Warner, Dec 26, 1864, NARA Ft. Worth RG: 21, New Orleans Admiralty Case No. 7959, U.S. vs Schooner *Morris*.

39. J.S. Palmer to G. Welles, Jan 18, 1865, *ORN* I: 21, 772; N.A.; Blume to C.H. Brown to Jan 11, 1865, *ORN* I: 21, 773; D. Augustin to G. Welles, Dec 27, 1864, *ORN* I: 21, 773–774; G.F. Emmons to G. Welles, Dec 29, 1864, *ORN* I: 21, 777–778; Price, "Ships That Tested the Blockade of the Gulf Ports, 1861–1865," *The American Neptune*, Vol. 12, No. 3 (Jul 1952), 229; "Galveston, Dec. 27, 1864," *Tri-Weekly Telegraph* (Houston), Dec 28, 1864, p 1, col 3; "Galveston, Dec 28th, 1864," *Galveston Weekly News* (Houston), Jan 4, 1865, p 1, col 3; Depositions Joseph Dixon & Harry Brayson [Henry Blessen], Jan 3, 1865, NARA Ft. Worth RG: 21, New Orleans Admiralty Case No. 7962, U.S. vs Schooner *Belle*.

40. J.K. Jouett to G. Welles, Dec 31, 1864, *ORN* I: 21, 779–800; Depositions of Pierre Tauréguiberry

& John Johnson, Jan 21, 1865, NARA Ft. Worth RG: 21, New Orleans Admiralty Case File No. 7975, U.S. vs. *Sea Witch*.

41. B.B. Taylor to G. Welles, Jan 3, 1865, & Jan 7, 1865, *ORN* I: 22, 5; U.S. Government, *CLD*, 216, 247.

42. U.S. Government, *CLD*, 213, 245; Auctioneer's Report, Apr 3, 1865, NARA Ft. Worth RG: 21, New Orleans Admiralty Case No. 7766, U.S. vs Schr *Lilly*.

43. A.G. Clary to G. Welles, Jan 14, 1865, *ORN* I: 22, 11; Deposition of Peter O'Meare, Jan 30, 1865, NARA Ft. Worth RG: 21, New Orleans Admiralty Case No. 7985, U.S. vs Schr *Josephine*.

44. Watson, *Adventures of a Blockade Runner*, 215 (quoted material).

45. L. Smith to E.P. Turner, Sep 8, 1863, *ORN* I: 20, 555–557; Silverstone, *Civil War Navies*, 77; Wilson, *Civil War Scoundrels*, 99, 155, 162, 170, 175–176.

46. Wilson, "Blockade Runner *Union*," 33–34; "Galveston, March 22, 1864," *Houston Daily Telegraph*, Mar. 23, 1864, p 2, col 3; "The Galveston News," *Galveston Tri-Weekly News* (Houston), Mar 23, 1864, p 2, col 1; "Charles W. Austin Dead," *The Savannah Morning News*, Apr 18, 1889, p 8, col 6; A.F. Warley to G.N. Hollins, Oct 12, 1861, *ORN* I: 16, 730a; Find a Grave, "Capt. Charles William Austin," findagrave.com/memorial/43897674/charles-william-austin [accessed May 5, 2024].

47. Wilson, *Civil War Scoundrels*, 99, 155, 162, 175–176.

48. "Puerto de la Habana" &" Pasageros Llegados," *Diario de la Marina* (Havana), Nov 30, 1864, p 1, col 3–4; "Puerto de la Habana," *Diario de la Marina* (Havana), Jan 18, 1865, p 1, col 3; Wise, *Lifeline of the Confederacy*, 273–275; W.T. Minor to W.H. Seward, Jan 19, 1865, NARA RG: 59, Havana Consular Despatches, Vol. 47, No. 31, pp 787–788; Wilson, *Civil War Scoundrels*, 99, 155, 162, 175–176.

49. M.D.L. Lane to W.H. Seward, Dec 31, 1864, NARA RG: 59, Vera Cruz Consular Despatches, Vol. 9, No. 53, pp 129–131; City and Port of Vera Cruz, Health Clearance, Feb 3, 1865, NARA Ft. Worth RG: 21, New Orleans Admiralty Case No. 8004, U.S. vs. *Eco*. *Will 'o the Wisp* sometimes appears as *Will of the Wisp*.

50. *Will 'o the Wisp* Shipping Account sheets, Jan 5, 1865, Henry Sampson Papers, Box 2, FF 10, Rosenberg Library, Galveston, TX; M.D.L. Lane to W.H. Seward, Jan 23, 1865, NARA RG: 59, Vera Cruz Consular Despatches, Vol. 9, No. 55, pp 134–135. Although well-documented, this run into and out of Galveston does not appear in Wise, *Lifeline of the Confederacy*.

51. H. d'Oleire & Co. Rabidens to T.W. House, Dec 1, 1864, BCAH, T.W. House Papers, Box 2R 43, Vol. 2.

52. City and Port of Vera Cruz, Health Clearance, Feb 3, 1865 & Crew List, Feb 4, 1865, NARA Ft. Worth RG: 21, New Orleans Admiralty Case No. 8004, U.S. vs. *Eco*; B.C. Dean to G. Welles, Feb 24, 1865, *ORN* I: 22, 49.

53. L. Smith to E.P. Turner, Sep 8, 1863, *ORN* I: 20, 555–557; Silverstone, *Civil War Navies*, 77; H. d'Oleire & Co to T.W. House, Dec 1, 1864, BCAH, T.W. House Papers, Box 2R 43, Vol. 2; Wilson, *Civil War Scoundrels*, 99, 155, 162, 175–176.

54. "Galveston Oct. 31, 1864," *Galveston News Tri-Weekly* (Houston), Nov 2, 1864, p 1, col 5; H. d'Oleire & Co to T.W. House, Dec 1, 1864, BCAH, T.W. House Papers, Box 2R 43, Vol. 2; "Puerto de la Habana," *Diario de la Marina (Havana)*, Dec 23, 1864, p 1, col 1.

55. H. d'Oleire & Co. to T.W. House, Dec 1, 1864, BCAH, T.W. House Papers, Box 2R 43, Vol. 2; "Puerto de la Habana," *Diario de la Marina* (Havana), Dec 23, 1864, p 1, col 1.

56. "Military and Naval Intelligence," *The Times* (London, England), Aug 15, 1862 p 22, col 3; T. Savage to W.H. Seward, Sep 17, 1864, NARA RG: 59, Havana Consular Despatches, No. 205, Vol. 47, pp 634–639; M.D.L. Lane to W.H. Seward, Dec 31, 1864, NARA RG: 59, Vera Cruz Consular Despatches, Vol. 9, No. 53, pp 129–131; J. Sorley to A.C. Hutchinson & A.B. Cammack to unknown, Nov 30, 1864 & J. Sorley to Carr Brothers & Watson, Dec 1, 1864, NARA Ft. Worth RG: 21, New Orleans Case No. 7962 U.S. vs *Belle*; Wise, *Lifeline of the Confederacy*, 275; "Death of Cap. Barnard," *Galveston Civilian*, Dec 10, 1877, p 1, col 3–4.

57. F. Chase to W.H. Seward, Dec 25, 1864, NARA RG: 59, Tampico Consular Despatches, Vol 7, No. 48, pp 350–351; M.D.L. Lane to W.H. Seward, Dec 31, 1864, & Jan 9, 1865, NARA RG: 59, Vera Cruz Consular Despatches, Vol. 9, No. 53, pp 129–131, & No. 15, pp 731–732; W.T. Minor to W.H. Seward, NARA RG: 59, Havana Consular Despatches, Vol. 47, No. 21, pp 758–759.

58. Shipping Account sheets, *Will 'o the Wisp*, Jan 5, 1865, Henry Sampson Papers, Box 2. FF 10, Rosenberg Library, Galveston, TX; Confederate Federal Supply Office Shipments, W.C. Black Letter Book, 1: 182, 278, 455, NARA RG: 365, cited in Davis, *Colin J. McRae*, 122, 125, 157–158; H. Sampson to Confederate Federal Supply Office (Shipping account sheets *Will 'o the Wisp*), May 19, 1865, Rosenberg Library, Henry Sampson Papers, Box 2, FF 11; M.D.L. Lane to W.H. Seward, Jan 23, 1865, NARA RG: 59, Vera Cruz Consular Despatches, Vol. 9, No. 55, pp 134–135.

59. "Galveston, March 6, 1865," *Galveston Daily News*, Houston, Mar 7, 1865, p 2, col 4; Special Order No. 88.1, Mar 29, 1865, NARA RG: 109, Special Orders, District of Texas, Chap. 2, Vol. 103, p 59.

60. Watson, *Adventures of a Blockade Runner*, 279, 280 (quoted material).

61. M.D.L. Lane to W.H. Seward, Feb 1, 1865, & Feb 23, 1865, NARA RG: 59, Vera Cruz Consular Despatches, Vol. 9, No. 56, pp 136–137, & No. 57, p 142–144.

62. "Buques que han Abierto Registro," *Diario de la Marina* (Havana), Feb 16, 1865, p 1, col 2.

Chapter 15

1. Watson, *Adventures of a Blockade Runner*, 280.
2. *Ibid.*, 282 (1st quote), 283 (2nd quote).
3. Galveston Special Orders No. 106.2, Sep 12, 1864, & 107.1, Sep 13, 1864, & 112.3, Sep 26, 1864, BCAH, Ashbel Smith Papers, Box 4L262; "Puerto de la Habana," *Diario de la Marina* (Havana), Feb 14, 1865, p 1, col 2; U.S. Government, *CLD*, 203, 240; Special Order No. 157.1, Aug 7, 1863, NARA RG: 109, Special Orders, Eastern Sub-District of Texas, Chap. 2, Vol. 105, p 187; *Eliza Catharine* Shipping Account Sheets, Mar 22, 1865, Rosenberg Library, Henry Sampson Papers, Box 2 FF 10; "Loss of the Schooner *Eliza Catherine* and Six Lives," *Galveston Daily News* (Houston), Apr 13, 1865, p 2, col 2.
4. Watson, *Adventures of a Blockade Runner*, 290–291, 306 (quoted material).
5. *Ibid.*, 291, 298, 305.
6. *Ibid.*, 292, 294, 302, 304.
7. *Ibid.*, 306.
8. *Ibid.*, 290, 306, 307.
9. *Ibid.*, 306, 307 (quoted material); Eric J. Graham, *Clyde Built, Blockade Runners, Cruisers, and Armoured Rams of the American Civil War* (Edinburgh: Berlinn, 2006), 47, 117, 158, 192–193. Watson says that *Eagle/Jeannette* was a paddle steamer. Graham says she was a screw steamer. Wise in *Lifeline of the Confederacy* describes *Eagle/Jeannette* as both a screw and a side-paddlewheel steamer (see pages 297 & 306). When captured in May 1863, the captain of the USS *Octorara* described her as an iron-hulled paddlewheel steamer.
10. Watson, *Adventures of a Blockade Runner*, 309 (1st quote), 310–312, 313 (2nd quote). The new moon phase in late March 1865, was on the 26th and 27th. By the 29th, its illumination was about 20%. See: moongiant.com/calendar/march/1865/ [accessed Jan 23, 2024].
11. "Puerto de la Habana," *Diario de la Marina* (Havana), Jan 10, 1865 & Jan 18, 1865, p 1, col 3; W.T. Minor to W.H. Seward, Jan 19, 1865, NARA RG: 59, Havana Consular Despatches, Vol. 46 & 47, No. 31, pp 787–788; Thorp, *Mersey Built*, 365–366; "Importacion de Ultramar," *Diario de la Marina* (Havana), Feb 11, 1865, p 1, col 4; W.T. Minor to W.H. Seward, NARA RG: 59, Havana Consular Despatches, Vol. 47, No. 41, p 804–805; Wise, *Lifeline of the Confederacy*, 273, 275. Henry Scherffius took *Lark* from Havana to Galveston.
12. "Puerto de la Habana," *Diario de la Marina* (Havana), Feb 7, 1865, p 1, col 3 & Feb 18, 1865, p 1, col 2; Special Order No. 111.17, NARA RG: 109, Special Orders, District of Texas, Chap. 2, Vol. 103, p 127; Galveston Special Order No. 60, BCAH, Ashbel Smith Papers, Box 4L262; J. Sorley, Register of Galveston Cotton Export Duty, Mar 20, 1865, NARA RG: 109, Confederate Citizens File, James Sorely; W. McCraven to A. Smith, Mar 21, 1865, BCAH, Ashbel Smith Papers, Box 2G225; Telegram Expense, Shipping Account Sheets, Mar 23, 1865, Henry Sampson Papers, Rosenberg Library, Box 2 FF 10; "Puerto de la Habana," *Diario de la Marina* (Havana), Mar 26, 1865, p 1, col 2; "Havana, April 1, 1865," *New York Tribune*, Apr 6, 1865, p 8, col 5; Wise, *Lifeline of the Confederacy*, 273, 275. Captain Samuel Marcy relieved Capt. Scherffius in Galveston.
13. "Puerto de la Habana," *Diario de la Marina* (Havana), Mar 26, 1865, p 1, col 2 & Apr 4, 1865, p 1, col 4; "Galveston, May 3d., 1865," *Galveston Daily News* (Houston, TX), May 6, 1865, p 1, col 5: Wise, *Lifeline of the Confederacy*, 273, 275; Shipping Account sheets, Mar 9, 1865, Henry Sampson Papers, Rosenberg Library, Box 2, FF 10.
14. W.T. Minor to W. Hunter, May 19, 1865, NARA RG: 59, Havana Consular Despatches, Vol. 47, No. 86, pp 882–883; J.B. Magruder telegrams to A. Smith, May 22, 1865 & May 23, 1865, BCAH, Ashbel Smith Papers, Box 2G225; Galveston Special Order No. 114, BCAH, Ashbel Smith Papers, Box 4L262; "Special to the Daily Telegraph," *Tri-Weekly Telegraph* (Houston), May 24, 1865, p 3, col 4; "News from Cuba," *New York Daily Herald*, Jun 6, 1865, p 1, col 5; Wise, *Lifeline of the Confederacy*, 273, 275; T. Savage to W.H. Seward, Sep 7, 1864, NARA RG: 59, Havana Consular Despatches, No. 202, Vol. 47, pp 625–627; F. Chase to F.W. Seward, Jan 27, 1865, NARA RG: 59, Tampico Consular Despatches, Vol. 8, No. 6, pp 379–381.
15. "Puerto de la Habana," *Diario de la Marina* (Havana), Mar 31, 1865, p 1, col 2 & Apr 4, 1865, p 1, col 5; Galveston Special Order Nos. 96.8 & 96.9, May 5, 1865, BCAH, Ashbel Smith Papers, Box 4L262; "Importacion de Ultramar," *Diario de la Marina* (Havana), May 11, 1865, p 1, col 3. Wise in *Lifeline of the Confederacy* p 315, omitted this evidence confirming that *Owl* ran into Galveston.
16. "The Situation," *New York Herald*, May 17, p 4, col 1; "Puerto de la Habana," *Diario de la Marina* (Havana), p 1, col 2; Wise, *Lifeline of the Confederacy*, 273, 275.
17. "Puerto de la Habana," *Diario de la Marina* (Havana), Jul 31, 1864, p 1, col 2; T. Savage to Capt. T.P. Green, Aug 25, 1864, NARA RG: 59, Havana Consular Despatches, Vol. 47, pp 629–631; Houston Signal Reports, Aug 29, 1864, & Sep 10, 1864, NARA RG: 109, Chap. 8, Vol. 7, p 401 & 415; Wise, *Lifeline of the Confederacy*, 273, 275.
18. "Puerto de la Habana," *Diario de la Marina* (Havana), Sep 16, 1864, & Sep 24, 1864, & Oct 28, 1864, p 1, col 2; Wise, *Lifeline of the Confederacy*, 273, 275.
19. "Puerto de la Habana," *Diario de la Marina* (Havana), Oct 28, 1864, & Nov 8, 1864, p 1, col 2; T. Savage to W.H. Seward, Nov 14, 1864, NARA RG: 59, Havana Consular Despatches, No. 180, Vol. 47, No. 221, p 686; Galveston Special Order No. 159.4, BCAH, Ashbel Smith Papers, Box 4L262; Wise, *Lifeline of the Confederacy*, 273, 275.
20. "Puerto de la Habana," *Diario de la Marina* (Havana), Dec 15, 1864, p 1, col 2; W.T. Minor to W.H. Seward, Jan 19, 1865, NARA RG: 59, Havana Consular Despatches, Vol. 47, No. 2, pp 785–786; "We were very glad," *Tri-Weekly Telegraph*

(Houston), Jan 27, 1865, p 4, col 3; W.T. Minor to W.H. Seward, Feb 11, 1865, NARA RG: 59, Havana Consular Despatches, Vol. 47, No. 41, pp 804–805; "Puerto de la Habana," *Diario de la Marina* (Havana), Feb 7, 1865, p 1, col 3; Wise, *Lifeline of the Confederacy*, 273, 275.

21. "Puerto de la Habana," *Diario de la Marina* (Havana), Feb 7, 1865, p 1, col 3 & Mar 25, 1865, p 1, col 2; W.T. Minor to W.H. Seward, Feb 24, 1865, NARA RG: 59, Havana Consular Despatches, Vol. 47, No. 47, pp 813–814; Wise, *Lifeline of the Confederacy*, 273, 275.

22. "Puerto de la Habana," *Diario de la Marina* (Havana), Mar 25, 1865, p 1, col 2 & Apr 4, 1865, p 1, col 4; "Importacion de Ultramar," *Diario de la Marina* (Havana), Mar 29, 1865, p 1, col 5; Galveston Special Order No. 79.4, Apr 19, 1865, BCAH, Ashbel Smith Papers, Box 4L262; Wise, *Lifeline of the Confederacy*, 273, 275.

23. W.T. Minor to W.H. Seward, May 1, 1865, NARA RG: 59, Havana Consular Despatches, Vol. 47, No. 76, pp 861–862; W.T. Minor to Wm. Hunter, May 19, 1865, NARA RG: 59, Havana Consular Despatches, Vol. 47, No. 86, pp 882–883; "Puerto de la Habana," *Diario de la Marina* (Havana), May 20, p 1, col 2; "Galveston, May 24, 1865," *Tri-Weekly Telegraph* (Houston), May 26, 1865, p 2, col 5; Wise, *Lifeline of the Confederacy*, 273, 275. *Denbigh* ran aground on Bird Key and was destroyed.

24. "The Blockade Runner *Lizzie*," *Illustrated London News*, Aug 6, 1864, p 136, col 3; "Puerto de la Habana," *Diario de la Marina* (Havana), Oct 18, 1864, p 1, col 2; T. Savage to W.H. Seward, Oct 20, 1864, NARA RG: 59, Havana Consular Despatches, RG: 59, Vol. 47, No. 217, pp 673–677; Port of LaSalle Weekly Abstract of Export Duties, Jan 9–14, 1865, NARA RG: 109, Confederate Citizens File, Darwin M. Stapp.

25. F. Chase to F.W. Seward, Jan 21, 1865, NARA RG; 59, Tampico Consular Despatches, Vol. 8, No. 1, pp 367–368; F. Chase to F.W. Seward, Feb 14, 1865, NARA RG: 59, Tampico Consular Despatches, Vol. 8, No. 8, pp 383–385.

26. LaSalle Weekly Abstract of Export Duties, Apr 29, 1865, NARA RG: 109, Confederate Citizens File, Darwin M. Stapp; "Puerto de la Habana," *Diario de la Marina* (Havana), May 21, 1865, p 1, col 1; Wise, *Lifeline of the Confederacy*, 275. Wise and Graham (*Clyde Built*) were unable to find the references cited here and elsewhere that confirm *Lizzie* did indeed run into and out of Texas on four separate occasions.

27. William Watson, *Adventures of a Blockade Runner* (1892; College Station: Texas A&M University Press, 2001), iii–ix; David A. Ivry, "Historical Development of Some Basic Life Insurance Terminology," *The Journal of Insurance*, Vol. 28, No. 3 (Sep 1961), 65–69.

28. "For Sale, The fine steel-twin screw Steamer *Pelican*," *Liverpool Daily Post*, Nov 1, 1864, p 4, col 1.

29. Watson, *Adventures of a Blockade Runner*, 291 (quoted material); Bulloch, *Secret Service*, 2: 241–243; Wilson & McKay, *James D. Bulloch*, 273, 323 fn85; Bennett, *The London Confederates*, 64. John Gilliat's wife was Louisa Ann Frances ("Fanny").

30. "Trial Trip, a Double-Screw Steamship," *Manchester Courier*, Jan 27, 1865, p 3, col 2; "Puerto de la Habana," *Diario de la Marina* (Havana), Mar 16, 1865, p 1, col 3; "Importacion de Ultramar," *Diario de la Marina* (Havana), Mar 18, 1865, p 1, col 5; Bennett, *The London Confederates*, 64; Wilson & McKay, *James D. Bulloch*, 193, 194, 293; Georgiana Gholson Walker, *The Private Journal of Georgiana Gholson Walker, 1862-1865*, ed. Dwight Franklin Henderson (Tuscaloosa, AL: Confederate Publishing, 1963), 12, 25, 28, 44, 124.

31. Glen N. Wiche (ed.), *Dispatches from Bermuda: The Civil War Letters of Charles Maxwell Allen, United States Consul at Bermuda, 1861-1888* (Kent: The Kent State University Press, 2008), 176–177; Frank E. Vandiver (ed.), *Confederate Blockade Running through Bermuda, 1861-1865, Letters and Cargo Manifests* (Austin: University of Texas Press, 1947), 148; Walker, *The Private Journal of Georgiana Gholson Walker*, 124; "General News" & "From Havana," *New York Times*, Mar 23, 1865, p 4, cols 1–2 & p 8, col 1; W.T. Minor to W.H. Seward, Mar 24, 1865, NARA RG: 59, Havana Consular Despatches, Vol. 47, No. 61, pp 836–837.

32. J. Sorely to J.B. Magruder, Apr 6, 1865, NARA RG: 109, Confederate Vessel Papers, L-120, Roll: 20, *Lavinia*.

33. "This Day's Shipping News," *London Evening Standard*, Dec 6, 1865, p 5 col 6; "Shipping Intelligence," *Western Daily Mercury* (Plymouth, UK), Dec 7, 1864, p 3, col 4; "Puerto de la Habana," *Diario de la Marina* (Havana), Mar 28, 1865, p 1, col 2; Special Order No. 108.5, NARA RG: 109, Special Orders, District of Texas, Chap. 2, Vol. 103, p 115. The Havana paper and Confederate orders misspelled Scherffius as "Sherffins" and "Scherffins."

34. Watson, *Adventures of a Blockade Runner*, 306 (quoted material); W.T. Minor to W.H. Seward, Jan 19, 1865, NARA RG: 59, Havana Consular Despatches, Vol. 47, No. 31, p 787–788; "Puerto de la Habana," *Diario de la Marina* (Havana), Jan 18, 1865, p 1, col 3; Special Order No. 111.17, Apr 21, 1865, NARA RG: 109, Special Orders, District of Texas, Chap. 2, Vol. 103, p 127.

35. Puerto de la Habana" and "Pasageros Llegados," *Diario de la Marina* (Havana), Nov 30, 1864, p 1, col 3–4; "From Havana," *New York Times*, Mar 30, 1865, p 8, col 2; Watson, *Adventures of a Blockade Runner*, 292; J. Sorely to J.B. Magruder, Apr 6, 1865, NARA RG: 109, Confederate Vessel Papers, L-120, Roll: 20, Seq.: *Lavinia*; "Puerto de la Habana," *Diario de la Marina* (Havana), Mar 12, 1865, p 1, col 3.

36. B.F. Sands to H.K. Thatcher, Apr 2, 1865, *ORN* I: 22, 126.

37. Wilson, *Civil War Scoundrels*, 99, 155, 162, 175–176.

38. Special Order No. 108.5, Apr 18, 1865, NARA RG: 109, Special Orders, District of Texas,

Chap. 2, Vol. 103, p 115; Special Order No. 109.13, Apr 19, 1865, NARA RG: 109, Special Orders, District of Texas, Chap. 2, Vol. 103, p 118; Galveston Special Orders No. 78.1, Apr 17, 1865 and No. 86.5, Apr 25, 1865, BCAH, Ashbel Smith Papers, Box 4L262; Regimental Return, William Leopold, April 1864, NARA RG: 109, U.S., Civil War Service Records (CMSR), Confederate, Texas; Ancestry, "Wilhelm (William) Edward Leopold, 1839–1893," ancestry.com [accessed Apr 20, 2024].

39. P.N. Luckett to E.P. Turner, Sep 27, 1863, *ORA* I: 26/2, 263–264; Deposition of F. Downs, Oct 3, 1864, NARA Ft. Worth RG: 21, New Orleans Admiralty Case No. 7913, U.S. vs. *John*; J. Bates to E.P. Turner, Oct 11, 1863, NARA RG: 109, Confederate Vessel Papers, R-24, Roll: 25, *Rob Roy*; Watson, *Adventures of a Blockade Runner*, 35–38, 44–46, 54, 69, 72; Galveston Quarterly Customs Report, Jan–Mar 1864, NARA RG: 365, cited in Davis, *Colin J. McRae*, 173.

40. Shipping Account Sheets, Jan 31, 1865, Rosenberg Library, Henry Sampson Papers, Box 2, FF 10.

41. *Ibid.*, Jan 25, 1865, & Feb 1, 1865; "Puerto de la Habana," *Diario de la Marina* (Havana), Jul 8, 1865, p 1, col 3. Steamship *Lark* sold *Jeannette* 10 tons of coal on Jan 31, 1865.

42. "Puerto de la Habana," *Diario de la Marina* (Havana), Mar 28, 1865, p 1, col 2; B.F. Sands to H.K. Thatcher, Apr 2, 1865, *ORN* I: 22, 126; W.T. Minor to W.H. Seward, May 1, 1865, NARA RG: 59, Havana Consular Despatches, Vol. 47, No. 76, pp 861–862; "By Flag of Truce," *Galveston Weekly News* (Houston), May 31, 1865, p 1, col 2–3; Wise, *Lifeline of the Confederacy*, 273, 275.

43. "Foreign Ports," *Journal of Commerce, jr.* (New York), May 10, 1865, p 4, col 5; Special Order No. 108.5, NARA RG: 109, Special Orders, District of Texas, Chap. 2, Vol. 103, p 115; "Important from Mexico," *New York Times*, May 10, 1865, p 5, col 2; W.T. Minor to W.H. Seward, May 1, 1865, NARA RG: 59, Havana Consular Despatches, Vol. 47, No. 76, pp 861–862; "Marine News," *Charleston Daily News*, Mar 20, 1867, p 4, col 3; "Blockade Runners," *Evening Telegraph* (Philadelphia), Feb 5, 1867, p 1, col, 2.

44. "Puerto de la Habana," *Diario de la Marina* (Havana), Sep 24, 1864, p 1, col 2, & Jul 8, 1865, p 1, col 3; "Galveston, Oct. 28. 1864," *Galveston Weekly News* (Houston), Nov 2, 1864, p 2, col 5; Galveston Special Orders No. 151.1 & 151.2, Nov 29, 1864, BCAH, Ashbel Smith Papers, Box 4L262.

45. Matamoros Consular Note, Dec 12, 1864, BCAH, José San Román Papers, Box 2G72; Galveston Special Orders No. 22.2, Jan 30, 1865, BCAH, Ashbel Smith Papers, Box 4L262.

46. W.T. Minor to W.H. Seward, Jan 19, 1865, NARA RG: 59, Havana Consular Despatches, Vol. 47, No. 31, pp 787–788; "Puerto de la Habana," *Diario de la Marina* (Havana), Jan 15, 1865, p 1, col 3; F. Chase to F.W. Seward, Jun 27, NARA RG: 59, Tampico Consular Despatches, Vol. 8, No. 24, pp 426–427; "Puerto de la Habana," *Diario de la Marina* (Havana), Jul 8, 1865, p 1, col 3.

47. Watson, *Adventures of a Blockade Runner*, 316 (quoted material).
48. *Ibid.*, 315, 316.
49. *Ibid.*, 316, 317.
50. *Ibid.*, 317, 318. 319.
51. "Puerto de la Habana," *Diario de la Marina* (Havana), May 12, 1865, p 1, col 2; Wilson & McKay, *James D. Bulloch*, 184–199; "Wednesday, March 8, 1865," Galveston News (Houston), Mar 8, 1865, p 4, col 1 (quoted material).

Chapter 16

1. "Importacion Ultramar," *Diario de la Marina* (Havana), Dec 14, 1864, p 1, col 4.

2. "Buques que han Abierto Registro," *Diario de la Marina* (Havana), Feb 16, 1865, p 1, col 2; Special Order No. 103, May 14, 1865, BCAH, Ashbel Smith Papers, Box 4L262.

3. "Buques que se han Despachado" *Diario de la Marina* (Havana), Feb 19, 1865, p 1, col 2; "Puerto de la Habana," *Diario de la Marina* (Havana), Feb 25, 1865, p 1, col 2 (quoted material).

4. Watson, *Adventures of a Blockade Runner*, 130, 286 (quoted material).

5. J. Sherrill to G. Welles, Mar 12, 1865, *ORN* I: 17, 825 (quoted material).

6. U.S vs the Schooner *Rob Roy* & Cargo, Apr 4, 1865, NARA RG: 21, Southern District of Florida (Key West) Admiralty Case No. 350, pp 656–659; "Naval Capture," *National Republican* (Washington), Mar 25, 1865, p 2, col 4; J. Sherrill to G. Welles, Mar 12, 1865, *ORN* I: 17, 825 (quoted material); U.S. Government, *CLD*, 221, 250.

7. Edward C. Stiles to S.R. Mallory, Mar 31, 1865, *ORN* I: 27, 194–195; "Puerto de la Habana," *Diario de la Marina* (Havana), Mar 31, 1865, p 1, col 2 and Apr 4, 1865, p 1, col 4.

8. *Ibid.*, Apr 28, 1865, p 1, col 3; "Carriers' North Dock," *Liverpool Shipping Telegraph and Daily Commercial Advertiser*, May 25, 1865, p 1, col 1; "At Liverpool," *Shipping and Mercantile Gazette* (London), Jun 19, 1865, p 1, col 4.

9. Watson, *Adventures of a Blockade Runner*, 324 (quoted material).

10. Skelmorlie Villas skelmorlievillas.co.uk/people-of-local-interest/william-watson/ [accessed Jan 31, 2024].

11. Watson, *Life in the Confederate Army*, 22–25; Mitchell, *William Watson, 1st Sergeant, 3rd Louisiana Infantry, Pelican Rifles* acwscots.co.uk/watson.htm [accessed Jan 31, 2024]; Discharge and pay account for William Watson, Jul 16 & 20, 1862, NARA, RG: 109, Confederate Soldiers from Louisiana, William Watson; Allan Mitchell, *William Watson, 1st Sergeant, 3rd Louisiana Infantry, Pelican Rifles*, Scots in the American Civil War acwscots.co.uk/watson.htm [accessed Jan 31, 2024]; "In the Confederate Army," *Boston Herald*, Dec 4, 1887, p 19, col 7–8 (quoted material).

12. Graham, *Clyde Built*, 158–159.

13. "New Books," *The Scotsman* (Midlothian, UK), July 10, 1892, p 2, col 2.
14. "Books and Authors," *The Echo* (London), July 14, 1892, p 1, col 5.
15. Watson, *Life in the Confederate Army*, v (1st quote); *Adventures of a Blockade Runner*, xi (2nd quote).
16. Ancestorium Family Tree Collaboration, "William Watson," ancestorium.com/tng/getperson.php?personID=I051130&tree=1 [accessed Feb 1, 2024]; Ancestry, "*1891 Scotland Census*, William Watson, Henry Watson," ancestry.com [accessed Apr 20, 2024].

Appendix 1

1. Proofs of Citizenship Seamen's Protection Certificates Port of New Orleans, Louisiana, 1850–1851, NARA RG: 36, Nov 15, 1850, Henry Laverty; *WPA Ship Registers*, Vol. V, No. 277.
2. New Orleans Customs Clearances, May 15—Aug 10, 1861, Ramsdell, Pickett Papers, BCAH; "Marine News," *Times-Picayune* (New Orleans), May 30, 1861, p 4, col 1; H. Eagle to W. Mervine, Aug 8, 1861, *ORN* I: 16, 617, 618.
3. "Marine News," *Times-Picayune* (New Orleans) Jul 3, 1861, p 4, col 1; Henry Eagle to Wm. Mervine, Aug 8, 1861, *ORN* I: 16, 617, 618.
4. Paul H. Silverstone, *Civil War Navies, 1855–1883* (Annapolis, MD: Naval Institute Press, 2001), 97; Henry Eagle to Wm. Mervine, Aug 8, 1861, and to Wm. McKean, Oct 19, 1861, *ORN* I: 16, 617, 618, 733.
5. United States vs. Schooner *C.P. Knap* [sic] & cargo, Sep 16, 1861, NARA Atlanta, RG: 21 Southern District of Florida, Key West Division, Admiralty Order Book, Apr 1861—Jul 1863; "A Curious Complaint," *New York Times*, Dec 18, 1861, p 5, col 1.
6. Lance E. Davis and Stanley L. Engerman, *Naval Blockades in Peace and War; An Economic History Since 1750* (New York: Cambridge University Press, 2006), 116–121; Historic Hansards, *Hansard's Parliamentary Debates*, Ser. 3, 162 & 166, 2077–2082, api.parliament.uk [accessed May 20, 2020]; "A Curious Complaint," New York *Times*, Dec 18, 1861, p 5, col 1.
7. "A Curious Complaint," New York *Times*, Dec 18, 1861, p 5, col 1 (quoted material); Ch. J. Helm to Wm. M. Browne, May 6, 1862, Havana *Mercantile Weekly Report* extracts, *ORN* II: 3, 412–413.
8. Proofs of Citizenship Seamen's Protection Certificates Port of New Orleans, Louisiana, 1850–1851, NARA RG: 36, Nov 15, 1850, Henry Laverty; Watson, *Adventures of a Blockade Runner*, 14, 17; Enrique Laverty Invoice for the *C.P. Knapp*; Jan 27, 1862, BCAH, José San Román Papers, Box 2G61; WPA, *Ship Registers*, Vol VI, No. 496; WPA, *Ship Registers*, Vol. V, No. 277; "Below Coming up" & "Marine News," *Times-Picayune* (New Orleans), Apr 1, 1863, p 4, col 3 & Apr 7, 1863, p 4, col 2.

Appendix 2

1. Wilson, *Civil War Scoundrels*, 83–85; Davis and Engerman, *Naval Blockades in Peace and War;* *an Economic History Since 1750*, 116–121; Historic Hansards, *Hansard's Parliamentary Debates*, Ser. 3, 162 & 166, 2077–2082, api.parliament.uk [accessed May 20, 2020].
2. *Ibid.*; Bernath, *Squall Across the Atlantic*, 11–12, 19–20. Note: The accomplished historians Lance Davis, Engerman, and Surdam are among those who erroneously equate blockade running with smuggling.
3. J. Bates to E.P. Turner; Wilson, *Civil War Scoundrels*, 83–85; Carlin, *Captain James Carlin*, 28–33.
4. Wilson, *Civil War Scoundrels*, 83–85.
5. *Ibid.*

Appendix 7

1. Lindsay W. Bristowe and Philip B. Wright, *Handbook of British Honduras, 1888–89* (Edinburgh: William Blackwood and Sons, 1888), 49; ShipIndex CLIP Appropriation Books, *Rob Roy*, Official Number 4641 crewlist.org.uk/ [accessed May 20, 2020]; Watson, *Adventures of a Blockade Runner*, 14.
2. Phil Essex, Craig S. Mork, Craig A. Pomeroy "An Owner's Guide to Tonnage Admeasurement 1998–2003" Jensen Maritime Consultants, Inc.
3. Gross Registered Tonnage = ((Length—.6 × Beam) × Beam × Draft) ÷ 94 [UK] or ÷ 95 [U.S.].
4. Essex, "An Owner's Guide to Tonnage Admeasurement 1998–2003." If the formula substitutes the draft (4 feet 9 inches) in place of the depth of hold (6 feet) the GRT is 73 32/94.
5. "Marine News," *Times-Picayune* (New Orleans), Apr 7, 1863, p 4, col 2; WPA, *Ship Registers and Enrollments of New Orleans, Louisiana*, Vol. V, 1851–1860, No. 466. & 617; Enrique Laverty Invoice for the *C.P. Knapp*; Jan 27, 1862, BCAH, José San Román Papers, Box 2G61.
6. American Lloyd's, *Register of American and Foreign Shipping 1865* (New York: E. & G. Blunt, 1863), 420; Bristowe, *Handbook of British Honduras, 1888–89*, 49; "Official No. 46416, *Rob Roy*," Crew List Index Project, *Mercantile Navy List*, 1872 (also 1873–1920 editions), p 283 (*John Douglas*) & 403 (*Rob Roy*) crewlist.org.uk/data/viewimages? [accessed Jun 12, 2020]; J.M. Jackson to Wm. H. Seward, May 18, 1863, No. 18, NARA RG: 59, Halifax Consular Despatches, p 48; Belize Certificate of Sale for *Concordia*, Aug 14, 1863, BCAH, José San Román Papers Box 2G65; C.A. Leas to F.W. Seward, May 30, 1863, No. 37. NARA RG: 59, Belize Consular Despatches Vol. 2, No. 37, p 9–11; Appraiser's Report, Feb 18, 1865, NARA Ft. Worth RG: 21, New Orleans Admiralty Case No. 7961, U.S. vs Schooner *Cora*; WPA, *Ship Registers and Enrollments of New Orleans, Louisiana*, Vol. VI, 1861–1870 (Baton Rouge, LA: Louisiana State University, March 1942), No. 564. It is possible, but unlikely, that *Rob Roy's* erroneous length was a typesetting error on the part of Watson's publisher. The New Orleans appraiser measured *Cora* as 62' × 21' × 6' and 65 73/95 tons.

Bibliography

Archives, Official Government Publications, Diaries, Journals, and Primary Sources

Allen, Charles Maxwell. *Dispatches from Bermuda: The Civil War Letters of Charles Maxwell Allen, United States Consul at Bermuda, 1861–1888*. Glen N. Wiche (ed.), Kent, OH: Kent State University Press, 2008.

American Lloyd's. *Register of American and Foreign Shipping 1865*. New York: E. & G. Blunt, 1863.

Anderson, Edward C. *Confederate Foreign Agent: The European Diary of Major Edward C. Anderson*, William S. Hoole (ed.), Tuscaloosa: Confederate, 1976.

Blatchford, Samuel. *Reports of Cases in Prize, Argued and Determined in the Circuit and District Courts of the United States, for the Southern District of New York, 1861–'65*. Washington: Government Printing Office, 1866.

Bulloch, James D. *Secret Service of the Confederate States in Europe*, Vol. 1–2. New York: G.P. Putnam's Sons, 1884.

Dana, Richard Henry. *To Cuba and Back: A Vacation Voyage*. London: Smith, Elder & Co., 1859.

David M. Rubenstein Rare Book & Manuscript Library, Duke University, Appleton Oaksmith Papers, 1840–1885,

Dolph Briscoe Center for American History, The University of Texas at Austin: Ashbel Smith Papers, José San Román Papers, William Pitt Ballinger Papers, Thomas W. House Papers, John Baptiste LaCoste Papers, Henry Sampson Papers, and Charles Ramsdell Collection.

Ford, John Salmon. *Rip Ford's Texas*. Stephen B. Oates (ed.), Austin: University of Texas Press, 1963.

Forrest, Douglas French. *Odyssey in Gray: A Diary of Confederate Service, 1863–1865*. William N. Still, Jr. (ed.), Richmond: Virginia State Library, 1979.

Fort, T.A. "Steamboats on the Lower Rio Grande." Unpublished manuscript, 2015, courtesy the author.

Fremantle, Sir Arthur James Lyon. *The Fremantle Diary, Being the Journal of Lt. Col. Fremantle Coldstream Guards on his Three Months in the Southern States*. Walter Lord (ed.), Boston: Little, Brown, 1954.

Gardner, Charles (comp.). *Gardner's New Orleans Directory, 1861*. New Orleans: Charles Gardner, 1861.

Great Britain, Foreign Office. *Correspondence on the Slave Trade with Foreign Powers: Parties to Treaties and Conventions, Under Which Captured Vessels Are to Be Tried by Tribunals of the Nation to which They Belong*. London: William Clowes and Sons for Her Majesty's Stationery Office, 1844.

Green, T.J. *Journal of the Texian Expedition Against Mier*. New York: Harper and Brothers, 1845.

Gregory, Sir William Henry. *Sir William Gregory, K.C.M.G., Formerly Member of Parliament and Sometime Governor of Ceylon: an Autobiography*, 2nd ed. Lady Gregory (ed.), London: John Murray, Albemarle St., 1894.

Hill Memorial Library, Louisiana State University Libraries, Baton Rouge, Louisiana and Lower Mississippi Valley Collections Special Collections, Thomas O. Moore Papers Inventory.

Houghton Library, Harvard University, Cambridge, MA, Charles Stillman Business Papers.

James C. Jernigan Library, The South Texas Archives & Special Collections, Texas A&M University Kingsville, Kingsville: Kenedy Family Collection; Mifflin Kenedy Papers.

King Ranch Archives, Kingsville, TX.

Mayo, John J. (comp.). *Mercantile Navy List and Maritime Directory for 1872*. London: Sir William Mitchell, 1873.

McNeil, Sallie. *The Uncompromising Diary of Sallie McNeil 1858–1867*. Ginny McNeill Raska and Mary Lynne Gasaway Hill (eds.), College Station: Texas A&M University Press, 2009.

National Archives and Records Administration, Fort Worth, RG: 21: New Orleans Admiralty Case Files.

National Archives and Records Administration, Fort Worth, RG: 36: Proofs of Citizenship Seamen's Protection Certificates Port of New Orleans, Louisiana, 1850–1851.

National Archives and Records Administration, Fort Worth, RG: 59: Belize Consular Despatches, Vol. 2, 3;

Halifax Consular Despatches, Vol. 10; Havana Consular Despatches, Vol. 44–48; Matamoros Consular Despatches, Vol. 8; St John, NB Consular Despatches, Vol. 5; Tampico Consular Despatches, Vol. 7, 8; Vera Cruz Consular Despatches, Vol. 9.
National Archives and Records Administration, RG: 21: Admiralty Papers, Southern District of Florida.
National Archives and Records Administration, RG 24: Muster Rolls of Naval Ships; Records of the Bureau of Naval Personnel.
National Archives and Records Administration, RG: 45: Operations of Naval Ships and Fleet Units.
National Archives and Records Administration, RG: 94: Amnesty Papers.
National Archives and Records Administration, RG: 109: M345 Confederate Citizens File; M346 Confederate Citizen Files Business; M347 Confederate Service Records, Texas Muster Rolls & Confederate Army Casualty Lists; M258 Confederate Engineers; M331 Confederate Officers & Enlisted Men; M320 Confederate Soldiers from Louisiana; M323 Confederate Soldiers from Texas; Papers Pertaining to Vessels of or involved with the Confederate States of America "Vessel Papers"; T817 List of the Adjutant General's Office for carded records of military organizations (The Ainsworth List).
National Archives and Records Administration, RG: 109: Military Departments—District of Texas, New Mexico and Arizona: Chief Signal Reports from Houston Observatory Relating to Meteorological Conditions and Enemy Vessels, Chap. 8, Vol. 7; General Orders, Chapter 2, Vol. 246; Letters Sent, Chapter 2, Vol. 122, 124, 129, 131, 132, 135, & 148; Letters Sent in the Field, Chap. 2, Vol. 123, 127, & 128; Special Orders, Chap. 2, Vol. 102–106, 106.5, 108, 110, 111, & 118; Telegrams Sent, Chap. 2, Vol. 136–138; Confidential Letters and Telegrams Sent, and Special Orders Issued, Chap. 2, Vol. 125.
National Archives and Records Administration, RG: 109: Military Departments—Special Orders, Eastern Sub-District of Texas, Chap. 2, Vol. 102, & 105.
North, Thomas. *Five Years in Texas; or, What You Did Not Hear During the War from January 1861 to January 1866. A Narrative of His Travels, Experiences, and Observations in Texas and Mexico.* Cincinnati: Elm Street Printing Co., 1871.
Parisot, Pierre Fourier. *The Reminiscences of a Texas Missionary.* San Antonio: St. Mary's Church, 1899.
Richardson, W. (comp.). *Galveston City Directory, 1866–1867.* Galveston: W. Richardson & Co., 1866.
Richardson, W., and D. *Galveston City Directory, 1859–1860.* Galveston: News Book and Job Office, 1859.
Rosenberg Library, Galveston, TX: Henry Sampson Papers, Box 2, FF10, & FF11; Richardson, W., and D. *Galveston City Directory, 1859–1860*; J.O.L.O. Observatory record book, 1861: 27–0701; Log of the *Royal Yacht*, 1862–1863: 53–0001.
Sand, Henry Augustus. *Crossing Antietam: The Civil War Letters of Captain Henry Augustus Sand, Company A, 103rd New York Volunteers.* Peter H. Sand and John F. McLaughlin (eds.), Jefferson, NC: McFarland, 2015.
Semmes, Raphael. *Memoirs of Service Afloat, during the War Between the States.* Baltimore: Kelly Piet & Co., 1869.
Smith, Ralph J. *Reminiscences of the Civil War, and other Sketches.* Waco: W.M. Morrison, 1962.
Texas A&M University-Kingsville, Kingsville, James C. Jernigan Library, The South Texas Archives & Special Collections.
Texas State Library and Archives Commission, Austin: Civil War Muster Rolls Index Cards (both Confederate and Union); Texas, US, Bonds and Oaths of Office, 1846–1920.
United States. *Compilation of Laws and Decisions of the Courts Relating to War Claims.* Washington, D.C.: Government Printing Office, 1908.
United States, 41st Congress, 3rd Session, 1870–1871, vol. 1, Senate Ex. Doc. No. 10, Parts 1–4, *Letters of the Secretary of the War, Unlawful traffic with rebels in the State of Texas*; No. 377, *Alleged Traffic with Rebels in Texas.* Washington, D.C.: Government Printing Office, 1871.
United States, 48th Congress, 1st Session, 1883–1884, House Ex. Doc. No. 103, *Mexican Claims*, Washington, D.C.: Government Printing Office, 1884.
United States. *Official Records of the Union and Confederate Navies in the War of the Rebellion*, 30 vols. Washington, D.C.: Government Printing Office, 1894–1922.
United States, 62nd Congress, 3rd Session, Senate Doc. No. 987, *Cotton Sold to the Confederate States,* Washington, D.C.: Government Printing Office, 1912.
United States, 63rd Congress, 1st Session, Apr 7–Dec 1, 1913, Senate Doc., No. 181 *Quotations from Statutes at Large of the Confederate States of America.* Washington: GPO, 1913.
United States, 38th Congress, 2nd Session, 1864–1865, Washington, D.C.: Government Printing Office, 1865: House Report No. 25, *New York Custom-House*; Part 2, *Papers Relating to Foreign Affairs.*
United States. *The War of the Rebellion: A Compilation of the Official Records of the Union and Confederate Armies*, 70 vols. Washington, D.C.: Government Printing Office, 1880–1901.
The University of Texas at Arlington Library, Special Collections, Samuel Maas Papers.
Vandiver, Frank E. (ed.). *Confederate Blockade Running Through Bermuda, 1861-1865, Letters and Cargo Manifests.* Austin: University of Texas Press, 1947.
Watson, William. *Adventures of a Blockade Runner; or, Trade in Time of War.* London: Fisher Unwin, 1892.

Watson, William. *The Civil War Adventures of a Blockade Runner*. 1892 reprint. College Station: Texas A&M University Press, 2001 (Introduction by J. Barto Arnold III).
Watson, William. *Life in the Confederate Army, Being the Observations and Experiences of an Alien in the South During the American Civil War*. 1887. Reprint. Baton Rouge: Louisiana State University Press, 1995 (Introduction by Thomas W. Cutrer).
Work Projects Administration. *Ship Registers and Enrollments of New Orleans, Louisiana*, Vol V (1851–1860) & VI (1861–1870). Baton Rouge: Louisiana State University, 1941.
Yale Class Committee. *Biographical Record of the Class of 1850, of Yale College*. New Haven: Tuttle, Morehouse, & Taylor, Printers, 1877.
The Young-Sanders Center, Franklin, Louisiana.

Online Resources

American Battlefield Trust (battlefields.org).
Ancestorium Family Tree Collaboration (ancestorium.com).
Ancestry (ancestry.com): 1891 Scotland Census; James B. McConnell passport application, May 14, 1866; Texas, Marriage Collection, 1814–1909, Texas Department of State Health Services, Austin, TX; US Federal Census for 1850 and 1860.
Boston Public Library, Norman B. Leventhal Map & Education Center (leventhalmap.org).
El Correo (elcorreo.com).
Crew List Index Project (crewlist.org.uk).
Encyclopedia Britannica (britannica.com).
Encyclopedia Virginia (encyclopediavirginia.org).
Find a Grave (findagrave.com).
Fold3 (fold3.com).
Genealogy Bank (genealogybank.com).
Geneanet (gw.geneanet.org).
The Handbook of Texas Online (tshaonline.org/handbook/online).
Historic Hansards (api.parliament.uk).
Historical Marker Database (hmdb.org).
Justia US Supreme Court (supreme.justia.com).
Louisiana Cemeteries (la-cemeteries.com).
Maine Historical Society (mainehistory.wordpress.com).
The Maritime Post (themaritimepost.com).
Mr. Lincoln's White House (mrlincolnswhitehouse.org).
Moongiant (moongiant.com).
National Museum United States Army (armyhistory.org).
Naval History and Heritage Command (history.navy.mil).
Poetry Foundation, Poems & Poets (poetryfoundation.org).
The Portal to Texas History, University of North Texas Libraries (texashistory.unt.edu).
Reaveley, Peter. "Navigation and Logbooks in the Age of Sail." U.S. Naval Academy, Historic Shipwrecks: Science, History, and Engineering, Spring 2012 Syllabus (Jan 8, 2012) (usna.edu/Users/oceano/pguth/website/shipwrecks/published_syllabus.htm).
Scots in the American Civil War (acwscots.co.uk).
Ship Index (shipindex.org).
Skelmorlie Villas (skelmorlievillas.co.uk).
United States Coast Guard (history.uscg.mil).
University of Florida George A. Smathers Libraries Digital Collections (ufdc.ufl.edu): Title Set: *Diario de la Marina* (Havana).
Walker, Georgiana Gholson. *The Private Journal of Georgiana Gholson Walker, 1862–1865*. Dwight Franklin Henderson (ed.), Tuscaloosa: Confederate, 1963.
White, Ryan. "History: Cats in the Navy." *Naval Post*, Mar 1, 2021 (navalpost.com/ship-cat-navy-history-simon-oscar-tiddles-blackie).
WolframAlpha Computational Intelligence, Dollar/Pound inflation calculator (wolframalpha.com).
The Young-Sanders Center for the Study of the War Between the States in Louisiana (http://www.youngsanders.org/).

Newspapers

Austin *Texas State Gazette*
Baltimore *Sun*
Barcelona (SP) *El Lloyd Español*
Bellville (TX) *Countryman*
Boston *Daily Advertiser*
Boston *Herald*

Charleston *Daily News*
Cincinnati *Commercial Tribune*
Columbia (TX) *Democrat and Planter*
Corpus Christi *Ranchero*
Dallas Morning News
Galveston *Civilian*
Galveston *Commercial and Weekly Prices Current*
Galveston *Daily News* (Houston, TX)
Galveston *Flake's Daily Bulletin*
Galveston *News Tri-Weekly*
Galveston *Tri-Weekly News* (Houston, TX)
Galveston *Weekly Civilian and Gazette*
Galveston *Weekly News* (Houston, TX)
Havana (Cuba) *Diario de la Marina*
Houston *Daily Post*
Houston *Daily Telegraph*
Houston *Post-Dispatch*
Houston *Tri-Weekly Telegraph*
Houston *Weekly Telegraph*
Las Vegas (NM) *Daily Optic*
Liverpool *Gore's General Advertiser*
Liverpool *Daily Post*
Liverpool *Mercury*
Liverpool *Shipping Telegraph and Daily Commercial Advertiser*
London *Daily News*
London *Echo*
London *Evening Standard*
London *Guardian*
London *Illustrated London News*
London *Shipping and Mercantile Gazette*
London *Times*

Manchester (UK) *Courier*
Middletown, CT *The Daily Constitution*
Midlothian (UK) *The Scotsman*
Nashville Daily Union
New Albany (IN) *Daily Ledger*
New-Orleans Commercial Bulletin
New Orleans Daily Crescent
New Orleans *Daily Delta*
New Orleans *Daily True Delta*
New Orleans *Era*
New Orleans *Sunday Delta*
New Orleans *Times-Picayune*
New York *Commercial Bulletin*
New York Daily Herald
New York *Evening Post*
New York *Herald*
New York *Journal of Commerce, jr*
New York *Times*
New York *Tribune*
Philadelphia *Evening Telegraph*
Philadelphia *Times*
Plymouth (UK) *Western Daily Mercury*
Providence, RI *The Evening Bulletin* (RI)
Providence, RI *Evening Press*
The Record (Bridge City, TX)
Savannah Morning News
Shiner (TX) *Gazette*
Washington, D.C. *Daily National Intelligencer and Washington Express*
Washington (D.C.) *National Republican*
Washington (D.C.) *Weekly National Intelligencer*
Williamsburg *Virginia Gazette*

Periodicals, Journals, Theses, Compilations

Bernard, Samantha. "Searching for the Schooner *Rob Roy*: An Historical Archaeological Analysis of a Civil War Blockade Runner." Thesis. East Carolina University, Greenville, 2020.
Day, James M. "Leon Smith: Confederate Mariner." *East Texas Historical Journal* 3, no. 1 (Mar 1965): 34–49.
Ellis, L. Tuffly. "Maritime Commerce on the Far Western Gulf, 1861–1865." *Southwestern Historical Quarterly* 72, no. 2 (Oct 1973): 167–226.
Garner, Stanton. "Thomas Bangs Thorpe in the Gilded Age: Shifty in a New Country." *The Mississippi Quarterly* 36, no. 1 (Winter 1982-1983): 35–52.
Gaul, Patrick. "Trading in the Shadow of Neutrality: German-Speaking Europe's Commerce with Union and Confederacy During the American Civil War." *Bulletin of the German Historical Institute* 67 (Fall 2020): 41–70.
Grimsley, Mark. "Inside a Beleaguered City: A Commander and Actor, Prince John Magruder." *Civil War Times Illustrated* 21 (Sep 1982): 14–17, 33–35.
"The Houston of the Daring Plungers." *The Houston Review* 2, no. 2 (Summer 1980), 104–111.
Ivry, David A. "Historical Development of Some Basic Life Insurance Terminology." *The Journal of Insurance* 28, no. 3 (Sep 1961): 65–69.
Kinney, Michele Anders. "'Doubly Foreign' British Consuls in the Antebellum South, 1830-1860." Thesis, University of Texas at Arlington, Arlington, 2010.
Kneupper, Chris. "Chronological and Archaeological History of the Forts Velasco." Unpublished manuscript, Jan 19, 2021.
Milledge, L. Bonham, Jr. "The British Consuls in the Confederacy." *Studies in History, Economics and Public Law* 43, no. 3 (1911): 28–35.
Price, Marcus. "Ships That Tested the Blockade of the Gulf Ports, 1861–1865." *American Neptune* 11, no. 4 (Oct 1951): 262–290; "Part 2," Vol. 12, no. 1 (Jan 1952): 52–59; "Part 3," Vol. 12, no. 2 (Apr 1952): 154–161; "Part 4," Vol. 12, no. 3 (Jul 1952): 229–238.
Stern, Philip Van Doren. "The Unknown Conspirator," *American Heritage* 8, Issue 2 (Feb 1957): 54–59.
TePaske, John J. "Appleton Oaksmith, Filibuster Agent." *The North Carolina Historical Review* 35, no. 4 (Oct 1958): 427–447.

Wilson, Walter E. "Blockade Runner Union (Later *Rosita* and *Carolina*)." *Civil War Navy, The Magazine* (Spring 2024): 32–43.

Wilson, Walter E. "Captain King's Cotton, The Civil War Blockade-Running Adventures of Richard King and Mifflin Kenedy." In *Supplementary Studies in Rio Grande Valley History*, 15, edited by Milo Kearney et al., 91–130. Edinburg: The University of Texas Rio Grande Valley, 2017.

Wilson, Walter E. "The Civil War Blockade Running Adventures of the Louisiana Schooner William R. King." *Louisiana History* 56 (Summer 2015): 294–314.

Wilson, Walter E. "'Sail Ho!' A Civil War Surgeon and the Texas Blockade," *Southwestern Historical Quarterly* 124, no. 4 (April 202): 1437–1463.

Secondary Sources

Bennett, Frank P. *History of American Textiles: With Kindred and Auxiliary Industries*. Boston: American Wool and Cotton Reporter, 1922.

Bennett, John D. *The London Confederates*. Jefferson, NC: McFarland, 2008.

Block, W.T. *Schooner Sail to Starboard: Confederate Blockade Running on the Louisiana-Texas Coastlines*. Woodville, TX: Dogwood Press, 1997.

Bristowe, Lindsay W., and Philip B. Wright. *Handbook of British Honduras, 1888–89*. Ediburgh: William Blackwood and Sons, 1888.

Brown, John Henry. *Indian Wars and Pioneers of Texas*. Austin: L.E. Daniell, 1896.

Byron, George Gordon. *Don Juan: in Sixteen Cantos, with Notes*. London: H.G. Bohn, 1849.

Carlin, Colin. *Captain James Carlin; Anglo-American Blockade Runner*. Columbia: University of South Carolina Press, 2017.

Casdorf, Paul D. *Prince John Magruder, His Life and Campaigns*. New York: John Wiley & Sons, 1996.

Cluster, Dick, and Rafael Hernández. *The History of Havana*. New York: Palgrave Macmillan, 2008.

Cotham, Edward T., Jr. *Sabine Pass: The Confederacy's Thermopylae*. Austin: University of Texas Press, 2004.

Daddysman, James W. *The Matamoros Trade, Confederate Commerce, Diplomacy, and Intrigue*. Newark: University of Delaware Press, 1984.

Dalzell, George Walton. *Flight from the Flag*. Chapel Hill: University of North Carolina Press, 1940.

Davis, Charles S., and J. Barto Arnold, III. *Colin J. McRae: Confederate Financial Agent: Blockade Running in the Trans-Mississippi as Affected by the Confederate Government's Direct European Procurement of Goods*. College Station: Institute of Nautical Archeology, Texas A&M University, 2008.

Davis, Lance E., and Stanley L. Engerman. *Naval Blockades in Peace and War: An Economic History Since 1750*. New York: Cambridge University Press, 2006.

Debray, X.B. (Xavier Blanchard). *A sketch of the history of Debray's (26th) Regiment of Texas Cavalry*. Austin: E. von Boeckmann, 1884.

De Cordova, Jacob. *Texas: Her Resources and Her Public Men, A Companion for J. De Cordova's New and Correct Map of the State of Texas*. Waco: Texian Press, 1858.

Edwards, John N. *Shelby's Expedition to Mexico, an Unwritten Leaf of the War*. Kansas City, MO: Kansas City *Times* Steam Book and Job Printing House, 1872.

Eicher, John H., and David J. Eicher. *Civil War High Commands*. Stanford: Stanford University Press, 2001.

Essex, Phil, Craig S. Mork, and Craig A. Pomeroy. *An Owner's Guide to Tonnage Admeasurement 1998–2003*. Jensen Maritime Consultants, 2003.

Evans, Clement A. (ed.) *Confederate Military History*, Vol. 10: *A Library of Confederate States History*. Atlanta: Confederate, 1899.

Faust, Albert B. *Guide to the Material for American History in Swiss and Austrian Archives*. Washington, D.C.: Carnegie Institution of Washington, 1916.

Frazier, Donald S. *Cottonclads! The Battle of Galveston and the Defense of the Texas Coast*. Abilene: McWhitney Foundation Press, 1998.

Gallaway, B.P. (ed). *The Dark Corner of the Confederacy: Accounts of Civil War Texas as Told by Contemporaries*. Dubuque: W.M. Brown Book Co., 1968.

Graham, Eric J. *Clyde Built, Blockade Runners, Cruisers, and Armoured Rams of the American Civil War*. Edinburgh: Berlinn, 2006.

Hall, Andrew W. *Civil War Blockade Running on the Texas Coast*. Charleston, SC: The History Press, 2014.

Hall, Andrew W. *The Galveston-Houston Packet Steamboats on Buffalo Bayou*. Charleston, SC: The History Press, 2012.

Hearn, Chester G. *Gray Raiders of the Sea, How Eight Confederate Warships Destroyed the Union's High Seas Commerce*. Camden, ME: International Marine Publishing, 1992.

Hearn, Chester G. *When the Devil Came Down to Dixie: Ben Butler in New Orleans*. Baton Rouge: Louisiana State University Press, 2000.

Irby, James A. *Backdoor at Bagdad: The Civil War on the Rio Grande*. El Paso: Texas Western Press, 1977.

Kennedy, Charles Stuart. *The American Consul: A History of the United States Consular Service 1776 –1924*, 2nd ed. Washington, D.C.: New Academia Publishing, 2015.

Krick, Robert E.L. *Staff Officers in Gray: A Biographical Register of the Staff Officers in the Army of Northern Virginia*. Chapel Hill: University of North Carolina Press, 2003.

Lea, Tom. *The King Ranch*. Boston: Little, Brown, 1957.

Lisarelli, Danial F. *The Last Prison, The Untold Story of Camp Groce CSA*. Parkland, FL: Universal, 1999.

Maffitt, Emma Martin. *The Life and Services and Services of John Newland Maffitt*. New York: Neale, 1906.

Owsley, Frank Lawrence, Jr. *The C.S.S. Florida, Her Building and Operations*. Philadelphia: University of Pennsylvania Press, 1965.

Pérez, Louis A., Jr. *Imitations of Modernity Civil Culture in Nineteenth-Century Cuba*. Chapel Hill: University of North Carolina Press, 2017.

Robinson III, Charles M. *Shark of the Confederacy*. Annapolis: Naval Institute Press, 1995.

Scheina, Robert L. *Latin America's Wars: The Age of the Caudillo: 1791–1899*, vol. 1. Washington, D.C.: Brassey's, 2003.

Schmidt, James M. *Galveston and the Civil War: An Island City in the Maelstrom*. Charleston, SC: The History Press, 2012.

Settles, Thomas M. *John Bankhead Magruder, a Military Reappraisal*. Baton Rouge: Louisiana State University Press, 2009.

Shingleton, Royce. *High Seas Confederate: The Life & Times of John Newland Maffitt*. Columbia: University of South Carolina Press, 1994.

Silverstone, Paul H. *Civil War Navies, 1855–1883*. Annapolis: Naval Institute Press, 2001.

Sprunt, James *Chronicles of the Cape Fear River, 1660–1916*, 2nd ed. 1916 reprint. Wilmington: Broadfoot, 1992.

Taylor, Walter Herron. *General Lee: His Campaigns in Virginia, 1861–1865, with Personal Reminiscences*. Brooklyn: Press of Braunworth & Co., 1906.

Tenkottr, Paul A., and James C. Claypool (eds.). *The Encyclopedia of Northern Kentucky*. Lexington: University Press of Kentucky, 2009.

Thompson, Jerry, and Lawrence T. Jones, III. *Civil War and Revolution on the Rio Grande Frontier; A Narrative and Photographic History*. Austin: State Historical Association, 2004.

Thompson, Samuel Bernard. *Confederate Purchasing Operations Abroad*. Chapel Hill: University of North Carolina Press, 1935.

Thorp, Robert. *Mersey Built, the Role of Merseyside in the American Civil War*. Wilmington, DE: Vernon Press, 2017.

Way, Frederick, Jr. (comp.) *Way's Packet Directory, 1848–1994, Passenger Steamboats of the Mississippi River System Since the Advent of Photography in Mid-Continent America*. Rev. ed. Athens: Ohio University Press, 1983.

White, Jonathan W. *Shipwrecked: A True Civil War Story of Mutinies, Jailbreaks, Blockade-Running, and the Slave Trade*. Lanham, MD: Rowman & Littlefield, 2023.

Wilson, Walter E. *Civil War Scoundrels and the Texas Cotton Trade*. Jefferson, NC: McFarland, 2020.

Wilson, Walter E., and Gary L. McKay. *James D. Bulloch, Secret Agent and Mastermind of the Confederate Navy*. Jefferson, NC: McFarland, 2012.

Wise, Stephen R. *Lifeline of the Confederacy, Blockade Running During the Civil War*. Columbia: University of South Carolina Press, 1988.

Wooster, Ralph A. (ed.). *Lone Star Blue and Gray, Essays on Texas in the Civil War*. Austin: Texas State Historical Association, 1995.

Index

Numbers in **_bold italics_** indicate pages with illustrations

A. Isaac, Levy & Co. 79
A.C. Dana 122, 181
USS *Admiral* 84, 187
admiralty court 3, 57, 58, 65, 75, 76, 81, 83, 87, 121, 122, 128, 129, 139, 146, 155, 159, 160, 162, 170, 174, 181, 208n43
Agnes (John Arthur) 59, 63, 67, 68, 79, 170, 181
Alabama 14, 20, 29, 32, 35, 37, 88, 165, 169, 173, 176, 192; *see also* Mobile; Mobile Bay; Montgomery
CSS *Alabama* 18, 64, 65, **_70_**, 181, 187, 192
Alabama (Ida Duvere) 128, 129, 139, 168, 181, 183
Albert Edward (Uncle Bill) 181, 198
SS *Alice* (SS *Matagorda*) 4, 83–85, 110, 132, 163, **_164_**, 176, 181, 187, 208n25
Alma 75, 167, 168, 171, 181
Amanda 86, 87, 98, 173, 175, 181, 188
Ann Giberson (Anna Gibberson) 59, 61, 63, 64, 67–69, 79, 114, 170, 181, 210n23
Anne Sophia (Annie Sophia, Anna Shepherd) 122, 181
Antoinetta (Antoinette) 122, 181
Appomattox Courthouse 151
Aransas (Pass, Bay) **_8_**, 15
Archer, Edward Richard 155, 165
Argyle Street, Glasgow 156
Arizona 93, **_96_**, 105, 172, 178
SS *Arizona (Caroline, Carolina,* USS *Arizona)* 53, 182
Arkansas 12, 35, 131, 149, 169, 172, 173, 192
Army of Northern Virginia 13, 151, 171
USS *Aroostook* 57, 100, 182, 188
Ashby (Ashbey), Joseph Henry 67, 165, 185
Askins, William E. 139, 165, 193

Atakapa tribe 87
Atchafalaya (Bay, River) **_7_**, 159
Atlantic (Coast, Ocean, ports) 16, 18, 70, 125, 152
SS *Austin (Donegal)* 53, 182
Austin, Charles William 4, 139, 140, **_141_**, 165, 184, 193, 194
Austin, TX 3, 166, 167, 178
Avendaño Brothers (Francisco Peregrino, aka Francisco Pablo Peregrino De Avendaño Y López; José Maria, aka Luis María de Avendaño y López; Miguel; Teodomiro) 77, 86, 124, 143, 165, 212n17
Ayrshire, Scotland 11, 20, 178
Azores 147

Bagdad, MX 22–24, 65, 119
Bahamas *see* Nassau
Ball, Hutchins, & Co. 50, 51, 68, 69, 169, 170
Baltimore, MD 37, 80–82, 183, 185, 186, 191–194
Banks, Nathaniel 88
SS *Barcelona* 124, 125, 136, 140, 141, 148, 182
Barnard, Joseph C. 142, 165, 194
Barrios, Appolonaria (Polly) 54, 55, 74, 83, 165
Bates, Joseph 3, 29, **_30_**, 31, 33, 34, 36–38, 44, 68, 88, 104, 163
Baton Rouge, LA 11–13
Bayly (Baily), William 139, 141, 142, 165, 183
CSS *Bayou City* 90, 172, 177, 182
Bayport, FL **_7_**, 143
Beauregard, Pierre Gustave Toutant 11, 165
Bee, Hamilton Prioleau 65, 165, 174
Beechgrove, Skelmorlie 157
Beissner, Charles Ludwig 153, 154, 166
Belgium (Belgian) 112, 132
Belize **_7_**, 56, 58–60, 62, 63, 67,

68, 75, 81, 82, 85, 98, 129, 130, 139, 154, 155, 168, 169, 171, 184, 189, 196, 197, 198, 211n4
Bell, George Panton 78, **_79_**, 166
Belle (Gipsey, Zouave) 134, 139, 166, 182
SS *Belle Sulphur* 53, 174, 182
Bermuda 11, 16, 148, 155, 178
USS *Bermuda* 86, 182
Berndt, Charles 139, 166, 191
Berwick Bay, LA 53, 112, 182, 187, 188, 193, 206n4
Birkenhead, UK 181, 184, 189, 195
SS *Black Joker (C. Vanderbilt, Cornelius Vanderbilt)* 53, 182, 207n11
Blakely, George 147, 166, 189, 195
Blanche see *General Rusk*
Blanchet, Pierre Constant 139, 166, 189,
Bloomfield, Benjamin Seton 32, 33, 132, 166
Boca Chica, TX 120
Boca del Rio *see* Rio Grande
Bolivar (Peninsula, Point), TX 83, 87–89, 109, 134, 220n20
Booth, John Wilkes 151, 166
Bordeaux, France 193
Borner, Paul 3, **_96_**, 100, 101, **_102_**, 103–105, 166
Boston, MA 81, 141, 174, 183, 189, 192, 194
Boston Sunday Herald 156
Bragg, Braxton 11, 166
Brazoria County, TX 3, 26, **_30_**
Brazos River, TX **_7_**, **_8_**, 15, 24–26, **_27_**, 28–30, 33, 34, 36, 39, 40, 43, 44, 46–59, 61, 63, 64, 66, **_67_**, 68, 69, 73, 75, 76, 81, 82, 88, 90, 98–100, 103–106, 108–111, 114, 122, 132, 139, 143, 150, 155, 163–168, 172, 176, 177, 181, 183–185, 187–190, 193, 196, 208n43, 211n4, 220n20
Brazos Santiago Pass, TX **_8_**, 15,

237

238 Index

53, 54, 120, *121*, 122, 139, 177, 182, 186, 188, 191, 206n7
Breckenridge, John 37, 169
British 5, 11, 12, 14, 15, 17, 18, 20, 21, 23, 25, 26, 29, 31, 33, 36–38, 40–42, 49, 57, 65, 74, 75, 78, 92, 94, 100, 110, 114, 119, 124, 125, 128, 129, 131, 144, 153, 154, 159, 166–169, 171–174, 177, 178, 180–194, 197, 198, 201n16, 207n10, 221n14; *see also* England; United Kingdom (UK)
British Honduras *see* Belize
British North America 121, 168
British Red Ensign 15, *16*, 49
Brooklyn, NY 128, 184, 187
Brown, James 11, 139, 166, 182
Brown, John 37
Brownsville, TX 3, *7*, 22, 24, 34, 41, 42, 46, 120, 122, 130, 139, 175, 185, 187, 191, 206n7
Buchanan, James 37, 169, 187
Buchel, August Carl 50, 51, 68, 166
Buckley, Cornelius W. 110, 167
Buffalo Bayou, TX 94, 97, 108, 188
Bulloch, James Dunwoody 147, 152, 167, 169, 189, 190, 193
Burgess, Francis 154, 167
Butler, Benjamin Franklin 13, 87, 165, 167, 187
Butler, John Henry 189
Byron, Lord (George Gordon Noel) 135, 167

SS *C. Vanderbilt* see SS *Black Joker*
Calcasieu, LA *8*, 53, 184, 189, 192
SS *California* 53, 54, 182
Campbell, Andrew Donaldson 11, 167
Campbell, Janet Maria, 11, 167
Canada 37, 76, 121, 122, 168–170, 173, 181, 190; *see also* British North America; Montreal; New Brunswick; Nova Scotia; St. John; Toronto
Canary Islands 147
Caney Creek, TX *8*, 15, 28, 43, 50, 61, 62, 67, 69, 184, 192, 200n23
Cape San Antonio, Cuba 123
Caplen Mound 87
Carbajal, José María Jesús 201n2
cards (for cotton) 67, 216n34
SS *Carolina* (*Caroline, Union, Rosita*) 81, 110, 111, 174, 183
Caroline 120, 183
Caroline Goodyear 65
Carrie Mair (*Carrie Muir*) 121–124, 128, 136, 139, 173, 174, 183, 189, 198
Carrington, William Thornton 94, 167
carte de visite (CDV) 81, 82, 105
Carter, William Fitzhugh 148, 167, 189
Castle Morro (*Castillo de los Tres Reyes Magos del Morro*, Castle of the Three Magi Kings of the Moor) 77
Catharine *see* Eliza Catharine
USS/CSS *Cavallo* (*Henrietta*) 91, 183
Cayce, Henry Petty 103, 167
Celda, Francis 75, 167, 181
Ceylon (Sri Lanka) 204n42
Chaos (*Vigilant, Fairy, Velocity, Nellie Blair*) 79, 110, 114, 137–139, 141, 142, 165, 168, 170, 183, 184
Charles Russell (*Maria W. Lawson*) 59, 67, 68, 109, 114, 137–139, 141, 142, 165, 183
Charles Street Jail 81
Charleston, SC *7*, 165
Chase, Franklin 48, 49, 75, 118, 119, 120, 137, 138, *138*, 150, 167, 221n14
Cherbourg, France 70, 181
Chicago, IL 37
USS *Chocura* 128, 129, 183, 189
Chubb, Thomas Beaverstock 90, 167
Cincinnati, OH 37
Civil War Adventures of a Blockade Runner; or, Trade in Time of War 3, *6*, *26*, *64*, *117*, *118*, *146*, 156, 199n1
Clarinda (USS/CSS *Sachem, Vera Cruz*) 30, 140–142, 148, 150, 170, 175, 177, 183, 184, 192, 194
Clark, Edward 29, 167
Clark, William 106, 107, 167
USS/CSS *Clifton* 30, 140, 165, 168, 170, 174, 184
Clyde River *see* River Clyde
Coahuila, MX 93, 177
Columbia, TX 28, 29, 33, 34, 36, 39–44, 50, 51, 54, 59, 61, 66, 68, 69, 105
Concordia 184, 198
Confederate Army 11, 26, 28, 29, 33, 36, 43, 45, 48, 62, 66, 90, 96, 97, 138, 148, 156, 168, 169, 172–176, 178, 182, 185
Confederate Congress 78, 161
Confederate Navy 70, 90, 147, 148, 155, 159, 165, 167, 174, 185, 186, 189
Confederate States of America (Confederacy) 12, 22, 35, 37, 38, 45, 49, 50, 60, 61, 65, 66, 72, 78, 83, 93, 111, 148, 152, 155, 161, 162, 168, 172, 178, 180
Conklin, Matthias Dayton 41, 46, 125, 132, 167
Connecticut 170, 181, 182, 183, 188, 192, 194
Cooper, William S. 81, 82, 139, 168, 189, 190
Corinth, MS, Battle of 13, 31, 32, 168
Cora (*Snow Drift*) 24, 25, 26, 53, 54, 67, 109, 110, 114, 139, 169, 175, 184, 198, 230ap7n6
USS *Cornubia* 138, 184, 185, 186
Corpus Christi Bay, TX *7*, *8*, 15, 54, 98, 175, 181
Cosmopolite (*Henrietta*) 171
cotton 7, 14, 15, 19–21, 23, 24, 28, 31, 34, 35, 39, 40, 42, 44–47, 49, 51, 56–58, 61–63, *64*, 68, 72, 73, 75, 76, 83, 89, 92, 98, 106–109, 111, 113, 115, 119, 120, 122, 124–126, 131, 132, 134, 136–138, 140–143, 147–151, 153, 160, 162, 170, 171, 173, 174, 177, 181, 183–190, 192, 193, 194, 208n34, 208n43, 210n23
Cotton Bureau (Office) 78, 109, 134, 170
cotton-clad 89, 90, 93
County Cork, Ireland 40
County Galway, Ireland 38, 169
C.P. Knapp 14, 24, 159, 160, 171, 184
Cross, Abraham 30, 31, 34, 36, 168
Cuba (Cubans) *7*, 42, 54, 62, 65, 69, 76, 91, 100, 123, 125, 126, 127, 128, 149, 174, 183, 186, 191, 207n18; *see also* Cape San Antonio; Havana
Cuca (*Lone*) 75, 122, 139, 168, 184
Curry (Currie), John M. 74–76, 83, 122, 139, 154, 168, 184, 192, 193
custom(s) (Confederate) 14, 28, 39, 40, 44–46, 49, 56, 63, 90, 94, 107, 109, 113, 134, 147, 150, 159, 161
custom(s) (Cuban) 85, 98, 154
custom(s) (Mexican) 159, 177
custom(s) (U.S.) 16, 17, 20, 82, 83, 175, 177

Dahlia *see* Delia
Danish Virgin Islands 61
Davidson, James 59, 67, 183
Davidson, Joseph 138, 142, 165, 168, 183
Davis, Jefferson 165, 166, 172
Davis, J.H. 139, 168, 181
Davison, James H. 139, 168, 189
Dazzle 120, 184

Index

Deadman's Bay, FL 154
Debray, Xavier Blanchard 29, 30, 88, 168
Deer 24, 26, 28, 175, 184
Delia (Dahlia) 143, 184
SS *Denbigh* 76, 144, 145, **146**, 147, 169, 185, 186, 228*n*23
Denmark 152; *see also* Danish Virgin Islands
CSS *Diana* 90, 177, 185
Diario de la Marina 85, 124, 128, 142, 153
Dover, UK 147
Dowling, Richard "Dick" William 30, 38, 167, 168
Downs, J. Francis 40, 41, 44, 56–59, 82, 114, 168, 177, 182, 185, 188, 194

SS *Eagle see* SS *Jeannette*
Eagle (Sybil) 139, 165
Eagle, Henry 159
Eagle Pass, TX 46
Eco (Echo) 141, 142, 185
Eliza Catharine 39–41, 63, 143, 173, 177, 183, 185
Emily 98, 110, 114, 166, 177, 185, 191
Emma 128, 129, 185
Enfield rifles 65, 66, 69, 82, 86, 189
England 37, 84, 147, 169, 170, 173, 174, 178, 181, 182, 184, 185, 189–193, 195
Ennis, Cornelius 82, 168, 187
Era No. 3 44, 45, 55, 185
Espiritu Santo Pass, TX 86
Essayons 7, 174, 185, 214*n*42
Essex, MA 184, 189–191
Eureka (Enriquita) 40, 41, 56, 57, 114, 168, 182, 185
Europe (European) 15, 66, 119, 124, 152
Evans, Colonel *see* Bates, Joseph
Exchange 67, 165, 185

Farragut, David Glasgow 111
Ferdinand 120, 122m 185
Fernandez, Joseph 101, 103, 168
Fisher Unwin **2**, **6**, **26**, **64**, **117**, **118**, **146**, 156, 199*Int*1*n*1
Flash 107, 126, 139, 167, 168, 177, 178, 185
Fleigh (Flagg), William Henry 107, 126, 127, 132, 168, 193
Florida 1, 7, 14, 20, 80, 154, 155, 165, 167, 170, 186, 192, 196, 200*n*24, 211*n*4; *see also* Bayport; Deadman's Bay; Gainesville; Key West; St. Marks; Steinhatchee River; Suwanee River; Tallahassee; Tampa Bay

CSS *Florida* 18, 64, 65, 70, 172, 185
Florida (schooner) 155
Fly, George Washington Lafayette **32**, 35, 168, 203*n*15
Ford, John 71
Ford, John Salmon "Rip" 32, 34, 42, 93, 168, 172
Fort Bates, TX 29, 43
Fort Cedar Bayou, TX 69
Fort Fisher, NC 70
Fort Jackson, LA 17
Fort Lafayette, NY 81
Fort St. Philip, LA 17
Fort Sulakowski, TX 29, 43
Fort Warren, MA 81
USS *Fox (Alabama)* 154, 167, 186, 192
Fox, Catherina "Kate" 109, 175
France, (French) 29, 40, 65, 70, 73, 74, 93, 119, 120, 137, 152, 166, 168, 169, 171, 173, 174, 177, 185; *see also* Bordeaux; Brest; Cherbourg; French Foreign Legion; Paris
Freemason 31
Fremantle, Sir Arthur James Lyon 22, 168, 169
French, Alonzo Frank 55, 77
French, James D. 187
French Foreign Legion 50, 166

G. Pauvert & Son 34, 41, 55
Gainesville, FL 154
Galveston (City, Harbor, Island), TX 3, **7**, **8**, 15–18, 28, 29, 31, 34, 38–42, 45–49, 51–53, 59, 62, 63, 65, **67**, 71, 72, 79–82, 84, 85, 87, 89, 90, 92–94, 96, 98, 107, 108, 110–115, 119, 121, 122, 125–130, **131**, 132, 134–151, 153–155, 159, 164–178, 181–196, 203*n*15, 208*n*25, 208*n*43, 213*n*33, 216*n*34, 220*n*14, 220*n*19–20, 222*n*9, 226*n*50, 227*n*11–12, 227*n*15
Galveston Bay, TX **7**, **8**, 44, 46, 49–53, 59, 62, 71, 75, 79–83, 87, 88, **89**, 90, 91, 96–99, 106, 108–111, **112**, 113–116, 118, 119, 121, 126, 136, 139, 163, 164, 166, 172, 181–183, 185, 187, 189–191, 193, 194, 208*n*43, 216*n*34, 220*n*19
SS *General Rusk (Blanche)* 42, 53, 54, 112, 174, 176, 186, 191, 208*n*21, 220*n*19*n*21
CSS *Georgia* 18, 186
German 24, 50, 62, 91, 109, 110, 166, 170, 175, 178
USS *Gertrude* 136, 186
Geziena Hilligonda 139, 170, 186
Gilliat, Algernon 147, 169, 190

Gilliat, Louisa Ann Frances "Fanny" 189, 228*n*29
Gilliat, John Saunders 147, 169, 228*n*29
Glasgow, Scotland 11, 145, 156, 178, 186, 193
Godfrey, Abner Melchior 142, 147, 169, 185, 194
Gordon, John 99, 103, 169
SS *Grampus No. 2* 53, 186
Greeley, Horace 45, 169
Greenock, Scotland 144, 156, 157, 193
Greenough, John 139, 169, 184
Gregory, William Henry 37, 38, 169, 204*n*45
Griffin, John 101, 103, 169
Griffiths, Thomas 146, 169
Gulf of Mexico 1, 5, **7**, **8**, 15–18, 25, 54, 63–65, 74, 76, 78, 83, 84, 86–88, 92, 106, 117, 119, 120, 123, 124, 128, **139**, 143, 147, 154, 159, 166, 175, 185, 189, 200*n*23–24
Gulf Stream 139

Harpers Ferry, VA 137
USS/CSS/SS *Harriet Lane (Lavinia, Elliott Richie)* 83–85, 89–91, 96, 130, 132, 148, 151, 165, 170, 175, 186, 187
Harris County, TX 175
Harrisburg, TX 96, 97, 217*n*54
USS *Hatteras* 18, 65, 176, 181, 187
Hatteras Inlet, NC 187
Havana, CU **7**, 14, 16, 24, 40, 42, 51, 53, 54, 57–69, 71–73, 75–82, 84–87, 90, 91, 94, 97–100, 107, 108, 110–112, 115, 116, 120–132, 134, 136–155, 159, 160, 163, 165, 166, 169, 170, 174, 175, 177, 178, 181–191, 193–196, 207*n*18, 222*n*9, 223*n*30, 224*n*19, 227*n*11, 228*n*33
Hawes, James Morrison 90–92, 95–97, 107, 108, 169, 170
Haynes, Samuel Barker 66, 169
Hébert, Paul Octave 93, 113, 169
Helm, Charles John 60, 61, 64–66, 70, 77, 79, 80, 83, 94, 101, 125, 127, 169, 170
Hendley, Joseph J. 92, 170, 216*n*34
Hendley, William 92, 170
Hennessy, Daniel 101, 103, 170
Her Britannic Majesty (Queen Victoria) 17, 18, 31, 38, 159, 166
High Island, TX 87
Holland (Netherlands) 186
Holland, Gustavus (or Gustave) Aldolphus 91, 92, 94, 95, 108, 170

Index

Hotel de Inglaterra, Havana 132
House, Thomas William 24, 28, 51, 56, 58, 63, 79, 98, 110, 113, 114, 125, 137, 138, **140**, 145, 148, 149, 151, 170, 177, 185, 189, 190, 210n23, 217n2
Houston, Sam 167, 168
Houston, TX **7**, 24, 28, 31, 34, 35, 39, 41, 50, 67, 69, 82, 93–99, 104, 105, 107, 108, 110, 111, 113, 131, 137, 145, 149, 167, 168, 170, 172, 175, 176, 224n20
Howe, James 99, 102, 103, 170, 217n2
Hubbard, George N. 59, 67, 170, 181
Huke, Emile Alvin 61–64, 66, 68, 69, 170
Hulburt, John E. 24, 67, 170
Hunter, Charles 186, 191
Hunter, William W. 90
USS *Huntsville* 132
Hurley, Charles William 184
Hutchins, William J. 78, 170; *see also* Ball, Hutchins, & Co.
Hyland, Jim 83, 111, 114, 127, 170, 223n18

Illinois 37, 173; *see also* Chicago
Indian (schooner) 79
SS *Indian No. 2* (*Indian Queen No. 2*) 53, 54, 187, 207n19
Indian Ocean 70
Indiana 182, 188, 193
Indianola, TX 166
Ireland (Irish) 14, 17, 25, 38, 40, 43, 55, 69, 81, 83, 110, 111, 121, 124, 127, 159, 169, 171, 174, 175, 201n16; *see also* County Cork; County Galway
SS *Isabel* 84, 132, 187
CSS *Island City* 94–97, 171, 187

Jacobs, John 25, 190, 201n16
Jamaica *see* Kingston
James Williams 49, 110, 167, 187, 191
Jansen, Bernardas Peter 139, 170
Jansen, Frederick 44, 54, 74, 83, 116, 127, 170
Jauréguiberry (Tauréguiberry), Pierre 139, 171, 192
SS *Jeannette* (*Eagle*, *Josie*) 82, 145–150, **151**, 152–155, 174, 187, 188, 227n9, 229n41
John 56, 58, 59, 82, 150, 168, 174, 177, 188, 208n43
John A. Hazard 139, 173, 188
USS *John Anderson see* USS *William G. Anderson*
John Arthur see Agnes

John Douglas (*Gino*) 67, 171, 188, 191, 198
SS *John F. Carr* 171
Johnson, Amos 184
Johnson, Andrew 176
Johnson, August A. 62, 67, 171, 192
Johnson, Peter 201n16
Johnson, Robert D. 172
Johnson, William 190
Jolly, David Leitch 49, 171
Jolly, Stewart L. 147, 171
J.O.L.O. 168, 170, 216n34
Jonah 116, 117, 171
Jordan, Levi 61, 62, 192
Jordan, Sarah Stone 61, 192
Joseph, Ferdinand Maximilian *see* Maximilian
Josephine 134, 139, 177, 188
SS *Josiah H. Bell* (*J.H. Bell*) 47, 53, 173, 188
Juárez, Benito (Juárista) 65, 119, 171, 177
Julia (*Thomas R. Hughlett*) 129, 139, 175, 183, 188

USS *Kanawha* 86, 87, 98, 175, 188
Kenedy, Mifflin 3, 130, 171, 175, 186
Kenney, Joseph Allen 67, 171, 188
Key West, FL **7**, 76, 81, 83, 154, 159, 160, 176, 183, 184, 194
USS *Kineo* **100**, **101**, 102–106, 166, 168–170, 174, 176, 178, 179, 188
King Neptune 116
King, Richard 3, 24, 130, 171, 175
King, William Rufus 192
King Ranch 3
Kingston, Jamaica **7**,
Kingsville, TX 3
USS *Kittatinny* 25, 26, 28, 176, 188
Knights Templar 31
Kuhn, Jacob Conrad 49, 171, 187, 190–192, 194

Lady Hurley (*Lote* or *Lottie Hurley*) 122, 139, 166, 189
Lafayette, Marquis de 219n5
Laguna del Madre, TX **8**
Lamar, Henrietta *see* Maffitt, Henrietta (Lamar)
Lamar, Mirabeau B. 71, 172
Lane, Marquis de Lafayette 109, 110, 137–139, 141, 142, 171, 219n5
SS *Lark* 125, 141, 144, 145, **146**, 147–150, 166, 169, 172, 175, 189, 227n11, 229n41
Laura Edwards 25, 189, 201n16

Laverty, Henry 14, 15, 17, 19–21, 23, 24, 159, 160, 171, 184, 192, 196, 198
Lavinia see CSS *Harriet Lane*)
Lawless, John Y. 94, 171, 182, 187, 190
Lee, Robert Edward 13, 93, 151, 171, 172, 177
Lee, William 75, 171, 181
Leopold, Wilhelm (William) Edward 150, 171, 172
Letts, Caleb 61, 62, 192
Life in the Confederate Army 156
Lightfoot (*Light Foot*) 114, 189
Lilly (*Lily*) 34-ton 107, 118, 119, 122, 126, 139, 168, 171, 189, 191, 221n14
Lilly (*Lily*, *Lily No. 2*) 44-ton 81, 82, 168, 189
Lilly 61-ton 98, 189
Lincoln, Abraham 45, 151, 161, 166, 169, 172, 173, 176
Little, George W. 67, 172, 193
Liverpool, UK 26, 49, 130, 139, 147, 155, 167–169, 185, 189–191, 194
SS *Lizzie* **144**, **146**, 147, 172, 189, 228n26
London, UK **2**, 5, **6**, **26**, 38, **64**, **70**, **117**, **118**, **144**, **146**, 147, 148, 169, 175, 189, 190, 203n42
Lone Star 59, 189
SS *Louisa Ann Fanny* 147, 148, 155, 167, 169, 174, 178, 189, 190
Louisiana 3, 11, 14, 20, 21, 28, 32, 35, 37, 75, 82, 83, 88, 93, 112, 113, 132, 149, 159, 160, 163–167, 169, 173–176, 178, 180, 182–184, 188, 189, 192, 193, 204n8; *see also* Baton Rouge; Berwick Bay; Calcasieu; Milliken's Bend, Battle of; New Orleans; Pelican State
Louisville, KY 37, 182, 189
Louvre Café 80, 81
Love Bird 65
Lowood (*Witchie*) 139, 178, 189
Lubbock, Francis Richard 51, 167, 172
Lubbock, Henry Schultz 130, 172, 182
Luckett, Philip Noland 33–36, 61, 172, 176
Luna (*Lunar*) 125, 129, 130, 190, 222n9
Lynn, Arthur Thomas 31, 33, 36–38, 40, 92, 94, 114, 172, 178
Lyon, Samuel C. 26, 56, 57, 172

MacGregor, Rob Roy 14, 172
Mack Canfield 49, 190
Madeira 147

Index

Maffitt, Caroline Matilda (Johnson) 71, 172
Maffitt, Henrietta (Lamar) 71, 172
Maffitt, John Newland, Jr. 64, 65, 70, **71**, 72, 147, 155, 172
Magruder, John Bankhead 30–33, 35–38, 46, 50, 52, 56, 60–68, 70, 71, 77–79, 88–94, **95, 96**, 97, 104, 109, 112, 113, 131, 149, 166, 167, 169, 170, 172, 173, 176, 177, 178, 204n45
Maine 81, 182, 184, 191, 193, 219n5
Mallory, Stephen Russell 70, 172
Maloney, John 65, 174
Marcy, Samuel 146, 147, 149, 166, 172, 189, 227n12
SS *Maria* (*Montpelier*) 125, 129, 130, 190, 222n9
Marmion, James Roger 52, 173
Marquez, Jr, Francis 3, 14, 19–21, 155, 159, 160, 171, 173, 192, 196–198
Marsden, Charles Poole 67, 173, 194
Martinique 70
Mary Ann 139, 190
Mary Augusta 147, 169, 190
Mary Elizabeth (*Mary Eliza*) 63, 79, 108–111, 114, 116–119, 122, 125, 140, 175, 190
Mary Ella (*Mary Ellen*, *Orion*) 82, 83, 174, 190
SS *Mary Hill* 44, 59, 66, 67, 68, 104, 174, 190
Mary Louise (*Mary Louisa*) 51, 79, 190
Mary P. Burton (*Pet*, *Phenix*) 122, 171, 190, 191
Maryland (Baltimore) 129, 183, 184, 186, 188, 191–193, 195
Mason *see* Freemason
Mason, Charles M. 97, 173
Mason, James Murray 37, 38, 173, 204n45
Mason, Thomas E. 35, 173
Massachusetts 12, 174, 176, 183, 184, 189–192; *see also* Boston
SS *Matagorda see* SS *Alice*
Matagorda Bay, TX **7, 8**, 36, 41, 43, 50, 52, 53, 54, 62, 64, 96, 112, 121, 128, 147, 173, 183, 186, 189, 190, 200n23, 207n18
Matagorda Island, TX 86
Matamoros, MX **7**, 14, 15, 19–22, 24, 26, 34, 46, 49, 63, 65, 73, 75, 78, 86, 87, 100, 101, 120, 122, 128–130, 139, 151, 159, 160, 165, 167, 171, 174–176, 184, 188, 193, 195, 196, 201n2, 201n16
Matthews, Asa Carrington 86, 173

Maximilian, Emperor 65, 93, 119, 120, 152, 171, 172, 173, 177
McBurney, Alex 40, 41, 43, 173, 204n5
McClellan, George Brinton 93, 173
McClusky, David 47–52, 67, 79, 80, 82, 83, 85, 90, 96, 99–107, 126, 166–168, 173, 175, 178, 188, 190–193, 205n1, 206n14, 213n27
McConnell, James Britton 80, 81, 91, 107, 108, 173, 190, 193
McCormick, John 181, 190
McCormick, Michael 189
McNamara, Thomas 139, 173, 183
McPherson, William 191
Methodist 172, 175
Mexican War 34, 50, 61, 92, 96, 165, 166, 168–172, 175–177
Mexico (Mexican) **7**, 15, 19, 22–24, 26, 46–49, 51, 53, 57, 65, 67, 73, 75, 76, 86, 87, 93, 100, 107–110, 119, 120, 123, 125, 126, 136, 137, **138**, 139, 141, 142, 146–148, 151, 152, 153, 161, 166, 167, 171, 174, 175, 177, 178, 181, 182, 184, 185, 186, 193, 204n8; *see also* Gulf of Mexico; Matamoros; Mexican War; Santana River; Sisal; Tampico; Tuxpan; Vera Cruz
Meyers, Henry 139, 173, 188
Mier Expedition 26
Milliken's Bend, Battle of 96
Mills, Andrew 173
Mills, David Graham 40, 44, 55, 62, 66, 173
Mills, John Robert 40, 44, 55, 62, 66, 97, 98, 113, 173, 174
Mills, Robert 40, 66, 68, 69, 76, 77, 79, 83, 97, 125, 136, 142, 143, 144, 155, 173; *see also* Mills Brothers; Mills' Plantation; R. & D.G. Mills & Co.
Mills, William 174
Mills Brothers 40, 43, 44, 45, 46, 54, 55, 62, 67, 68, 69, 77, 78, 107, 112, 113, 114, 125, 132, 142, 166
Mills' Plantation 69
Mississippi 12, 31, 32, 173, 184; *see also* Corinth; Vicksburg
Mississippi River 17, 84, 159, 169, 180, 186, 191, 192
Missouri 12
USS *Mobile* (*Tennessee*) 98, 185, 191
Mobile, AL **7**, 14, 20, 75, 76, 81, 88, 125, 163, 164, 166, 169, 182, 183, 193, 208n25, 220n14
Mobile Bay, AL 14, 111, 182, 195

Monterrey, MX 177
USS *Montgomery* 42, 186, 191
Montgomery, AL 37
SS *Montpelier see* SS *Maria*
Montreal, Canada 121, 122, 190
Moore, Andrew Jackson "Jack" 58, 81–83, 87, 145, 150, 151, 174, 185, 187, 188, 194, 195
Moore, Thomas Overton 11, 174
Moorsom 18, 20, 197, 198, 200n40
Morgan, Charles 84, 174
Morgan, William 101, 103, 104, 174
Morgan City, LA 159
Morris 139, 174, 191
Morris, Charles M. 186

Nassau, Bahamas **7**, 16, 76, 128, 148, 152–154, 181, 193, 194
National Archives 3, 8, 36, 94, 112, 175
Navy, Confederate 70, 90, 147, 148, 155, 159, 165, 167, 172, 174, 185, 186, 189
Navy, Royal 17, 166, 192
Navy, Texas 3, 178
Navy, U.S. **7**, 8, 15, 18, 25, 29, 36, 42, 43, 45–49, 51, 53, 57, 62–64, 67, 70, 73, 76, 80, 81, 83, 84, 86, 87, 89, 96, 98, 99, 103, 105, 106, 110, 115, 121, 122, 127, 130, 134–136, 138, 140, 143, 152, 154, 159–162, 165–170, 174, 176, 178, 179, 182–188, 191–196, 204n45, 206n7
Neptune (schooner) 139, 166, 191
CSS *Neptune No. 2* 90, 177, 191
Netherlands 152, 186
New Brunswick, Canada 73, 119, 121, 169, 190
New Brunswick, NJ 185
New Jersey 175, 181, 184, 185, 194
New Orleans, LA 1, 7, 12–17, 19–21, 25, 28, 32, 37, 40, 49, 53, 57, 58, 75–77, 80–82, 86, 87, 119–122, 127–129, 136, 139, 159, 160, 163–167, 170–172, 174–176, 178, 180–184, 187–192, 195, 196, 198, 199n15, 201n16, 204n8, 208n43, 223n18, 230Ap7n6
New York (City, Harbor, State) 24, 37, 42, 62, 81, 82, 105, 128, 129, 137, 140, 145, 150, 165, 166, 168–170, 173–177, 182–184, 186, 187, 191, 193, 194; *see also*; Niagara Falls
New York Public Library *121*
New York Times 160
New York Tribune 169
Newport, RI 129. 190
Newport News, VA 186

242 Index

Niagara Falls, NY 37
Nicaragua 81, 178
Nina 46, 191
North Carolina 16, **27**, 70, 82, 148, 165, 166, 174, 194; *see also* Wilmington
Nova Scotia 74, 185, 194
Nuevo León 93, 177

Oakhill, MO 12, 156
Oakhill, Skelmorlie 156
Oaksmith, Appleton 81, 174, 183
Oetling, George Gottlieb 120, 151, 174, 186
O'Hagan, James 55, 74, 83, 116, 117, 120–123, 128, 132, 136, 174
O'Sullivan, John 65, 68, 77, 174
Owl (*Foam*) 70–72, 80, 144, **146**, 147, 150, 155, 165, 172, 178, 191, 227n15

Page, John 181
Page, Thomas Jefferson 152, 174, 193
Panuco River, MX 120
Paris, France 80
Parizot, Ernest 34, 35, 41, 43, 113, 143, 174, 203n26
Parliament 37, 38, 169, 203n42
Pascagoula, MS 184
Pass Cavallo, TX **8**, 15, 86, 139, 190, 200n23
Payne, John W. 104, 174, 182, 184, 188
Pea Ridge, AR 12, 35, 156, 173
Pea Ridge, Skelmorlie 156
SS *Pelican* 84, 125, 147–150, **151**, 152–155, 172, 175, 177, 191
Pelican Rifles 12
Pelican Spit, TX 89, 215n21
Pelican State 11
Pennefather, Frederick A. 189, 190,
Pennsylvania 183, 185–187, 191, 192
USS *Penobscot* 57, 81, 110, 191, 193
percussion caps 53, 78, 82
Pet (*Phenix*) *see* Mary P. Burton
Philadelphia, Pa 183
SS *Phoenix* 9, 144, 145, 147–150, **151**, 152–155, 189, 191
Phoenix Fire and Pelican Life Insurance Company 147
Pinchon, William Glenford 174, 189
Plymouth, UK 147, 193
Polish 30, 44, 63, 177
Port Lavaca, TX 36, 146, 147, 166, 191, 208n21
Portugal (Portuguese) 103, 147, 152, 168, 194
Potter, Jesse F. 139, 174

Price, Marcus Wesley 75, 175, 206n5, 206n6, 207n9–13, 207n15, 208n23–24, 211n7
prize (court, crew, vessel) 24, 47, 50, 51, 57, 65, 67, 84, 86, 96, 100–102, 104, 105, 126, 128, 129, 139, 145, 154, 155, 166, 168–170, 174–179, 181, 188, 194
Providence, RI 129, 190
Prussian 119, 120, 122, 137, 166, 171, 174, 190, 193
Purdie, William A. 86, 87, 175

USS *Quaker City* 54, 192

R. & D.G. Mills & Co. 40, 44, 45, 56, 61, 63, 66, 68, 69, 76, 77, 83, 112–114, 131, 153, 166, 169, 173, 174, 175, 185, 192, 220n31
railroad (rail, railhead) 16, 28, 29, 34, 68, 105, 156, 170, 174, 176, 178
Read, Thomas 114, 175
Red Fish Bar, TX 91
Red River 187
Red River campaign 88, 166, 178
Reed Walter 91, 175
Reichman, Moses 107
Renshaw, William Bainbridge 89, 90, 175, 194
Reserve 49, 191
Rhett, Thomas Grimke 112, 175
Rhode Island 129, 190
Richard H. Vermilyea (*R.H. Vermilyea*) 75, 79, 168, 191
HBMS *Rinaldo* 17, 18, 192
Rio Grande (Boca del Rio) 1, 2, **8**, 14, 15, 19, 21–26, 28, 34, 41–43, 46, 50, 52–54, 60, 64, 65, 73, 75, 85, 86, 108, 119, 120, 130, 136, 139, 155, 159–161, 166, 168, 170–175, 177, 181, 183, 184, 186, 189, 190, 192, 200n23, 201n16, 220n20
River Clyde 145, 228n26
Rodriguez, José 86, 87, 175, 181
Rogues Gallery 105, 218n26
Ross, Richard 139, 175, 188
Rothesay, Scotland 145
Roubien, Pascalis 204n8
Royal Mail steamer 60
Royal Navy *see* Navy, Royal

SS *Sabine* 53, 192
Sabine Lake (Pass, River) **7**, **8**, 15, 30, 38, 44, 53, 54, 61–63, 65, 87, 88, 93, 114, 138, 140, 142, 148, 150, 163, 164, 167, 168, 182–184, 187, 188, 192, 194
USS/CSS *Sachem* see SS *Clarinda*
St. Gall, Switzerland 49, 171

St. John, New Brunswick (Canada) 73, 119, 121, 122, 190
St. Louis, MO 37
St. Marks, FL 155, 178
San Antonio, TX 61, 166, 170
San Bernard River, TX **8**, 15, 29, 43, 50, 51, 61, 62, 66–69, 200n23
San Francisco, CA 170, 176
USS *San Jacinto* 173
San Jose Island, TX 86
San Luis Pass, TX **8**, 15, 49, 51, 59, 62, 67, 68, 83, 84, 98, 106, 109, 129, 134, 139, 168, 181, 185, 191, 193, 206n14
San Román, José 3, 19, 23, 24, 86, 130, 175
Santana River, MX 220n20
Sarah 48–52, 67, 68, 99, 166, 171, 173, 192, 206n14
Sarah Jordan 61–63, 66–69, 170, 171, 192
Saunders, William 98, 103, 175
Scherffius, Catherina "Kate" Fox *see* Fox, Catherina "Kate"
Scherffius, Emily Branard 175
Scherffius, Georgius "George" 63, 108, 109, 111, 114, 116–118, 122, 125, 140, 175, 190
Scherffius, Henricus "Henry" Ervin 24, 26, 28, 42, 63, 109, 110, 125, 140–142, 146–151, 169, 170, 172, 175, 177, 184, 189, 191, 201n12, 227n11–12
Scotland (Scotsman, Scottish) 5, 11–14, 20, 29, 42, 43, 47, 55, 167, 229n11; *see also* Greenock; Skelmorlie
Scott, Hugh Trann 94, 132, 175
Scott, Robert B. 148, 149, 175
Scott, Winfield 92, 171, 175
Scribner & Welford 156
Scrimgeour, William **42**, 43, 176, 181, 186
Scurry, William Reed 33, 34, 172, 176
Sea Witch (*Pizarro*) 139, 171, 192
Sellin, Felix 103, 176
Semmes, Raphael 18, 64, 65, **70**, 176, 181
Seward, Frederick William 118, 176
Seward, William Henry 66, 68, 81, 137, 176
Seyburn, Isaac Declar 25, 28, 176, 188
Sherrill, John 176, 192
SS *Sir William Peel* (*Don Pedro Segundo*) 23, 25, 192
Sisal, MX 54, 124, 136, 182, 183
Skelmorlie 11, 156, 157, 167, 178

Index

Slaughter, James Edwin 49, 176
slave (slavery) 11, 43, 44, 45, 81, 97, 126, 174
smallpox 151, 155
Smith, Edith 3, *141*
Smith, Edmund Kirby 94, 112, 171, 176
Smith, George Levin 50, 176, 206*n*14
Smith, John 101, 102, 103, 176
Smith, Leon 42, 55, 64, 89, 91, 94, 96, 97, 105, 106, 130, **131**, 132, 172, 173, 176, 177, 186, 187
Smith, Ralph Julius 69, 176
Smith, Vincent Eastman 4, *141*
Snow Drift see *Cora*
South Carolina 172
USS *South Carolina* 159, 192
South Hampton, UK 147
Southern Flora 53, 192
Southern Methodist University 3, *32*
Southern Pacific Railroad 176
Southern Steamship Company 84, 174
Spain 19, 25, 42, 60, 68, 69, 76, 77, 124, 126, 136, 142, 148, 152, 165, 166, 175, 182, 187, 183, 194; see also Havana
Stafford, John C. 97, 177
USS *Stars and Stripes* 154, 176, 192
Steinhatchee River, FL 154, 192, 196
Sterrett, John H. 90, 177, 182, 185, 191
Stillman, Charles 130, 171, 175
Stingaree 79, 80, 83, 85, 90, 99–107, 126, 166–170, 173–176, 178, 179, 188, 191, 193, 206*n*14, 213*n*27
Stingray (*Sting Ray*) 67, 79, 107, 172, 191, 193, 206*n*14, 213*n*27
CSS *Stonewall* 148, 152, 174, 193
Sulakowski, Valery 29, 30, 43, 44, 177
SS *Susannah* (*Mail*, *Susanna*) 80, 91, 92, 107, 108, 110, 111, 125, 139, 140, 165, 168, 170, 173, 193
Suwanee River, FL 154
Sweden (Swede, Swedish) 55, 74, 83, 110, 116, 127, 170
Switzerland (Swiss Confederation, Swiss) 49, 68, 171, 187, 190–192, 194
Sybil (*Eagle*) 139, 165, 193
Sylphide (*Sylfide*, *Selphide*, *Sylphyde*) 75, 76, 168, 193, 211*n*7
Sylvia 73, 74, 76, 85, 86, 87, 98, 193

SS *Talisman* 156, 193
Tallahassee, FL 155
Tampa Bay, FL 154
Tampico, MX 7, 46, 48–51, 58, 60, 65–68, 73, **74**, 75, 76, 79, 80, 83, 84, 98, 106, 107, 110, 112, 115, 116, **117**, 118–121, **122**, 123–126, 128, 137, **138**, 139–142, 145–147, 149–151, 153–155, 167, 168, 171, 174, 181–185, 187, 189, 190, 191, 192, 193, 194, 196, 211*n*4, 220*n*20
Taylor, Fred 56, 58
Taylor, George (alias A. Brotherton) 55, 56, 177
Taylor, Walter Herron 93, 177
Taylor, Zachary 166
Texas A&M University 1, 3, 166
Texas City High School 213*n*27
Texas Marine Department 45, 47, 52, 53, 55, 56, 71, 94–97, 105, 106, 130, 131, 140, 149, 172–174, 176, 177, 182, 184–189
Texas Ranger 34, 93, 168, 172
SS *Texas Ranger* (*Ranger*) 53, 112, 193, 206*n*4, 220*n*19–20
Thames River, UK 148
Thompson (or Thomson), George 83, 116, 117, 211*n*4
Thorpe, Thomas Bangs 87
Timmins, James Gregory 150, 177
Toronto, Canada 37
Townsend, Samuel L. 139, 177, 188
Trans-Mississippi Department 112, 134, 172, 175, 176
Trinity Episcopal Cemetery, Galveston, TX 38
Trinity River, TX 79, 190
SS *Triton* 141, 142, 165, 193, 194
Tucker, William Rogers 58, 82, 142, 177, 185, 188
Tupelo, MS 12
Turbert, August 40, 41, 177, 185
Turkey 50, 166
Turner, Edmund Pendelton 50, 51, 67–69, 177

SS *Union* 53, 112, 140, 165, 194, 207*n*9, 208*n*25, 220*n*19; see also SS *Carolina*
United Kingdom (UK) 17, 22, 122, 148, 152, 155, 156, 173, 178, 198; see also British; Dover; England; Kent; Liverpool; London; Plymouth; South Hampton
United States Navy see Navy, U.S.
University of Texas at Austin 3
University of Texas Rio Grande Valley 1, 2

Vaughn, Robert 139, 177, 185
Velasco, TX 7, 24, 29, 36, 43, 54, 56, 60, 61, 68, 98, 100, 101, 103, 129, 139, 167, 174, 185, 188
Velocity see *Chaos*
SS *Vera Cruz* see SS *Clarinda*
Vera Cruz, MX 7, 58–60, 65, 67, 68, 98, 107–110, 124, 125, 134, 136–141, **142**, 147, 148, 150, 171, 181, 182, 184, 185, 188, 189, 191, 192, 194, 219*n*5
Vicksburg, MS 32, 173, 184
SS *Victoria* 53, 54, 194, 207*n*20
Victoria, TX 213*n*27
Vidaurri, Santiago 93, 177
Virginia 13, 32, 37, 51, 93, 151, 159, 166, 167, 171, 173, 176–178, 186; see also Norfolk; Richmond
USS *Virginia* 50, 134, 166, 176, 206*n*14

Walker, John George 112, 113, 131, 132, 177, 178
Walker, Norman Stewart 148, 178
Walker, William 81, 178
Ward, Edward 139, 178
Washington, D.C. 37, 90, 175
Washington Hotel, Galveston 93
Watson, Agnes Milligan 157, 178
Watson, David Shelton 178
Watson, Helen Milligan 156, 157, 178
Watson, Henry 11, 178
Watson, Henry (Harry) 157, 178
Watson, Margaret Hamilton 11, 178
Watson, Maria 11
Watson, Mary Milligan 157, 178
Watson, Robison Gilmour McLean 11, 178
Watters, John 100, **101**, 102–104, 178, 188
Wave 49, 194
W.D.S. Hyer (*William D.S. Hyer*) 59, 61, 63, 67–69, 79, 110, 114, 137–139, 141, 142, 173, 194
Wegmann, Louis Edward 34, 174, 203*n*26
West Columbia, TX 28
West Florida 165, 196
West Indies 11, 103, 167, 168
USS *Westfield* 89, 90, 175, 194
Wild Horse Desert, TX 23
SS *Will o' the Wisp* 141, 142, 169, 194
William D.S. Hyer see *W.D.S. Hyer*

USS *William G. Anderson* 73, 116, 190, 194
William R. Kibby 53
William R. King 82, 174, 194
Williams, John Howell 92, 178
Wilmington, DE 181, 182, 186, 187, 195
Wilmington, NC 16, 147, 148, 194
Windlass 111, 220n17

Wisconsin 183, 188
Wolfean, Frederick Alexander 99, 102, 103, 178
SS *Wren* 130, 149, 195

yellow fever 25, 40, 91, 108, 109, 114, 127, 170, 175, 189
Yorktown, VA 93
Yucatan (Channel, Peninsula), MX 7, 76, 83, 88, 100, 123, 126, 139

SS *Zephine* (*Frances, Francis, Marian, Zephyr, Neptune*) 110, 129, 130, 195, 223n30
Zimmerman, Charles 101, 103, 179
Zouave see *Belle*

www.ingramcontent.com/pod-product-compliance
Lightning Source LLC
Chambersburg PA
CBHW060340010526
44117CB00017B/2900